T0240472

Lecture Notes in Computer Science

Vol. 1: GI-Gesellschaft für Informatik e.V. 3. Jahrestagung, Hamburg, 8.–10. Oktober 1973. Herausgegeben im Auftrag der Gesellschaft für Informatik von W. Brauer. XI, 508 Seiten. 1973.

Vol. 2: GI-Gesellschaft für Informatik e.V. 1. Fachtagung über Automatentheorie und Formale Sprachen, Bonn, 9.–12. Juli 1973. Herausgegeben im Auftrag der Gesellschaft für Informatik von K.-H. Böhling und K. Indermark. VII, 322 Seiten. 1973.

Vol. 3: 5th Conference on Optimization Techniques, Part I. (Series: I.F.I.P. TC7 Optimization Conferences.) Edited by R. Conti and A. Ruberti. XIII, 565 pages. 1973.

Vol. 4: 5th Conference on Optimization Techniques, Part II. (Series: I.F.I.P. TC7 Optimization Conferences.) Edited by R. Conti and A. Ruberti. XIII, 389 pages. 1973.

Vol. 5: International Symposium on Theoretical Programming. Edited by A. Ershov and V. A. Nepomniaschy. VI, 407 pages. 1974.

Vol. 6: B. T. Smith, J. M. Boyle, J. J. Dongarra, B. S. Garbow, Y. Ikebe, V. C. Klema, and C. B. Moler, Matrix Eigensystem Routines – EISPACK Guide. XI, 551 pages. 2nd Edition 1974. 1976.

Vol. 7: 3. Fachtagung über Programmiersprachen, Kiel, 5.–7. März 1974. Herausgegeben von B. Schlender und W. Frielinghaus. VI, 225 Seiten. 1974.

Vol. 8: GI-NTG Fachtagung über Struktur und Betrieb von Rechensystemen, Braunschweig, 20.–22. März 1974. Herausgegeben im Auftrag der GI und der NTG von H.-O. Leilich. VI, 340 Seiten. 1974.

Vol. 9: GI-BIFOA Internationale Fachtagung: Informationszentren in Wirtschaft und Verwaltung. Köln, 17./18. Sept. 1973. Herausgegeben im Auftrag der GI und dem BIFOA von P. Schmitz. VI, 259 Seiten. 1974.

Vol. 10: Computing Methods in Applied Sciences and Engineering, Part 1. International Symposium, Versailles, December 17–21, 1973. Edited by R. Glowinski and J. L. Lions. X, 497 pages. 1974.

Vol. 11: Computing Methods in Applied Sciences and Engineering, Part 2. International Symposium, Versailles, December 17–21, 1973. Edited by R. Glowinski and J. L. Lions. X, 434 pages. 1974.

Vol. 12: GFK-GI-GMR Fachtagung Prozessrechner 1974. Karlsruhe, 10.–11. Juni 1974. Herausgegeben von G. Krüger und R. Friehmelt. XI, 620 Seiten. 1974.

Vol. 13: Rechnerstrukturen und Betriebsprogrammierung, Erlangen, 1970. (GI-Gesellschaft für Informatik e.V.) Herausgegeben von W. Händler und P. P. Spies. VII, 333 Seiten. 1974.

Vol. 14: Automata, Languages and Programming – 2nd Colloquium, University of Saarbrücken, July 29–August 2, 1974. Edited by J. Loeckx. VIII, 611 pages. 1974.

Vol. 15: L Systems. Edited by A. Salomaa and G. Rozenberg. VI, 338 pages. 1974.

Vol. 16: Operating Systems, International Symposium, Rocquencourt 1974. Edited by E. Gelenbe and C. Kaiser. VIII, 310 pages. 1974.

Vol. 17: Rechner-Gestützter Unterricht RGU '74, Fachtagung, Hamburg, 12.–14. August 1974, ACU-Arbeitskreis Computer-Unterstützter Unterricht. Herausgegeben im Auftrag der GI von K. Brunnstein, K. Haefner und W. Händler. X, 417 Seiten. 1974.

Vol. 18: K. Jensen and N. E. Wirth, PASCAL – User Manual and Report. VII, 170 pages. Corrected Reprint of the 2nd Edition 1976.

Vol. 19: Programming Symposium. Proceedings 1974. V, 425 pages. 1974.

Vol. 20: J. Engelfriet, Simple Program Schemes and Formal Languages. VII, 254 pages. 1974.

Vol. 21: Compiler Construction, An Advanced Course. Edited by F. L. Bauer and J. Eickel. XIV. 621 pages. 1974.

Vol. 22: Formal Aspects of Cognitive Processes. Proceedings 1972. Edited by T. Storer and D. Winter. V, 214 pages. 1975.

Vol. 23: Programming Methodology. 4th Informatik Symposium, IBM Germany Wildbad, September 25–27, 1974. Edited by C. E. Hackl. VI, 501 pages. 1975.

Vol. 24: Parallel Processing. Proceedings 1974. Edited by T. Feng. VI, 433 pages. 1975.

Vol. 25: Category Theory Applied to Computation and Control. Proceedings 1974. Edited by E. G. Manes. X, 245 pages. 1975.

Vol. 26: GI-4. Jahrestagung, Berlin, 9.–12. Oktober 1974. Herausgegeben im Auftrag der GI von D. Siefkes. IX, 748 Seiten. 1975.

Vol. 27: Optimization Techniques. IFIP Technical Conference. Novosibirsk, July 1–7, 1974. (Series: I.F.I.P. TC7 Optimization Conferences.) Edited by G. I. Marchuk. VIII, 507 pages. 1975.

Vol. 28: Mathematical Foundations of Computer Science. 3rd Symposium at Jadwisin near Warsaw, June 17–22, 1974. Edited by A. Blikle. VII, 484 pages. 1975.

Vol. 29: Interval Mathematics. Procedings 1975. Edited by K. Nickel. VI, 331 pages. 1975.

Vol. 30: Software Engineering. An Advanced Course. Edited by F. L. Bauer. (Formerly published 1973 as Lecture Notes in Economics and Mathematical Systems, Vol. 81) XII, 545 pages. 1975.

Vol. 31: S. H. Fuller, Analysis of Drum and Disk Storage Units. IX, 283 pages. 1975.

Vol. 32: Mathematical Foundations of Computer Science 1975. Proceedings 1975. Edited by J. Bečvář. X, 476 pages. 1975.

Vol. 33: Automata Theory and Formal Languages, Kaiserslautern, May 20–23, 1975. Edited by H. Brakhage on behalf of GI. VIII, 292 Seiten. 1975.

Vol. 34: GI – 5. Jahrestagung, Dortmund 8.–10. Oktober 1975. Herausgegeben im Auftrag der GI von J. Mühlbacher. X, 755 Seiten. 1975.

Vol. 35: W. Everling, Exercises in Computer Systems Analysis. (Formerly published 1972 as Lecture Notes in Economics and Mathematical Systems, Vol. 65) VIII, 184 pages. 1975.

Vol. 36: S. A. Greibach, Theory of Program Structures: Schemes, Semantics, Verification. XV, 364 pages. 1975.

Vol. 37: C. Böhm, λ-Calculus and Computer Science Theory. Proceedings 1975. XII, 370 pages. 1975.

Vol. 38: P. Branquart, J.-P. Cardinael, J. Lewi, J.-P. Delescaille, M. Vanbegin. An Optimized Translation Process and Its Application to ALGOL 68. IX, 334 pages. 1976.

Vol. 39: Data Base Systems. Proceedings 1975. Edited by H. Hasselmeier and W. Spruth. VI, 386 pages. 1976.

Vol. 40: Optimization Techniques. Modeling and Optimization in the Service of Man. Part 1. Proceedings 1975. Edited by J. Cea. XIV, 854 pages. 1976.

Vol. 41: Optimization Techniques. Modeling and Optimization in the Service of Man. Part 2. Proceedings 1975. Edited by J. Cea. XIII, 852 pages. 1976.

Vol. 42: James E. Donahue, Complementary Definitions of Programming Language Semantics. VII, 172 pages. 1976.

Vol. 43: E. Specker und V. Strassen, Komplexität von Entscheidungsproblemen. Ein Seminar. V, 217 Seiten. 1976.

Vol. 44: ECI Conference 1976. Proceedings 1976. Edited by K. Samelson. VIII, 322 pages. 1976.

Vol. 45: Mathematical Foundations of Computer Science 1976. Proceedings 1976. Edited by A. Mazurkiewicz. XI, 601 pages. 1976.

Vol. 46: Language Hierarchies and Interfaces. Edited by F. L. Bauer and K. Samelson. X, 428 pages. 1976.

Vol. 47: Methods of Algorithmic Language Implementation. Edited by A. Ershov and C. H. A. Koster. VIII, 351 pages. 1977.

Vol. 48: Theoretical Computer Science, Darmstadt, March 1977. Edited by H. Tzschach, H. Waldschmidt and H. K.-G. Walter on behalf of GI. VIII, 418 pages. 1977.

Lecture Notes in Computer Science

Edited by G. Goos and J. Hartmanis

70

Semantics of Concurrent Computation

Proceedings of the International Symposium, Evian, France, July 2–4, 1979

Edited by Gilles Kahn

Springer-Verlag
Berlin Heidelberg New York 1979

Editorial Board
P. Brinch Hansen D. Gries C. Moler G. Seegmüller
J. Stoer N. Wirth

Editor
Gilles Kahn
IRIA
Domaine de Voluceau
Rocquencourt, B.P. 105
78150 Le Chesnay/France

AMS Subject Classifications (1970): 68-02, 68A05, 68A20
CR Subject Classifications (1974): 4.0, 4.3, 5.0

ISBN 3-540-09511-X Springer-Verlag Berlin Heidelberg New York
ISBN 0-387-09511-X Springer-Verlag New York Heidelberg Berlin

This work is subject to copyright. All rights are reserved, whether the whole or part of the material is concerned, specifically those of translation, reprinting, re-use of illustrations, broadcasting, reproduction by photocopying machine or similar means, and storage in data banks. Under § 54 of the German Copyright Law where copies are made for other than private use, a fee is payable to the publisher, the amount of the fee to be determined by agreement with the publisher.

© by Springer-Verlag Berlin Heidelberg 1979
Printed in Germany

Printing and binding: Beltz Offsetdruck, Hemsbach/Bergstr.
2145/3140-543210

FOREWORD

The International Symposium on Semantics of Concurrent Computation was organized in response to a growing need for a better understanding of the theoretical issues surrounding parallel computation. These Proceedings should help the reader to compare existing approaches, both recent and established. It is hoped that they will be a step towards a uniform theoretical basis which would inform the future design, expression and analysis of concurrent systems.

The Program Committee for the Symposium was chaired by G. Kahn and R. Milner and comprised :

J.B. Dennis	C.A.R. Hoare	S. Owicki
H. Genrich	A. Mazurkiewicz	G. Roucairol
C. Hewitt	G. Plotkin	

In addition the following people spent time and effort in the refereeing process :

N. Abdallah	S. Finkelstein	J.J. Lévy	W. Polack
W. Ackerman	T. Gross	K. Marzullo	B. Robinet
S. Andler	B. Hailpern	M. Mayburv	W.P. De Roever
J.D. Brock	M. Hennessy	G. Milne	L. Valiant
R. Bryant	R. Karp	T. Mowbray	C. Van Wyck
B. Courcelle	S. Kudlak	D. Park	D. Wall
J. Dean	K. Lautenbach	V. Pratt	N. Yamanouchi
J. Feldman	A. Lansky	F. Preparata	

CONTENTS

THE TEMPORAL SEMANTICS OF CONCURRENT PROGRAMS

Amir Pnueli
Tel-Aviv University
Computer Science Division
Tel-Aviv, ISRAEL

ABSTRACT

The formalism of Temporal logic is suggested as an appropriate tool for formalizing the semantics of concurrent programs. A simple model of concurrent program is presented in which n processors are executing concurrently n disjoint programs under a shared memory environment. The semantics of such a program specifies the class of state sequences which are admissible as proper execution sequences under the program.

The two main criteria which are required are

a) Each state is obtained from its predecessor in the sequence by exactly one processor performing an atomic instruction in its process.

b) Fair Scheduling: No processor which is infinitely often enabled will be indefinitely delayed.

The basic elements of Temporal Logic are introduced in a particular logic framework DX. The usefulness of Temporal Logic notation in describing properties of concurrent programs is demonstrated. A construction is then given for assigning to a program P a temporal formula W(P) which is true on all proper execution sequences of P. In order to prove that a program P possesses a property R, one has only to prove the implication $W(P) \supset R$.

An example of such proof is given. It is then demonstrated that specification of the Temporal character of the program's behavior is absolutely essential for the unambiguous understanding of the meaning of programming constructs.

INTRODUCTION AND OVERVIEW

The approaches to definition of mathematical semantics of programs can be roughly classified into the following categories:

a. <u>Operational</u>. In this approach we regard programs as generators of execution sequences. Each execution sequence is a sequence of program states. The set of execution sequences associated with a program can be specified by describing an interpreter which generates the sequences, given the program, or by specifying the successor relation which holds between consecutive states in any execution sequence.

b. Denotational. Here we regard a program as a function from the initial state into the final state, or more generally a relation between initial and final states. The semantics is specified by a mapping from programs to the functions or relations they compute.

c. Deductive. Here the stress is not so much on what a program is or what it does, but on what can be proved about its behavior, or about the function or relation it computes. Hoare's axiomatic system, Predicate transformers, Dynamic logic and Program logic all belong to this class.

For sequential deterministic programs, all three approaches have proved very useful and fruitful. Preference for one approach to the other is usually dictated by the specific need one has for a formal semantics. Thus implementors of a language would probably prefer the operational approach, already presenting some kind of an interpreter. The denotational approach is quite useful in resolving delicate and intractable issues in language design such as recursion and parameter transfer mechanisms in an implementation independent way. It is also very beneficial when considering transformations or translation between different languages when both languages have a common semantic range. The deductive approach is of course very attractive to someone interested in verifying the correctness of programs, directly providing him with the needed tools. With the hopeful coming of age of the "systematic programmer", these tools are increasingly used for the proper construction of programs by a systematic human or machine.

Unfortunately the attempts to extend all these approaches to deal also with nondeterministic, and in particular, parallel programs, are fraught with difficulties. Following is a partial unordered list of some of these difficulties:

1. In a deterministic program there is only one possible execution path which may either reach the exit point with some final result, or fail or abort in some intermediate state, terminating in an error state. Alternately it may loop forever. In a nondeterministic program there are many possible execution paths each of which may display any of the options listed above. What is then the proper notion of a correct termination? Should we require that at least one path terminates and not care about the others? or perhaps require all paths to terminate with correct answers? how about all paths either terminating or aborting (sometimes we mean blocking) but none looping? These problems have been partially dealt with by different power domain constructions

and a special mechanism in Dynamic Logic.

2. A parallel program can no longer be considered as a function from initial to terminal states. There are two reasons for that, one syntactic and the other semantic. The syntactic reason is that the modularity inherent in the Denotational Semantics method requires that for every programming construction operator which constructs a new program segment $c(P_1,P_2)$ from two smaller segments P_1,P_2 there exists a semantic operator $\mathcal{C}$ which relates the semantics of P_1 and P_2 to that of $c(P_1,P_2)$. Denoting the semantics of P by $\mathfrak{M}(P)$ we need a commutation rule:

$$\mathfrak{M}(c(P_1,P_2)) = \mathcal{C}(\mathfrak{M}(P_1),\mathfrak{M}(P_2)).$$

If we consider $\mathfrak{M}(P)$ as the function computed by P there exists no semantic operator which can relate the function computed by $P_1 \| P_2$ (P_1 run in parallel with P_2) to the functions computed respectively by P_1 and P_2. This is so since when considering P_i separately we assume its instructions to be executed consecutively while in the execution of $P_1 \| P_2$ the instructions of P_1 are interleaved with those of P_2 creating new effects. The obvious solution is to consider $\mathfrak{M}(P)$ no longer as a function into finite states but as a function into the execution sequences generated by P.
Then $\mathfrak{M}(P_1 \| P_2) = M(\mathfrak{M}(P_1),\mathfrak{M}(P_2))$ where M is a merging operator. This means that the execution sequences generated by $P_1 \| P_2$ are all possible merges between execution sequences of P_1 and P_2.

The semantic inadequacy associated with the functional description of programs is that together with parallel programs we naturally consider programs which are models for operating systems. These programs are not run for their final result but rather for maintaining some continuous behavior. Consequently for these programs halting is synonymous with failure and in the non-failing case the notion of a terminal state is meaningless. Again the obvious extension is to consider the complete execution sequence and discuss its properties. On second inspection it seems rather fortunate that we could get away with functions into just the terminal state in the sequential case. We cannot manage with such simple range when considering parallel or even cyclic programs.

3. The Fair Merge problem. One of the basic assumptions laid down by Dijkstra in his basic model of parallel programs is that the execution of any particular processor might be delayed for any arbitrarily long finite period, (alternately any instruction may take arbit-

rarily long to terminate) but may not be delayed forever. This worked beautifully in enabling us to separate qualitative from quantitative analysis and analyse properties which are completely independent of any relative rates of speeds between different processors. However, mathematically this assumption is most troublesome in its being discontinuous. Thus in considering the fair merge of two execution sequences S_1 and S_2, we include a set of sequences which have an increasingly long prefix taken from S_1 before any element of S_2 is taken, but exclude their limit which is S_1 alone. Consequently the operator M introduced above is discontinuous. Since continuity is a basic underlying assumption of the Denotational approach it seems questionable whether this operator can be accomodated within the framework of the denotation approach.

In this paper I suggest an approach to the semantics (and verification) of parallel programs which can be described as deductive-operational. It is operational in the sense that the semantic range is that of **execution** sequences, i.e. sequences of states arising during execution of a (parallel) program. These states include also the location in the program in which the state arises as one of their components. However, to single out only these sequences which are actually realized during a possible computation I use deductive methods. A special logic apparatus called Temporal logic is used in order to reason about these sequences, and list their properties.

This approach to semantics was primarily motivated by the problem of verification of the properties of parallel programs. In [PNU] and earlier work, a clear classification is made of properties which one may want to establish for parallel programs according to the complexity of their time dependence. The simplest in this classification are the invariant properties (safety properties in [LAM]). This class of properties corresponds to the partial correctness notion of sequential programs and covers the important properties of partial correctness, mutual exclusion, deadlock freedom, clean execution and data integrity, for concurrent programs. Several methods have been proposed for verifying such properties by Keller, Owicki, Ashcroft and Lamport which on closer inspection prove to be very close to one another, and seem highly adequate and reasonably efficient for proving such properties (as much as can be expected under the inherent complexity of the problem). When we consider the class of more time dependent properties, those that relate two events at different instants, we get a class that contains the notions of termination and total correctness for sequential programs, and the concepts of termination for terminating concurrent programs, and those of responsiveness, accessibility, liveness [LAM] and eventual fairness (in scheduling or responding) for the general concurrent programs. When we get to verifying this class of properties we find that there are very few suggestions, and the only property studied seriously is that of termination. The difficulty stems from the lack of tools for even expressing these properties formally. Temporal Logic provides an excellent and natural tool for expressing these and other properties which depend on development in time. Thus, the temporal semantics of a program is given by a formula W(P) expressing the temporal properties of all its possible and legal execution sequences. Then in order to prove that a temporal property R holds for a program we only have to prove the validity of the implication.

$$W(P) \supset R.$$

This implication is interpreted as stating that any sequence of states, which is a realizable execution sequence of the program P (and hence satisfy W(P)) must also satisfy R.

The lack of tools for specifying any but the invariant properties of concurrent and cyclic programs also led to confusion and ambiguity in the introduction of new synchronization primitives. To the extent that some formal definition was given for these primitives it was at best partial. It usually specified under what conditions these primitives may be activated (such as $x>0$ for $p(x)$) and what happens when it is activated (x decremented by 1), but not the frequency at which it must be activated (can it be delayed forever?). We will illustrate in the sequel at least one case in which a wrong implementation of a construct has been "proven" correct. The problem lies in that the proof only covered the invariant property but not the temporal property which in this case should have been that of (eventual) fairness.

To summarize the benefits of the Temporal logic approach to Semantics and Verification:

a) Temporal Logic enables us to express temporal properties for which no previous formalism existed. Consequently, it:

b) Provides us with semantics of programs which takes into account these properties and presents a semantic specification which is complete.

c) Provides a formalism for proving temporal properties of programs based on their temporal semantics.

A SIMPLE MODEL OF CONCURRENT PROGRAMS

We will present now a simple model of concurrent program which we will study and for which we will present semantics.

A concurrent program consists of n disjoint processes:

$$P = P_1 \| P_2 \| \ldots \| P_n$$

which execute concurrently, plus a set of initial conditions.

Each process can be represented as a single entry transition graph. This is a directed labeled graph whose nodes are labeled by node labels $m_i^0, m_i^1, \ldots$ for process P_i. The edges are labeled by commands of the form $c \to \alpha$ where c is a (guard) condition which may be missing and then interpreted as true. α is a statement which may be an assignment of the form $\bar{y} \leftarrow f(\bar{y})$ for the set of program variables $\bar{y} = \{y_1, \ldots, y_p\}$. α may also be empty. We denote the set of labels for process P_i by $L_i = \{m_i^0, m_i^1, \ldots\}$. An example of a concurrent program is given in fig. 1.

In our model all variables are accessible to all processors. Thus synchronization is accomplished via shared memory. In the graph we preclude self loops, i.e. edges from a node to itself.

A state in our model is a pair $\langle \bar{m}, \bar{\eta} \rangle$ where $\bar{m} = (m_1, m_2, \ldots, m_n)$ is a vector of labels, $m_i \in L_i$ and $\bar{\eta} = (\eta_1, \ldots, \eta_p)$ is a set of values currently assigned to the program variables $y_1, \ldots, y_p$.

An execution sequence for a program is any sequence satisfying the following conditions:

1. The initial state is $\langle (m_1^0, \ldots, m_n^0), (\eta_1^0, \ldots, \eta_p^0) \rangle$ where m_0^i are the entry labels and η_j^0 the initial values of the y's.
2. (Multiprogramming Assumption) - A successive state is obtained from its predecessor by exactly one processor executing one transition which is enabled. Thus let

$$s = \langle (m_1, \ldots, m_n), \bar{\eta} \rangle .$$

If processor i contains an edge from node m_i to node m_i' which is labeled by $c(\bar{y}) \to [\bar{y} \leftarrow f(\bar{y})]$ and $c(\bar{\eta})$ is true then s' is a possible successor of s where

$$s' = \langle (m_1, \ldots, m_{i-1}, m_i', m_{i+1}, \ldots, m_n), \ f(\bar{\eta}) \rangle .$$

Alternately we may allow idling at any stage, i.e. $s' = s$.

Note that any command is considered atomic. It is now commonly accepted that if we split the instructions in a program into small enough commands then the multiprogramming model even though simulating concurrency by interleaving is adequate in modelling any desired concurrent situation.

3. (Fair Scheduling Assumption). Let E denote the exit condition of a node m of process i i.e. the disjunction of all guards on all edges departing from m. In most of the cases this is equivalent to true, but this is not the case for example for nodes m_1^2 and m_2^2 in fig. 1 where: $E = (x>0)$. A sequence is fair if whenever processor i is stuck at m, i.e. from a certain point on $m_i = m$ then E is true only at a finite number of states thereafter. Stated negatively: no processor whose exit condition is true infinitely often may be deprived forever. Note that we concentrate here on infinitely executing programs. In order to analyze terminating programs we can introduce terminal nodes which have no exits.

In the frequent case that E = true we may replace the above claim by a simpler one: Every processor is eventually scheduled for execution. We only admit fair sequences among our execution sequences.

Consider now the representation of conventional programming elements in our model. Consider any program which may be run in parallel with another and contains assignment statements, tests and unconditional transfers (go to's). The corresponding graph model will contain a node for each statement representing the state just before the execution of this statement. Corresponding to each statement which is the successor of this statement, i.e. may be reached by the execution of the statement, we draw an edge from the statement node to its successor. The label of this edge depends on the statement.

1. For a test statement of the form "if $p(\bar{y})$ ℓ,r" we label the edge from m (being the current node) to ℓ with the label $p(\bar{y})\rightarrow$, and the one to r by $\sim p(\bar{y})\rightarrow$.
2. For a "go to ℓ" statement we draw an edge from m to ℓ which may remain unlabeled or labeled by true $\rightarrow$.
3. For an assignment statement of the form "$\bar{y}_i \leftarrow f(\bar{y})$", let m' denote the node following m in the program. If we want to faithfully model a possible interference between the fetching and storing of operands, we may have to break an assignment statement into a chain of simpler assignments. Thus to fully model $y_2 \leftarrow g(y_1,y_3)$ we need the chain

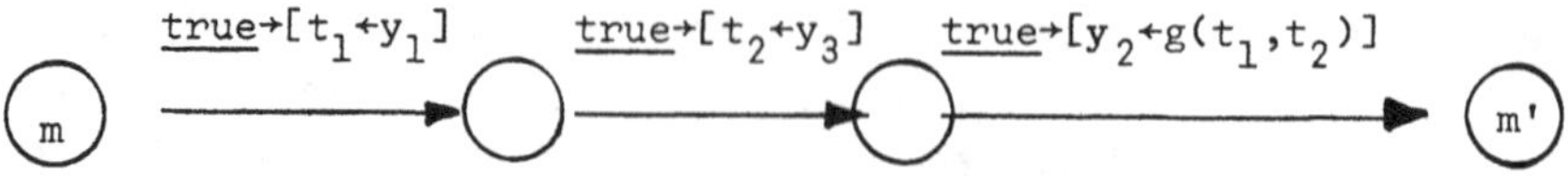

t_1 and t_2 are auxiliary variables local to the process P_i. Frequently we are assured that no interference may occur and then a single edge labeled by the full assignment will suffice.

For statements of the type 1-3 the exit condition of a node (i.e. the disjunction of all outgoing guards) is always *true*. Hence the implication of fair scheduling for such a node is that a processor waiting at such a node will eventually be scheduled resulting in one of the transitions being taken and a new node reached.

Consider now the case that a program contains a synchronization primitive such as p(x), v(x), *with* r *when* B *do*.. etc.

4. For a "p(x)" statement, the node from m to m' will be labeled by "$x>0\to[x\leftarrow x-1]$".
5. A "v(x)" is simply represented as "$x\leftarrow x+1$".
6. "*with* r *when* B" *do* is represented as

$$r > 0 \;\&\; B \to [r\leftarrow r-1]$$

with a corresponding "$r\leftarrow r+1$" at the end of the block.

For statements of this sort the exit condition is not identically *true*. Fair scheduling has to be interpreted as ensuring that if the exit condition is true infinitely often, the processor cannot remain trapped at the node. The crucial observation is that it is not sufficient to require that the processor will eventually be scheduled, because it might always get scheduled when the condition is false and no transition is possible. The stronger condition ensures that it will eventually be scheduled when the exit condition is *true*.

TEMPORAL LOGIC OR REASONING ABOUT SEQUENCES

Temporal Logic is a branch of Modal Logic which was designed in order to discuss the variability of situations (or states) over time. It enables us to discuss from within one state the truth of statements either in this state or in states lying in the future or in the past of this state. The full Temporal logic (as presented say in [PRI] or [RES]), contains operators for referring to both past and future. In our work we found it sufficient to consider only the future fragment. Different Temporal systems exist in order to discuss different models of time such as time measured by integers, branching (non-deterministic) time, etc. In our case we concentrate on integer like time which is deterministic. Note that since we intend to reason within execution sequences, each execution sequence is deterministic (each state having exactly one successor) even though the program generating them is a non-deterministic program and hence many different execution sequences are possible.

We introduce three Temporal operators: X which states truth of properties in the next instant, F which states existential truth in the future, and G which states universal truth in the future. Let σ denote the sequence $\sigma = s_0, s_1, \ldots,$ then ${}_i\sigma$ is the suffix subsequence ${}_i\sigma = s_i, s_{i+1}, \ldots$ for any $i \geq 0$.

Consider first a well formed Temporal formula constructed from propositions $p_1, \ldots, p_\ell$, the classical connectives, and the Temporal operators F,G,X. We assume that each state contains truth assignment to all the propositions $p_1, \ldots, p_\ell$. We may proceed to define the validity of a temporal formula on a sequence $\sigma = s_0, s_1, \ldots$ We will denote $\sigma \mathrel{|}\!\approx W$ the fact that the formula W is true on the sequence σ. This is defined inductively as follows:

For a proposition p, $\sigma \mathrel{|}\!\approx p$ iff $s_0 \mathrel{|}\!\approx p$ i.e. p is true in the state s_0

$\sigma \mathrel{|}\!\approx W_1 \vee W_2$ iff $\sigma \mathrel{|}\!\approx W_1$ or $\sigma \mathrel{|}\!\approx W_2$

$\sigma \mathrel{|}\!\approx \sim W$ iff $\sigma \mathrel{|}\!\not\approx W$ i.e. it is not the case that $\sigma \mathrel{|}\!\approx W$.

$\sigma \mathrel{|}\!\approx XW$ iff ${}_1\sigma \mathrel{|}\!\approx W$ i.e. W is true for the sequence $s_1, s_2, \ldots$

$\sigma \mathrel{|}\!\approx GW$ iff for every $i \geq 0$ ${}_i\sigma \mathrel{|}\!\approx W$.

$\sigma \mathrel{|}\!\approx FW$ iff there exists an $i \geq 0$ such that ${}_i\sigma \mathrel{|}\!\approx W$.

A formula W is valid if for all sequences σ, $\sigma \mathrel{|}\!\approx W$ is true. Thus $\sim Fp \equiv G(\sim p)$ is a valid formula.

The definition of interpretation for sequences can be extended to cover Temporal formulas containing predicates instead of just propositions. It reduces again to the ability to evaluate predicates on states.

The intuitive interpretation derived from the above is that XW is true at a state iff W is true at the next immediate state; GW is true at a state iff W is true at <u>all</u> future states; and FW is true at a state iff W is true at <u>some</u> future state (possibly the present). With this interpretation for the basic operators, we may interpret slightly more complex expressions:

$p \supset Fq$ - If p is presently true, q will eventually become true.

$G(P \supset Fq)$ - Whenever p becomes true it will eventually be followed by q.

FGp - At some future instance p will become permanently true.

$F(p \& Xp)$ - There will be a future instant such that p is true at that instant but false at the next.

GFp - Every future instant is followed by a later one in which p is true. Thus p is true infinitely often.

We will illustrate now how some important properties of programs can be expressed as Temporal formulas valid on their execution sequences.

Recall that an execution state is a tuple of the form $s = \langle (m_1,\ldots,m_n), (y_1,\ldots,y_p)\rangle$, $m_i \in L_i, y_1,\ldots,y_p$ are program variables.

In our formulas we will use propositions $m_1^1,\ldots,m_n^k$, one for each label in the graph. m_i will be true in s if it appears in the tuple $\bar{m}$, and false otherwise. This double use of m as a label and a proposition should cause no confusion. The proposition m_i being true in s means that s represents a state in which the processor P_i currently executes at m_i. In addition we will use arbitrary predicates over the $\bar{y}$ variables.

We consider first the class of properties which can be expressed as formulas of the form GW where W is classic (i.e. contains no Temporal operators). This is an <u>invariance</u> property.

Properties expressible by invariances are:

1. Partial correctness. Consider a single sequential program with entry m^0 and exit m^e. Let Ψ be a formula specifying the correctness of the program, i.e. Ψ is to hold on termination. Then partial correctness can be stated as:

$$G(m^e \supset \Psi).$$

This claims that it is invariantly true that whenever we reach the exit point Ψ holds. We can also add the effect of an input restriction φ by writing $m^0 \& \varphi \supset G(m^e \supset \Psi)$, meaning that if φ is initially true then the program is partially correct.

2. Clean behavior. For every instruction in the program we can write a condition which will ensure a lawful termination of the instruc-

tion. Thus if the instruction contains division this condition will include a claim that the divisor is non-zero (or not too small). If the instruction contains array reference then the condition will claim that the subscript expression is within the array bounds. Let λ_i be the legality condition for the statement departing from m^i. Then a statement assuring peaceful behavior of a program is

$$G(\bigwedge_i (m^i \supset \lambda_i)).$$

That is: whenever we reach m^i, λ_i holds.

3. Mutual Exclusion. Let each of the processes P_1, P_2 contain a critical section. For simplicity assume that it consists of the single nodes m_1 in P_1 and m_2 in P_2. To claim that these sections are never simultaneously accessed we write:

$$G(\sim(m_1 \& m_2))$$

i.e. it is never the case that both m_1 and m_2 are true.

4. Deadlock Freedom. (Absolute) Deadlock in this context means that all processors are locked and none can move. Obviously in our model a processor can be locked in a node only if its exit condition is not identically true. Let $m_1, \ldots, m_n$ be any set of nodes with exit conditions $E_1, \ldots, E_n$ none of which is identically <u>true</u>. Then the statement that deadlock never occurs at $m_1, \ldots, m_n$ is that

$$G(m_1 \& m_2 \& \ldots \& m_n \supset E_1 \vee E_2 \vee \ldots \vee E_n)$$

i.e. whenever we simultaneously get to $m_1, \ldots, m_n$, at least one of the exit conditions must be true. In order to exclude deadlock at all possible $(m_1, \ldots, m_n)$ tuples we should take the conjunction of all such candidate combinations. In practice only very few combinations are not identically false anyway.

Next we advance to a class of properties which require a more complicated Temporal structure for their expression. These are properties expressible by the Temporal implication: $W_1 \supset FW_2$ or more generally $G(W_1 \supset FW_2)$.

1. Total Correctness. Consider again a sequential program with entry m^0 and exit m^e and input-out specification (φ, Ψ). The statement of its total correctness with respect to (φ, Ψ) is given by:

$$m^0 \, \& \, \varphi \supset F(m^e \& \Psi)$$

i.e. if currently the program is at m^0 and the input values satisfy φ it is guaranteed to reach m^e and satisfy Ψ there.

2. Accessibility. In the context of critical sections we often want to prove that any program wishing to enter its critical section will be granted permission to do so. Let m be a location (node) just before the entrance to the critical section expressing the wish of the program to enter its critical section. Let m' be a location inside the critical section, The property of accessibility is then expressible as

$$G(m \supset Fm')$$

i.e. whenever P is at m it will eventually get to m'.

3. Responsiveness, Suppose that our program models an operating system which receives requests for some resource from many external agents. A request from customer i is signalled by a variable r_i turning <u>true</u>. The program allocates the resource between the different customers and signals a granted request by setting a variable g_i to <u>true</u>, A reasonable correctness statement for such a situation is that every request is eventually honored:

$$G(r_i \supset Fg_i).$$

Once it has been demonstrated that the Temporal Logic language is a useful tool for expressing and formulating interesting properties of concurrent and cyclic programs (as well as some sequential programs), our next step is to present an axiomatic system in which proofs of these properties can be carried out. Such an axiomatic system called DX is presented below:

THE SYSTEM DX

<u>Axioms</u>:

Take G and X as primitive operators (F derived as $FW = \sim G(\sim W)$).

A1. $G(p\supset q) \supset (Gp\supset Gq)$

A2. $Gp\supset p$

A3. $X(\sim p) \equiv \sim Xp$

A4. $X(p\supset q) \supset (Xp\supset Xq)$

A5. $Gp\supset Xp$

A6. $Gp\supset XGp$

A7. $G(p\supset Xp)\supset(p\supset Gp)$

Inference Rules:

R1. (TAU) If A is an instance of a classical tautology then $\vdash A$.
R2. (MP) If $\vdash A$ and $\vdash (A \supset B)$ then $\vdash B$.
R3. (GEN) If $\vdash A$ then $\vdash GA$.

A1, A4 give distributivity of the logical implication over all future instances and over the next instant. A3 specifies the uniqueness of the next instant. A2 claims that the present is part of the future (a convention adopted in this system); and A5 claims that the next instant is part of the future. A7 is the induction axiom. The rule (GEN) is based on the assumption that all time instants are symmetric and hence anything provable about the present (not just true in the present) is equally provable for any other time instant and hence provable for all future instants.

Similar but not identical systems appear in [PRI]. Other systems, which do not take X as primitive (it can be defined in terms of a stricter F, one which does not include the present) have been more extensively studied under the name D by Dummet and Lemmon ([DUM] [HUG]). An equivalent system is classified in the general Modal Logic context as S4.3.1 [HUG].

A proof given by Bull [BUL] for D can be modified to show that indeed DX captures a natural number like time model. This is to say that any model of DX can be embedded in a natural numbers model in which G, F and X assume their intuitive roles.

When we restrict ourselves to propositional Temporal Logic, the validity of formulas can be shown to be decidable by using a tableaux method. When considering the full first order theory, additional axioms are required to distribute quantifiers over the Temporal operators. These are the Barcan formulas [HUG]. Augmented by them the DX system is certainly sound and should prove to be complete for proving general Temporal formulas.

THE TEMPORAL SEMANTICS OF PROGRAMS

Having at our disposal the Temporal tools we will proceed to formalize the class of execution sequences generated by the concurrent programs of our model.

Consider a node in any of the processes P_i:

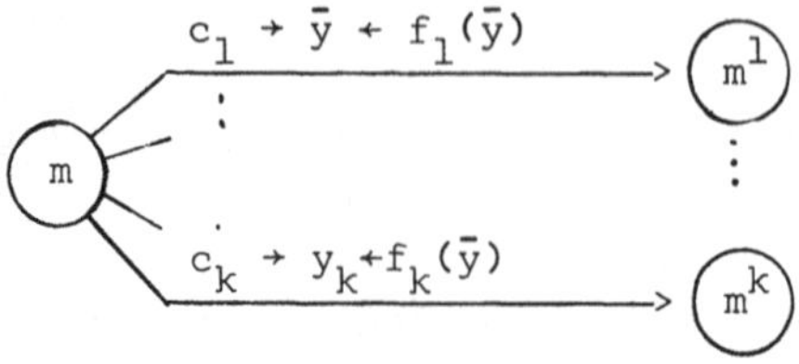

We denote the exit condition of m by $E = c_1 \vee c_2 \vee \ldots c_k$. For the node m define first a clause:

(1) $N_m\colon\ m \wedge \bigvee_{i=1}^{k} [c_i \wedge Xm^i \wedge X\bar{y} = f_i(\bar{y})]$.

This clause describes the instant of an active transition taken from node m. It states that one of the conditions c_i is true in the current state and that in the next state execution is at m^i and the next $\bar{y}$ is obtained by applying f_i to the current $\bar{y}$. This formulation by $X\bar{y} = f(\bar{y})$ is not strictly in our language but it can be expressed as $[(\bar{a}=\bar{y}) \supset X(\bar{y}=f(\bar{a}))]$. Alternately when the program is a finite state program all variables may be assumed to have only boolean variables. Then f is a boolean function and we may write $X\bar{y} \equiv f(\bar{y})$ which is within the language.

Define next the claim of fair scheduling for node m.

(2) $F_m\colon \sim[Gm \wedge GF(\bigvee_{i=1}^{k} c_i)]$

i.e. it is impossible to remain stuck at m while the exit condition $E = \bigvee_{i=1}^{k} c_i$, enabling at least one of the exits to be taken, becomes true infinitely often. In the frequent cast that E=<u>true</u> this is equivalent to $\sim Gm$ or $F(\sim m)$ i.e. we can never get stuck at m. Note that if a program contains an exit node, i.e. a node which has no outgoing transitions then $E =$ <u>false</u> and F_m is identically true for that node, allowing execution of the relevant program to remain at the exit node.

Having defined the basic clauses for each statement we assemble them into statements about complete processes. In that assembly we make use of the following abbreviation: If $w_1,\ldots,w_k$ are formulas then the statement $\sum_{i=1}^{k} w_i = 1$ claims that exactly one of $w_1,\ldots,w_k$ is true while all the others are false.

Consider process P_j with label set L_j.

(3) $A_j: \sum_{m \in L_j} N_m = 1$

Expresses the situation that process P_j is active, i.e. some transition in it is taking place.

(4) $I_j : \sum_{m \in L_j} (m \wedge Xm) = 1$

Expresses the situation that process P_j is idle, i.e. one of the label propositions is true and will remain so in the next instant.

(5) $B_j : \bigwedge_{m \in L_j} F_m$.

Expresses the conjunction of all the fair scheduling requirements for all statements within P_j.

We may assemble now the statements for each process to a statement for the complete program $P = P_1 \| P_2 \| \ldots \| P_n$.

Define first

(6) $I : \bigwedge_{j=1}^{n} I_j \,\&\, \bar{y} = X\bar{y}$.

This expresses the fact that all processes are idle, and hence the values of all variables remain the same.

Assume that the initial labels in all programs are $\bar{m}^0 = m_1^0, \ldots, m_n^0$, and that the initial values of the variables are $\bar{y} = \bar{\xi}$.

Then the formula expressing the semantics of the program is:

(7) $W(P): \bar{m}^0 \& (\bar{y}=\bar{\xi}) \,\&$

$$G\left(\bigwedge_{j=1}^{n} (A_j+I_j=1) \,\&\, \left(\left(\sum_{j=1}^{n} A_j\right)+I = 1\right) \,\&\, \bigwedge_{j=1}^{n} B_j\right).$$

The first clause requires the correct initial conditions of the execution sequence. The second contains three subclauses which have to be invariantly maintained. The first states that at any instant each process is either active or idle. The second subclause maintains that at most one process may be active at any time, and if all are idle then the values of all variables stay the same. The third subclause ensures fair scheduling for all the statements in the program.

Note first that our semantics allows instants of complete inaction or idling. This is necessary in order to accomodate terminating programs as well as incorrect programs which may inadvertently lead to deadlocks. Even though a program is incorrect it should still have some execution sequences. However the fair scheduling clause will prevent endless idling while there is still some possible action in one of the processes.

Another important point is the strict interleaving discipline imposed by the second subclause. At most one process may be active at any moment. This is essential since otherwise two p(x) operations may be permitted to occur simultaneously allowing two processes to enter their critical sections at the same time.

The formula expressing the semantics of a program W(P) imposes restrictions on possible sequences which are satisfied only by proper (and fair) execution sequences of the program. Then in order to prove that a property R expressed by a Temporal formula holds we have only to prove the statement: $W(P) \supset R$ ...(8)

i.e. all execution sequences which satisfy W(P) and hence are proper execution sequences of P must also satisfy R.

If indeed (8) is the basic proof principle we should be able to use it to justify all other proof methods suggested for proving properties of concurrent programs, such as [OWI], [LAM], [PNU] etc.

Consider for example the simplest and most important proof rule, that of establishing global invariants. It states that if $Q(\xi)$ is true (i.e. initially true) and Q is inductive, i.e. preserved along each transition in each of the processes, it is invariantly true.

From Q being inductive we infer that for any statement m in any of the processes it is true that $Q \& N_m \supset XQ$. Thus for every process j, $Q \& A_j \supset XQ$. Obviously also $Q\&I \supset XQ$ since no change is taking place. Thus $Q\&(\sum_{j=1}^{n} A_j+I = 1) \supset XQ$ and hence $W(P) \supset G(Q \supset XQ)$. Since W(P) implies that initially $\bar{y} = \xi$ it also implies Q. Thus we have that

$$W(P) \supset Q \& G(Q \supset XQ)$$

which by A7. yields $W(P) \supset GQ$.

In a similar way (8) can be used to argue soundness for all the other proof principles expounded in [PNU], [LAM], [KEL] and any newly suggested ones.

The use of DX in conjunction with (8) for proving accessibility will be illustrated below as an example.

Consider Fig. 1. We wish to prove that once P_1 gets to m_1^2 it will eventually arrive at m_1^3. This represents the fact that whenever one of the processes wishes to access its critical section, this access will eventually be granted. In this case it is sufficient to prove that we never get stuck at m_1^2, i.e. $\sim G(m_1^2)$. Note that this is not an immediate consequence of the fair scheduling policy since the exit condition from m_1^2 is not identically true. The proof proceeds by assuming $G(m_1^2) \& W(P)$ and deriving a contradiction to W(P). Hence $W(P) \supset GF(\sim m_1^2)$, i.e. we will always get to a state in which $\sim m_1^2$. The proof below enumerates only the major steps:

1. Gm_1^2 — Hypothesis
2. $G(m_1^3+m_2^3+x=1)$ — Can be derived by the invariance rule from W(P). Incidentally this proves the mutual exclusion for m_1^3 and m_2^3.
3. $m_2^3 \supset F(m_2^0 \& x>0)$ — By the $F_{m_2^3}$ clause of fair scheduling
4. $m_2^3 \supset F(x>0)$ — Consequence of 3.
5. $\sim m_2^3 \& \sim m_1^3 \supset (x=1)$ — By 2. Hence $F(x>0)$
6. $m_1^2 \supset \sim m_1^3$ — by W(P).
7. $\sim m_2^3 \& m_1^2 \supset (x=1)$ — by 5,6 hence $F(x>0)$
8. $m_1^2 \supset F(x>0)$ — by 4 and 7.
9. $Gm_1^2 \supset [Gm_1^2 \& GF(x>0)]$ — by GEN applied to 8.
10. $Gm_1^2 \& GF(x>0)$ — by 1,9 and MP

(10) is a contradiction of the fair scheduling clause at m_1^2 hence contradicting W(P). We conclude then that

$$W(P) \supset GF(\sim m_1^2)$$

as required.

In conclusion I would like to illustrate the absolute necessity of having a semantic description which specifies not only the partial correctness properties of constructs (such as our N_m) but also their Temporal Properties (the F_m clause). In a recent report Gries [GRI] analyzes a proposed implementation of the conditional critical section construct using semaphores. The suggested solution is essentially using semaphores to maintain a queue of all processes which have already expressed a wish to gain access of the resourse using a statement:

<u>with</u> r <u>when</u> B_j <u>do</u>...

B_j may vary from one process to another. The implementation guarantees that after termination of a critical section by any of the processes all processes currently in the queue are given a chance to test their B_j condition before any outsider is allowed into the queue. In order to prove correctness of the implementation, the following facts are established:

1. Mutual exclusion is maintained - Only one process is admitted to a critical section.
2. In the next cycle of testing their conditions, inside processes have higher priority than any outsiders.
3. Any interested outsider is eventually admitted into the queue.

However these are not sufficient to guarantee the correct Temporal behavior of the construct which I believe to also include:

4. It is impossible for a process P_j to be indefinitely delayed while $r>0\&B_j$ is true infinitely often.

Indeed this property is not satisfied by the proposed implementation, which therefore should make it incorrect (if we accept 4. to be an essential property of the <u>with</u>-<u>when</u> construct). The failure is due to the fact that a strict queue discipline cannot be maintained using semaphores only. Further Temporal analysis of this and improved algorithms will be forthcoming in [KRA].

This example was sketchily discussed in order to emphasize the importance of Temporal Conceptology and tools in both formulating desired properties of programs, and analysing and proving their behavior. It shows that in the absence of proper tools and standards an incorrect implementation can be "proved" correct. It also strongly urges that semantics of programming (and synchronization) constructs should specify both their invariance properties and also their Temporal properties. Of particular importance is their scheduling or fairness policy.

CONCLUSION

The Temporal approach to programs semantics and verification draws our attention to the richness of the class of properties that one may want to prove about programs and their behavior. It provides us with tools for formulating these properties, and then for formally proving them. The present paper concentrated on expressing the correct behavior of concurrent programs and thus specifying their semantics. This semantic specification can be used to prove other Temporal properties of the programs. It is also of great importance in the specification, study and implementation of new programming constructs and features.

In the present system the level of description is very low. Consequently, proofs of the simplest cases require many minute steps.

It is hoped that a systematic experience with proofs in the system will lead to a list of derived meta-rules which will facilitate reasoning on a much higher level.

REFERENCES

[BRI] Brinch Hausen, P.: "A Comparison of Two Synchronizing Concepts", Acta Informatica 1(1972) 190-199.

[BUC] Büchi, J.R.: "On a Decision Method in Restricted Second Order Arithmetic", International Congress on Logic Methodology and Philosophy of Science, Stanford, California (1960).

[BUL] Bull, R.A.: "An Algebraic Study of Diodorean Modal Systems", Journal of Symbolic Logic 30(1965) 58-64.

[BUR] Burstall, R.M.: "Formal Description of Program Structure and Semantics of First Order Logic", Machine Intelligence 5(1970) 79-98.

[DUM] Dummet, M.A. and Lemmon, E.J.: "Modal Logic between S4 and S5" Zeitschrift für Math. Logik ünd Gründ, der Mathematics 5(1959) 250-264.

[FRA] Francez, N. and Pnueli, A.: "The Analysis of Cyclic Programs", Acta Informatica 9(1978) 133-157.

[GRI] Gries, D.: "A Proof of Correctness of Reim's Semaphore Implementation of the With-When statement". Technical Report TR 77-314, Cornell University, Ithaca, N.Y. 14853.

[HOA] Hoare, C.A.R.: "Towards a Theory of Paralle Programming" in Hoare, Perrot (Eds.): Operating Systems Techniques (1972) Academic Press.

[HUG] Hughes, G.E. and Creswell, M.J.: "An Introduction to Modal Logic", Methuen and Co. London 1972.

[KEL] Keller, R.M.: Formal Verification of Parallel Programs". CACM 19 (7) 1976.

[KRA] Krablin, L: "A Temporal Analysis of Fairness", a forthcoming M.Sc. thesis, University of Pennsylvania.

[KRO] Kröger, F: "LAR: A Logic of Algorithmic Reasoning", Acta Informatica 8(1977) 243-266.

[LAM] Lamport, L.: "Proving the Correctness of Multiprocess Programs", IEEE Transactions on Software Engineering 3(2) 1977, 125-143.

[MAN] Manna Z: "Properties of Programs and First Order Predicate Calculus", JACM 16 (2) 244-255.

[OWI1] Owicki, S. and Gries, D.: "An Axiomatic Proof Technique for Parallel Programs", Acta Informatica 5, 319-339.

[OWI2] Owicki, S. and Gries, D.: "Verifying Properties of Parallel Programs: An Axiomatic Approach", CACM 19 (5) 1976, 279-284.

[PNU] Pnueli, A.: "The Temporal Logic of Programs", 19th Annual Symposium on Foundations of Computer Science, Providence R.I. Nov. 1977.

[PRI] Prior, A.: "Past, Present and Future", Oxford University Press 1967.

[ASH1] Ashcroft, E.A.: "Proving Assertions About Parallel Programs", JCSS 10, 1(1975) 110-135.

[ASH2] Ashcroft, E.A. and Wadge, W.W.: "Intermittent Assertion Proofs in Lucid," IFIP, Toronto 1977.

[KAH] Kahn, G: "The Semantics of Simple Language for Parallel Programming", Proceedings IFIP 14, North Holland.

[HAR] Harel, D. and Pratt, V.R.: "Nondeterminism in Logics of Programs", Proc. 5th ACM Sumposium on Principles of Programming Languages. Tucson, Ariz. Jan. 1978.

[LAM1] Lamport, L.: "Sometime is sometimes "not never", Technical Report CSL-86, SRI International' Menlo Park, California, Jan. 1979.

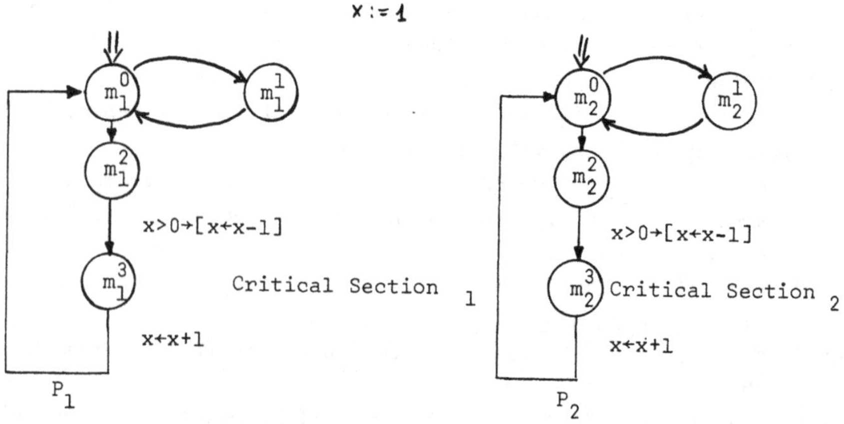

Fig. 1: Mutual Exclusion

MODAL LOGIC OF CONCURRENT NONDETERMINISTIC PROGRAMS*

Karl Abrahamson
Department of Computer Science
University of Washington
Seattle, Wa., 98195/USA

Abstract

This paper describes a logic, L, for reasoning about concurrent programs. Programs are similar to those of dynamic logic, with a shuffle operator included. L is a modal logic including the modalities [], meaning "throughout the future," and $<>^{+}$, meaning "sometime in the future." These modalities are extended by constraints, so that they can be used to express assertions such as "p holds as long as q does." Programs contain labels. Using labels, it is possible to isolate the behavior of a single process or segment of a process, while at the same time keeping the segment in the context of the whole parallel system. A certain subset of the propositional case of L is known to be decidable.

1. Introduction.

After writing many a bug-ridden program, many computer scientists and programmers have come to the conclusion that some formal verification method for programs is needed. Consequently, a number of logics of (sequential) programs have been developed [4,6,8,12]. When programs run concurrently, they are enormously more complex, and formal verification is proportionately more desirable. A number of concurrent program logics have been proposed [1,7,9,10,11]. I will assume familiarity with some of them. Some desirable properties of concurrent program logics are described below.

1) The fundamental properties of sequential programs are comparatively simple. Basicly, we wish to know about program A:

Does A always halt?

When A halts, will P be true?

The situation is not so cut and dried when programs are running concurrently. Con-

---

*This Research was supported by the National Science Foundation under Grant No. MCS77-02474.

current processes can interact with each other in complex ways. In order to describe their interaction we must be able to make statements about what a program does while it is running. Desirable properties of programs may be quite complex. For example, we may require A to eventually set condition P true, provided request Q is held true by B until acknowledgement R becomes true.

2) For the purposes of this paper, I will assume that sequential proofs are relatively well understood. It is therefore desirable to apply sequential program proof techniques to concurrent programs. Owicki [9] gives a method for doing this. In her method, one must show that two proofs are "interference-free." But the property to be proved, namely the non-interference of two proofs, cannot itself be stated within the logic! This is more than a matter of elegance. Because of it, the <u>shortest</u> proof of any statement about any n line concurrent program has $O(n^2)$ steps. A reasonable logic of concurrent programs should be powerful enough that the intermediate steps in proofs, as well as the ultimate goals, are expressible.

3) As noted, we wish to apply sequential proof techniques to concurrent programs. Therefore a sequential logic should be a subset of our concurrent program logic. Many sequential program logics,for example those of Hoare [6], Pratt [12], Manna and Waldinger [8] have programs as syntactic entities. A concurrent logic containing these must also have syntactic programs. This is in contrast to the logics of [7,10,11].

This paper describes a logic, denoted L, which at least approaches the goals of 1 - 3. L is a temporal logic of programs, as described by Lamport [14]. L is described in detail in sectios 2 and 3. Section 4 briefly considers proofs in L. Section 5 gives some theorems concerning decidability and expressiveness in L.

2. Programs of L.

Programs are built from some set of basic programs. These could include assignment statements, synchronization primitives, or just about anything else. Their exact nature does not concern us. There is one restriction on the semantics of basic programs; they are indivisible, in both the sense that they cannot be interrupted by other programs, and that intermediate steps are invisible when considering such properties as global invariance. This is not an unreasonable restriction. Assignment statements can be thought of as indivisible provided they contain at most one instance of any shared variable. At any rate, interleaving must take place at some levle of detail. It is simplest to make that level the level of basic programs.

Programs are built from basic programs using the operations ?, ;, $\cup$, * of dynamic logic [12], plus the parallel operator //. Dynamic logic-type programs have some advantages over the usual Algol-like programs.

1) Programs are nondeterministic. Dijkstra [2] has shown that nondeterminism is a useful concept, even in sequential programming. Also, since concurrent programs are inherently nondeterministic, we have a symmetry which can be exploited.

2) The concepts of sequencing, choice, looping and testing are separated. The familiar if-then-else construct does both a test and a choice (based on the outcome of the test.) Both the formal semantics and proofs can be simpler if we deal with only one type of action at a time.

I will briefly describe the operations of sequential (regular) dynamic logic programs before going on to parallel programs.

Tests. If p is a formula then p? is a program. p? acts as a no-op when p is true, and may not be executed when p is false. p? is an indivisible program. For example, $(p \vee q)$? tests the values of both p and q instantaneously. Tests which are not indivisible can be written, if desired, using p?$\cup$q? for $(p \vee q)$? and p?;q? for $(p \wedge q)$? Examples of programs with tests are given under "choice" and "looping" below. I should point out that any formula can be tested (actually any closed formula.) p could, for instance, be a partial correctness assertion about a program. My reason for allowing arbitrary tests is not so much a practical one as a matter of elegance. I don't need to define separate "testable" and "writable" formulas.

Sequencing. A;B means simply run A then run B.

Choice. Since programs are nondeterministic, this operation is simple. A$\cup$B means "nondeterministically choose to execute either A or B." The familiar construct "if p then A else B" is simulated by the program (p?;A)$\cup$(~p?;B).

Looping. The program A* means "repeat A zero or more times, the choice being made nondeterministically." The familiar construct "while p do A" is simulated by the program (p?;A)*;~p?.

Concurrent programs differ in syntax from sequential programs in two respects.

1) There is one more operator, //. A//B denotes the interleaving of execution sequences of A with those of B. The interleaving is not assumed to have the

finite delay property.

2) Every program in given a unique label. This both facilitates the formal semantics definition, and gives us a means of identifying points and regions of a program. Non-essential labels are omitted for readability.

Syntax of concurrent programs.

If ℓ is a label, α a basic program, p a closed formula, A and B programs, then the following are also programs.

1. ℓ:α 2. ℓ:p?
3. ℓ:(A $\cup$ B) 4. ℓ:(A;B)
5. ℓ:(A*) 6. ℓ:(A//B)

provided no label appears twice in the same program.

Semantics of concurrent programs.

A sequential program can be completely described by a set of transitions between states which the program can make. Essentially, because there are no other processes, it does no harm to consider the entire program as one indivisible step. The relational semantics of [3] exploit that. Relational semantics will not work for concurrent programs. Pratt [13] has described a semantics of processes based on trajectories. A trajectory is a finite or infinite sequence of states, through which a program can travel. However, as Pratt has noted, even trajectories are inadequate for concurrent programs, if programs are to be built using an operator such as //. There is not enough information in a trajectory to tell how it interleaves with other trajectories. The semantics of L gets around this problem by letting a program describe a set of sequences of moves. A move is an indivisible transition between two states. The move sequence ...(u,v)(w,z)... contains a move from state u to state v, followed by a move from state w to state z. For a sequential program this sequence would make sense only if v = w. But we must take into account the fact that the "phantom" move from v to w may have been made by some other process. For example, suppose A has semantics {(u,v)(w,z)}, and B has semantics {(v,w)}. Then the semantics of A//B is {(v,w)(u,v)(w,z), (u,v)(v,w)(w,z), (u,v)(w,z)(v,w)}. There is only one legal sequence in A//B, namely (u,v)(v,w)(w,z). Illegal sequences are ignored when the semantics of formulas are defined.

3. Formulas.

There are two kinds of formula, open and closed. An open formula makes a statement about a single program, G. Open formulas can make complex statements about G, without ever having to state explicitly what G is. The same formula may be true for many different programs. Open formulas are described in detail below.

A closed formula simply applies an open formula to an explicitly mentioned program. Pnueli [11] describes program logics as either endogenous, where sentences apply to a single, known, program, or exogenous, where programs are explicitly mentioned. He discusses the merits of both. Basicly, in an endogenous logic, it is easier to make complex statements about the program in question. Exogenous logics allow for statements about equivalence of programs. Programs are more a part of the logic, rather than special outside objects. Since most sequential program logics are exogenous (e.g. those of Hoare [6], Pratt [12,13]), an exogenous concurrent program logic can include a sequential one. In a sense, the open formulas form an endogenous logic, and the closed formulas form a powerful exogenous logic.

Open formulas.

An open formula describes how the state evolves with time, starting in the current state, during the execution of program G. In addition to such important information as variable values, the state includes program counter(s) values. Program counters change in the obvious way as G executes. Since G is generally nondeterministic, from any current state, there may be several different paths which G can take, each a different evolution of the state with time. By a future, I mean a sequence of states through which G could possibly travel, starting in the present state. When an open formula makes an assertion about the future behavior of G, it always considers all possible futures. The open formulas of L are as follows. Let P be a closed formula, E and F open formulas, and let ℓ be a label.

1. P is an open formula. G is ignored.

2. $\sim E$, $E \vee F$, $E \supset F$, etc. are open formulas.

3. a) before(ℓ) is an open formula, meaning "some program counter is at the point labeled by ℓ in G."

   b) in(ℓ) is an open formula, meaning "some program counter is within the region labeled by ℓ in G." If G contains ℓ:(ℓ_1:a; ℓ_2:b), in(ℓ) would mean before ℓ_1 or before ℓ_2.

c) after(ℓ) is an open formula, meaning "some program counter is at the point immediately following region ℓ."

4. (Special case of rule 5.)

a) []E is an open formula meaning "E is true now and in every state of every possible future."

b) $\langle\rangle^{+}E$ is an open formula meaning "Every possible future contains some state where E holds."

c) The duals of [] and $\langle\rangle^{+}$ are defined as $\langle\rangle E = \sim[]\sim E$, and $[]^{+}E = \sim\langle\rangle^{+}\sim E$.

Closed formulas

We assume a base logic, such as propositional or predicate calculus. Closed formulas are just sentences of the base logic, augmented with the "closures" of open formulas. If q is an open formula and a is a program, then A.q is a closed formula meaning "apply q to program A." A.q can be combined with other formulas in the usual ways of the base logic.

Constraints

The modalities [] and $\langle\rangle^{+}$, and their duals, allow one to proceed blindly into the future. Constraints give a means of "watching the states as they go by." More precisely, constraints restrict the allowable futures of G. A constraint restricts not just the individual states in the future, but the sequence of states as a whole.

5. If c is a constraint, then

a) [c]E is an open formula, meaning "in every possible future, E will remain true as long as c does."

b) $\langle c\rangle^{+}E$ is an open formula, meaning "in every possible future, E becomes true before c becomes false."

We still have left unanswered the question of just what a constraint is. I will give three kinds of constraints below. There may be others which are useful, and for that reason constraints are left loosely defined.

No constraints.

Many interesting statements about programs can be made without any constraints at all. When there are no constraints, boxes and diamonds are left empty.

1. (Global invariance.) A.[]p means "p is true throughout the execution of A."

2. (Partial correctness.) (ℓ:A).[](after(ℓ) ⊃ p) means "whenever A halts, p is true."

3. (A preserves p.) A.[](p⊃[]p) means "once p becomes true, it remains true during execution of A."

4.(no divergences.) (ℓ:A.)<>$^+$after(ℓ) says that all paths of A terminate.

5. We can state that, in A//B, whenever A halts, p is true, regardless of what B has done. This is written ((ℓ:A)//B).[](after(ℓ)⊃ p). This sort of explicit label referencing is handy in isolating the behavior of a single process. Another method of isolating a process is discussed under label constraints.

Label constraints.

Constraints apply to prefixes of paths. The constraint "ℓ" means "every move within the path is made by some program within the region labeled by ℓ." The constraint "$\ell_1,\ell_2,\ldots,\ell_n$" allows moves to be made by programs within ℓ_1 or ℓ_2 or ... or ℓ_n. Label constraints are particularly useful when the label applies to a single component of a parallel program, for then the moves made by that component can be isolated. Another use of label constraints is discussed under proofs. Notice that [ℓ]p is not the same as [in(ℓ)]p. The latter states only that one process must remain within region ℓ. [ℓ]p states that every move is made by that process which is in region ℓ. Other processes are suspended.

Example. Suppose program A works according to specifications provided concurrent programs preserve the truth of Q. A itself does not preserve Q. We can state thet B preserves Q in A//B by (A//(ℓ:B)).[](Q ⊃ [ℓ]Q). This says "after running A//B for any number of steps, if Q is found true, then running B any further will leave Q true."

The section on single step constraints gives another example using label constraints.

Formula Constraints.

Owicki [10] has developed a logic which includes the statement "p while q", meaning "p remains true as long as q remains true." If we say that constraint q on paths means that every point on the path satisfies q, then p while q can be written [q]p.

Single step constraints.

Let the constraint ss mean "the path is of length 2" (involving one state transition.) Some interesting formulas are

1. A cannot deadlock: $A.[]<ss>true$. This says "no matter how A runs, it can always go one more step."

2. In A//B, A never waits: $((\ell:A)//B).[]<ss,\ell>true$.

3. In A//B, A cannot starve: $((\ell_A:A)//(\ell_B:B)).[]<>^{+}(<ss,\ell_A>true \wedge \sim<ss,\ell_B>true)$

4. We might say that a program inherently deadlocks if it can never reach a state where it is free from deadlock. "A inherently deadlocks" can be stated as ID= $A.[]<>\sim<ss>true$. ID involves alternation of quantifiers of paths. In Owicki's logic [10], paths are always implicitly universally quantified. Hence neither ID nor its negation can be stated in her logic.

4. Proofs.

I have as yet no proof system for L. This section will briefly describe how partial correctness assertions might be proved. The basic idea is to modify sequential proof methods to make them work for parallel programs. This is the approach taken by Owicki [9], and others [1,7]. In Owicki's method, a sequential proof is done for each process of a parallel system, and then each step of each proof is shown not to be invalidated by other processes. In L, it is possible to integrate the non-interference proof with the sequential proofs. Suppose, for example, I wish to use the Hoare-style rule

$$(1) \qquad \frac{P\{A\}Q \ , \ Q\{B\}R}{P\{A;B\}R}$$

Suppose A;B occurs in process C of C//D. Assuming that the proofs of P{A}Q and Q{B}R have been carried out with due consideration to the action of process D, rule (1) can be applied provided it is proved that D preserves the truth of Q. Thus, tentatively, $D.[](Q \supset \Box Q)$ becomes another condition for rule (1). But it is not just D which must preserve Q, it is D, running concurrently with C, which must preserve Q. The additional condition should be $(C//\ell_D{:}D).[](Q \supset [\ell_D]Q)$. Above it was assumed that P{A}Q was proved with due consideration for process D. That assumption should not be part of the proof rule. Rather, it should be part of the statement of what has been proved, namely P{A}Q. Ordinarily P{A}Q is written in L as $(\ell_A{:}A).((\mathrm{before}(\ell_A) \wedge P) \supset [](\mathrm{after}(\ell_A) \supset Q))$. To show that D was accounted for, we could change the program to $(\ell_A{:}A//D)$. But the actions of D can be affected by the rest of C. The correct way to state P{A}Q is $(\underbrace{(\ldots\ell_A{:}A\ldots)}_{C}//\ell_D{:}D).((\mathrm{before}(\ell_A) \wedge P) \supset [\ell_A,\ell_D](\mathrm{after}(\ell_A) \supset Q)$. The labels in the box prevent C from exitting A and then looping back through A. Rule (2), related to rule (1), can now be stated. Let $E = (\ldots\ell{:}(\ell_A{:}A;\ell_B{:}B)\ldots)//\ell_D{:}D$.

$$\begin{array}{lrl} & \text{prove:} & E.((\mathrm{before}(\ell_A) \wedge P) \supset [\ell_A,\ell_D](\mathrm{after}(\ell_A) \supset Q), \\ (2) & & E.((\mathrm{before}(\ell_B) \wedge Q) \supset [\ell_B,\ell_D](\mathrm{after}(\ell_B) \supset R), \\ & & E.\ [](Q \supset [\ell_D]Q) \\ & \text{conclude:} & E.((\mathrm{before}(\ell) \wedge P) \supset [\ell,\ell_D](\mathrm{after}(\ell) \supset R). \end{array}$$

Rule (2) is certainly not simple. In fact, the statements of seemingly simple ideas, such as P{A}Q, are rather long. Other proof rules for L are bound to be at least as complex. I offer the following defense of these rules.

1. Abbreviations can be used to shorten the rules and simplify statements.

2. Consider rule (2). $E.[](Q \supset [\ell_D]Q)$ needs to be proven only once, even though it may be used many times, for instance to prove P{A;B}R, P{S;T}R, and so on. Short proofs are possible in some cases.

<u>Label Constraints in proofs</u>.

Rule (2) makes use of label constraints. There is good reason for this. An elegant way to do sequential proofs is inductively on program structure. Rule (1) is such an inductive rule. First we prove a statement about A, then one about B, and we combine them to get a statement about A;B. Concurrent programs are more difficult to handle inductively. Unless explicit reference is made to how the proofs of P(C) and Q(D) are carried out, we can conclude nothing from them about a statement R(C//D). We can't conclude anything about R((A;B)//D) from P(A//D) and Q(B//D), since it may be the interaction of A and B which causes disaster in D. A solution is to use label constraints. Statements are made about E = C//D, and, as was the case with rule (2), programs are referred to by their labels. The "label structure" can be built up inductively without constantly changing programs. In rule 2, a statement about ℓ_A is combined with one about ℓ_B to obtain a statement about ℓ, which covers both ℓ_A and ℓ_B. ℓ represents the program A;B. It appears that labels can play a useful role in proofs.

5. Decidability and Expressiveness.

This section states some theorems concerning the propositional case of L, denoted L_0. Proofs and other results will appear later. The appendix contains a formal semantics of L_0. For these theorems, all of the constraint types mentioned so far can be in L_0. The base logic for L_0 is propositional calculus. Basic programs are uninterpreted program letters, with no inputs or outputs. A program modifies a "global environment" in some unknown way. A formula of L_0 is valid if it holds under all interpretations and propositional variable values. Let L_0^- be L_0 without $<>^+$ and $[]^+$.

Theorem 1. The validity problem for L_0^- is decidable, and is in Co-NTIME($2^{2^{c^n}}$) for some c.

PDL is the propositional case of (sequential regular) dynamic logic [3,13]. It appears on the surface that much more can be said in L than in PDL. While that is true if formulas are to be kept short, every formula of L_0^- is equivalent to a (possibly very long) formula of PDL.

Theorem 2. Every length n formula of L_0^- is equivalent to some PDL formula Q of length at most $2^{2^{c^n}}$ for some c.

Theorem 3. Let PDL^+ be PDL augmented with the formula loop(A) = "A can diverge," for every program A (see [5]). Theorem 2 holds with L_0^- replaced by L_0 and PDL replaced by PDL^+.

Acknowledgement. I would like to thank Michael J. Fischer for many helpful suggestions. It was he who suggested the general form of constraints.

Appendix - Formal Semantics of L_0.

Preliminaries

Σ_0 = basic programs

Φ_0 = basic formulas (propositional variables)

Γ = labels

A structure (or interpretation) is a triple (W,π_0,ρ_0) consisting of a set of "worlds", or states, W, a function $\pi_0:\Sigma_0 \rightarrow \mathcal{P}(W)$ assigning to each basic formula the worlds where it holds, and a function $\rho_0:\Phi_0 \rightarrow \mathcal{P}(W\times W)$, assigning to each basic program a set of transitions between worlds.

$M = W \times \mathcal{P}(\Gamma) \times W$ (the set of labeled moves);

$H = M^{\infty}$ = the set of paths, finite and infinite sequences of labeled moves;

$H_r = \{h \in H : h = \ldots(u_1,t_1,v_1)(u_2,t_2,v_2)\ldots \Rightarrow v_1 = u_2\}$

= the set of legal paths.

The paths in H are "discontinuous." The path X= (u,s,v)(w,t,z) is in H, even if v $\neq$ w. X denotes a move from state u to state v, followed by a move from state w to state z. Only continuous paths, members of H_r, are of ultimate interest. However, since interleaving discontinuous paths can result in a continuous path, discontinuous paths cannot be ignored. The label set s in (u,s,v) denotes that this move is made by a program with all of the labels in s. A program can have several labels. For example, A is labeled by both ℓ_1 and ℓ_2 in $\ell_1:(\ell_2:A \cup \ell_3:B)$.

If X is a set of paths, then $[X]_\ell$ is defined as the set of paths in X, with every label set s of every move replaced by $s \cup \{\ell\}$.

Programs.

The set Σ of programs, and semantics $\rho:\Sigma \rightarrow \mathcal{P}(H)$, assigning to each program a set of paths, are given inductively below. Let $\alpha \in \Sigma_0$, $A,B \in \Sigma$, $p \in \Phi$, $\ell \in \Gamma$. Then

1. $\ell:\alpha \in \Sigma$, $\rho(\ell:\alpha) = \{(u,\ell,v) : (u,v) \in \rho_0(\alpha)\}$
2. $\ell:p? \in \Sigma$, $\rho(\ell:p?) = \{(u,\ell,u) : u \in \pi(p)\}$
3. $\ell:(A \cup B) \in \Sigma$, $\rho(\ell:(A \cup B)) = [\rho(A) \cup \rho(B)]_\ell$
4. $\ell:(A;B) \in \Sigma$, $\rho(\ell:(A;B)) = [\rho(A)\cdot\rho(B)]_\ell$ (concatenation of sequences. $a\cdot b = a$ if $|a| = \infty$)
5. $\ell:(A^*) \in \Sigma$, $\rho(\ell:A^*) = [\lambda \cup \rho(A)\cdot\rho(A^*)]_\ell$, and is the least solution which is closed under least upper bound of prefix chains.[1]
6. $\ell:(a//B) \in \Sigma$, $\rho(\ell:(A//B)) = [\text{shuffle}(\rho(A), \rho(B))]_\ell$, where shuffle interleaves

---

[1] This says that a program which can make arbitrarily much progress can make infinitely much progress. A prefix chain is an infinite chain of sequences $s_1 \leq s_2 \leq \ldots$, where $\leq$ denotes the prefix relation.

sequences.

Open Formulas.

Ω is the set of open formulas. For every $G \in \mathcal{P}(H)$, there is a function $\delta_G : \Omega \rightarrow \mathcal{P}(W \times H_r)$ assigning to each open formula the complete states where it holds. A complete state consists of a world and a prefix computation, which essentially encodes all program counter values. Let $p \in \Phi$, $q, r \in \Omega$, $\ell \in \Gamma$, and let c be a constraint. The semantics of constraints is omitted. Then

1. $p \in \Omega$, $\delta_G(p) = \{(w,h) \in W \times H_r \ : \ w \in \pi(p) \}$.
2. $\sim q \in \Omega$, $\delta_G(\sim q) = W \times H_r - \delta_G(q)$.
3. $q \vee r \in \Omega$, $\delta_G(q \vee r) = \delta_G(q) \cup \delta_G(r)$.
4. a) $in(\ell) \in \Omega$, $\delta_G(in(\ell)) = \{(w,h) \in W \times H_r \ : \exists u, r \in W,\ t \in \mathcal{P}(\Gamma), h' \in H.$
$[h(u,t,v)h' \in G, \ell \in t] \}$.

   Note that h(u,t,v) does not have to be in H_r. The process at ℓ may be blocked.

   b) $before(\ell) \in \Omega$, $\delta_G(before(\ell)) =$
$\{(w,h) \in W \times H_r \ : \exists u_1, u_2, v_1, v_2 \in W,\ t_1, t_2 \in \mathcal{P}(\Gamma),\ h', h'' \in H.$
$[((h = h''(u_1,t_1,v_1) \wedge \ell \notin t_1) \vee h = \lambda)$
$\wedge\ h(u_2,t_2,v_2)h' \in G \wedge \ell \in t_2] \}$

   c) $after(\ell) \in \Omega$, δ_G is similar to δ_G for $before(\ell)$.

5. a) $[c]q \in \Omega$, $\delta_G([c]q) =$
$\{(w,h) \in W \times H_r \ : \ (\forall h_2.\ hh_2 \in G)(\forall h_1$ prefix of h_2, $hh_1 \in H_r$, h_1 satisfies c)
$[(w', hh_1) \in \delta_G(q)$, where w' is the second world of the last move of hh_1 ($w' = w$ if $hh_1 = \lambda$)] }.

   b) $\langle c \rangle^+ q \in \Omega$, semantics same as for $[c]q$, but replace $\forall h_1$ by $\exists h_1$.

Closed formulas.

The closed formulas Φ, and their semantics $\pi : \Phi \rightarrow \mathcal{P}(W)$, are given below. Let $A \in \Sigma$, $r \in \Omega$, $p, q \in \Phi$, $P \in \Phi_0$. Then

1. $P \in \Phi$, $\pi(P) = \pi_0(P)$.
2. $\sim p \in \Phi$, $\pi(\sim p) = W - \pi(p)$.
3. $p \vee q \in \Phi$, $\pi(p \vee q) = \pi(p) \cup \pi(q)$.
4. $A.r \in \Phi$, $\pi(A.r) = \{w \in W \ : \ (w,\lambda) \in \delta_{\rho(A)}(r) \}$.

References.

1. Aschcroft, E. A. and Z. Manna. "Formalization of Properties of Parallel Programs." Machine Intelligence 6, Edinburgh University Press.
2. Dijkstra, E. W. "Guarded Commands, Nondeterminacy and Formal Derivation of Programs," C.A.C.M. 18,8, 1975.
3. Fischer, M. J. and R. E. Ladner. "Propositional Modal Logic of Programs," Proc. 9th ann. ACM Symp. on Theory of Computing, 286-294, Boulder, Col., May, 1977.
4. Floyd, R. W. "Assigning Meaning to Programs," Proc. AMS Symp. Appl. Math. 19, 1967, 19-32.
5. Harel, D. and V. R. Pratt. "Nondeterminism in Logics of Programs," Proc. 5th ann ACM Symp. on Principles of Prog. Lang., 203-213, Tuscon, Arizona, Jan., 1978.
6. Hoare, C. A. R. "An Axiomatic Basis for Computer Programming," C.A.C.M. 12,10, 1969, 576-580.
7. Lamport, L. "Proving the Correctness of Multiprocess Programs," Mass. Computer Associates, Inc. Mass. 01880.
8. Manna, Z. and R. Waldinger. "Is 'Sometime' Sometimes Better than 'Always'?," C.A.C.M. 21,2, 1978.
9. Owicki, S. and D. Gries. "An Axiomatic Proof Technique for Parallel Programs I," Acta Informatica 6, 319-339.
10. Owicki, S. Colloquium presentation, Dept. of Comp. Sci., University of Washington, Nov. 16, 1978.
11. Pnueli, A. "The Temporal Logic of Programs," 18th IEEE Symp. on Foundations of Computer Science, 46-57, Oct. 1977.
12. Pratt V. R. "Semantical Considerations on Floyd-Hoare Logic," 17th IEEE Symp. on Foundations of Computer Science, 109-121, 1976.
13. Pratt V. R. "A Practical Decision Method for Propositional Dynamic Logic," Proc. 10th ACM Symp. on Theory of Computing, 326-337, 1978.
14. Lamport, L. "'Sometime' is Sometimes 'Not Never'," S.R.I. International Report, Menlo Park, California, January, 1979.

NON-DETERMINISTIC SYSTEM SPECIFICATION

J.R. ABRIAL* and S.A. SCHUMAN**

Abstract

This paper presents an elementary formal approach (or rather, a catalog of definitions) which provides a general framework for non-deterministic system specification : definitions are given for a system, a halting system, abstraction and implementation, and finally for the extension and refinement of a system. The notion of an invariant function is extended to that of an almost invariant function.

In a second part, we apply this formalism to the specification of a disk handler and of a small "on-line" query system.

----

* Consultant 42, rue Descartes 75005 PARIS

** IRIA Domaine de Voluceau B.P. 105 78150 LE CHESNAY

1. Introduction

Various proposals have recently been made ([1],[2],[3]) for introducing language mechanisms suited to parallel programming.

On the other hand, Hoare's proof techniques ([6]) have been generalized to parallel programming ([4],[5]) ; as a result some difficult algorithms (like the "on-the-fly garbage collector", ([7],[8])) have been "proven" correct.

Finally, it is now strongly felt ([10]) that actual programming must be preceded by a rigorous (formal) specification of the intended system.

This paper aims at a modest contribution in these domains :

- in a first part we propose an elementary formal approach (or rather, a catalog of definitions) which provides a general framework for non-deterministic system specification.
- in a second part we apply the formalism to the specification of various examples. We use, as a tool, the Z specification language ([11]).

2. An elementary system description formalism

Inspired, among others, by Sintzoff's ideas ([9]) we say that a system is characterized by it state, which evolves under the influence of various events. Starting with an initial state, the history (or trace) of a system, is therefore defined as the sequence of states and events that eventually leads to a final state.

Actually, we study all the possible histories of a system whose initial state is choosen in a set of starting states, whose various events are members of a finite set and whose final state is choosen in a set of ending states.

For a given state, only a limited number of events may occur : to each event is therefore associated a domain, representing the subset of states in which it may be fired (for example, an interruption may only be taken into account if the computer is in a state where it is unmasked).

We assume that the transition between two states (as a consequence of an event) is "instantaneous" : in other words, each event is independent from the others ; more precisely, no two events may occur at the "same" time. In practice, this mutual exclusion constraint is handled either by the basic hardware synchronism or by special mechanisms, like the masking of interupts.

There is no guarantee, however, that a system, once started, will ever reach any final state. Various incidents may occur :

- no further event may be possible (deadlock) ;
- the system enters a periodic cycle (loop) ;
- the system continues "ad infinitum".

As a consequence, we say that a system is a halting system if all its possible histories are finite and end in a final state.

It is interesting to compare two systems Σ_1 and Σ_2 built on the same set of states but with different events : if, for all histories h_1 of Σ_1, there exists a history h_2 of Σ_2, such that h_1 and h_2 have the same initial and final states, and that all states of h_1 also occur in h_2 in the same order (with posibly more states in h_2), we say that Σ_1 is an abstraction of Σ_2 and conversely that Σ_2 is an implementation of Σ_1.

Finally, if one replaces an event e of a system Σ_1 with other events, in such a way that the new system Σ_2 is an implementation of Σ_1, we say that Σ_2 is a refinement of Σ_1 for the event e.

2.1 Definition of a system

Let S be a set (the set of states of the system) and I be a finite set (the set of event names).

Let S_i (for $i \in I$) be a family of subsets of S and e_i be a family of total functions from S_i into S (the events) :

$$e_i : S_i \rightarrow S \qquad (1) \qquad\qquad (\text{for } i \in I)$$

such that :

$$\forall i \in I.\ \forall s \in S_i . e_i(s) \neq s \qquad (2)$$

Let S_b and S_f (beginning and final states) be two subsets of S such that :

$$S_b \subset (S_f \cup \bigcup_{i \in I} S_i) \qquad (3)$$

$$(S_f \cap \bigcup_{i \in I} S_i) = \emptyset \qquad (4)$$

The 6-tuple (S,S_b,S_f,I,S_i,e_i) is called a system.

Example : An "arithmetic" producer-consummer (APC)

$S = \mathbb{N} \times \{0,\dots,n\} \times \mathbb{N}$ ($n \in \mathbb{N}^+$ is the "buffer" size)
$I = \{p,c\}$ (for produce and consumme)
$S_b = \mathbb{N} \times \{0\} \times \{0\}$
$S_f = \{0\} \times \{0\} \times \mathbb{N}$
$S_p = \mathbb{N}^+ \times \{0,\dots,n-1\} \times \mathbb{N}$
$S_c = \mathbb{N} \times \{1,\dots,n\} \times \mathbb{N}$
$e_p(in,buf,out) = (in-1,buf+1,out)$
$e_c(in,buf,out) = (in,buf-1,out+1)$

It is easy to verify that APC is a system

2.2. Successor function. Domain of a system

Let Σ be a system (we denote its components as previously). The total function S_Σ from the power set of states into itself :

$$S_\Sigma : \mathcal{P}(S) \rightarrow \mathcal{P}(S) \qquad (5)$$

defined by

$$S_\Sigma(E) = \bigcup_{(i,s) \in I \times E} N(i,s) \qquad (6)$$

where

$$N(i,s) = \begin{cases} \text{if } s \in S_i \text{ then } \{e_i(s)\} \\ \text{if } s \in S_f \text{ then } \{s\} \\ \text{otherwise } \emptyset \end{cases} \qquad (7)$$

is called the Successor function of Σ.

We denote by S^*_Σ the function from the power set of states into itself defined by :

$$S^*_\Sigma\ (E) = \bigcup_{n \in \mathbb{N}} S^n_\Sigma\ (E) \qquad (8)$$

The <u>domain</u> D_Σ of a system is definied by

$$D_\Sigma = S^*_\Sigma (S_b) \qquad (9)$$

Note that the relation "$s' \in S^*_\Sigma$ ({s})" is a preorder relation (reflexive and transitive).

<u>Example</u> : The graph of S^*_{APC} ({(3,0,0)}) where n = 2 is

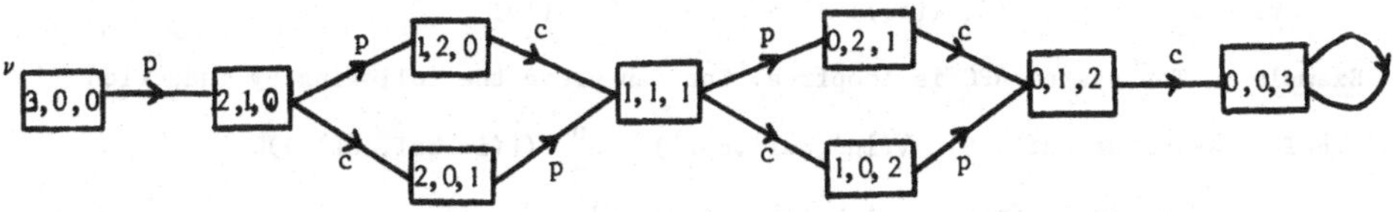

2.3. <u>Deterministic system</u>

A system Σ is said to be <u>deterministic</u> if the following holds

$$\forall s \in D_\Sigma .\mathrm{card}(S_\Sigma (\{s\})) \leq 1 \quad (10)$$

2.4. <u>Deadlockfree system</u>

A system Σ is said to be <u>deadlock-free</u> if the following holds

$$\forall s \in D_\Sigma .S_\Sigma \ (\{s\}) \neq \emptyset \qquad (11)$$

By the very definition of S_Σ, the condition (11) is equivalent to

$$D_\Sigma \subset (S_f \cup \bigcup_{i \in I} S_i) \qquad (12)$$

<u>Sufficient condition</u> : A system Σ is deadlockfree if the following holds

$$\forall i \in I.e_i(S_i) \subset (S_f \cup \bigcup_{i \in I} S_i) \quad (13)$$

<u>Example</u> : The system APC is deadlockfree ; it is easy to verify that

$$S_c \cup S_p \cup S_f = S$$

2.5. <u>Invariance</u>

Let Σ be a system. A total function g from S into a set X

$$g : S \rightarrow X \qquad (14)$$

is said to be <u>invariant throughout Σ</u> if the following holds

$$\forall i \in I. \forall s \in S_i .g(s) = g(e_i(s)) \qquad (15)$$

Example : The following function

$$inv : S \to \mathbb{N}$$

where

$$inv(in,buf,out) = in + buf + out$$

is invariant throughout the system APC.

2.6. Loop-free system

A system Σ is said to be loop-free if the relation "$s' \in S^*_\Sigma(\{s\})$" is an order relation i.e. if it is antisymetric.

Necessary and sufficient condition : The system Σ is loop-free iff the following holds

$$\forall s \in D_\Sigma . s \in S^*_\Sigma (S_\Sigma (\{s\})) \to s \in S_f \qquad (16)$$

Example : The system APC is loopfree. One can prove the following by induction

$$\forall n \in \mathbb{N} . \quad \forall (in,buf,out) \in S. \quad \forall (in',buf',out') \in S^n_\Sigma (\{(in,buf,out)\}).$$

$$(in'<in) \vee (out'>out) \vee (in'=0 \wedge buf'=0)$$

This formula leads directly to (16).

2.7. Finite system

A system Σ is said to be finite if the following holds

$$\forall s \in D_\Sigma . S^*_\Sigma (\{s\}) \text{ is finite} \qquad (17)$$

Example : The system APC is finite. Using the invariant "inv" (§ 2.5.) one gets

$$\forall s \in S.card(S^*_{APC}(\{s\})) \leq \frac{(p+1).(p+2)}{2}$$

where $p=inv(s)$

2.8. Variance

Let Σ be a system. A total function v of S into $\mathbb{N}$

$$v : S \to \mathbb{N} \qquad (18)$$

where

$$\forall s \in \bigcup_{i \in I} S_i . v(s) > 0 \qquad (19)$$

$$\forall s \in S_f . v(s)=0 \qquad (20)$$

$$\forall i \in I. \quad \forall s \in S_i . v(e_i(s)) < v(s) \qquad (21)$$

is a variant of Σ .

Sufficient condition for "loop-freeness" and finiteness" :
A system Σ is loop-free and finite if there exists a variant.

Example : The following is a variant of the system APC

$$v(in,buf,out) = 2.in+buf$$

2.9. Halting system

A system Σ is said to be halting if the following holds

$$\forall s \in S_b . \exists\, n \in \mathbb{N} . S_\Sigma^n (\{s\}) \subset S_f \wedge S_\Sigma^n (\{s\}) \neq \emptyset \qquad (22)$$

The sequence :

$$\{s\},\ S_\Sigma(\{s\}),\ S_\Sigma^2(\{s\}),\ \ldots$$

is therefore stationary ; we denote its limit by $M_\Sigma(\{s\})$.

Necessary and sufficient halting condition : A system is halting iff it is loop-free, finite and deadlockfree.

Proof of the direct part :

Let "$E \leq F$" be the relation (over subsets of D_Σ) defined by

$$\exists n \in \mathbb{N} . F = S_\Sigma^n (E) \qquad (23)$$

a) If Σ is loop-free then the relation $\leq$ is an order relation. Its antisymmetry comes from (16).

b) If Σ is finite then

$$\forall s \in S_b . \mathcal{P}(S_\Sigma^* (\{s\})) \text{ is finite}$$

Therefore the set $\mathcal{P}(S_\Sigma^*(\{s\}))$ is a finite set ordered by $\leq$. The sequence :

$$\{s\} \leq S_\Sigma(\{s\}) \leq S_\Sigma^2(\{s\}) \leq \ldots$$

is therefore stationary and its limit $M_\Sigma(\{s\})$ is such that $M_\Sigma(\{s\}) = S_\Sigma(M_\Sigma(\{s\}))$; as a consequence $M_\Sigma(\{s\}) \subset S_f$

c) If Σ is deadlockfree then $M_\Sigma(\{s\}) \neq \emptyset$ (by induction)

Consequence on an invariant function : If a system Σ is halting and if g is invariant throughout Σ then the following holds

$$\forall s \in S_b . g(M_\Sigma(\{s\})) = \{g(s)\} \qquad (24)$$

2.10. Externally deterministic system

A halting system Σ is said to be externally deterministic if the following holds

$$\forall s \in S_b . \mathrm{card}(M_\Sigma(\{s\})) = 1 \qquad (25)$$

Sufficient condition : A halting system is externally deterministic if there exists an invariant function whose restriction to S_f is injective.

Example : The system APC is externally deterministic because the restriction of "inv" (§ 2.5.) to S_f is injective.

2.11. Induced topology

Let Σ be a system. We construct a topology top_Σ on D_Σ by defining the closure $\bar{E}$ of all subsets E of D_Σ to be

$$\bar{E} = S_\Sigma^* (E) \qquad (26)$$

We obviously have for all subsets E and F of D

$$\overline{E \cup F} = \bar{E} \cup \bar{F}$$
$$E \subset \bar{E} \qquad (27)$$
$$\emptyset = \bar{\emptyset}$$
$$\bar{E} = \bar{\bar{E}}$$

This closure operation therefore defines (see[12]) a topology on D_Σ whose closed sets C are such that :

$$C = S^*_\Sigma (C)$$

Example : In the system APC the following are closed sets :

$\{(0,0,3)\}$, $\{(0,1,2) , (0,0,3)\}$, $\{(0,2,1)(0,1,2),(0,0,3)\}$ etc.

2.12. Abstraction and implementation

Let $\Sigma = (S,S_b,S_f,I,S_i,e_i)$ and $\Sigma' = (S,S_b,S_f,I',S',e'_i)$ be two halting systems (notice that their states, beninning states and final states are the same) such that

$$\forall s \in S_b . M_\Sigma (\{s\}) = M_{\Sigma'}(\{s\}) \qquad (29)$$

$$D_\Sigma \subset D_{\Sigma'} \qquad (30)$$

Let "$id_{\Sigma\Sigma'}$" be the total function from D_Σ into $D_{\Sigma'}$

$$id_{\Sigma\Sigma'} : D_\Sigma \to D_{\Sigma'} \qquad (31)$$

defined by $id_{\Sigma\Sigma'}(s) = s \qquad (32)$

If "$id_{\Sigma\Sigma'}$ is continuous then Σ is said to be an abstraction of Σ' and conversely Σ' is an implementation of Σ. In other words, if C' is a closed set of top Σ' then so is $C' \cap D$ with respect to top Σ.

Notice that the relation "Σ is an abstraction of Σ'" is a preorder relation.

Example : Let ACM (for arithmetic copy machine) be the following system

$S = \mathbb{N} \times \{0,\dots,n\} \times \mathbb{N}$

$J = \{copy\}$

$S_b = \mathbb{N} \times \{0\} \times \{0\}$

$S_f = \{0\} \times \{0\} \times \mathbb{N}$

$S_{copy} = \mathbb{N}^+ \times \{0\} \times \mathbb{N}$

$e_{copy}(in,buf,out) = (in-1,buf,out+1)$

It is easy to verify that ACM is an abstraction of APC ($e_{copy} = e_p \circ e_c$)

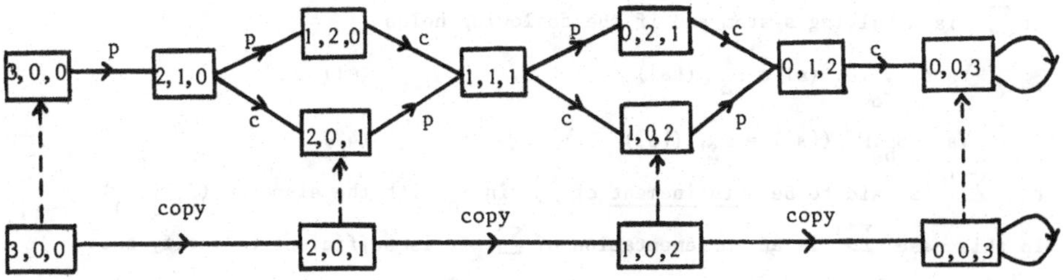

Influence on an invariant function : If g is an invariant function throughout Σ and if Σ is an abstraction of Σ' then g is almost invariant through Σ'. In other words the function g is may-be not invariant on $D_{\Sigma'} - D_{\Sigma}$ but it "recovers" its invariance on D_{Σ}.

Example : The function "inv2(in,buf,out)=in+out", invariant throughout ACM, is almost invariant throughout APC.

2.13. Trivial extension of a system

Let Σ be a system, T_i (for $i \in I$) a family of subsets of a set T and T_b a subset of T such that

$$T_b \subset \bigcap_{i \in I} T_i \qquad (33)$$

the 6-tuple $(SxT, S_b xT_b, S_f xT_b, I, ST_i, e_i')$

where $ST_i = S_i x T_i$ (34)

and $e_i'(s,t) = (e_i(s),t)$ (35)

is obviously a system, which we call a trivial extension of Σ by (T_b, T_i).

2.14. Refinement of a system

Let Σ be a halting system, i_o an event name of Σ, J a new set of events (i.e., $I \cap J = \emptyset$) and T_j (for $j \in J$) a family of total functions from T_j into S

$$g_j : T_j \rightarrow S \qquad (36)$$

such that

$$\forall j \in J. \forall s \in T_j . g_j(s) \neq s \qquad 39$$

$$S_f \cap \bigcup_{j \in J} T_j = \emptyset$$

the 6-tuple $\Sigma' = (S, S_b, S_f, I-\{i_o\} \cup J, S_i', e_i')$

where $S_i' = \begin{cases} \text{if } i \in I-\{i_o\} \text{ then } S_i \\ \text{if } i \in J \text{ then } T_i \end{cases}$ and $e_i' = \begin{cases} \text{if } i \in I-\{i_o\} \text{ then } e_i \\ \text{if } i \in J \text{ then } g_i \end{cases}$

is obviously a system.

If Σ' is a halting system and if the following holds

$$\forall s \in S_{i_o}.e_{i_o}(s) \in S^{*}_{\Sigma'}(\{s\}) \qquad (41)$$

$$\forall s \in S_b.M_{\Sigma}(\{s\}) = M_{\Sigma'}(\{s\}) \qquad (42)$$

then Σ' is said to be a refinement of Σ in i_o with the elements (J,T_j,g_j).

In this case, Σ' is an implementation of Σ. It is sufficient to verify that

$$\forall C' \in \mathcal{P}(D_{\Sigma'}).C'=S^{*}_{\Sigma'}(C') \rightarrow (C' \cap D_{\Sigma})= S^{*}_{\Sigma}\ (C' \cap D_{\Sigma}) \qquad (43)$$

or better

$$\forall C' \in \mathcal{P}(D_{\Sigma'}).C'= S^{*}_{\Sigma'}\ (C') \rightarrow S_{\Sigma}\ (C' \cap D_{\Sigma}) \subset C' \cap D_{\Sigma} \qquad (44)$$

where this latter is a direct result of the definition of Σ' and (41).

Note : The proof of the halting of Σ' is less difficult in general than the one of Σ if, following [5] , the new events do not destroy the hypothoses used in the proof Σ.

3. Examples

We first specify a disk handler (§ 3.1.) which we shall further refine several times in order to obtain an on-line query system (§ 3.3.).

3.1. Specification of a disk handler : the "lift" system

A disk is made up of a finite number of concentric tracks. In order to optimize the arm movement, one organizes the disk scheduling in such a way that the arm goes regularly from the exterior to the interior and back (this is the "lift" algorithm) : the queries are therefore not served according to a FIFO strategy but rather by taking into account the current arm position and its next intended move (say "up" or "down").

With each track is associated a queue of recognized queries that have not yet been served.

Example :

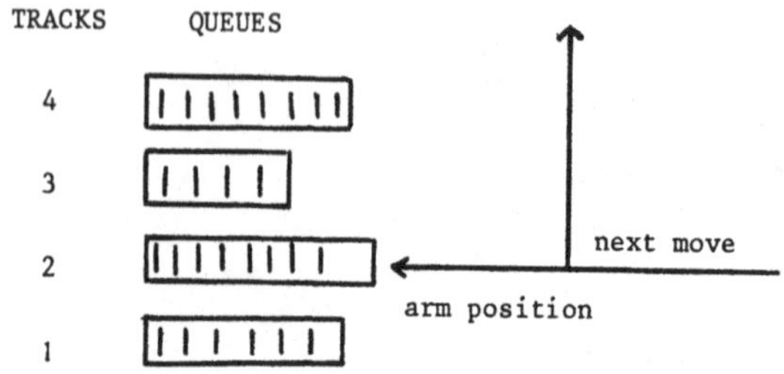

After serving the queries for track n°2, the arm moves to track n°3, serves its waiting queries, does the same for track n°4, then turns around to serve successively lower tracks, and so on.

More precisely, the state of such a system is characterized by :

- The ordered set of future queries (each query is defined by, say, a query name and a track name) : input

- The current arm position : current-track
- The next move of the arm : next-move
- The number of recognized queries to be served by the disk while its arm is on the current position : how-many
- For each track, an ordered set of recognized, but not yet served, queries for that track : queue
- The set of past served queries (where each track name is replaced by its content): output

Three events may occur :

- Recognizing a new query (when "input" is not empty) : ask
- Serving a recongnized query for the current arm position (when "how-many" is not null) : serve
- Moving the arm (when "how-many" is null and there exists a non empty "queue" of recognized queries) : move

This system is said to be correct if, when (and if) it halts, the final "output" set corresponds to the initial "input" set, i.e. each query of the initial "input" occurs in the final "output" (with the track name replaced by its content) and the final "output" does not contrain extra "ghost" answers. The order of the final "output" is meaningless.

The precise Z specification of this system follows.

```
specification lift
  type
    ordered TRACK ;
    MOVE = (up,down) ;
    QUERY-NAME ;
    VALUE
  assertion
    card (TRACK) in NAT     /*TRACK is finite*/
  relation
    disk : TRACK --- VALUE
  definition
    QUERY = prod (q-name : QUERY-NAME, track : TRACK) ;
    ANSWER = prod (q-name : QUERY-NAME, value : VALUE) ;

    GENERAL-STATE =
      prod (input : ordered set (QUERY),
           |current-track : TRACK,
           |next-move : MOVE,
           |how-many : NAT,
           |queue : func (TRACK, ordered set (QUERY)).
           |output : set (ANSWER)
           );
    STATE = subset s in GENERAL-STATE where
             | card (input(s)) in NAT and                              /*p is the*/
             | how-many(s) ≤ card (queue(s)(current-track(s))) and /*maximum*/
             | (sigma t in TRACK of card (queue(s)(t))end) ≤ p     /*size of all*/
             end                                                       /*queues*/

    INIT-STATE = subset s in STATE where
                  | how-many(s) = 0 and
                  | queue(s) = lambda t in TRACK => EMPTY end and
                  | output(s) = EMPTY
                  end

    FINAL-STATE = subset s in STATE where
                   | input(s) = EMPTY and
                   | how-many(s) = 0 and
                   | queue(s) = lambda t in TRACK => EMPTY end
                   end
  type
    EVENT-NAME = (ask,move,serve)
  relation
    set DOMAIN : EVENT-NAME --- STATE ;
    event : EVENT-NAME --- func (STATE,STATE)
  assertion
    DOMAIN(ask) = subset s in STATE where
                   | input(s) ≠ EMPTY and
                   | (sigma t in TRACK of card (queue(s)(t))end < p
                   end ;
    DOMAIN(move) = subset s in STATE where
                    | how-many(s) = 0 and
                    | exist t in TRACK where queue(s)(t) ≠ EMPTY end
                    end ;
    DOMAIN(serve) = subset s in STATE where how-many(s) ≠ 0 end ;
```

```
event(ask) =
  lambda s in DOMAIN(ask)==>
  | replace s with
  | | input : tail(input(s)),
  | | queue : given q = first(input(s)) then
  | |           | subst(queue(s),track(q),cat(queue(s)(track(q)),{q}))
  | |           end
  | end
  end ;

event(serve) =
  lambda s in DOMAIN(serve)=>
  | replace s with
  | | how-many : how-many(s)-1,
  | | queue : subst(queue(s),current-track(s),
  | |                             tail(queue(s)(current-track(s)))),
  | | output : given q = first(queue(s)(current-track(s))) then
  | |            | output(s) ∪ {(q-name : q-name(q),
  | |            |                   value : disk(track(q)))}
  | |            end
  | end
  end ;

event(move) =
  lambda s in DOMAIN(move) =>
  | if next-move(s) = up then
  | | if forall t in TRACK then
  | | |     t >  current-track(s) → queue(s)(t) = EMPTY
  | | |   end
  | | then given  /*notice that t is defined*/
  | | |     | t = sup t' in TRACK where
  | | |     |
  | | |     |         | t' ≤ current-track(s) and queue(s)(t') ≠  EMPTY
  | | |     |         end
  | | |     then
  | | |     | replace s with
  | | |     |   current-track : t,
  | | |     |   next-move : down,
  | | |     |   how-many : card(queue(s)(t))
  | | |     | end
  | | |     end
  | | else given  /* notice that t is defined*/
  | | |     | t = inf t' in TRACK where
  | | |     |       | t'> current-track(s) and queue(s)(t') ≠ EMPTY
  | | |     |       end
  | | |     then
  | | |     | replace s with
  | | |     | | current-track : t,
  | | |     | | how-many : card(queue(s)(t))
  | | |     | end
  | | |     end
  | | end
  | else
  | | ...
  | end
  end
relation
  set INVARIANT : STATE --- ANSWER ;
  variant : STATE --- NAT
```

```
assertion
  INVARIANT =
    lambda s in STATE =>
    [ union q in (input(s) ∪ union t in TRACK of queue(s)(t)end) of
    |   {(q-name :q-name(q), value : disk(track(q)))}
    | end ∪ output(s)
    end ;

   variant =
     lambda s in STATE =>
     | 3 x card(input(s))
     | + 2 x sigma t in TRACK of card(queue(s)(t)) end
     | - (if how-many(s) = 0 then 0 else 1 end)
     end
```

3.2. Correctness of the "lift" system

It is easy to verify that "lift" is a halting system :

a) "lift" is a system (§2.1.)

The three events are well defined (1) and obey (2).
The sets INIT-STATE, FINAL-STATE, DOMAIN(ask), DOMAIN(move), and DOMAIN(serve) obey (3) and (4)

b) "lift" is deadlock-free (§ 2.4.)

One may immediatly check that :

```
event(ask)(DOMAIN(ask)) ⊂ DOMAIN(ask) ∪  DOMAIN(move)  ∪  DOMAIN(serve)
event(move)(DOMAIN(move)) ⊂  DOMAIN(ask) ∪  DOMAIN(serve
event(serve)(DOMAIN(serve)) ⊂  DOMAIN(ask) ∪  DOMAIN(move) ∪  DOMAIN(serve) ∪
                               FINAL-STATE
```

c) "lift" is loop-free and finite (§ 2.8.)

It is sufficient to verify that "variant" is indeed a variant (conditions (19), (20) and (21)).

It is easy to check that INVARIANT is indeed an invariant function throughout "lift" (condition (15)). Since "lift" halts one may apply (24) and hence verify that it is correct according to the above informal definition of correctness.

Note : "lift" is not externally deterministic (§ 2.10.).

3.3. Specification of a complete system : the system "query"

We now refine the "lift" system several times in order to obtain an on-line "query" system, as shown by the following drawing :

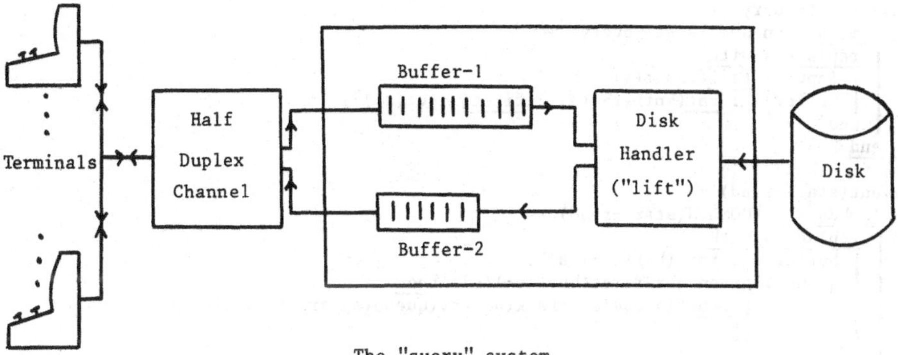

The "query" system

3.3.1. Trivial extension of "lift"

We add the following "fields" to the GENERAL-STATE

buffer-1 : ordered set (QUERY)
buffer-2 : ordered set (ANSWER)
Channel-Status : {in,out,free}

The following condition is added to the definition of STATE

card(buffer-1(s)) ≤ m and card(buffer-2(s)) ≤ n and
(channel-status(s) = out → buffer-2(s) ≠ EMPTY) and
(channel-status(s) = in → input(s) ≠ EMPTY and card(buffer-1(s)) < m)

Where m and n are positive integers representing the maximum size of the buffers.

The sets INIT-STATE and FINAL-STATE are restricted by the following condition

buffer-1(s) = EMPTY and buffer-2(s) = EMPTY and channel-status(s) = free

3.3.2. Tentative refinement of the "ask" and "serve" events

We replace the events "ask" and "serve" with {get-query, start-read} and {read,put-answer} respectively.

The new domains are the following

```
DOMAIN(get-query) =
  subset s in STATE where
  | input(s) ≠ EMPTY and
  | card(buffer-1(s)) < m
  end

DOMAIN(start-read) =
  subset s in STATE where
  | buffer-1(s) ≠ EMPTY and
  | (sigma t in TRACK of card(queue(s)(t)end) < p
  end

DOMAIN(read) =
  subset s in STATE where
  | how-many(s) ≠ 0 and card(buffer-2(s)) < n
  end

DOMAIN(put-answer) = subset s in STATE where buffer-2(s) ≠ EMPTY end
```

The new events are the following

```
event(get-query) =
  lambda s in DOMAIN(get-query) =>
  | replace s with
  | | input : tail(input(s)),
  | | buffer-1 : cat(buffer-1(s), {first(input(s))})
  | end
  end

event(start-read) =
  lambda s in DOMAIN(start-read) =>
  | replace s with
  | | buffer-1 : tail(buffer-1(s)),
  | | queue : given q = first(buffer-1(s)) then
  | |         | subst(queue(s),track(q),cat(queue(s)(track(q)),{q}))
  | |         end
  | end
  end

event(read) =
  lambda s in DOMAIN(read) =>
  | replace s with
  | | how-many : how-many(s)-1,
  | | queue : subst(queue(s),current-track(s),
  | |                            tail(queue(s)(current-track(s)))),
  | | buffer-2 : given q = first(queue(s)(current-track(s)) then
  | |              | cat(buffer-2(s),{(q-name : q-name(q),value : disk(track(q))})
  | |              end
  | end
  end

event(put-answer) =
  lambda s in DOMAIN(put-answer) =>
  | replace s with
  | | buffer-2 : tail(buffer-2(s)),
  | | output : output(s) ∪ {first(buffer-2(s))}
  | end
  end
```

3.3.3. Further tentative refinement of the "get-query" and "put-answer" events

Taking into account the "half-duplex" channel, we replace the events "get-query" and "put-answer" with {start-get-query, end-get-query} and {start-put-answer, end-put-answer } respectively,

The new domains are the following

```
DOMAIN(start-get-query) =
  subset s in DOMAIN(get-query) where
  | channel-status(s) = free
  end

DOMAIN(end-get-query) =
  subset s in DOMAIN(get-query) where
  | channel-status(s) = in
  end

DOMAIN(start-put-answer) =
  subset s in DOMAIN(put-answer) where
  | channel-status(s) = free
  end
```

```
DOMAIN(end-put-answer) =
  subset s in DOMAIN(put-answer) where
  | channel-status(s) = out
  end
```

The new events are the following

```
event(start-get-query) =
   lambda s in DOMAIN(start-get-query) =>
   | replace s with
   | | channel-status : in
   | end
   end

event(end-get-query) =
  lambda s in DOMAIN(end-get-query) =>
  | replace event(get-query)(s)) with
  | | channel-status : free
  | end
  end

event(start-put-answer) =
  lambda s in DOMAIN(start-put-answer) =>
  | replace s with
  | | channel-status : out
  | end
  end

event(end-put-answer) =
  lambda s in DOMAIN(end-put-answer) =>
  | replace event(put-answer)(s)) with
  | | channel-status : free
  | end
  end
```

3.4. Correctness of the "query" system

The "query" system is a halting system

a) Deadlock : Condition (13) holds hence "query" is deadlock-free

b) Loop and finiteness : The following function is a variant of "query".

```
variant' = lambda s in STATE =>
           | 7 x card(input(s))
           | + 5 x card(buffer-1(s))
           | + 4 x sigma t in TRACK of card(queue(s)(t))end
           | + 2 x card(buffer-2(s))
           | - (if how-many(s) = 0 then 0 else 1 end)
           | - (if channel-status(s) = free then 0 else 1 end)
           end
```

It is possible to show that "lift" is an abstraction of "query". As a consequence the function INVARIANT is almost invariant (§ 2.12.) throughout the halting system "query". One can again apply (24) thus completing the correctness proof of the system "query".

4. Conclusion

We have presented an elementary formalism for the specification of non-deterministic systems. A few examples showed the use of this formalism.

Other examples, like the classical "reader-writer" or even the "on-the-fly-garbage-collector" can be specified using the same method.

However much work remains to be done in this domain. In particular, it might be interesting to define sufficient conditions for refinements.

REFERENCES

1. DIJKSTRA, E.W. Guarded commands, nondeterminacy and formal derivation of programs. Comm. ACM 18,8 (Aug. 1975)
2. HOARE, C.A.R. Communicating sequential processes. Comm. ACM 21,8 (Aug. 1978)
3. BRINCH HANSEN, P. Distributed processes : A concurrent programming concept. Comm. ACM 21,11 (Nov. 1978)
4. OWICKI, S. GRIES, D. An axiomatic proof technique for parallel programs. I. Acta Informatica 6 (1976)
5. OWICKI, S. Axiomatic proof techniques for parallel programs Dept. C.S. Cornell University TR 75-251 (1975)
6. HOARE, C.A.R. An axiomatic basis for computer programming Comm. ACM 12,10 (Oct. 1969)
7. GRIES, D. An exercise in proving parallel programs correct. Comm. ACM 20,12 (Dec. 1977)
8. DIJKSTRA, E.W. et al. On-the-fly garbage collection : An exercise in cooperation Comm. ACM 21,12 (Nov. 1978)
9. SINTZOFF, M. Inventing program construction rules in Constructing quality Software North-Holland/IFIP (1978)
10. MEYER, B. DEMUYNCK, M. Specification languages : A critical survey and proposal. Submitted for publication.
11. ABRIAL, J.R. Z : A specification language. Proceedings of the international conference on mathematical studies of information processing. Kyoto, Japan (Aug. 1978)
12. KURATOWSKI, K Introduction à la théorie des ensembles et à la topologie. Dunod.

ON PROPERTIES PRESERVED BY CONTRACTIONS OF CONCURRENT SYSTEMS

John S. Gourlay*
William C. Rounds*
Richard Statman†
*Department of Computer and Communication Sciences
†Department of Philosophy
The University of Michigan
Ann Arbor, Michigan 48109

Abstract

We propose a definition of representation map between concurrent systems called a contraction, which is intended to capture the notion of a safe simulation of an abstract by a concrete system. We give several examples and investigate some specific behavioral properties (such as nontermination) which might be preserved by contractions or their inverses. In the second part of the paper, we use model theory to study the decidability properties of the set of sentences preserved by contractions.

1. Introduction

The Dijkstra notion of "levels of abstraction" is a popular way to visualize the design and analysis of software systems. Combined with the modularity ideas championed by Parnas, the notion seems to lead in practice to systems more easily modifiable and verifiable than ones without this structure. One case where the methodology has been applied is the work on secure operating systems at SRI [11], in which a hierarchy formalism was introduced to guide level design and implementation. Software design languages like DREAM [9] and SARA [2] try to take the idea into account, and of course the notion of abstraction, deriving from Hoare, is central to the new programming languages.

Recently two papers have appeared which formalize the notion of abstraction for concurrent programs. Brand [1] discusses an extension of Milner's work on "simulation" [7] between programs, and Kwong [5] gives general conditions under which one program is a "reduction" of another. Kwong's work is a simplification and generalization of work of Lipton [6].

We would like to emphasize the relevance of both of these papers to the understanding of concurrent systems. The first part of our paper unifies and extends the results of both authors. The second part is a model-theoretic investigation of the properties of transition relations which remain generally true whenever we abstract one system from another. We are motivated by the fact that properties of abstractions are easier to prove than those of implementations. Our results attempt to characterize those properties which are always preserved by abstractions (our technical term is contraction). We do not give a complete solution of the problem, but we can give deciability results about the set of sentences expressing such properties.

We feel that definitions like these are worth considering as possibilities for representing one level of abstraction by another. The work at SRI, with its mappings between levels, is a case in point. The mappings considered in that work are not required to be contractions; thus, although proofs can be carried out that a mapping satisfies certain conditions, the conditions which it does satisfy may not be enough to transfer properties from the abstract to the concrete system. (Brand and Kwong make this point as well [1, pp. 8-9]; [5, p. 26].) We do not mean to suggest, however, that the definitions are unique. In special cases there will likely be strengthened conditions which are much more useful.

2. Contractions

Our objective is to model the behavior of asynchronous systems. We begin by describing virtual machines, which are variations of the transition systems in Keller [4]. Our formalization evolved from the work of Riddle [9] on descriptions of software systems, and can be regarded as a step towards providing a semantics for this and similar software design languages. Next we introduce the idea of a contraction between virtual machines, giving examples. We conclude with some representative theorems on specific properties like nontermination [5], liveness [4], and Church-Rosser [13], which might be preserved under contractions. These theorems generalize results in Kwong, who studied the special case of reductions.

2.1. Virtual Machines as Concurrent Algebras

We picture a virtual machine in the following diagram:

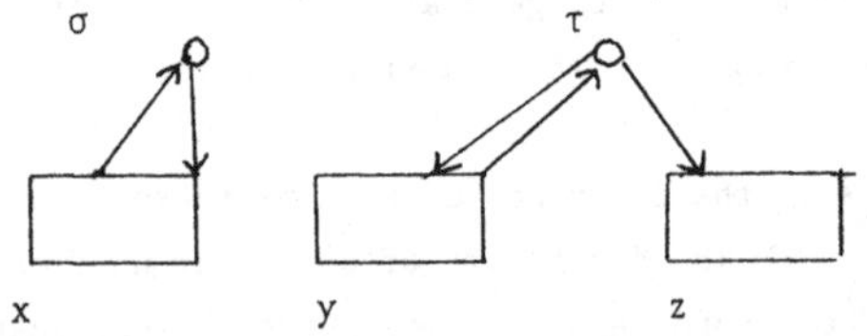

Here, σ and τ are names of abstract operations on the abstract data in the boxes x, y, and z. At this level, σ and τ are indivisible commands, although their "implementations" may be nonatomic and interleavable. An important point is that σ and τ are nondeterministic (i.e., not functions). Another is that σ may fire iff the inputs to σ are in the domain of σ. Thus, we have an abstract Petri net.

2.1.1. Definition. A virtual machine is a 4-tuple $<X, \{A_x\}_{x\varepsilon X}, \Sigma, Int>$ where X is a set of variables (chosen as a subset of some universe $V = \{v_1, v_2 \ldots\}$); $\{A_x\}$ is a collection of abstract sets indexed by X (the domains over which variables take their values). Σ is a graded alphabet of operation names, and Int is an interpretation of Σ as appropriate abstract "actions". Σ is a graded by the following maps:

$V : \Sigma \to P(X)$: the input variables for σ form $V(\sigma)$

$C : \Sigma \to P(X)$: the output variables for σ form $C(\sigma)$

Note: we use sets instead of sequences of variables -- no "aliasing" allowed at a given level.

If for a subset Y of X we let A^Y denote the product $\prod_{y\varepsilon Y} A_y$, then we may specify the interpretation as a function Int such that for each $\sigma \varepsilon \Sigma$, $Int(\sigma) \varepsilon P(A^{V(\sigma)} \times A^{C(\sigma)})$, i.e., Int (σ) is a relation between two Cartesian product sets.

For a given virtual machine we can define the global state space $Q = A^X$, and we can define the extension $\hat{\sigma}$ of an operation σ to the whole state space in a componentwise fashion by letting the extension $\hat{\sigma}$ act as the identity on those variables not changed by σ. Thus, $\hat{\sigma} \subseteq Q \times Q$. We will refer to a virtual machine as an automaton $<Q, \Sigma>$, where Q is understood to be the global state space.

A behavior string of $<Q, \Sigma>$ is just an element $w \varepsilon \Sigma^*$ such that for some (q, q') $\varepsilon Q \times Q$, we have $(q, q') \varepsilon Int(w)$, where

$Int(w) = Int(\sigma_1) \circ \ldots \circ Int(\sigma_n)$ if $w = \sigma_1 \ldots \sigma_n$. (We will write $q\ w\ q'$.)

A computation is a triple $<q_0, \sigma_0, q_1, \sigma_1, \ldots, q_{n-1}, \sigma_{n-1}, q_n>$ such that the q_i's are appropriately related by the σ_i's.

2.1.2. Definition. Let $A = <X, \{A_x\}, \Sigma, I>$ and $B = <Y, \{B_y\}, \Gamma, J>$. We assume $\Sigma \cap \Gamma = \phi$ but that X and Y may overlap. If so, we require that $v \varepsilon X \cap Y \Rightarrow A_v = B_v$. (Intuitively, we would like to capture the notion of shared variables between two systems running concurrently.) The concurrent product of A and B is then just

$$A \Delta B = <X \cup Y, \{A_x\} \cup \{B_y\}, \Sigma \cup \Gamma, I \cup J>.$$

Define $L(A) = \{w |\ w$ is a behavior of $A\}$. What is the relationship between L(A), L(B) and $L(A \Delta B)$? Unfortunately, we cannot say anything if $X \cap Y \neq \phi$, but if A and B are really independent (i.e., $X \cap Y = \phi$), then $L(A \Delta B) = L(A) \Delta L(B)$, where Δ on the right is the shuffle operator on formal languages. (Notice that this construction occurs in Petri net theory [3] just to prove closure of Petri net languages under Δ.)

2.1.3. Example. Figure 1 (Appendix) is taken from Riddle [10] and represents a spooling system with several user processes, a virtual memory system, and several other components. In this diagram (ignore specific names -- they are irrelevant) we imagine the program processes (in cirles) interacting with each other by message passing (the square boxes represent message buffers) but the internal structure of the processes is unspecified at this point. Thus the action of a particular process will be a relation on the Cartesian product space formed by taking the message boxes as components.

We might imagine a specification of this system given by some conditions on the variables associated with each component, or a behavioral specification given by listing allowable interleavings of operations. The problem of interest then would be to show that when more detail is given for each component, that the allowed actions of the concrete system in some sense realize the specifications of the abstract system. "More detail" could mean giving a program for each process (thus introducing program counters as components of the global state) or expanding a particular component such as the address translator as an asynchronous subsystem. Thus, we now turn to the definition of realization by contractions.

2.1.4. Definition. Let $<Q_A, \Sigma_A>$ and $<Q_B, \Sigma_B>$ be virtual machines. Let $\rho_A(\rho_B)$ be the relation on $Q_A(Q_B)$ defined by $(q_A, q'_A) \in \rho$ iff for some $w \in \Sigma^*$, $q_A\ w\ q_A'$. A partial surjective mapping h: $Q_B \rightarrow Q_A$ is a contraction if it satisfies the two conditions

2.1.4 (1) $h \circ \rho_A \subseteq \rho_B \circ h$

2.1.4 (2) $h^{-1} \circ \rho_B \circ h \subseteq \rho_A$

where $\circ$ is relation composition (i.e., $R \circ S$ means perform R, then S).

We say that a map satisfying (1) alone is a weak contraction; a weak contraction is not necessarily a contraction.

Informally, A is the more abstract system, and h is a representation map. We wish every state (configuration) of A to have some representation in B, so h is surjective, but we do not wish states of B to represent more than one state of A, so h is a function. Condition (1) says that every computation of A can be simulated by one of B, and condition (2) asserts that the reverse is also true, at least with respect to those B states which represent configurations in A.

We notice that Brand's definition differs from ours: First, h is not required to be a function; second, he does not require condition (1); and last, he replaces (2) with the stronger condition

(2B) $h^{-1} \circ \rho_B \subseteq \rho_A \circ h^{-1}$.

Using the fact that h is a function, it is easy to check that (2B) $\Longrightarrow$ (2) but not conversely. (If h is total, then (2B) is equivalent to (2).) Thus, our definitions, when h is partial a surjection, are weaker than Brand's. Later on, we will require a condition called domain reachability on our systems in order to obtain certain mapping properties.

The definitions can be illustrated in the following diagrams: for (1) we have

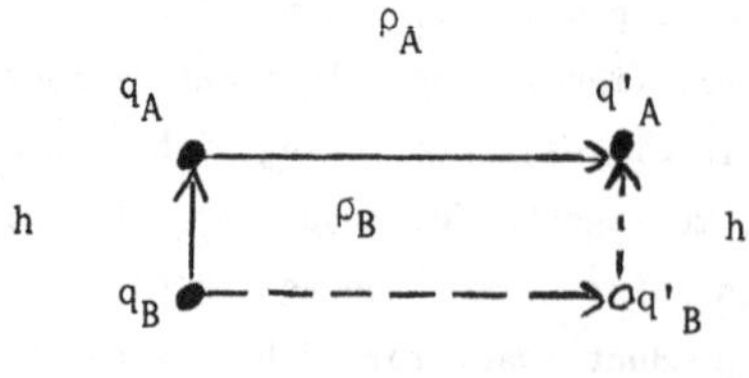

where the solid lines and circles represent given (universally quantified) information, and the dotted lines and open circle can be filled in (existential information). Similarly, for (2) we have

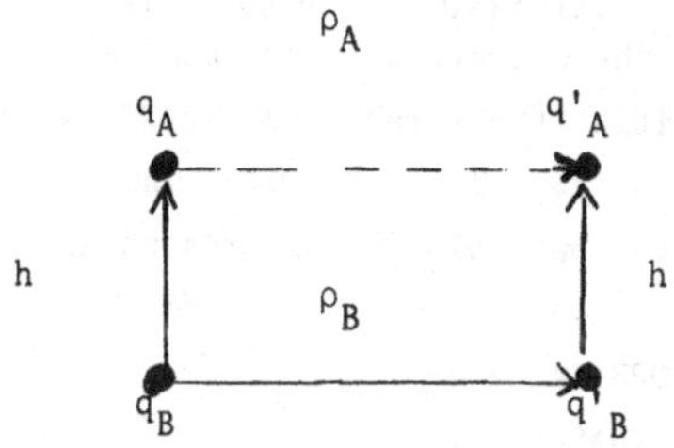

Since our abstract machines are "higher-level", we have inverted the usual commutative diagrams.

2.2 Examples

Referring to the spooling system example (2.1.3), imagine that we wished to expand the address-translator component as in Figure 2 (Appendix). We notice that several new data boxes have been added to the system (Enable, Mutex, etc.) Ignoring the control structure involved, we can see that an appropriate representation map h would be the projection from the new Cartesian space onto the old one. (That is, just ignore the values of Mutex, etc.) Of course, the B transition relation will be much more detailed than A's. It turns out, however, that projections are contractions, so that we may apply our general theorems.

For another example, we examine a situation not explicitly involving asynchronous systems, but involving shared memory space. Imagine the value of a stack of integers to be a finite sequence $\langle n_1,\ldots n_k\rangle$. Pushing an integer n onto this stak means forming the sequence $\langle n_1,\ldots,n_k,n\rangle$. (Our stacks can only be pushed.) At the abstract level A, assume we have two independent stack variables STACK1 and STACK2 with domains $\mathbb{N}^*$, and an integer variable N. We have two PUSH operations

PUSH1 : STACK1 x N → STACK1

PUSH2 : STACK2 x N → STACK2

(Of course, these would be parameterized into a single operation in any language.) In addition, suppose we have a READ operation: N → N which changes N to an arbitrary value. Thus, the state space of A is $\mathbb{N}^* \times \mathbb{N}^* \times \mathbb{N}$. Any sequence of READs and PUSHes is allowable.

We realize this machine by a machine B with a semi-infinite integer array $S[1::\infty]$ for a memory. The two stacks will be subarrays of S, and B will have some extra variables not part of S. In particular, B has variables BASE1 and TOP1, giving the locations of the bottom and top of STACK1 in memory; similarly the variables BASE2 and TOP2 keep track of STACK2. B also has an integer variable BUF for reading in integers. As a first try at simulating A with B, we might equip B with the stack-simulating operations

A1 : TOP1 x BUF x S → S x TOP1

A2 : TOP2 x BUF x S → S x TOP2

where A1 sets TOP1 : = TOP1 + 1, then S[TOP1] : = BUF. (Similarly for A2).

It is clear that with only the operations described, B could not simulate A, because B would often be overwriting the array used for STACK2 when trying to PUSH STACK1 (assuming STACK1 stored to the left of STACK2). Thus, we equip B with a SHIFT operation which in one block move, puts STACK2's representing array a fixed distance c from the end of STACK1:

```
begin for i := 0 until TOP2-BASE2 do
      S[TOP2 + c + i] := S[BASE2 + i];
      BASE2 := TOP1 + c
end.
```

Suppose also that B has a "Read" operation R : BUF → BUF.

The representing map h is then defined componentwise:

STACKi = <S[BASEi],...,S[TOPi]>

N = BUF.

As defined, h is a weak contraction, because (trivially) PUSH1 can be realized by SHIFT ∘ A1, PUSH2 by SHIFT ∘ A2, and READ by R. However, h is not a contraction since nothing constrains the B machine from overwriting. There are many ways to redefine the system B to make h into a contraction. One obvious way is to let the operation A1 be conditional:

```
if TOP1 + 1 ≥ BASE2 then SHIFT;
TOP1 := TOP1 + 1;
S[TOP1] :=BUF.
```

In addition, we restrict the domain of h to be those states in which TOP1 < BASE2. It is then easy to see that the new h is a contraction.

We conclude our examples by showing how the Lipton-Kwong reductions fit our definitions. According to [5, Def. 4.1] a <u>reduction</u> of B to A is a situation in which

(2.2.1) $Q_A \subseteq Q_B$;

(2.2.2) $\rho_B \restriction Q_A = \rho_A$

where $\restriction$ denotes the restriction of ρ_B to states in Q_A. There are additional conditions on initial states and non-null transitions which we ignore here; (2.2.1) and (2.2.2) express the essential conditions. Notice that we can choose for a contraction from Q_B to Q_A the partial-identity function on Q_A; 2.1.4 (1) and 2.1.4(2) then follow directly from (2.2.1) and (2.2.2). Another way of stating (2.2.1) and (2.2.2) is that the structure (Q_A, ρ_A) is a substructure of (Q_B, ρ_B), where the relations are reflexive and transitive. We will exploit this fact in the second part of the paper.

2.3 General Algebraic Facts about Contractions

2.3.1. The class of contractions (and the class of weak contractions) is closed under composition.

We will write A $\leq$ B if there is a contraction from B onto A. A corollary of 2.3.1 is that $\leq$ is transitive.

2.3.2. Definition. Virtual machines A and A' are independent if $X_A \cap X_{A'} = \phi$.

2.3.3. If A $\leq$ B and A' $\leq$ B' and A is independent of A' and B of B' then A Δ A' $\leq$ B Δ B'.

This fact gives us a way to synthesize contractions; see Brand for some sufficient conditions under which one may do the same thing when variables are shared.

2.3.4. Definition. A is a component of B if $\Sigma_A = \Sigma_B$, $X_A \subseteq X_B$. $A_x^A = A_x^B$ for all $x \in X_A$, and $\mathrm{Int}_A(\sigma)) = \pi_A(\mathrm{Int}_B(\sigma))$ for all $\sigma \in \Sigma$. In this definition, π_A is the natural projection from $Q_B \to Q_A$, and if ρ is a relation on Q_B, then $\pi_A(\rho) = \{(\pi_A(q), \pi_A(q')) \mid (q,q') \in \rho\}$.

2.3.5. If A is a component of B, then A $\leq$ B (projection is a contraction).

2.4. Predicates Preserved under Contractions.

In this subsection we consider the notion of invariant and specific properties of concurrent systems like nontermination and so on. Proofs are straightforward consequences of the definitions and are omitted for brevity. The relation ρ will denote the reflexive transitive closure of the state transition relation defined by individual actions σ in a virtual machine <Q, Σ>.

2.4.1. Definition. If P is a predicate on Q ($P \subseteq Q$) then

$$\Box P = \{q \in Q \mid (\forall r \in Q)\ (q \,\rho\, r \Longrightarrow r \in P)\}$$

$$\Diamond P = {}^{\sim}\Box{}^{\sim}P$$

These are exactly the Kripke modal operators "necessarily" and "possibly". See Pratt [8] for an extensive use of these operators in a logic of programs. The importance of them for us is that they can be used to state Keller's [4] definition of invariant: a predicate P is invariant with respect to a state $q \in Q$ iff $q \in \Box P$.

2.4.2. Definition. If h is a partial map $Q_B \to Q_A$ with domain D, we say h satisfies the domain reachability condition

$$\mathrm{DRC}(h) \Longleftrightarrow D \subseteq \Box\Diamond D.$$

This says: starting in D, no matter what happens, it's always possible to get back to D. This condition, if satisfied by a contraction h, provides an analogue of Brand's strong definition (2.1.4 (2B)).

2.4.3. Definition. Given h: $Q_B \to Q_A$, and $P \subseteq Q_A$ or Q_B, we wrote

$h[P] = \{h(q) \mid q \in P\}$

$h^{-1}[P] = \{q \mid h(q) \in P\}$.

2.4.4. If h is a weak contraction then $h[\Box P] \subseteq \Box h[P]$

2.4.5. If h is a contraction with domain D then $h[\Diamond (P \cap D)] \subseteq \Diamond h[P]$.

2.4.6. If h is a contraction and DRC(h) then $h[\Diamond P] \subseteq \Diamond h[P]$.

2.4.7. If h is weak, then
$h^{-1}[\Diamond P] \subseteq \Diamond h^{-1}[P]$;
$\Box h^{-1}[P] \subseteq h^{-1}[\Box P]$.

2.4.8. If h is a contraction then
$h^{-1}[\Diamond P] = D \cap \Diamond h^{-1}[P]$.

Corollary: if h is a total contraction, then 2.4.7 can be strengthened to equality.

2.4.9. Given contractions h: $C \to B$, k: $B \to A$ with DRC(h) and DRC(k). Then DRC($h \circ k$).

We now generalize Kwong's results to the case of contractions.

2.4.10. Definition. The virtual machine <Q, Σ> has the nontermination property with respect to $Q_o \subseteq Q$ iff the predicate $P = \{q \mid \exists q' \neq q \text{ such that } q \, \rho \, q'\}$ is Q_o - invariant. (This is the negation of the halting property in Lipton [6].)

2.4.11. Suppose h: $B \to A$ is a contraction with DRC(h) holding. If as has the nontermination property, then B has the same property with respect to $h^{-1}[Q_o]$.

2.4.11 is the conclusion reached by Lipton [6]. It is the type of result one desires: the ability to infer properties of a complex system (B) from a simple one (A). The property of nontermination is only a weak form of the non-halting behavior which is desirable in operating systems, however. Two stronger properties are liveness and deadlock-freeness, the first is defined using process structure, which we ignore in this paper.

2.4.12. Definition (Keller [4]). Given virtual machine <Q, Σ> the state q is live if for each $\sigma \in \Sigma$, $q \in \Box \Diamond$ domain (σ).

Unfortunately, the inverse images of live states under contractions need not be live. Let h be a contraction with DRC (h) holding; suppose in addition to (2.1.4) we have $\rho_B \subseteq h \circ \rho_A \circ h^{-1}$. Then:

2.4.13. If h(q) is live in A, then for all σ_B such that domain(σ_B) $\cap$ domain (h) $\neq \phi$, we have $q \in \Box \Diamond$ domain (σ_B). Thus q is live with respect to those states and operations of B which "make sense" in A.

Our final theorem conserns the Church-Rosser property.

2.4.14. Definition. Given virtual machine <Q, Σ> and $P \subseteq Q$, with ~ an equivalence relation on P. <Q, Σ> has the partial Church-Rosser property with respect to ~ and P iff for each q, q' in P with $q \sim q'$, and for each r, $r' \in Q$ with $q \, \rho^* \, r$ and $q' \overset{\rho}{\to}{}^* r'$, there are s, $s' \in P$ with $s \sim s'$, $r' \rho \, s'$.

If P = Q, then we say <Q, Σ> is Church-Rosser with respect to ~.

2.4.15. Let h: $Q_B \to Q_A$ be a contraction, and suppose $\sim_A$ is an equivalence relation on Q_A. Define $\sim_B$ on Q_B by $q \sim_B q' \Longleftrightarrow h(q) \sim_A h(q')$. If B is partial Church-Rosser with respect to $\sim_B$ and D, then A is Church-Rosser with respect to $\sim_A$. Conversely, if h satisfies the DRC and A is Church-Rosser with respect to $\sim_A$, then B is partial Church-Rosser with respect to D and $\sim_B$.

3. Logical Properties Preserved by Contractions

This section is devoted to a much more general study of contractions than in Section 2. Here we consider sentences expressing properties of the transition relation ρ itself. These will be expressed in a first order logical language L having ρ as a binary predicate symbol, and perhaps other predicates as well. A typical formula, expressing the classical Church-Rosser property, is

$$\forall q\ r\ s\ (q\ \rho\ r \wedge q\ \rho\ s \supset (\exists t)\ (r\ \rho\ t \wedge s\ \rho\ t)).$$

Another, asserting the existence of a "terminating" state, is

$$(\exists q\ (\forall r)\ (q\ \rho\ r \supset q=r)$$

This formula requires the use of equality as an additional predicate. Our language might have still other predicates: for example, a unary predicate expressing that a state is initial, etc. We will interpret these forumlas in standard first-order mathematical structures. Our virtual machines thus are thought of as structures $\langle Q\ \rho\rangle$ where ρ is assumed to be a transitive, reflexive relation. The lanugage L will always have ρ as a predicate and we will always assume the axioms of L stating that ρ is reflexive and transitive. We may assume other axioms, but we restrict them to be universal and to be finite in number.

We are interested in sentences "preserved" by contractions in all models of T, the axiomatic theory just described. These are therefore the properties that we get "for free" whenever we have any contraction. It is unfortunately the case that few such properties exist of any practical interest. However, the set of sentences C expressing these properties still has an interesting structure.

3.1. Definition

Let L be the language described above containing ρ and = as symbols, and let T be a universal finitely axiomatized theory which contains the reflexivity and transitivity of ρ. If A is a structure for L, let A* be its reduct to just the relation ρ (i.e., ignore all other predicates). A sentence S in L is preserved under contractions if for all A and B, models of T, whenever we have a contraction from B* onto A* and B $\models$ S, then A $\models$ S.

Example. The property of ρ being symmetric is preserved under contractions. The sentence in this case is $\forall xy(x\rho y \supset y\rho x)$; it is easy to check that the sentence is preserved. The sentence $\forall xy(x\rho y \vee y\rho x \supset x=y)$, however, is not preserved. (Map $\langle \mathbb{Z}\leq\rangle$ onto $\langle \mathbb{Z}_2, U\rangle$ when U is the universal relation).

Of course, we wish in general to lift properties from abstract to concrete systems. We thus define a sentence to be preserved under inverse contractions by reversing the implication in the foregoing definition to read: when A $\models$ S then B $\models$ S.

Then we have the observation:

3.2.

S is preserved under contractions iff $\tilde{}S$ is preserved under inverse contractions.

By 3.2, it is sufficient to study the set of senteances C preserved under contractions in order to establish decidability properties of both sets. Our next observation is a step in this direction:

3.3

If S is preserved under contractions, then there is a universal sentence U such that $T \vdash S \longleftrightarrow U$. This is a direct consequence of the Los-Tarski theorem [14, p. 76]. Recall that every reduction (substructure) is a contraction, and hence if S is preserved under contractions it must be preserved under substructures. The observation follows (T is universal).

3.4. Theorem

The set of sentences $C \subseteq L$ preserved under contractions is not recursive.

Proof. Consider the set L' of sentences formed just from the relation ρ, and let Tr and Ref the formulas expressing the transitivity and reflexivity of ρ. Rogers, in his thesis [12], showed that the set $\{A \in L' \mid Tr \wedge Ref \to A\}$ is not recursive. But $Tr \wedge Ref \to A$ is a theorem iff the one element partial order satisfies A and $\tilde{}A$ is preserved under contractions. Since the first assertion is clearly decidable the second cannot be. Thus the set $\{A \in L' \mid A \text{ preserved}\}$ is undecidable, and therefore so is C.

C is not recursive, but we have the next best thing.

3.5 Theorem

The set C is recursively enumerable.

The proof of 3.5 involves two lemmas.

3.6 Lemma

If U is a universal formula, then we can effectively find $A_1,\ldots,A_k$, models of T, such that if U is not preserved then for some i there is a model A_i of T and a model B of T, and there is a contraction from B* onto A_i* for which $B \models U$ and $A_i \models \sim U$.

Proof. Since U is universal, we may construct a sentence $S \longleftrightarrow \sim U$ and S is a disjunction of sentences S_i, each of which is the $\exists$-closure of a conjunction of literals. Let B' and A' be models of T, and h a contraction $: B'^* \to A'^*$. Suppose also that $B' \models U$ and $A' \models \sim U$. Then for some j, $A' \models S$; Let $S_j = \exists x_1 \ldots x_n R$ where R is a conjunction of literals, and select $a_1,\ldots,a_n \in A'$ such that $A', a_1,\ldots,a_n \models R$. Let A be the substructure of A' generated by $\{a_1,\ldots,a_n\}$. Let B be the substructure of B' generated by $h^{-1}[\{a_1,\ldots,a_n\}]$. Then h restricted to $h^{-1}[\{a_1,\ldots,a_n\}]$. is a contraction of B* onto A*, $B \models T \wedge U$ because $T \wedge U$ is universal, $A \models T \wedge \tilde{}U$ because T is universal. Thus for $A_1,\ldots,A_k$ it suffices to construct all models of $T \wedge \tilde{}U$ of size $\leq$ number of quantifiers in U.

3.7. Lemma

Let A with domain Q_A be a countable model of T; then there is a theory T_A which is recursive in A, (in an extension of the language L) such that for every B, B is a model of T and there is a contraction from B* onto A* if an only if B is a reduct of a model of T_A.

Proof. For each a εQ_A introduce a monadic predicate P_a. The axioms of T_A are then

for each a ε Q_A : $\exists x\ P_a(x)$

for a, b ε Q_A and a $\neq$ b : $\forall x\ \tilde{}(P_a(x) \wedge P_b(x))$

for a, b ε Q_A and $\tilde{}a\rho b$: $(\forall xy\ (P_a(x) \wedge P_b(y) \rightarrow \tilde{}(x\rho y))$

for a, b ε Q_A and a b : $(\forall x \exists y)\ (P_a(x) \rightarrow x\rho y \wedge P_b(y))$

It is each to chech that T_A has the desired properties.

Now for the proof of theorem 3.5. Given a sentence S which is (hopefully) preserved, start enumerating universal sentences U, halting when T $\vdash$ S$\longleftrightarrow$U. By Los-Tarski, if S is preserved, such a U will be found. Given U, construct the $A_1,\ldots,A_k$ given by lemma 3.6 and the finitely axiomated $T_{A_1},\ldots, T_{A_k}$ given by lemma 3.7. Then by 3.6 and 3.7, S is preserved iff for all i $\leq$ k, $T_{A_i} \vdash$ S, which is again an enumerable property. This completes the proof.

By our examples, not every universal sentence is preserved under contractions. We can show, however, that the set of universal sentences built just from ρ and which are preserved is in fact a recursive set.

3.8. Theorem

If U is universal and built from ρ alone, and if U is not preserved, then we may construct finite partial orders B and A depending on U such that B $\models$ U, A $\models$ $\tilde{}$U, and there is a contraction from B onto A.

(In fact, the construction and resulting decision procedure will run in double exponential time.)

Note: From now on, our discussion is devoted to formulas involving only the relation ρ.

3.9. Lemma

If A and B are transitive reflexive structures and h is a contraction from B onto A, then there are partial orders A' and B' elementarily equivalent to A and B and a contraction h' : B' $\rightarrow$ A'.

Proof. Since ρ is transitive and reflexive, the relation $\equiv$ defined by q $\equiv$r iff q ρr and rρ q is a congruence relation on the structures A and B. Let A' and B' be quotient structures A/$\equiv$ and B/$\equiv$. These structures are elementarily equivalent to A and B. It is easy to check that the map h' defined by h' defined by h'(a/$\equiv$) = b/$\equiv$ iff $\exists$ x$\equiv$a such that h(x)$\equiv$b is well defined, and is contraction from A' to B'

The proof of theorem 3.8 can now be given. Let U be a sentence not preserved under contractions. Write U as $\tilde{}$S, where S = $\exists x_1 \ldots x_n R$ and R is in full disjunctive normal form. Let $R_1,\ldots,R_n$ be the disjuncts of R. For each R_i let R^*_i be the result of performing the following operations as often as possible:

(1) if $x_j\rho x_k$ and $\sim x_j\rho x_\ell$ are conjuncts replace the entire disjunct by $\bot$.

(2) if $x_j\rho x_k$, $x_k\rho x_\ell$ and $\sim x_j\rho x_\ell$ are conjuncts replace the entire disjunct by $\bot$.

(3) if $x_j\rho x_k$, $x_k\rho x_\ell$ and $\sim x_j\rho k_\ell$ are conjuncts replace the entire disjunct by $\bot$.

(4) if $x_j\rho x_k$ and $x_k\rho x_j$ are conjuncts replace x_k by x_j throughout the disjunct.

If A is a partial order, then $A \models \exists x_1 \ldots x_n R$ iff $A \models \exists x_1 \ldots x_n R^*$. Now if U is not preserved, we may apply lemma 3.9 to obtain partial orders A and B such that $B \models \sim S$, and for some i, $A \models \exists x_1 \ldots x_n R^*_i$ and a contraction h from B onto A. As in theorem 3.5, choose $a_1, \ldots a_n$ such that $A, a_1, \ldots, a_n \not\models R^*_i$ and let A_1 be the substructure of A generated by $a_1, \ldots, a_n$. Let h_1 be the restriction of h to h^{-1} $[\{a_1, \ldots, a_n\}]$ and B_1 be the substructure of B generated by this inverse image. B_1 may not have finite domain, so more work is still needed. However, A_1 and B_1 are partial orders such that $B_1 \models \sim S$, $A_1 \models \exists x_1 \ldots x_n R^*_i$, and h_1 is a total contraction from B_1 onto A_1. Now assume that $a_1, \ldots, a_n$ are topologically sorted: $i \leq j \Rightarrow a_i \rho a_j$. Define a sequence $\langle \underline{B}_i \rangle_{1 \leq i \leq n}$ of finite subsets of the domain of B_1 as follows:

(1) $\underline{B}_1 = \{b\}$ where b is arbitrarily chosen in h_1^{-1} $[a_1]$.

(2) if $\underline{B}_1, \ldots, \underline{B}_{i-1}$ are defined, and each $\underline{B}_j \subseteq h_1^{-1}[a_j]$, then we construct $\underline{B}_i$ by choosing for each $j < i$ and $b \in \underline{B}_j$ some b' in h_1^{-1} $[a_i]$ such that $b \rho b$. If $\underline{B}_i$ is still empty, then select an arbitrary b in $h_1^{-1}[a_i]$ to put into $\underline{B}_i$. Let $\underline{B} = \bigcup_{i \leq n} \underline{B}_i$.

Then $|B| \leq 2^{n+1}$. Let B_2 be the substructure of B_1 generated by $\underline{B}$ and h_2 be restriction of h_1 to B_2. Then h_2 is a contraction of B_2 onto A_1. B_2 and A_1 are the structures required by the theorem, and h_2 is the required contraction.

This research was supported by NSF Grant MCS 76-07744.

REFERENCES

[1] Brand, D. Algebraic simulation between parallel programs. IBM Research Report RC 7206 (June, 1978).

[2] Estrin, G. and Campos, I. Concurrent software design supported by SARA at the age of one. Proc. 3rd Int'l. Conf. on Software Engineering, Atlanta, Ga. May 1978.

[3] Hack, M. Petri net languages. Computation Structures Group Memo 124, Project MAC, MIT, June 1975 .

[4] Keller, R.M. Formal verification of parallel programs. Comm. ACM 19 (1976), 371-384.

[5] Kwong, Y.S. On reduction of asynchronous systems. Theoret. Comp. Sci. 5 (1977), 25-50.

[6] Lipton, R. Reduction: a method of proving properties of parallel programs. CACM 12, December 1975, 717-721.

[7] Milner, R. An algebraic definition of simulation between programs. AI Memo 142, Computer Science Department, Stanford University: 1971.

[8] Pratt, V. Semantical consideration on Floyd-Hoare logic. Proc. 17th IEEE Symp. on Foundations of Comp. Sci., Houston, Tx, October 1976.

[9] Riddle, W.E., et al. Behavior modelling during software design. Proc. 3rd Intl. Symp. on Software Engineering, Atlanta, Ga, May 1978.

[10] Riddle, W.E. Hierarchical modelling of operating system structure and behavior. Proc. ACM National Conference, Boston, August 1972, 1105-1127.

[11] Robinson, L., et al. A formal methodology for the design of operating system software. In R. Yeh (ed.), Current Trends in Programming Methodology, Vol. I, Prentice Hall, 1977.

[12] Rogers, H. Certain logical reduction and decision problems. Ann. Math 64 (1956), 264-284.

[13] Rosen, B. Correctness of parallel programs -- the Church-Rosser approach. Theoret. Comp. Sci. 2 (1976), 183-207.

[14] Shoenfield, J.R. Mathematical Logic, Addison Wesley, Reading, Ma (1967).

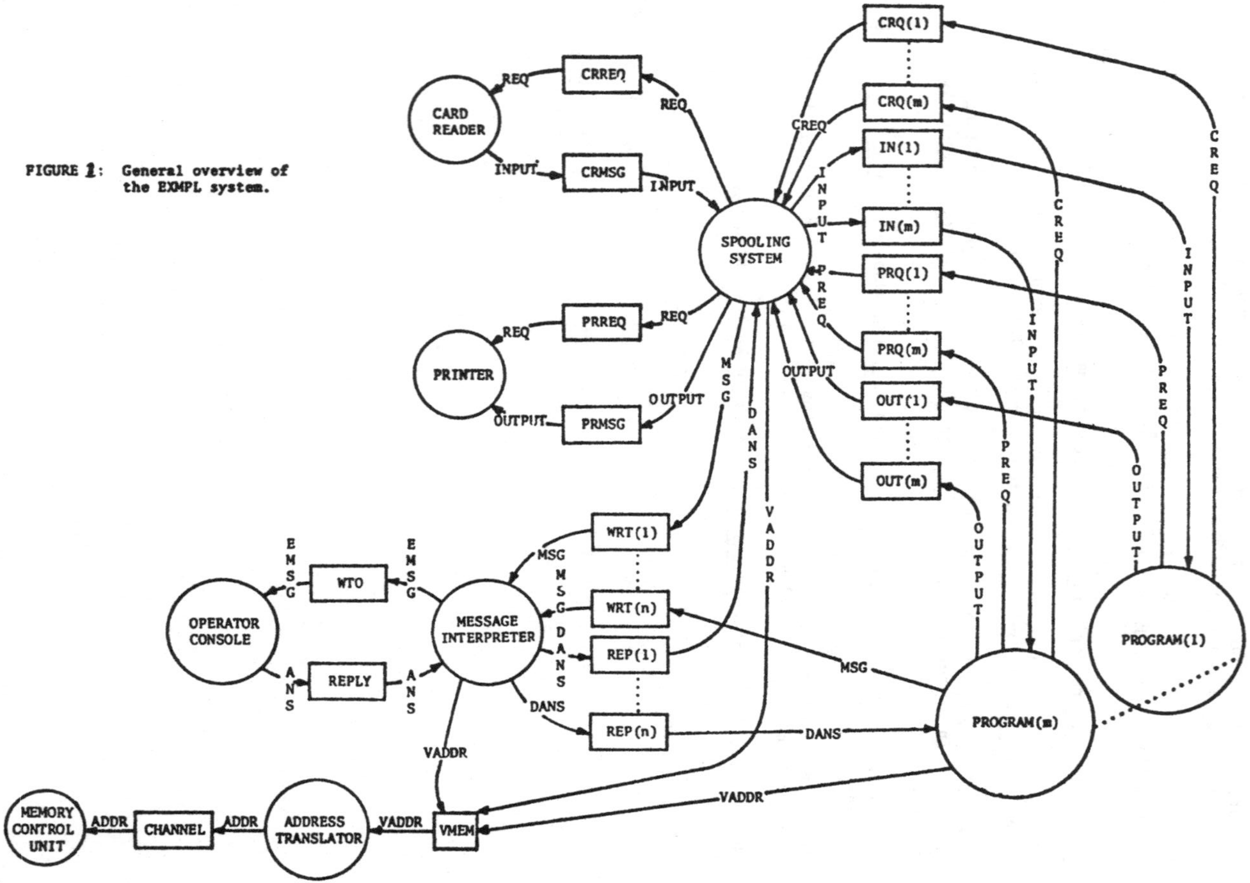

FIGURE 1: General overview of the EXMPL system.

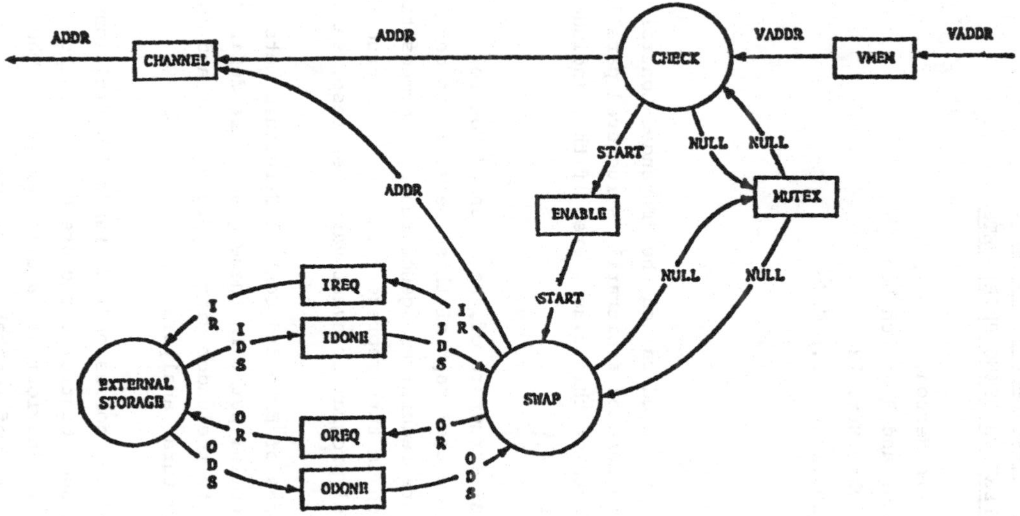

FIGURE 2: More detailed model of the ADDRESS_TRANSLATOR program process of the EXMPL system.

STATIC ANALYSIS OF CONCURRENT PROCESSES FOR DYNAMIC PROPERTIES USING PETRI NETS

Otthein Herzog
IBM Development and Research Lab.
Schönaicher Str. 220
D - 7030 Böblingen, F.R.G.

ABSTRACT

A new subclass of Petri Nets is presented called the "Extended Control Structure Nets". The control structure of arbitrarily structured parallel programs can be represented by nets of this class, even if they include operations on general semaphores.

First of all, the purely statical structure of the Extended Control Structure Nets is dealt with, i.e. the graph of these nets. It is defined, in which way these nets are recursively generated by a composition of connected state machines which in turn represent the control structure of sequential parts of a parallel program or event variables resp. semaphores.
Various properties of these graphs of Extended Control Structure Nets are stated. In addition, some special paths in these graphs are defined which are meaningful in respect to the underlying interpretation and thus are important for the later structural analysis.

By the inclusion of markings and the corresponding standard definitions, the full modelling power of Extended Control Structure Nets is introduced in respect to the dynamical behaviour of parallel programs. The notion of liveness is given in terms of reachable markings.

Finally, necessary and sufficient conditions are given for the liveness of Extended Control Structure Nets. This result offers the conceptual framework for the following proposal:

- Represent the control structure of parallel programs by Extended Control Structure Nets.
- Check (at compile-time) if all the seven liveness conditions are satisfied for a parallel program.
- If they are satisfied the analyzed program will be deadlock-free.

1. INTRODUCTION

There are various programming languages offering the feature of parallel programming like PL/I, BURROUGHS Extended Algol, ALGOL 68, Concurrent Pascal etc. While in the first two mentioned programming languages the synchronization is done by boolean event variables, variables of type "semaphore" /4/ are offered for that purpose in ALGOL 68 and the synchronization constructs of Concurrent Pascal /1/ can be implemented using semaphores.

In /8/ and /9/, a subclass of the Petri nets, the Control Structure Nets are studied suited to the modelling of parallel programs using only event variables for the synchronization between different tasks.

In this paper, the class of Extended Control Structure Nets is defined allowing the control structure representation of parallel programs including semaphore operations on general semaphore variables, where a parallel program is considered to be a set of cooperating sequential processes.

Accordingly, this new subclass is defined recursively by a composition of connected state machines. Some structural properties of Extended Control Structure Nets as well as necessary and sufficient conditions for the liveness are shown in a rather informal way. A more detailed and more formal approach is taken in /10/.

2. GRAPHS OF EXTENDED CONTROL STRUCTURE NETS

2.1 Basic definitions

Definition 1:

The graph of Petri net gpn = (P, T; PRE, POST) consists of

- the finite, nonempty set P ("places"),
- the finite set T ("transitions"),
  where $P \cap T = \emptyset$, and
- the functions PRE: $P \times T \rightarrow \mathbb{N} \cup \{0\}$
  and POST: $T \times P \rightarrow \mathbb{N} \cup \{0\}$.

According to this definition, a graph of a Petri net may consist of exactly one place.

As usual, in the graphical representation of Petri nets, places are drawn as circular and transitions as rectangular nodes. The value of PRE, resp. POST of a pair of places and transitions will be attached to that connecting arc.

The following well-known graph-theoretical notations are used throughout this paper:

Definition 2:

Let gpn = (P, T; PRE, POST) be the graph of a Petri net;
$x_i \in P \cup T$, $i = 1,\dots,n$

1. $(x_1,\dots,x_n)$ is called sequence of edges ("se") iff
   (i) $x_1, x_n \in P$
   (ii) $(\forall\, i \in 1,\dots,n-1): x_i, x_{i+1}$ are adjacent

2. A sequence of edges is called path ("pa") iff
   all edges are distinct.

3. A sequence of edges is called simple path ("sp") iff
   all vertices are distinct.

4. A path is called elementary circuit ("ec") iff
   all vertices are distinct except $x_1 = x_n$.

V(se) denotes the set of vertices of sequence of edges se.

Now, the graph of a connected Petri net is defined. An example is given following the definition.

Definition 3:

Let gpn = (P, T; PRE, POST) be a graph of a Petri net;
let $p_I \in P$ be an initial place, where $(\forall t \in T)$: $POST(t,p_I) = 0$,
$p_F \in P$ a final place, where $(\forall t \in T)$: $PRE(p_F,t) = 0$,
P_I the set of initial places, P_F the set of final places.

1. gpn is called graph of a connected Petri net ("gcpn") iff
   (i) $|P_I| = 1$, $|P_F| \geq 1$
   (ii) $(\forall p \in P)$ $(\exists$ simple path $sp_I)$: $sp_I = (p_I,\ldots,p)$
   (iii) $(\forall p \in P)$ $(\exists$ simple path $sp_F)$: $sp_F = (p,\ldots,p_F)$

2. GCPN := $\{$gpn$|$gpn is graph of a connected Petri net$\}$

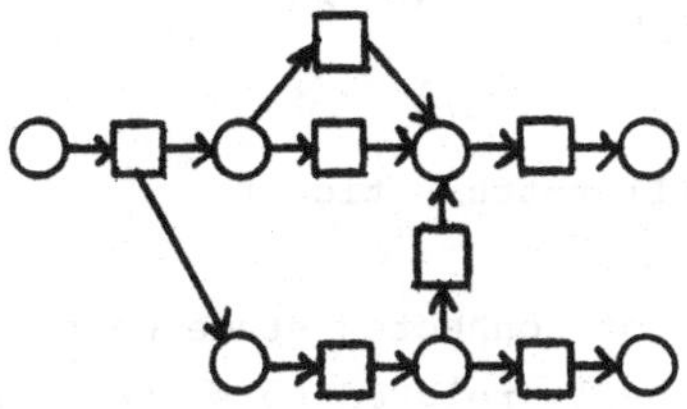

Fig. 1: Instance of a graph of a connected Petri net

Further notations:

Let gcpn $\in$ GCPN, gcpn = (P, T; PRE, POST); p $\in$ P, t $\in$ T.

1. $PRED(t) := \{p \in P \mid PRE(p,t) > 0\}$
   $SUCC(t) := \{p \in P \mid POST(t,p) > 0\}$
   $PRED(p) := \{t \in T \mid POST(t,p) > 0\}$
   $SUCC(p) := \{t \in T \mid PRE(p,t) > 0\}$

2. (i) t is called signal transition ("s-transition") iff $|SUCC(t)| > 1$
   (ii) $T \supseteq S := \{t \mid t \text{ is s-transition}\}$

3. (i) t is called receive transition ("r-transition") iff $|PRED(t)| > 1$
   (ii) $T \supseteq R := \{t \mid t \text{ is r-transition}\}$

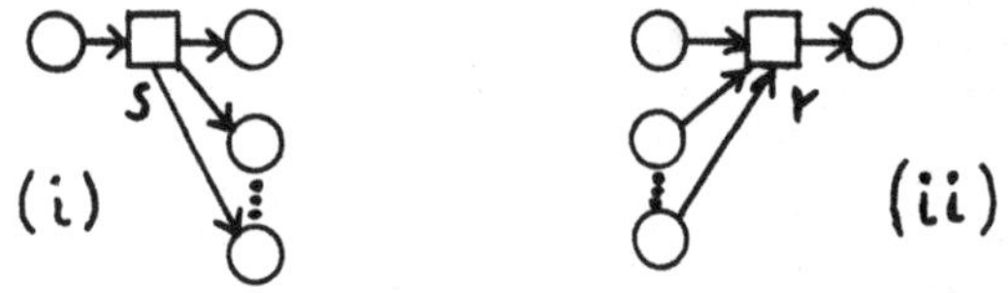

Fig.2: (i) s-transition s, (ii) r-transition r

By the next definition graphs of connected state machines (/6/ and /11/) are defined which are very closely related to state graphs of finite automata.

Definition 4:
Let gcpn $\in$ GCPN, gcpn = (P, T; PRE, POST).

1. gcpn is called graph of a connected state machine ("gcsm") iff
   (i) $(\forall p \in P)\ (\forall t \in T)$: $PRE(p,t) \leq 1$
   (ii) $(\forall t \in T)\ (\forall p \in P)$: $POST(t,p) \leq 1$
   (iii) $(\forall t \in T)$: $|PRED(t)| = |SUCC(t)| = 1$
   (iv) $|P_F| = 1$

2. $GCSM := \{gcpn \in GCPN \mid gcpn \text{ is a graph of a connected state machine}\}$

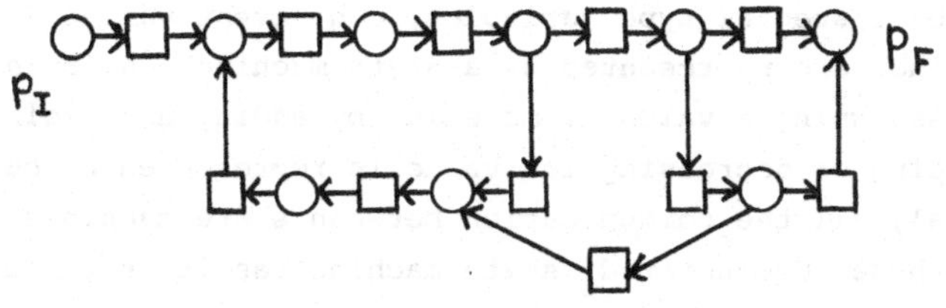

Fig. 3: Instance of a graph of a connected state machine

Such a connected state machine can be thought as representing a purely sequential part of a program like a sequential procedure. It is easy to see that arbitrary sequential control structures can be modelled far away from any structured programming.

Definition 5 explains the composition of two graphs of connected Petri nets:
- the sets of places and transitions have to be disjoint;
- the already existing arcs are preserved;
- if both graphs of connected Petri nets contain transitions then exactly one arc has to be added outgoing from an arbitrary transition of the first graph and entering the initial place of the second graph;
- if the second graph consists of only one place then arbitrary many arcs can be added
  - outgoing from the first graph and entering the only place of the second one,
  - as well as outgoing from the place of the second graph entering arbitrary transitions of the first one.

This composition seems to be quite restrictive, but after a look to the underlying motivation it appears to be rather natural:
the composition is intended to give the possibility of modelling the attaching of an asynchronously executing process to a calling process. This requires the representation of the attaching mechanism, namely starting this process at exactly the initial statement.

In many situations some synchronization has to be performed between concurrent processes: entering critical regions or the termination of an attached process might be examples. This synchronization can be achieved through the use of special type variables, e.g. event variables or semaphores. Both kinds are represented by a state machine consisting of a single place. Assigning a value is modelled by adding an ingoing arc to it whereas reading or decreasing its value is represented by outgoing arcs. In general, all the communication between state machines is assumed to be done by these "degenerated" state machines as it is reflected in the following definition.

Definition 5:

Let gpn = (P, T; PRE, POST) be a graph of a Petri net,
$gcpn_i \in GCPN$, $gcpn_i = (P^i, T^i; PRE^i, POST^i)$, (i=1,2),
where $P^1 \cap P^2 = T^1 \cap T^2 = \emptyset$;
P_I^i the set of initial places of $gcpn_i$;
$U^1 \subseteq T^1$: $|U^1| = 1$.

$gpn = gcpn_1 + gcpn_2$ is called composition of $gcpn_1$ and $gcpn_2$ iff

(i) $P = P^1 \cup P^2$

(ii) $T = T^1 \cup T^2$

(iii)

$$PRE := \begin{cases} (P^1 \cup P^2) \times (T^1 \cup T^2) \to \mathbb{N} \cup \{0\} \\ (p,t) \to \begin{cases} PRE^i(p,t), & \text{if } p \in P^i,\ t \in T^i \\ n \in \mathbb{N} \cup \{0\}, & \text{if } p = P^2,\ t \in T^i \\ 0 & \text{else} \end{cases} \end{cases}$$

(iv)

$$POST := \begin{cases} (T^1 \cup T^2) \times (P^1 \cup P^2) \to \mathbb{N} \cup \{0\} \\ (t,p) \to \begin{cases} POST^i(t,p), & \text{if } t \in T^i,\ p \in P^i \\ 1, & \text{if } \{t\} = U^1,\ \{p\} = P_I^2 \in P^2 \\ n \in \mathbb{N} & \text{if } \{t\} = U^1,\ \{p\} = P^2 \\ n \in \mathbb{N} \cup \{0\} & \text{if } \{t\} \in T^1,\ \{p\} = P^2 \\ 0 & \text{else} \end{cases} \end{cases}$$

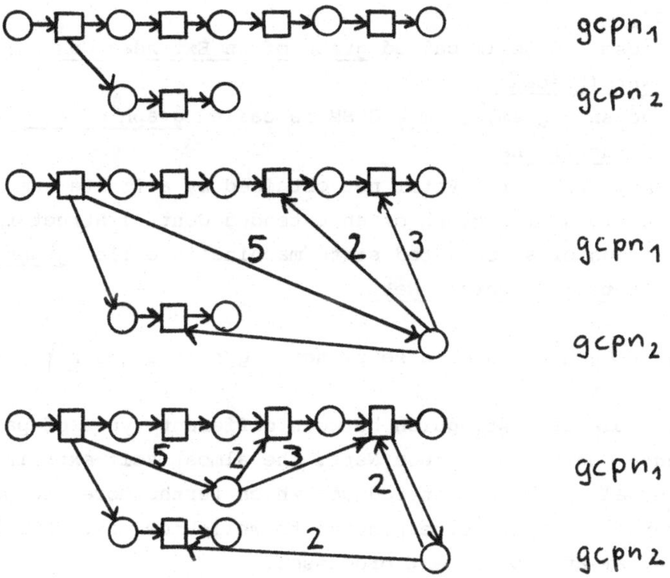

Fig.4: Examples for the composition

The following two properties of the composition can be proved very easily:

<u>Property 1:</u>
By the composition of any two graphs of connected Petri nets all "old" arcs are preserved and at least one "new" arc is added.

<u>Property 2:</u>
The resulting graph of such a composition is again a graph of a connected Petri net.

These structural preservation rules allow the following recursive definition of the subclass of Extended Control Structure Nets which is defined by composition of graphs of connected state machines.

Definition 6:

1. (i) gcsm $\in$ GCSM is called graph of an Extended Control Structure Net ("gecsn").

   (ii) gecsn + gcsm, gcsm $\in$ GCSM is called graph of an Extended Control Structure Net.

   (iii) Any graph of a Petri net obtained by a finite number of compositions of a graph of an Extended Control Structure Net and a graph of a connected state machine is called graph of an Extended Control Structure Net.

2. GECSN := $\{$gpn graph of a Petri net $|$ gpn is a gecsn$\}$

It is possible to distinguish between different types of paths in graph of Extended Control Structure Nets: the almost self-explaining "internal" and "external" paths are introduced which furthermore can be splitted into several subtypes corresponding to well-known structural properties of sequential and concurrent processes.

Definition 7:

Let gecsn $=(\biguplus_{i=1}^{l} P^i, \biguplus_{i=1}^{l} T^i$, PRE, POST) be the graph of an Extended Control Structure Net, where p, q are places.

1. A path pa = (p,...,q) is called internal path("ipa") iff all its vertices belong to the same graph of a connected state machine making up a component j of the Extended Control Structure Net.
   $IPA_j := \{ pa = (p,\dots,q) \mid V(pa) \in P^j \cup T^j \}$

2. An internal path ipa = (p,...,q) is called simple internal path iff ipa is a simple path.
   $SIPA_j := \{ ipa \in IPA_j \mid$ ipa is simple path $\}$

3. An internal path ipa = (p,...,q) is called loop ("l_p") iff ipa is an elementary circuit.
   $LP_j := \{ ipa \in IPA_j \mid$ ipa is elementary circuit $\}$

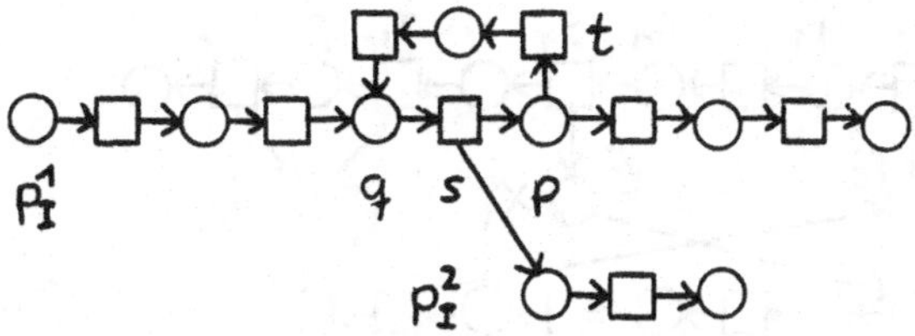

Fig.5: Internal paths

In fig.5, $(P_I^1,\ldots,q,s,p,t,\ldots,q) \in IPA_1$, $(P_I^1,\ldots,q,s,p) \in SIPA_1$, $(q,s,p,\ldots,q) \in LP_1$ and $(P_I^1,\ldots,q,s,p_I^2) \notin IPA_1$.

Definition 8:

Let gecsn $=(\biguplus_{i=1}^{l} P^i, \biguplus_{i=1}^{l} T^i;$ PRE, POST) be the graph of an Extended Control Structure Net where p, q, are places.

1. A path pa = (p,...,q) is called <u>external path ("epa")</u> iff there are at least two vertices belonging to two different components of the Extended Control Structure Net.
   $EPA_{j,k} := \{$ pa = (p,...,q) | pa is external path with vertices from components j and k $\}$

2. epa $\in EPA_{j,k}$ is called <u>simple external path</u> iff epa is a simple path.
   $SEPA_{j,k} := \{$ epa $\in EPA_{j,k}$ | epa is simple path $\}$

3. epa $\in EPA_{j,k}$, epa = (p,...,q) p $\in P^j$ is called <u>synchronization circuit ("sct")</u> iff (p,...,q) is an elementary circuit
   $SCT_j := \{$ epa $\in EPA_{j,k}$ | epa is synchronization circuit $\}$

The internal paths represent the control flow in sequential processes where the "loop" models the iterative constructs. External paths show synchronization links between concurrent processes where cycles may also appear but may lead to deadlocks if they are not resolved explicitely. These cycles are called synchronization circuits because of their synchronization properties.

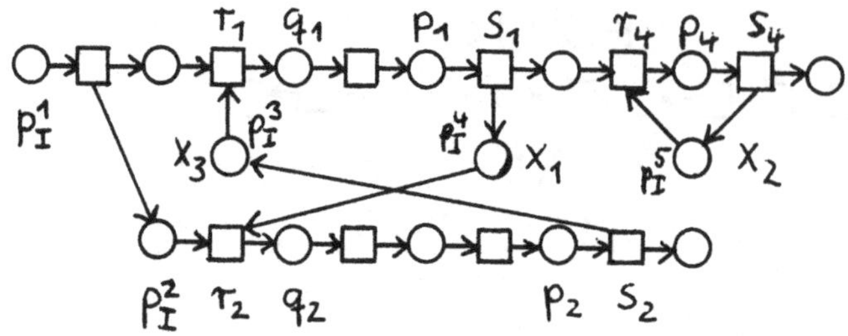

Fig.6: External paths

In fig.6, $(p_1,s_1,x_1) \in SEPA_{1,4}$, $(p_1,s_1,x_1,r_2,q_2,\ldots,p_2,s_2,x_3) \in SEPA_{1,3}$ $(p_4,s_4,x_2) \in SEPA_{1,5}$, $(p_1,s_1,x_1,r_2,q_2,\ldots,p_2,s_2,r_1,q_1,\ldots,p_1) \in SCT_1$ and $(p_4,s_4,x_2,r_4,p_4) \in SCT_1$

Definition 9 introduces the notion of simple control paths which turns out to be a rather important one for the later structural analysis. In general, the control of concurrent processes proceeds along simple control paths. This includes the attaching of concurrent subprocesses. Thus a certain simple control path may lead from one component of an Extended Control Structure Net through some components entered at their initial places and left where the new component is attached. In any case, if a simple control path includes a special state machine consisting of exactly one place, this place will be the final one of that simple control path.

Definition 9:

Let gecsn $=(\biguplus_{i=1}^{l} P^i \;,\; \biguplus_{i=1}^{l} T^i \;;$ PRE, POST) be the graph of an Extended Control Structure Net.

The simple path sp = (p,...,q) is called simple control path ("scop") iff

each transition on sp and its preceding place on sp belong to the same component.

$SCOP_{p,q} : \{ sp = (p,\ldots,q) \mid$ sp is simple control path $\}$

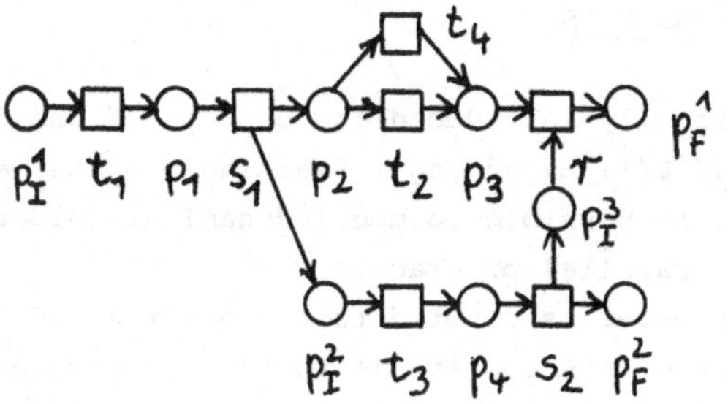

Fig.7: Simple control paths : example

In fig.7, $(p_I^1,t_1,p_1,s_1,p_2,t_2,p_3,r,p_F^1) \in SCOP_{p_I^1,p_F^1}$,
$(p_I^1,t_1,p_1,s_1,p_2,t_4,p_3,r,p_F^1) \in SCOP_{p_I^1,p_F^1}$,
$(p_I^1,t_1,p_1,s_1,p_I^2,t_3,p_4) \in SCOP_{p_I^1,p_4}$,
$(p_I^1,t_1,p_1,s_1,p_I^2,t_3,p_4,s_2,p_I^3,r,p_F^1) \notin SCOP_{p_I^1,p_F^1}$ because of $\{p_I^3\} = P^3, r \in T^1$.

Listed below are several properties of the graphs of Extended Control Structure Nets concerning mainly the ways different components are connected to each other.

Property 3:
For each s-transition there exists at least one output place which belongs to another component.

Property 4:
A component can only be entered in two ways:
- at its initial place from another component's s-transition or
- at an r-transition which is a successor of a single place state machine.

Property 5:
If there is a component consisting of a single place state machine, all predecessors of that place are s-transitions and all successors are r-transitions.

Property 6:
There is a simple control path to each place of the graph of an Extended Control Structure Net.

3. EXTENDED CONTROL STRUCTURE NETS

In this section there is finally introduced the concept of the dynamical behaviour of a Petri net (/18/). By adding a "marking" to the definition of graphs of Petri nets it is possible to model dynamical (discrete) concurrent systems such as parallel programs.
The remaining part of this paper is devoted to the question of "liveness" of Extended Control Structure Nets comparable to the "proper termination" of concurrent processes. It is shown that the analysis of the structural properties of an Extended Control Structure Net leads to necessary and sufficient conditions for the dynamical liveness property.
This result makes it possible to apply the following procedure to the analysis of a parallel program for proper termination (absence of deadlocks):

- Represent the control structure of concurrent processes by a graph of an Extended Control Structure Net,
- apply the algorithms based on the seven liveness conditions

In the proposed representation there is no way to model mutual decision dependencies. This leads to a worst case analysis but proves from the statical properties of a set of concurrent processes that there will always be a proper termination.

3.1 Basic notations and definitions

Definition 10:

Let gecsn $\in$ GECSN, gecsn = $(\biguplus_{i=1}^{l} P^i \quad \biguplus_{i=1}^{l} T^i;$ PRE, POST).

1. (i) A marking is a mapping m: $\biguplus_{i=1}^{l} P^i \rightarrow \mathbb{N} \cup \{0\}$

   (ii) An initial marking is denoted by m_I

2. t $\in \biguplus_{i=1}^{l} T^i$ is called activated at a marking m iff

   $(\forall\ p \in PRED(t)): m(p) \geq PRE(p,t)$

3. t $\in \biguplus_{i=1}^{l} T^i$, t activated at m, fires according to the firing rule, generating a new marking m':

   (i) $(\forall\ p \in PRED(t)): m'(p) = m(p) - PRE(p,t)$

   (ii) $(\forall\ q \in SUCC(t)): m'(q) = m(q) + POST(t,q)$

   Notation: $m \xrightarrow{t} m'$

4. A marking m_k ($k > 0$) is called <u>reachable from a marking m_o</u> iff $(\exists\, t_1,\ldots,t_k \in \bigcup_{i=1}^{l} T^i)$ $(\exists$ markings $m_1,\ldots,m_{k-1})$:

$$m_o \xrightarrow{t_1} m_1, m_1 \xrightarrow{t_2} m_2,\ldots,m_{k-1} \xrightarrow{t_k} m_k$$

<u>Notation:</u> $m_k \in [m_o]$ (m_k belongs to the reachability class of m_o)

<u>Definition 11:</u>

1. ecsn = (gecsn; m_I) is called <u>Extended Control Structure Net</u> iff
   (i) gecsn $\in$ GECSN: gecsn = $(\bigcup_{i=1}^{l} P^i, \bigcup_{i=1}^{l} T^i$; PRE, POST)

   (ii) $m_I(p) = \begin{cases} 1 \text{ if } p = p_I^1 \\ 0 \text{ else} \end{cases}$

2. ECSN: $= \{$ ecsn = (gecsn; m_I) $|$ ecsn is Extended Control Structure Net $\}$

Now, the liveness of Extended Control Structure Nets is defined and explained by an example (fig. 8).

<u>Definition 12:</u>

Let ecsn be an Extended Control Structure Net,
r an r-transition with preceding places q and q', where q belongs to the same component as r, whereas q' has to be identified to be a single place component.

Furthermore, let m be a marking reachable from the initial marking such that m (q) = k $\geq$ 1.

Then ecsn is called <u>live</u> iff
there exists a marking m' reachable from m such that m'(q) = k $\geq$ 1 and for all q' $\in$ PRED (r): m'(q') $\geq$ PRE(q',r)

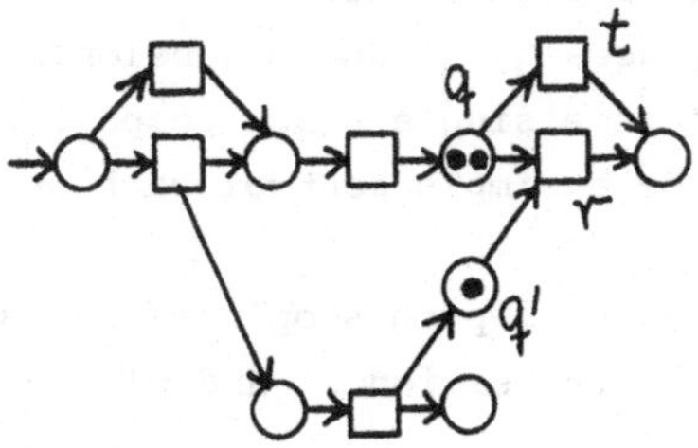

Fig. 8: Example

It follows from definition 12, that in a live Extended Control Structure Net at a marking $m(q) \geq 1$, there must exist a marking m' reachable from m such that r as well as t are activated at m'. Consequently the ecsn from fig. 8 is not live (let r fire once and try it again!).
There is an obvious interpretation of this definition: as places like q are representing decision statements in processes, each of the outgoing branches may be executed depending on the result of the performed test and all the synchronization signals for each branch have to be provided. It becomes clear now, too, why the liveness analysis is a worst-case analysis: all the tests are assumed to be independent from each other as the representing places do not contain any interpretation.

The following property can be shown quite easily using the known properties of graphs of Extended Control Structure Nets: In fact it shows the importance of simple control paths in respect to the propagation of markings.

Property 7:

Let scop = (p,...,q) be a simple control path in a live Extended Control Structure Net.
Then there are markings reachable from the initial marking m_I such that each transition on scop can fire.

The following property of live Extended Control Structure Nets assures the existence of certain simple control paths in respect to an r-transition which guarantee the delivering of enough tokens such that r can fire ultimately.

Property 8:

Let ecsn be a live Extended Control Structure Net,
r an r-transition with input places q, q' where q belongs to the same component as r whereas q' is a single place component;
furthermore let scop = $(p_I^1,\ldots,q)$ be a simple control path starting at the initial place of ecsn.
Then there is at least one simple control path scop' leaving scop at an s-transition s and terminating in an s-transition s' and q' such that

$$\sum_{s' \in \bigcup V(scop')} POST(s',q') \geq PRE(q'r)$$

The following definition 13 reflects the properties a place has to have if it is to represent a semaphore. Usually, semaphores are used in order to synchronize the sharing of resources which implies that there are not enough resources to satisfy each possible request. In fact, if there are sufficient many resources provided for the "users" there are no new problems. According to these facts, only these places are called semaphere places, where there cannot exist a marking such that all the r-transitions connected to such a place and modelling the P-operation (/4/) can fire at one time because of missing tokens in that place. The non-existence of that marking is expressed by statical properties avoiding to have to look for all possible markings reachable from the initial marking in order to be able to determine which places are semaphore places.

Definition 13:

Let ecsn be an Extended Control Structure Net,

$\{x\}$ be a single place component with output r-transitions

$\{r_1,\ldots,r_k \mid k > 2\}$ where each one belongs to a different component,

$SCOP_{P_I^1,x} := \{ scop = (p_I^1,\ldots,s,x) \mid \ V(scop) \cap \{r_1,\ldots,r_k\} = \emptyset \}$

x is called semaphore place iff

there is $SCOPSUB_{P_I^1,x} \subseteq SCOP_{P_I^1,x}$ such that $\sum_{s} POST(s,x) < \sum_{i=1}^{k} PRE(x,r_i)$

where $SCOPSUB_{P_I^1,x}$ is generated from $SCOP_{P_I^1,x}$ as follows:

if there are

$scop = (p_I^1,\ldots,\bar{p},t,\ldots,s,x)$, $\bar{s}cop = (p_I^1,\ldots,\bar{p},\bar{t},\ldots,s',x) \in SCOP_{P_I^1,x}$,

such that $|SUCC(\bar{p})| > 1$, $t \neq \bar{t}$ and $\bar{p},t,\bar{t}$ belong to the same component and $s \neq s'$,

then the one with the smallest POST (s,x), POST (s',x) is selected.

In order to give an easier and more understandable formulation of the liveness conditions, the notation of complete simple control paths is introduced now. This property turns out to appear in all the liveness conditions. Examples are given in fig. 9.

Definition 14:

Let ecsn be an Extended Control Structure Net,

r an r-transition with at least one single place component $\{q'\}$ as input place and with place q as input place belonging to the same component as r does.

Let p be a place and scop = (p,...,q) a simple control path.

scop is called a complete simple control path in respect to q' iff

(i) there is an scop' = (p,...,s',q'),

(ii) for every scop' = $(p,\ldots\bar{p},t,\ldots,s',q')$, where $|SUCC\ (\bar{p})| > 1$, there is a $\overline{scop}'$ = $(p,\ldots,\bar{p},\bar{t},\ldots,s'',q')$, where $t \neq \bar{t}$.

SCOP':= $\{$scop' = (p,...,s',q')| scop' satisfies (i) and (ii)$\}$

SCOPSUB': = scop' = (p,...,s',q') | scop'= $(p,\ldots\bar{p},t,\ldots,s',q') \in$ SCOPSUB' $\leadsto$ scop'= $(p,\ldots,\bar{p},\bar{t},\ldots,s',q') \notin$ SCOPSUB'$\}$

Shorthand notation: V(SCOPSUB'): = $\bigcup_{scop' \in SCOPSUB'}$ V(scop')

In other words, all the possible simple control paths from p to q' are gathered in SCOP',
whereas in SCOPSUB' $\subseteq$SCOP' these paths are omitted which start at a common decision place $\bar{p}$.

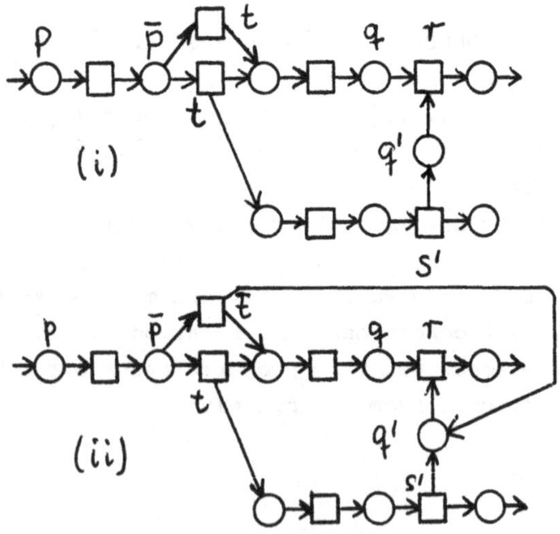

Fig. 9: Illustration of def. 14. (i): no complete simple control path (ii): complete simple control path.

Condition 1:

Let ecsn be a live Extended Control Structure Net, r an r-transition with at least one single place component $\{q'\}$ as input place and with place q as input place belonging to the same component as r does.

Then
every scop = $(p_I^1, \ldots, q)$ is a complete simple control path in respect to q'
such that for every V(SCOPSUB') holds:

$$\sum_{s' \in V(SCOPSUB')} POST(s',q') - \sum_{r' \in R'} PRE(q',r') \geq PRE(q',r)$$

where $R' := \{$ r-transition r' | r' $\in$ V(SCOPSUB') $\cup$ V(scop) and r' is output transition of q' $\}$

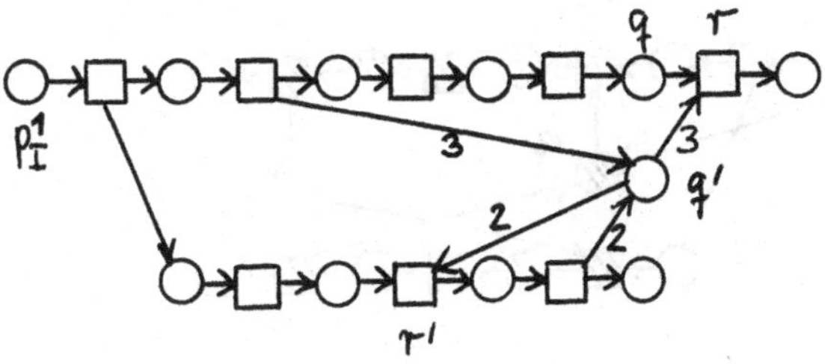

Fig. 10: Example for a satisfied condition 1.

In fig. 12, COMSCOPSUB'=COMSCOP' and it is always granted that there will be enough tokens on q' when q is marked.

Condition 2:

Let ecsn be a live Extended Control Structure Net,

r an r-transition with at least one single place component $\{q'\}$ as input place and with place q as input place belonging to the same component as r does.

In addition, $r \in V(sct)$, where sct=(q',r,...,q') is a synchronization circuit.

Then

there is an r-transition on sct such that it holds for every scopsub' $\in$ SCOPSUB' belonging to scop = $(p_r^1, \ldots, q)$:

$$V(\text{scopsub}') \cap V(\text{sct}) = \{q'\}$$

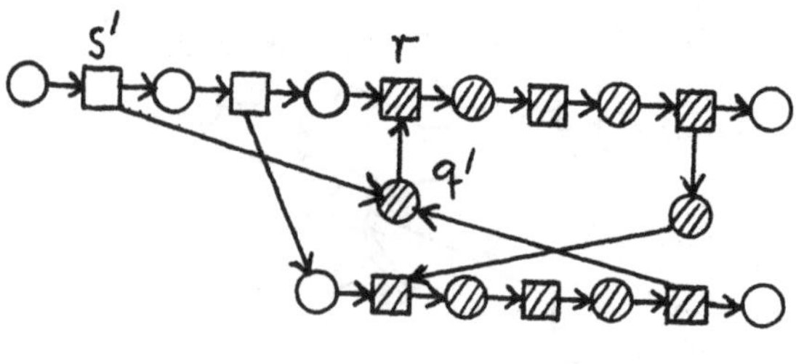

Fig. 11: Example for a satisfied condition 2

By condition 2 it is required in order to resolve a "deadlock" caused by a synchronization circuit, that the paths from which the tokens have to be put on q' do not belong to that synchronization circuit themselves.

Condition 3:

Let ecsn be a live Extended Control Structure Net,

r an r-transition with at least one single place component $\{q'\}$ as input place and with place q as input place belonging to the same component as r does.

In addition, r $\in$V(lp), where lp=(q,r,...,q) is a loop.

Then

lp=(q,r,...,q) is a complete simple control path in respect to q' such that for every V(SCOPSUB') holds:

$$\sum_{s' \in V(SCOPSUB')} POST(s',q') - \sum_{r' \in R'} PRE(q',r') \geq PRE(q',r)$$

where R':= $\{$ r-transition r' $|$ r' $\in$V(lp) and r' is output transition of q'$\}$

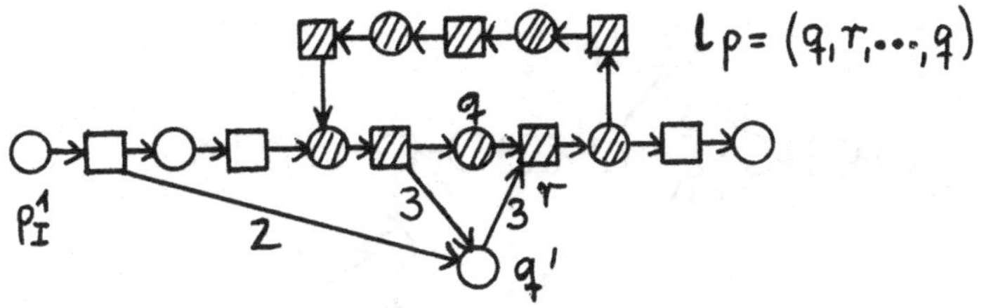

Fig. 12: Example for a satisfied condition 3

As it is not determined how many times a token will travel around a loop, the necessary tokens for q' have to be generated on the very same loop, too.

Condition 4:

Let ecsn be a live Extended Control Structure Net,

r an r-transition with at least one single place component {q'} as input place and with place q as input place and q'' as output place belonging to the same component as r does, say component j.

In addition, r is in a component which is attached from an s-transition s placed on a loop lp=(...,s,...).

Then

lp or every sipa=$(q'',\ldots,p_F^j)$, sipa $\in SIPA_j$ is a complete simple control path in respect to q'

such that for every $V(SCOPSUB'_{lp})$, $V(SCOPSUB'_{sipa})$ holds:

$$\sum_{s'\ V(SCOPSUB'_{lp})} POST(s',q') + \sum_{s'\ V(SCOPSUB'_{sipa})} POST(s',q') -$$

$$\sum_{r' \in R} PRE(q',r') \geq PRE(q',r)$$

where R' := { r-transition r' | r' $\in$ V(lp) or V($p_I^j,\ldots,q$) and r' is output transition of q' }

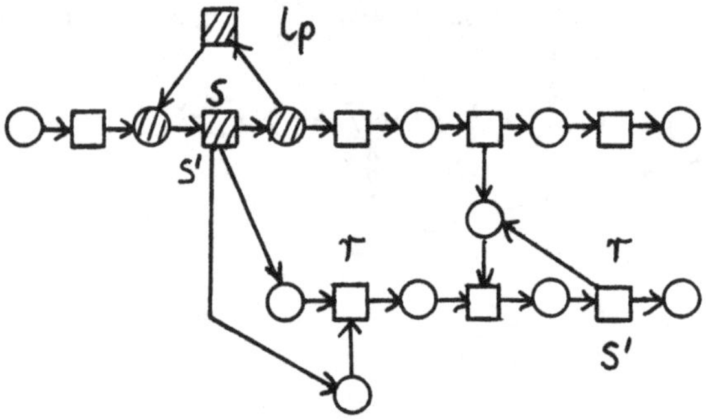

Fig. 13: Example for a satisfied condition 4

As there might be many tokens travelling in component j, r must be activated as many times. This is achieved by getting the tokens needed from the loop itself or from the remaining part of the component j.

Condition 5:

Let ecsn be a live Extended Control Structure Net,

$\{r_1, r_2, r_3, r_4\} \subset R$, where two of them belong to different components,

$\{x_1, x_2\} \subseteq$ SEMAP, where $r_1, r_4 \in SUCC(x_1)$, $r_2, r_3 \in SUCC(x_2)$;

Let $scop_1 \in SCOP_{p_I^1,q3}$: $scop_1 = (p_I^1, \ldots, q_1, r_1, \ldots, q_3)$,

$scop_2 \in SCOP_{p_I^1,q_4}$: $scop_2 = (p_I^1, \ldots, q_1, r_2, \ldots, q_4)$, where

q_3 and q_4 are input places of r_3 and r_4, resp., and belong to the same component as they do.

In addition, there is no forced sequentialization between $(p_I^1, \ldots, q_1)$ and $(p_I^1, \ldots, q_2)$.

Then

every $scop_1$ is a complete simple control path in respect to x_1 such that

$$\sum_{s' \in V(SCOPSUB')} POST(s', x_1) - \sum_{r' \in R'} PRE(x_1, r_1') \geq PRE(x_1, r_1) + PRE(x_1, r_4)$$

where $R' := \{$ r-transition $r' \mid r' \in V(scop_1)$ and r' is output transition of $x_1 \}$

or

every $scop_2$ is a complete simple control path in respect to x_2 such that

$$\sum_{s' \in V(SCOPSUB')} POST(s', x_2) - \sum_{r' \in R'} PRE(x_2, r') \geq PRE(x_2, r_2) + PRE(x_2, r_3)$$

where $R' := \{$ r-transition $r' \mid r' \in V(scop_2)$ and r' is output transition of $x_2 \}$

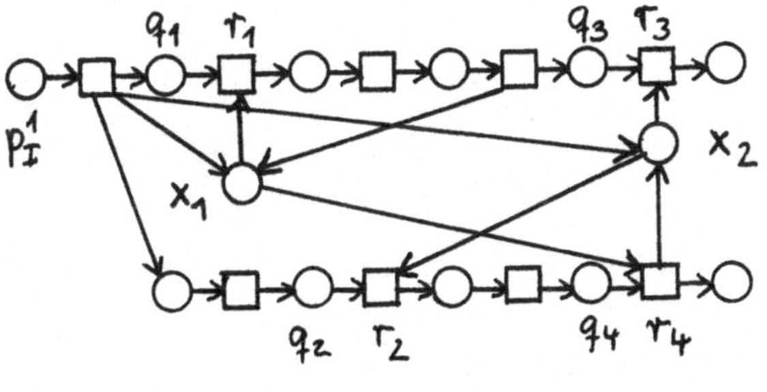

Fig. 14: Example for a satisfied condition 5

Condition 5 is set up in order to resolve the "cigarette smoker problem" /18/ which can occur if at least two r-transition require tokens from at least two semaphore places, but in a reversed order.

Theorem :

Let ecsn an Extended Control Structure Net.
ecsn is live iff the conditions 1 through 5 are satisfied.

The proof of this theorem can be found in /10/ where it is stated in a slightly changed way.

ACKNOWLEDGEMENTS

Part of this work was done while the author was as a research associate with the Computer Science Department of the University of Utah at Salt Lake City, Utah, supported by the Deutsche Forschungsgemeinschaft Bonn through grant He/989/2.
I have to thank Suhas Patil, Z. Kohavi and R.M. Keller for many helpful discussions during that time.
A refinement of the condition 5 is due to Edmund M. Clarke, Harvard University.

REFERENCES

/1/ P. BRINCH HANSEN: Concurrent Pascal - A Programming Language for Operating System design.- California Institute of Technology, Information Science, Technical Report No. 10 (April 1974)

/2/ BURROUGHS Corporation: BURROUGHS B 6700/B 7700 ALGOL Language Reference Manual.- 5000649 (1974)

/3/ V. G. CERF: Multiprocessors, Semaphores and a Graph Model of Computation.- University of California, Computer Science Department, UCLA-10P14-110 (Apr. 1972)

/4/ E. W. DIJKSTRA: Co-operating sequential Processes.- In: F. GENUYS (Ed.): Programming Languages.- London (1968), p. 43-112

/5/ H. J. GENRICH, K. LAUTENBACH: Synchronisationsgraphen.- Acta Informatica 2 (1973), p. 143-161

/6/ M. H. T. HACK: Extended State Machine allocatable Nets (ESMA) - an Extension of Free Choice Petri Nets Results.- M.I.T., Project MAC, Computations Structures Group Memo 78-1 (1974)

/7/ O. HERZOG, M. YOELI: Control Nets for Asynchronous Systems, Part 1.- Technion-Israel Institute of Technology, Computer Science Department, TR-74 (May 1976)

/8/ O. HERZOG: Zur Analyse der Kontrollstruktur paralleler Programme mit Hilfe von Petri-Netzen.- Universität Dortmund, Abteilung Informatik, Bericht Nr. 24/76 (1976)

/9/ O. HERZOG: Automatic Deadlock Analysis of parallel Programs.- In: E. MORLET, D. RIBBENS (Eds.): International Computing Symposium 1977.- Amsterdam (1977), p. 209-216

/10/ O. HERZOG: Liveness of Extended Control Structure Nets.- University of Utah, Dept. of Computer Science, CSUU-77-107 (August 1977)

/11/ A. HOLT, F. COMMONER: Events and Conditions.-
Applied Data Research Inc., New York (1970)

/12/ IBM Corporation: OS PL/I Checkout and Optimizing Compilers:
Language Reference Manual.-
GC33-0009-3 (1974)

/13/ R. M. KELLER: Generalized Petri Nets as Models for System Verification.-
Princeton University, Department of Electrical Engineering, Technical Report No. 200 (Dec. 1975)

/14/ R. M. KELLER: Formal Verification of parallel Programs.-
Comm. ACM 19,7 (1976), p. 371-394

/15/ H. C. LAUER: Correctness in Operating Systems.-
AD 753122 (1972)

/16/ K. LAUTENBACH, H. A. SCHMID: Use of Petri Nets for proving Correctness of concurrent Process Systems.-
Proceedings of the IFIP Congress 74.- Amsterdam (1974), p. 187-191

/17/ R. E. MILLER: Some Relationships between various Models of Parallelism and Synchronization.-
IBM Thomas J. Watson Research Center, RC 5074 (Oct. 1974)

/18/ S. S. PATIL: Limitations and Capabilities of Dijkstra's Semaphore Primitives for Coordination among Processes.-
M.I.T., Project MAC, Computation Structures Group Memo 57 (Feb. 1971)

/19/ C. A. PETRI: Concepts of Net Theory.-
In: Mathematical Foundations of Computer Science, Proceedings of Symposium and Summer School, High Tatras, Sept. 3-8, 1973.-
Mathematical Institute of the Slovak Academy of Sciences, Computing Research Center United Nations D.P. Bratislava (1973), p. 127-146

/20/ H. A. SCHMID: An Approach to the Communication and Synchronization of Processes.
In: Proceedings of the International Computing Symposium, Davos 1973.- Amsterdam (1973), p. 165-171

/21/ M. YOELI: Petri Nets and Asynchronous Control Networks.-
Unitversity of Waterloo, Department of Applied Analysis and Computer Science, Research Report CS-73-07 (1973)

NOTION DE DUALITE ET DE SYMETRIE DANS LES RESEAUX DE PETRI

Gérard MEMMI

Institut de Programmation (E.R.A. - C.N.R.S. N° 592)

4, Place Jussieu
75230 PARIS CEDEX 05 (FRANCE)

ABSTRACT

After having recalled some basic definitions and properties of the Petri nets, we synthesize some algebraic results, based upon a theorem of compatibility of linear inequalities systems (near of the Farkas lemma).

We find, as corollaries of equivalence theorems between algebraic propositions and Petri nets properties, two theorems synthesizing new results and scattered ones in the literature. Moreover, we refind a necessary condition for a Petri net to be live only based upon the structure of the graph, and also a symmetrical necessary condition for a Petri net to be bounded and live.

We recall, then, the leakage notion [10] and define the symmetrical notion of accumulator from where we derive a necessary condition for a Petri net to be bounded and live.

INTRODUCTION

Un réseau de Pétri permet, en particulier, de modéliser graphiquement des systèmes de processus asynchrones concurrents, évoluant dans le temps de façon discrète, et de décrire les principaux outils de synchronisation (du sémaphore aux expressions de chemins). De plus, ce modèle clair et propre permet à la fois la conception et l'analyse.

Notre recherche nous a conduit à étudier des phénomènes de conservation [11], de diminution systématique [10] [11] et, dualement, de possibilité d'accumulation de marques dans une partie quelconque du réseau de Pétri.
Schématiquement, nous avons prouvé que l'existence d'un phénomène de conservation est équivalente à ce que le réseau soit borné indépendamment du marquage et de l'orientation de sous-ensembles d'arcs déterminés par les transitions. L'existence d'un phénomène de diminution de marques implique que le réseau soit non vivant et l'existence d'un phénomène d'accumulation de marques suffit pour qu'un réseau vivant soit non borné.

Après avoir rappelé, dans une première partie, quelques définitions et propriétés fondamentales d'un réseau de Pétri, nous présentons une interprétation algébrique de ces dernières, basée sur un théorème de compatibilité des systèmes d'inéquations linéaires très proche du lemme de Farkas (voir annexe). Nous en tirons deux théorèmes de synthèse rassemblant et augmentant certains résultats jusque là épars dans la littérature [2] , [7] , [8] , [9] , [11] , [12] , [13] , [14] .
Tout en simplifiant notablement la plupart des preuves, nous retrouvons en corollaires en particulier, une condition nécessaire pour qu'un réseau de Pétri soit vivant, portant uniquement sur la structure du graphe constituant le réseau, ainsi qu'une condition nécessaire symétrique pour qu'un réseau de Pétri soit vivant et borné.

Dans la dernière partie, nous rappelons la notion de fuite et introduisons la notion symétrique de piège d'où nous tirons une condition nécessaire pour qu'un réseau de Pétri soit vivant et borné.

1. GENERALITES SUR LES RESEAUX DE PETRI

Rappelons tout d'abord la définition d'un réseau de Pétri et de ses propriétés principales.

Définition 1 -

Un *réseau de Petri* est le couple $\mathcal{R} = (\mathcal{G}, \mathcal{M})$ où $\mathcal{G} = (P\ T, \Gamma, V)$ est un graphe biparti valué;
les sommets de P sont appelés *places*,
les sommets de T sont appelés *transitions*,
Γ est la correspondance associant à un sommet ses successeurs.
V est une application de $P \times T \cup T \times P$ dans $\mathbb{N}$ telle que $V(x,y) > 0$ si, et seulement si (x,y) est un arc de $\mathcal{G}$.
$\mathcal{M}$ appelé marquage initial du réseau est une application de P dans $\mathbb{N}$.
Une place p contient k marques si, et seulement si $\mathcal{M}(p) = k$.

Posant $|P| = n$, $|T| = m$, une fois les éléments de P et T indexés; à tout graphe biparti valué et fini, nous associons la matrice caractéristique $\Delta(n \times m) = ((\delta_{ij}))$ telle que :
$\delta_{ij} = V(t_j, p_i) - V(p_i, t_j)$.

On fait alors évoluer le marquage d'un réseau de Pétri au moyen de déclenchements et de séquences de déclenchements, modélisant ainsi le fonctionnement d'un système de processus asynchrones.

Définition 2 -

Un déclenchement d_t associé à une transition t est une fonction de $\mathbb{N}^n$ dans $\mathbb{N}^n$ qui, à un marquage $\mathcal{M}$ associe un marquage $\mathcal{M}'$ tel que pour tout p de P :
$\mathcal{M}'(p) = \mathcal{M}(p) + V(t,p) - V(p,t)$.
Par convention, $d_t(\mathcal{M})$ est définie (t est déclenchable à partir de $\mathcal{M}$) si, et seulement si, pour tout p de $\Gamma^-(t)$: $\mathcal{M}(p) \geq V(p,t)$.
Une séquence de déclenchements σ est une composition de déclenchements
$\sigma = \dots \circ d_{t_n} \circ \dots \circ d_{t_1}$; soit $\mathcal{M}$ un marquage,
$\sigma(\mathcal{M})$ est définie si et seulement si $d_{t_1}(\mathcal{M})$ est définie et pour tout $i > 1$, t_i est déclenchable à partir du marquage $d_{t_{i-1}} \circ \dots \circ d_{t_1}(\mathcal{M})$.

Par convention, l'application identité id de $\mathbb{N}^n$ dans $\mathbb{N}^n$ est une séquence de déclenchement toujours définie.

Nous noterons $\mathcal{E}_{\mathcal{M}}$ l'ensemble des marquages atteints à partir de $\mathcal{M}$.
A chaque séquence de déclenchements σ, nous associons le vecteur $\bar{\sigma}$ de $\mathbb{N}^m$ tel que la $i^{\text{ème}}$ composante de $\bar{\sigma}$ soit égale au nombre d'occurrences de t_i.
Alors : $\sigma(\mathcal{M}) = \mathcal{M} + \Delta\bar{\sigma}$ (1)

Pour un système représenté statiquement par un graphe biparti, se pose la question de synchronisation de processus.

De cette question nait deux problèmes cruciaux :

1) *Problème de stabilité* : il s'agit de savoir si un processus du système produit plus que ses processus successeurs ne peuvent consommer et donner ainsi une infinité de ressources disponibles.

2) *Problème d'interblocage ou de verrou mortel* : il s'agit de déceler si deux ou plusieurs processus partageant des ressources vont se bloquer mutuellement, entraînant bien évidemment le mal fonctionnement de tout ou partie du système.

Le premier problème se modélise par la notion de réseau borné.

Définition 3 -

Dans un réseau de Pétri $\mathcal{R} = (\mathcal{G}, \mathcal{M})$.

Une place p est *bornée* si, et seulement si : $\exists\ n \in \mathbb{N}, \forall \mathcal{M}' \in \mathcal{E}_{\mathcal{M}} : \mathcal{M}'(p) < n$.

Un ensemble de places est borné si, et seulement si il ne contient que des places bornées.

Le réseau $\mathcal{R}$ est borné si, et seulement si P est borné.

Le graphe $\mathcal{G}$ est borné si, et seulement si, pour tout marquage $\mathcal{M}$, le réseau $(\mathcal{G},\mathcal{M})$ est borné.

Enfin, nous dirons que $\mathcal{G}$ est *intrinsèquement borné* si, et seulement si tout graphe obtenu en inversant le sens des arcs adjacents à tout sous-ensemble de transitions est un graphe borné.

Une propriété plus forte [11] est celle de graphe invariant qui permet, entre autre, de trouver des éléments de preuve de correction d'un réseau de Pétri [7].

Définition 4 -

Soit $\mathcal{G} = (P,T,\Gamma,V)$ un graphe biparti valué, Δ sa matrice caractéristique, nous appellerons *semi-flot*, toute solution de

$$(2) \begin{cases} f^T\Delta = 0 \\ f \in \mathbb{N}^n \end{cases}$$

Un *invariant* I est un sous-ensemble de P tel qu'il existe un semi-flot f avec $f_i \neq 0$ si et seulement si $p_i \in I$.

Nous notons $\|f\| = I$ et disons que I est le support de f.

Un invariant est dit *minimal*, si et seulement si, il ne contient d'autres invariants que l'ensemble vide et lui-même.

$\mathcal{G}$ est un invariant si, et seulement si P est un invariant.

Notons que $f^T \Delta = 0$ si, et seulement si :

$\forall t \in T : \quad \sum f(P).\ V(p,t) = \sum f(p).\ V(t,p)$

La loi de Kirchhoff est vérifiée aux sommets de T c'est pourquoi nous avons appelé semi-flot toute solution de (2).

Au problème d'interblocage correspond diverses notions. Nous nous interesserons à la notion de réseau vivant, de réseau finissant ou fortement finissant.

Commoner [5] a donné plusieurs définitions de transitions vivantes qu'il nomme $\mathcal{L}_1, \mathcal{L}_2, \mathcal{L}_3, \mathcal{L}_4$, et qui sont de plus en plus restrictives. Nous unifions ici son approche avec celle de Lien [8] sur les transitions finissantes.

Définition 5 -

Dans un réseau de Pétri $\mathcal{R} = (\mathcal{G}\ \mathcal{M})$, soit t une transition,

t est *morte* si et seulement si pour tout M de $\mathcal{E}_{\mathcal{M}}$, t n'est pas déclenchable.

t est $\mathcal{L}_1$ si, et seulement si il existe une séquence de déclenchements atteignant un marquage où t est déclenchable (t *est quasi-vivante*)

t est *finissante* si, et seulement si il existe un entier k tel que pour toute séquence de déclenchements σ, $\bar{\sigma}(t) \leq k$

t est $\mathcal{L}_2$ si, et seulement si pour tout entier k, il existe une séquence de déclenchements σ telle que $\sigma(\mathcal{M})$ soit définie et $\bar{\sigma}(t) \geq k$ (t *est tiède).*

t est $\mathcal{L}_3$ si, et seulement si il existe une séquence de déclenchements infinie telle que $\sigma(\mathcal{M})$ soit définie et $\bar{\sigma}(t) = \infty$ (t *est pseudo vivante)*

t est $\mathcal{L}_4$, nous dirons t est *vivante* si, et seulement si t est $\mathcal{L}_1$ pour tout marquage de $\mathcal{E}_{\mathcal{M}}$.

Commoner a démontré [5] que si t est $\mathcal{L}_4$ alors t est $\mathcal{L}_3$

si t est $\mathcal{L}_3$ alors t est $\mathcal{L}_2$

si t est $\mathcal{L}_2$ alors t est $\mathcal{L}_1$

toutes les propositions réciproques étant fausses.

Nous avons, clairement, si t est finissante, alors t est $\mathcal{L}_1$ et non $\mathcal{L}_2$ ou bien si t est non finissante, alors t est $\mathcal{L}_2$

Donnons un exemple tiré de Commoner [5] discernant une transition $\mathcal{L}_2$ d'une transition $\mathcal{L}_3$

Exemple 1

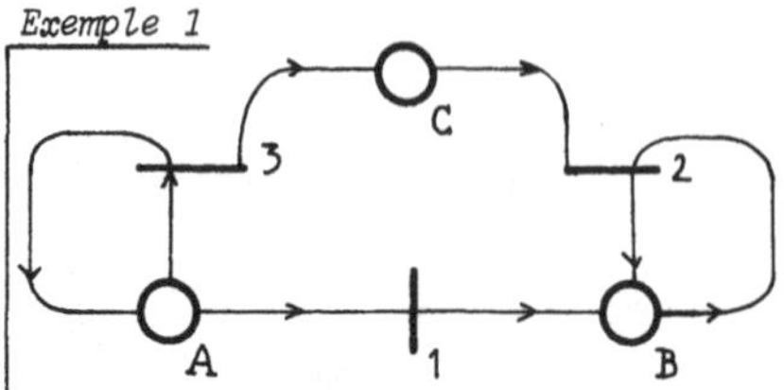

$V(x,y) = 1$ pour tout arc (x,y) de $\mathcal{G}$

$\mathcal{M}(A) = 1$, $\mathcal{M}(B) = \mathcal{M}(C) = 0$

3 est $\mathcal{L}_3$ et non $\mathcal{L}_4$

2 est $\mathcal{L}_2$ et non $\mathcal{L}_3$

Notons que pour tout marquage $\mathcal{M}$ le réseau $(\mathcal{G}, \mathcal{M})$ ne possède aucune transition vivante $(\mathcal{L}_4)$.

Définition 6 -

Nous dirons qu'un réseau $\mathcal{R} = (\mathcal{G}\ \mathcal{M})$ est *finissant* si, et seulement si toute transition est finissante, sinon $\mathcal{R}$ est *non-finissant*.

$\mathcal{R}$ est *fortement non finissant* si, et seulement si, il existe une séquence de déclenchements infinie σ telle que pour toute transition t_i, tout entier $k : \bar{\sigma}_i > k$.
Le graphe biparti valué $\mathcal{G}$ est *non finissant (fortement non finissant)* si, et seulement si il existe un marquage $\mathcal{M}$ tel que le réseau $(\mathcal{G}, \mathcal{M})$ soit non finissant (fortement non finissant).

$\mathcal{G}$ est intrinséquement fortement non finissant si, et seulement si tout graphe obtenu en inversant le sens des arcs adjacents à tout sous-ensemble de places est un graphe fortement non finissant.
Le réseau $\mathcal{R} = (\mathcal{G}, \mathcal{M})$ est *vivant* si, et seulement si toute transition est vivante.

Propriété 1 : soit $\mathcal{R} = (\mathcal{G}, \mathcal{M})$ un réseau de Pétri.

Si $\mathcal{R}$ est vivant, alors $\mathcal{G}$ est fortement non finissant.
Si $\mathcal{G}$ est fortement non finissant, alors $\mathcal{G}$ est non finissant.
Les propositions réciproques étant fausses.

Ces propositions sont évidentes; donnons simplement des contre exemples montrant que les réciproques sont fausses.

Le réseau représenté par le schéma de l'exemple 1 est non finissant puisque 3 est non finissante. Ce réseau n'est pas fortement non finissant puisque dans tout marquage, après les déclenchements de 1 vidant A de toutes ses marques, 3 est morte.

Exemple 2 -

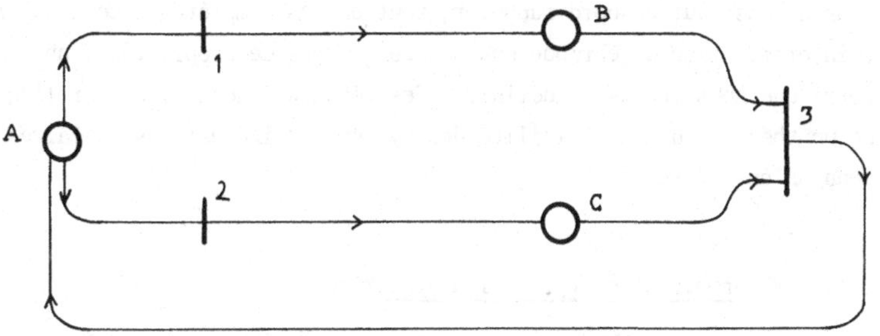

V(3,A) = 2; autrement V (x, y) = 1 pour tout arc (x,y).
La séquence de déclenchements infinie $(d_3 \circ d_2 \circ d_1)^n$ $n \to \infty$ existe bien avec le marquage $\mathcal{M}(A) = 2$, $\mathcal{M}(B) = \mathcal{M}(C) = 0$; et permet d'écrire que le réseau est fortement non finissant, pourtant après la séquence de déclenchements $d_1 \circ d_1$ toutes les transitions sont mortes, le réseau n'est donc pas vivant.

Une propriété plus forte que celle de graphe fortement non finissant est celle de graphe fortement répétitif où l'on impose à σ de retomber sur le marquage d'où elle s'est déclenchée.

Définition 7 - $\mathcal{G}$ est *répétitif (fortement répétitif* ou consistant selon Ramchandani [12])si et seulement si il existe un marquage $\mathcal{M}$ pour lequel il existe une séquence de déclenchements σ (déclenchant au moins une fois toutes les transitions de T) telle que $\sigma(\mathcal{M}) = \mathcal{M}$.

2. RESULTATS DE NATURE ALGEBRIQUE

Nous allons tout d'abord rappeler, tout en les complétant, certains résultats d'interprétation algébrique des quatre groupes de propriétés d'un réseau de Pétri que nous venons de définir. Ces résultats sont basés sur l'équation (1) et un théorème de compatibilité des systèmes d'inéquations linéaires que nous donnons en annexe.

2.1.- Théorèmes d'interprétation algébrique

Si x et y sont deux vecteurs ayant N composantes, $x = (x_i)_{i=1,\dots,N}$; $y = (y_i)$ $i=1,\dots,N$,

Nous notons $x \gneq y$ si et si seulement si $x \geq y$ et $x \neq y$

$x > y$ si et si seulement si $\forall i = 1, \dots, N$ $x_i > y_i$

Théorème 1 : les trois propositions suivantes sont équivalentes :

(1) $\mathcal{G}$ est fortement non finissant

(2) $\exists$ $g > 0$ $\Delta g \geq 0$

(3) $\nexists$ $f \geq 0$ $f^T \Delta \lneq 0$

L'équivalence de (1) et (2) se trouve dans Lien [8] ou bien dans Valk [14].

$2 \Rightarrow 3$: soit f de $\mathbb{N}^n$ et $g > 0$ tel que $\Delta g \geq 0$

nous avons donc $<g , f^T \Delta > >, 0$ donc $f^T \Delta \lneq 0$ est impossible.

$3 \Rightarrow 2$: $\nexists f \geq 0$ $f^T \Delta \lneq 0$ signifie que le système $\begin{cases} f^T \Delta \geq b \\ f > 0 \end{cases}$

est incompatible pour tout $b \gneq o$; donc (voir corollaire en annexe)

$$\begin{cases} u \geq 0 \\ \Delta u \leq 0 \\ <u,b> > 0 \end{cases}$$

est compatible pour tout $b \gneq 0$ donc $\exists g > 0$ $\Delta g \geq 0$ (Q.E.D.)

Théorème 2 : $\mathcal{G}$ est (fortement) répétitif si, et seulement si $\exists g \gneq 0$ $(g > 0)$ $\Delta g = 0$

Ce résultat est dû à Ramchandani [12] et à Lien [8] et est pris comme définition par Sifakis [13] . Remarquons que g est alors un semi-flot sur T vérifiant la loi de Kirchhoff sur P .

Théorème 3 : Les trois propositions suivantes sont équivalentes :

(1) $\mathcal{G}$ est borné

(2) $\nexists\ g \geq 0 \quad \Delta g \gneq 0$

(3) $\exists\ f > 0 \quad f^T\Delta \leq 0$

L'équivalence de (2) et (3) se démontre d'une façon duale à l'équivalence de (2) et (3) du théorème 1.

non (2) $\Rightarrow$ non (1) : soit $g \geq 0$ tel que $\Delta g \gneq 0$, alors il existe un marquage $\mathcal{M}$, une séquence de déclenchements σ telle que $\bar{\sigma} = g$ et $\sigma(\mathcal{M}) = \mathcal{M} + \Delta g$ nous avons donc $\sigma(\mathcal{M}) \gneq \mathcal{M}$; σ est définie à partir de $\sigma(\mathcal{M})$ donc $\mathcal{G}$ est non borné.

(3) $\Rightarrow$ (1) : soit $\mathcal{M}_0$ un marquage initial quelconque pour $\mathcal{G}$, soit $\mathcal{M} \in \mathcal{E}_{\mathcal{M}_0}$ donc $\exists\, g \in \mathbb{N}^m$ tel que $\mathcal{M} = \mathcal{M}_0 + \Delta g$.

Effectuons le produit scalaire par f : $< \mathcal{M}, f> = <\mathcal{M}_0 , f > + < g , f^T\Delta >$

$f^T\Delta \leq 0, \| f \| = P$ donc $\forall\, p \in P, \forall\, \mathcal{M} \in \mathcal{E}_{\mathcal{M}_0} : \mathcal{M}(p) \leq \dfrac{< \mathcal{M}_0, f >}{f(p)}$

D'où, non seulement $\mathcal{G}$ est borné, mais nous avons un majorant pour le marquage de toute place de $\mathcal{G}$ (Q.E.D.)

Sifakis [13] cite l'équivalence de non (1) et non (2).

D'une façon analogue, en notant $\mathcal{G}^-$ le graphe obtenu en inversant le sens de tous les arcs de $\mathcal{G}$ nous avons :

Théorème 4 : Les trois propositions suivantes sont équivalentes :

(1) $\mathcal{G}^-$ est fortement finissant

(2) $\exists\ g > 0 \quad \Delta g \leq 0$

(3) $\nexists\ f \geq 0 \quad f^T\Delta \gneq 0$

Les trois propositions suivantes sont équivalentes :

(1) $\mathcal{G}^-$ est borné

(2) $\nexists\ g \geq 0 \quad \Delta g \lneq 0$

(3) $\exists\ f > 0 \quad f^T\Delta \geq 0$

Théorème 5 : Les quatre propositions suivantes sont équivalentes :

(1) $\mathcal{G}$ est intrinséquement borné

(2) $\nexists g \quad \Delta g > 0$

(3) $\exists f > 0 \quad f^T \Delta = 0$

(4) $\mathcal{G}$ est un invariant

(1) ⟹ (2) : évident après la définition 3 et le théorème 3.

(2) ⟹ (3) : $\nexists g_n \Delta g > 0$ signifie que $\Delta x \geq b$ est un système incompatible pour tout b de $\mathbb{Q}^+ - \{0\}$, donc d'après le théorème de compatibilité

$\exists u \geq 0 \quad u^T \Delta = 0$ et $<u, b>>0$

Ceci, pour tout b de $\mathbb{Q}_+^n - 0$ donc $\exists f > 0 \quad f^T \Delta = 0$

(3) ⟹ (4) : par définition

(4) ⟹ (1) : en effet, si $\mathcal{G}$ est invariant, alors $\mathcal{G}$ est borné.

De plus, en inversant le sens des arcs adjacents à un sous-ensemble de transitions, $\mathcal{G}$ reste un invariant, donc borné (Q.E.D.).

Ce théorème achève de positionner la propriété de graphe invariant par rapport à celle de graphe borné.

Dualement, nous avons :

Théorème 6 : Les quatre propositions suivantes sont équivalentes :

(1) $\mathcal{G}$ est fortement répétitif

(2) $\exists g > 0, \ \Delta g = 0$

(3) $\nexists f \ , f^T \Delta = 0$

(4) $\mathcal{G}$ est intrinséquement fortement non finissant.

2.2.- Théorèmes de dualité et de forte connexité

D'une manière générale, nous partitionnons nos propositions en deux groupes se correspondant par dualité.

Groupe 1 :

1,1 (a) $\exists f > 0, \ f^T \ \Delta \leq 0$ (borné)

1,2 (b) $\exists f > 0, \ f^T \ \Delta \geq 0$ ($\mathcal{G}^-$ borné)

1,3 (a,b) $\exists f > 0, \ f^T \ \Delta = 0$ (invariant)

Groupe 2 (dual)

2,1 (a) $\exists g > 0, \ \Delta g \leq 0$ ($\mathcal{G}^-$ fortement non finissant)

2,2 (b) $\exists g > 0, \ \Delta g \geq 0$ (fortement non finissant)

2,3 (a,b) $\exists g > 0, \ \Delta g = 0$ (fortement répétitif)

Théorème 7 : Si une proposition du groupe 1 (a) et une proposition du groupe 2 (b) sont vraies, alors toutes le sont.

Si une proposition du groupe 1 (b) et une proposition du groupe 2 (a) sont **vraies**, alors toutes le sont.

Si deux propositions sont vraies sans être réparties d'une des deux façons ci-dessus, on ne peut rien dire en général.

La démonstration de ce résultat est simple et repose sur nos cinq théorèmes d'interprétation.
Nous retrouvons ainsi un résultat de Lien : $\mathcal{G}$ est fortement non finissant et invariant si, et seulement si $\mathcal{G}$ est borné et fortement répétitif.

Ou bien encore, un résultat de Sifakis : $\mathcal{G}$ est invariant et fortement répétitif si, et seulement si $\mathcal{G}$ et $\mathcal{G}^-$ sont bornés et fortement non finissant.

Nous allons maintenant nous préoccuper de la forte connexité de $\mathcal{G}$.

Théorème 8 : Si une proposition de chaque groupe (groupe 1(a) et groupe 2(b)) est vérifiée, alors $\mathcal{G}$ est fortement connexe.

D'après le théorème 7, nous avons en particulier $\mathcal{G}$ et $\mathcal{G}^-$ bornés et $\mathcal{G}$ fortement répétitif.

Soit C une composante fortement connexe source, $\mathcal{G}$ est fortement répétitif et borné, donc $C \cap T \neq \emptyset$ et $C \cap P \neq \emptyset$ (C n'est pas réduit à un seul élément).
De $\mathcal{G}$ fortement répétitif, nous tirons : il existe une séquence de déclenchements σ, un marquage $\mathcal{M}$ tels que $\sigma(\mathcal{M}) = \mathcal{M}$, σ étant composée de toutes les transitions de T . C étant une composante fortement connexe source, les transitions de C se déclenchent indépendamment du déclenchement des autres transitions de $\mathcal{G}$ (d'une façon persistante selon Ramchandani). $\mathcal{G}$ est borné : aucune transition de C ne peut envoyer de marques hors de C autrement écrit $\forall t \in C : \Gamma(t) \subset C$.

En inversant le sens des arcs, C devient une composante fortement connexe puits; $\mathcal{G}^-$ est borné; $\mathcal{G}^-$ reste fortement répétitif, par un raisonnement analogue, nous tirons $\forall p \in C$, $(\Gamma^-)^-(p) \subset C$ soit $\forall p \in C : \Gamma(p) \subset C$.
Ce qui achève de déconnecter C du reste du graphe; d'où $\mathcal{G}$ est fortement connexe (Q.E.D.).
En prenant $\mathcal{G}$ invariant et fortement répétitif, nous retrouvons un résultat de Lien [9]
En prenant $\mathcal{G}$ borné et fortement répétitif, nous retrouvons un résultat de Sifakis [13]
En prenant $\mathcal{G}$ invariant et fortement non finissant, nous retrouvons un résultat de [11].

2.3.- Corollaires

Des théorèmes 1 à 7, et de la propriété 1 (si un réseau de Pétri est vivant, alors il est fortement non finissant), nous tirons d'une façon immédiate les résultats de Lien et Sifakis suivants.

Corollaire 1 : si $\mathcal{G}$ est borné et s'il existe $\mathcal{M}$ tel que le réseau de Pétri $\mathcal{R} = (\mathcal{G}, \mathcal{M})$ soit vivant, alors $\mathcal{G}$ est fortement répétitif et invariant.

Corollaire 2 : s'il existe $f \geq 0, f^T\Delta \lneq 0$ alors :

(1) $\nexists\ \mathcal{M}$ tel que $(\mathcal{G},\mathcal{M})$ soit vivant

(2) $\mathcal{G}$ n'est pas fortement répétitif.

En effet, les propositions (3) des théorèmes 1 et 6 sont contredites, donc $\mathcal{G}$ n'est ni fortement finissant ni fortement répétitif, d'où (1) est vérifiée (Q.E.D.).

Corollaire 3 : S'il existe $f \geq 0, f^T\Delta \ngtr 0$ alors :

(1) S'il existe $\mathcal{M}$ tel que $(\mathcal{G},\mathcal{M})$ soit vivant, alors $(\mathcal{G},\mathcal{M})$ est non borné.

(2) $\mathcal{G}$ n'est pas fortement répétitif

(3) du théorème 6 est contredit, donc $\mathcal{G}$ n'est pas fortement répétitif.

S'il existe $\mathcal{M}$ tel que $(\mathcal{G},\mathcal{M})$ soit vivant, alors $\mathcal{G}$ est fortement non finissant, donc $\exists\ g>0,\ \Delta g \geq 0$, or $\mathcal{G}$ n'est pas fortement répétitif, donc $\nexists\ g>0,\ \Delta g = 0$
d'où $\exists\ g>0, \Delta g \ngtr 0$ donc $\mathcal{G}$ n'est pas borné (Q.E.D.)

D'une façon analogue, nous démontrons :

Corollaire 4 : S'il existe $g \geq 0,\ \Delta g \lneq 0$ alors

(1) Si $\mathcal{G}$ est borné, alors $\nexists\ \mathcal{M}$ tel que $(\mathcal{G},\mathcal{M})$ soit vivant

(2) $\mathcal{G}$ n'est pas un invariant.

Corollaire 5 : S'il existe $g \geq 0, \Delta g \ngtr 0$ alors

(1) $\mathcal{G}$ est non borné

(2) $\mathcal{G}$ n'est pas un invariant

Les corollaires 1, 2, 3, 4, sont dûs à Sifakis [13]
Rappelons un résultat voisin au corollaire 1, et dû à Ramchandani [12]

Théorème 9 : Si le réseau de Pétri ($\mathcal{G}$, $\mathcal{M}$) est vivant et borné, alors $\mathcal{G}$ est fortement répétitif.

Remarquons que $\mathcal{G}$ n'est alors ni nécessairement un invariant, ni borné.

Exemple 3

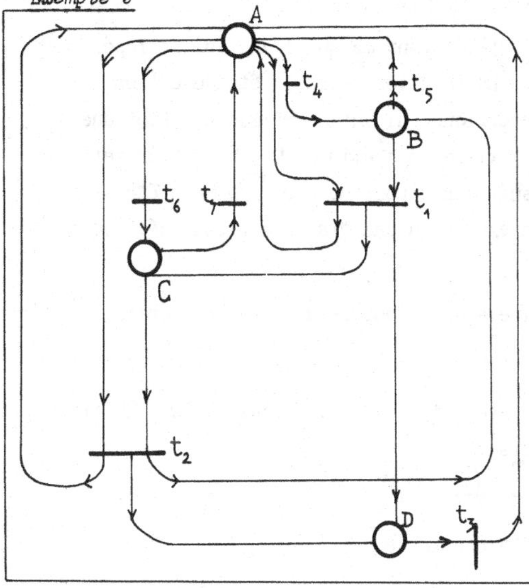

V (A, t_1) = V (D, t_3) = 2
V (C, t_7) = V (t_6, C) =
V (A, t_6) = V (t_7, A) = 3

Pour tout autre arc (x,y), V (x,y)=1
Pour $\mathcal{M}$ tel que $\mathcal{M}$(A) = 2; $\mathcal{M}$(B)=1
$\mathcal{M}$(C) = $\mathcal{M}$ (D) = 0 ; ($\mathcal{G}$, $\mathcal{M}$)

est vivant et borné, pourtant pour
$\mathcal{M}'$(A) = 1 ; $\mathcal{M}'$(B)=3; $\mathcal{M}'$(C)=
$\mathcal{M}'$(D) = 0 ; ($\mathcal{G}$, $\mathcal{M}'$) est non
borné.

3.- DEUX RESULTATS DE NATURE GRAPHIQUE

Les corollaires 2 et 3 sont symétriques du point de vue de l'existence d'un vecteur f . De plus, le corollaire 2 expose une condition nécesssaire pour qu'un réseau de Pétri soit vivant indépendamment de son marquage initial.

Dans [10], nous avons présenté une condition nécessaire analogue reposant sur la notion de fuite. Schématiquement, un ensemble à fuites C est un ensemble de places dont on sait diminuer le nombre de marques au point qu'il sera nécessaire de déclencher des transitions de Γ^-(C) - Γ (C) pour pouvoir continuer à déclencher des transitions de Γ (C). Nous rappelons ici ce résultat et présentons la notion symétrique de piège avec le même formalisme que dans [10].

Théorème 10 : soit $\mathcal{G}$ = (P, T, Γ, V) un graphe biparti valué,

$T_N = \{t \in T, \forall p \in P: V(p,t) = V(t,p)\}$ (nous dirons que T_N est l'ensemble des transitions neutres de $\mathcal{G}$), $D \subset P$ tel que $\Gamma^-(D) \subset \Gamma(D)$ (D est un verrou); une condition nécessaire et suffisante pour que les transitions de Γ (D) - T_N soient vivantes dans un réseau $\mathcal{R}$ = ($\mathcal{G}$, $\mathcal{M}$) est que dans le sous-graphe engendré par $P \cup T - T_N$, D ne soit pas un ensemble à fuites.

Définition 8 - Nous nommons *relation de choix étendu*, la relation suivante dans $T \times T$: $t_1 \xrightarrow{\sigma} t_2$ si, et seulement si, il existe une séquence de déclenchements σ telle que dans tout marquage $\mathcal{M}$ où $d_{t_1}(\mathcal{M})$ est définie, $\sigma(\mathcal{M})$ est définie et t_2 est déclenchable à partir de $\sigma(\mathcal{M})$.

Cette relation est évidemment indépendante de tout marquage initial et repose uniquement sur la structure du graphe. La relation de choix étendu est un préordre mais, n'est en général, ni symétrique, ni anti-symétrique. Pour une machine à états, $t \xrightarrow{\sigma} t'$ signifie qu'il existe un chemin de t à t'. Nous retrouvons alors qu'une condition nécessaire et suffisante pour qu'une machine à états soit vivante est qu'elle soit fortement connexe et qu'une transition soit déclenchable à partir du marquage initial.

Définissons enfin une constante relative à une séquence de déclenchements et à un ensemble de places.

Définition 9 - $N(\sigma, C)$ est *l'accroissement du nombre de marques de* C lors de la séquence de déclenchements σ. Alors :

$$N(\sigma, C) = \sum_{p \in C} (\Delta \bar{\sigma})(p)$$

Donnons une propriété immédiate de cette constante.

Propriété 2 : Si la séquence de déclenchements σ se décompose en deux séquences de déclenchements σ_1, σ_2 (i.e. $\sigma = \sigma_2 \circ \sigma_1$) alors C étant un ensemble de places, nous avons : $N(\sigma, C) = N(\sigma_1, C) + N(\sigma_2, C)$.

De plus : $N(\sigma, C) = \sum_{p \in C} N(\sigma, p)$

et si $\sigma = d_t$: $N(\sigma, C) = \sum_{p \in C} (V(t,p) - V(p,t))$

Nous allons définir un piège comme un ensemble de places qui aura une tendance à gagner des marques.

Les résultats ont une démonstration analogue aux résultats symétriques relatifs à la notion de fuite dans [10].

Définition 10 - Soit C un ensemble de places, $R \subset C$, R est un piège de C si, et seulement si : $\forall t \in \Gamma^-(R), \exists r \in \Gamma^-(R)$ telle que $t \xrightarrow{\sigma} r$ avec :

$$N(d_r \circ \sigma, R) > 0 \text{ et pour tout } p \text{ de } C - R, N(d_r \circ \sigma, p) \geq 0$$

Remarque 1 : soit R un piège de C, alors R est un piège de tout sous-ensemble C' tel que $R \subset C' \subset C$.

Propriété 3 : soit C un sous-ensemble de places, soit R_1, R_2 deux pièges de C, alors $R_1 \cup R_2$ est un piège de C.

De même que pour les fuites, l'union d'un piège d'un ensemble A et d'un piège d'un ensemble B n'est pas nécessairement un piège d'un quelconque ensemble de places. L'intersection de deux pièges de C n'est pas non plus un piège de C en général.

Nous pouvons alors définir le piège maximal d'un ensemble C.

Définition 11 - soit C un ensemble de places, le *piège maximal* de C est le piège formé par l'union de tous les pièges de C. Nous noterons R_C un tel piège, si C n'a pas de piège, nous avons $R_C = \emptyset$, si $R_C = C$, nous dirons que C est un piège.

D'après la remarque 1, tout piège d'un ensemble C est un piège.

Proposition 1 : soit R un piège de C, alors il existe des transitions de $\Gamma^-(R)$ telles que :

$$\sum_{p \in C} V(t,p) > \sum_{p \in C} V(p,t) \qquad \text{ou bien } \Gamma^-(R) = \emptyset .$$

L'existence d'un piège de C est donc bien liée à l'existence de transitions faisant croître strictement le nombre de marques de C.

Algorithme : soit C un ensemble de places, l'algorithme suivant permet de déceler le piège maximal de C.

1°) Initialisation : poser $R_0 = C$, $B_0 = \Gamma^-(C)$

2°) A l'étape i : pour chaque transition de B_{i-1} construire la correspondance $u_i(t) = \{r, r \in \Gamma^-(R_{i-1})$, telle que $t \xrightarrow{\sigma} r$ avec $N(d_r \circ \sigma, R) > 0$ et pour tout p de $C - R$, $N(d_r \circ \sigma, p) \geq 0\}$

Poser $M_i = u_i^{-1}(\emptyset)$, $B_i = B_{i-1} - M_i$, $R_{i-1} - \Gamma(M_i)$

3°) Test d'arrêt : si $R_i = R_{i-1}$ s'arrêter sinon passer à l'étape $i+1$.

Définition 12 - Soit C un ensemble de places du graphe $\mathcal{G} = (P, T, \Gamma, V)$, nous dirons que C est un *ensemble de pièges* si, et seulement si on peut partitionner C en k sous-ensembles $R_1, \ldots, R_k$ tels que

(i) R_1 est un piège

(ii) Pour tout $i > 1$, R_i est le piège maximal de $\bigcup_{l \leq i} R_l$

De l'existence de piège, nous tirons une condition suffisante pour qu'un réseau vivant soit non borné.

Théorème 11 : soit $\mathcal{R} = (\mathcal{G}, \mathcal{M})$ un réseau de Pétri vivant, T_N l'ensemble des transitions neutres, S un sous-ensemble de places tel que $\Gamma(S) \subset \Gamma^{-}(S)$; si dans le sous-graphe engendré par $P \cup (T - T_N)$, S est un ensemble de pièges avec $\Gamma^{-}(S) =$ alors des places de S sont non bornées.

Soit $\mathcal{G} = (P', T', \Gamma', V)$ le sous-graphe engendré par $P \cup T - T_N$, $\mathcal{M}'$ la restriction de $\mathcal{M}$ à P', $\mathcal{R}$ est vivant, donc $\mathcal{R}' = (\mathcal{G}', \mathcal{M}')$ l'est. Chaque fois qu'une transition de $\Gamma'^{-}(S)$ est déclenchable, on peut choisir de faire croître strictement le nombre de marques de S. Or $\Gamma'(S) \subset \Gamma^{-}(S)$, $\mathcal{R}'$ est vivant d'où l'existence d'une séquence de déclenchements infinie faisant croître à l'infini le nombre de marques de S. Cette séquence existe dans le réseau de Pétri initial, donc des places de S sont non bornées. (Q.E.D.)

4.- CONCLUSION

Nous avons rappelé et augmenté, tout en renouvelant le cadre des résultats de nature algébrique, dont les plus importants sont le théorème 7 et les corollaires 2 et 3 qui devraient, en particulier, permettre de simplifier les démonstrations de résultats tels que ceux de Hack [6] sur les réseaux à choix libre.

De plus, nous avons mis en évidence la correspondance duale entre propriétés de réseaux de Pétri, ce qui permet de transporter des résultats d'une sous-classe de réseaux de Pétri dans sa transformée par dualité ou par symetrie.

Nous avons présenté deux conditions nécessaires symétriques l'une de l'autre, indépendantes du marquage initial pour qu'un réseau de Pétri soit vivant d'une part, borné et vivant de l'autre.

Puis en rappelant la notion graphique de fuite, et en introduisant celle symétrique de piège, nous avons apporté deux résultats tout à fait analogues aux conditions de nature algébrique. Nous savons qu'elles ne sont pas identiques; il existe en effet, des graphes vérifiant l'une quelconque de ces conditions sans pour autant vérifier la condition analogue.

Nous conjecturons alors qu'il existe une structure plus générale permettant d'englober les deux résultats analogues que nous avons présentés.

5. REFERENCES

[1] J. ABADIE *"Problèmes d'optimalisation"* U.V. Informatique Opérationnelle Institut de Programmation Pub. n° 41 (1972-1973).

[2] E. BEST, H. SCHMID *"Systems of Open Paths in Petri Nets"* Proc. of the Symp. On M.F.C.S. 75 Lect. notes in Comp. Sc. n° 32 Springer Verlag 1975.

[3] P. CAMION *"Modules unimodulaires"* J. of Combinatorial theory 4, 1968, p. 301-362.

[4] F. COMMONER, A. HOLT, S. EVEN, A. PNUELI *"Marked Directed Graphs"* J. Comput. System Sci. 5 Oct. 1971, p. 511-523.

[5] F. COMMONER *"Deadlocks in Petri Nets"* CA-7206-2311, Applied Data Research, Wakefield, Mass. June 1972.

[6] M. HACK *"Analysis of Production Schemata by Petri Nets"* MS. Thesis Dept Electrical Engineering, MACTR 94, Project MAC, M.I.T. Cambridge, Mass. Sept. 1972 .

[7] K. LAUTENBACH, H. SCHMID *"Use of Petri Nets for Proving Correctness of Concurrent Process System"*. Information processing 1974. North Holland Publ. Co 1974, p. 187-191.

[8] Y.E. LIEN *"Termination Properties of Generalized Petri Nets"* S.I.A.M. J. Comput., June 1976, Vol 5, n° 2, pages 251-265.

[9] Y.E. LIEN *"A Note on Transition Systems"* J. Inf. Sciences 1976, Vol 10 N° 4, p. 347-362.

[10] G. MEMMI *"Fuites dans les réseaux de Pétri"* RAIRO Inf. Théorique, Vol 12 N° 12, p. 125-144 (Juin 1978).

[11] G. MEMMI *"Application of the semi-flow notion to the Boundeness and Liveness Problems in the Petri Nets Theory"* Proc. of the Conf. on Information Sciences and Systems, John Hopkins University, Baltimore, U.S.A., March 1978.

[12] C. RAMCHANDANI *"Analysis of Asynchronous Concurrent Systems by Timed Petri Nets"* Ph. D. Thesis, Project MAC. MAC-TR-120, Cambridge, Mass. Feb 1974.

[13] J. SIFAKIS *"Structural Properties of Petri Nets"* Lab. ass. au C.N.R.S. n° 7, R.R. n° 102, Grenoble Déc 1977 .

[14] R. VALK *"Prévention des bloquages aux systèmes parallèles"*

6.- ANNEXE

Le théorème que nous consentons de rappeler se trouve dans [1] où il est démontré sur $\mathbb{R}$. Dans sa thèse [3] Camion démontre ce résultat dans le cadre des modules unimodulaires. Tous les vecteurs et matrices que nous utilisons sont définis sur $\mathbb{Z}$; c'est donc la démonstration de Camion qu'il faut invoquer quoique la démonstration de Fourier-Abadie [1] légèrement remaniée aboutisse également au résultat sur $\mathbb{Z}$.

Théorème : (Théorème de compatibilité)

Des deux systèmes :

$$S1 : \quad Ax \geq b$$

$$S2 : \begin{cases} u \geq 0 \\ u^T A = 0 \\ \langle u, b \rangle > 0 \end{cases}$$

un, et un seul, est compatible.

Corollaire

Des deux systèmes :

$$S1 : \begin{cases} Ax \geq b \\ x \geq 0 \end{cases}$$

$$S2 : \begin{cases} u \geq 0 \\ u^T A \leq 0 \\ \langle u, b \rangle > 0 \end{cases}$$

un, et un seul, est compatible.

Où A est une matrice ayant ses coefficients dans $\mathbb{Z}$ $(A \in M_{m \times n}(\mathbb{Z}))$; x, u et b sont des vecteurs colonnes : $x \in M_{n \times 1}(\mathbb{Z})$;

u et $b \in M_{m \times 1}(\mathbb{Z})$.

7.- Remerciements : je tiens à remercier Messieurs les Professeurs Claude Girault et Gérard Roucairol, de leur soutien, leurs suggestions et leurs critiques positives.

Je remercie également la Société ECA AUTOMATION (315, Bureaux de la Colline, 92213 Saint-Cloud CEDEX) de son aide dans la réalisation matérielle de ce papier.

A CHARACTERIZATION OF CONCURRENCY-LIKE RELATIONS

Ryszard Janicki

Institute of Mathematics
Warsaw Technical University
Pl. Jedności Robotniczej 1
00-661 Warsaw / Poland

Abstract.

In the paper algebraic properties of symmetric and irreflexive relations (called sir-relations) are discussed. Such relations are of importance in the Petri nets theory (Best[1],Petri[11,12],Mazurkiewicz[7]).

It was proved that for every sir-relation $C \subseteq X \times X$ there is a family of functions (called representations of C) of the form $r: X \to 2^U$, where U is a set, such that $(a,b) \in C \iff r(a) \cap r(b) = \emptyset$. The properties of that family and the relationship between the theory of covers and the theory of sir-relations are discussed.

The notion of K-density for sir-relations is introduced, and some of its properties are proved.

1. Introduction.

The basic difference between sequential processes and concurrent processes is such that in the case of sequential processes for two events the earlier (and later) event is always defined, while in the case of concurrent processes there are events that the relation earlier-later is undefined between them. Other words, the most general model of sequential processes is the theory of linearly ordered sets, whereas the most general model of concurrent processes is the theory of partially ordered sets. The idea of describing sequential processes as linearly ordered sets of event occurrences originates from Pawlak[8], while the idea of describing concurrent processes as partially ordered sets of event occurrences is due to Genrich[2].

a sequential process

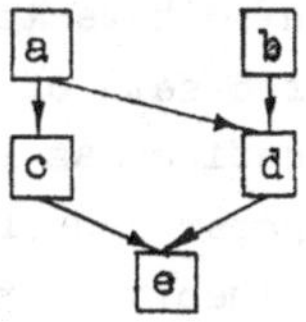

a concurrent process

About events for which the relation earlier-later is undefined we say that they can "occur concurrently". If by the state of process at the time t we mean a set of all events which occur at the time t, then every state of the process is a maximal set of events with the property that every two events may occur concurrently. Instead of saying that two events can occur concurrently we can say that they are in the concurrency relation.

The notion of the concurrency relation originates from Petri [11] and the original definition of that relation was formulated in terms of the theory of nets.

Petri nets theory (Petri [10,11,12], Peterson[9] and others) constitutes an axiomatic approach towards describing parallel systems and processes. The concurrency relation is one of the most important notions of that theory (Petri [11,12]). This is the relation that describes which elements can "coexist" and that generates parallelism. Petri has shown ([11,12]) that a sufficiently comprehensive theory of parallel systems and processes can be established on the basis of that relation.

The relation that describes which elements of processes can coexist is also of importance in the theory of traces, i.e. partially ordered sets of occurrence symbols. This relation is called the indenpendency relation in this case. Traces (introduced by Mazurkiewicz) play the same part in the theory of concurrency as strings in the theory of sequential processes and systems (see Mazurkiewicz [7], Janicki[4], Knuth[5]).

The Petri`s concurrency relation as well as the Mazurkiewicz`s indenpendency relation have such common property that both defines elements which can be executed or can coexist concurrently. They also have common mathematical properties. The concurrency relation is symmetric and reflexive, the indenpendency relation is symmetric and irreflexive. We leave the problem if an event is concurrent with oneself to philosophers, the more so as both assumptions are equivalent (in the sense that all results are the same, only formulations are different). The assumption of irreflexiveness is more conveniant for our purposes.

In the case when we have to do with concurrent processes, or with partially ordered sets of event occurrences, the relation of concurrency can be defined as a complement of the partial order relation. Then many properties of the concurrency relation follows from the well known theory of partially ordered sets. In particular, the greather part of properties of the concurrency relation given in the fundamental Petri's paper [11] follows from that fact.

In the case of concurrent systems the concurrency relation is not defined of the explicite form but as so called set of cases (Petri [10,11]).

Proving properties of concurrent systems is much difficult then the proving properties of concurrent processes. Among other things this follows from the fact that in the case of processes many notions can be defined in terms of partial orders. For example the sequential component of a concurrent process is a maximal chain, and the "case" or the cuts of the process at the time t is a maximal antichain (see Best [1], Petri [11]). In the case of systems these notions are defined much difficult and the theory of partial orders cannot be applied. There are some troubles with the description of dynamic properties of concurrent systems on the basis of "topological" properties of these systems only. To author's mind this follows from the fact that the properties of concurrency-like relations are not enough investigated. In the paper we shall deal with properties of such relations.

Assume that X is a set of objects representing a system (process), and there exists an symmetric and irreflexive relation $C \subseteq X \times X$ that describes which elements can "coexist" or are "independent". We do know nothing about other structures of X. What can we prove about this system (process).

Throughout the text we use standard mathematical notation as 2^X (the power set of X), $|X|$ (the ordinality of X) and so on.

Proofs of theorems are not given in the paper and will be published elsewhere.

2. Basic definitions.

Let X be a set.

By a sir-relation (from symmetric and irreflexive) we mean any relation $C \subseteq X \times X$ such that:

(1) $(a,b) \in C \iff (b,a) \in C$,

(2) $(a,b) \in C \Rightarrow a \neq b$.

For every $C \subseteq X \times X$, let $\overline{C} = X \times X - C$.

Let $lines_C \subseteq 2^X$ (or lines, if C is understood) be a family of subsets of X defined by the equivalence:

$$A \in lines \iff \begin{array}{ll} (1) & (\forall a,b \in A) \quad (a,b) \in \overline{C}\ , \\ (2) & (\forall c \notin A)(\exists a \in A) \quad (a,c) \in C. \end{array}$$

Let $cuts_C \subseteq 2^X$ (or cuts, if C is understood) be a family of subsets od X defined by the equivalence:

$$A \in cuts \iff \begin{array}{ll}(1) & (\forall a,b \in A)\ \ a=b \ \text{ or } \ (a,b) \in C, \\ (2) & (\forall c \notin A)(\exists a \in A)\ \ (a,c) \in \overline{C}\ .\end{array}$$

The fact that families lines and cuts are nonempty follows directly from well known Kuratowski-Zorn Lemma.

2. Representations of sir-relations.

Let X represent a computing system (process) and let $C \subseteq X{\times}X$ describe elements which are "independent". Since it is a computing system, to every element of X is assigned a piece of memory. Such a set of memory pieces is usually called the set of "resources" or "real resources". The parallelism of our system (process) is descri-by the relation C, so if $(a,b) \in C$ then a and b have no common piece of memory (c.f. Mazurkiewicz [7]). "Real resources" are only consistent with the relation C and there are usually such elements a,b that a and b use no common resources but $(a,b) \notin C$.

We prove that for every sir-relation $C \subseteq X{\times}X$ there is a set, called the set of "main abstract resources", with the following properties:

(1) $(a,b) \in C$ iff a and b have no common main abstract resources,

(2) every main abstract resource determinates one sequential component of X (one element of $lines_C$) unambiguously and vice versa.

Let $C \subseteq X{\times}X$ be a sir-relation fixed for the rest of this section.

Every function $r: X \mapsto 2^U$, where U is a set, such that:

$$(\forall a,b \in X) \qquad (a,b) \in C \iff r(a) \cap r(b) = \emptyset$$

is called a <u>representation</u> of sir-relation C.

The set U defined by the representation r is called a set of <u>abstract resources</u>.

A representation $r: X \mapsto 2^U$ of C is called <u>proper</u> iff: $(\forall u,v \in U)\ \ u=v \iff r^{-1}(u)=r^{-1}(v)$, where r^{-1} denotes the co-image.

For every representation r of C, let $li(r)$ be the following set of subsets of X: $li(r) = \{ r^{-1}(u) \mid u \in U \}$.

A proper representation r of C is said to be <u>main</u> iff

$$li(r) = lines_C .$$

<u>Lemma 3.1.</u>(follows from Marczewski [6])
For every sir-relation C there exists a representation r of C.

Unfortunately, the representation defined by means of Marczewski's construction is usually not main (see [3,6]).

Let $R: X \mapsto 2^{lines}$ be the function defined as follows:

$$(\forall a \in X) \quad R(a) = \{A \mid A \in lines \;\&\; a \in A\} .$$

<u>Theorem 3.2.</u> (on the existence of a main representation).

(1) $(\forall a,b \in X) \quad R(a) \cap R(b) = \emptyset \iff (a,b) \in C,$

(2) $(\forall A \in lines) \quad R^{-1}(A) = A .$

<u>Corollary 3.3.</u>
For every set U, if $|U| = |lines_C|$ then there is a main representation r of $C \subsetneq X \times X$ such that $r: X \mapsto 2^U$.

Every set U such that $|U| = |lines_C|$ is called a set of <u>main abstract resources of C</u>.

<u>Example.</u>

Let $X = \{1,2,3,4,a,b,c,d\}$, $C = \{1,3,a,b\} \times \{2,4,d,e\} \cup \{2,4,d,e\} \times \{1,3,a,b\}$. A main representation can be defined as follows:

$$r_{main}: X \longmapsto 2^{\{u,v\}}, \text{ and:}$$

$r_{main}(1)=r_{main}(3)=r_{main}(a)=r_{main}(b)= \{u\}$,

$r_{main}(2)=r_{main}(4)=r_{main}(d)=r_{main}(e)= \{v\}$,

$r_{main}(c)= \{u,v\}$.

The family $lines_C$ and the function R are of the following form:

$$lines_C = \{ \{1,3,a,b,c\} , \{2,4,c,d,e\}\} ,$$

$R(1) = R(3) = R(a) = R(b) = \{ \{1,3,a,b,c\} \}$,

$R(2) = R(4) = R(d) = R(e) = \{ \{2,4,c,d,e\} \}$,

$R(c) = \{\{1,3,a,b,c\} , \{2,4,c,d,e\}\}$.

4. Characterization of lines.

In this section we describe the family lines as a set of solutions of an equality.

Let $C \subseteq X \times X$ be a sir-relation.

Let $d : X \mapsto 2^X$ be the function defined as follows:

$$(\forall a \in X) \quad d(a) = \{ b \in X \mid (a,b) \in \overline{C} \}.$$

Theorem 4.1.

$$A \in \text{lines} \iff A = \bigcap_{a \in A} d(a).$$

Corollary 4.2.

$$(\forall a \in X) \quad R(a) = \{ A \in 2^X \mid a \in A \ \& \ A = \bigcap_{b \in A} d(b) \}.$$

5. Sir-relations and covers.

By a <u>cover</u> of a set X we mean any family of sets $\text{cov} \subseteq 2^X$ such that:

$$(\forall a \in X)(\exists A \in \text{cov}) \quad a \in A.$$

The families lines_C and cuts_C are obviously covers.

If every elements of a cover are separable then such a cover is called a partition. It is well known fact that any partition describes an equivalence relation and vice versa. For covers the part of the equivalence relation is played by the sir-relation (note that a complement of any equivalence relation is also a sir-relation).

It turns out that every cover of X describes a sir-relation and every sir-relation describes a specific family of covers. We shall deal with that problem in this section.

Let X be a set and let cov be a cover of X.

Let $r_{\text{cov}} : X \mapsto 2^{\text{cov}}$ be the function defined as follows:

$$(\forall a \in X) \quad r_{\text{cov}}(a) = \{ A \in \text{cov} \mid a \in A \}.$$

Let $C_{\text{cov}} \subseteq X \times X$ be the relation defined as follows:

$$(\forall a,b \in X) \quad (a,b) \in C_{\text{cov}} \iff r_{\text{cov}}(a) \cap r_{\text{cov}}(b) = \emptyset.$$

Note that C_{cov} is a sir-relation and r_{cov} is a proper representation of C_{cov}. The relation C_{cov} is called a sir-relation defined by the cover cov.

Let $C \subseteq X \times X$ be a fixed sir-relation.

Let COV(C) be the family of the following covers of X:

$$cov \in COV(C) \iff C_{cov} = C.$$

The set COV(C) is called a set of covers definable by sir-relation C. It is obvious that $lines_C \in COV(C)$.

Lemma 5.1.

For every representation r of C: $li(r) \in COV(C)$.

Let LINES (or $LINES_C$) be the following family of subsets of X:

$$A \in LINES \iff (\forall a,b \in A) \quad (a,b) \in \overline{C} .$$

Observe that the family LINES ddefines the family lines and vice versa, namely:

$$lines = \{A \in LINES \mid (\forall B \in LINES) \ A \subseteq B \Rightarrow A=B\} ,$$

$$LINES = \{A \in 2^X \mid (\exists B \in lines) \quad A \subseteq B\}.$$

Observe also, that the families LINES and lines are respectively the greatest and the least element of COV(C).

Theorem 5.2.

For every sir-relation $C \subseteq X \times X$:

$$(\forall\, cov \subseteq 2^X) \quad cov \in COV(C) \iff lines_C \leq cov \leq LINES_C .$$

Corollary 5.3.

For every cover cov of X:

$$lines_{C_{cov}} \leq cov \leq LINES_{C_{cov}} .$$

Let cov be an arbitrary cover of X. From the above considerations it follows that generally $lines_{C_{cov}} \neq cov$, and r_{cov} is not main representation.

Now, we define such a class of covers that the above properties will be fulfiled.

A cover cov of X is called a maximal sets cover (abbr. ms-cover) iff:

$$(\forall A \in cov)(\forall B \in 2^X) \qquad B \supsetneq A \Rightarrow B \notin cov.$$

For example the family $lines_C$ is a ms-cover.

Theorem 5.4.

cov is a ms-cover $\Leftrightarrow$ $\text{lines}_{C_{\text{cov}}} = \text{cov}$.

Corollary 5.5.

For every cover cov of X the following three conditions are equivalent:

(1) cov is a ms-cover,

(2) $\text{lines}_{C_{\text{cov}}} = \text{cov}$,

(3) $r_{\text{cov}} = R_{C_{\text{cov}}}$.

Corollary 5.6.

A representation $r : X \mapsto 2^U$ of $C \subseteq X \times X$ is main $\Leftrightarrow$ $|U| = \text{minimum}$.

From the above considerations it follows that from the point of view of the set of abstract resources main representations are the smallest representations.

The facts proved above have very simple interpretation. Let X be a set representing concurrent system or process. The sir-relation (a generalization of the concurrency relation) describes the set of sequential components and vice versa. It can be expected such a result. Assume that cov is a cover of X such that each element of cov is a set of elements with one common resource at least. If cov is not ms-cover that components designated by some resources can be contained in components designated by others, and some of resources define only subsets of sequential components.

The family lines_C defines a minimal set of abstract resources sufficient to define the parallelism of the system (process) X.

6. Regular sir-relations.

A cover cov of X is said to be minimal iff:

$(\forall A \in \text{cov})$ $\text{cov} - \{A\}$ is not a cover of X.

Sometimes the family COV(C) contains a minimal cover, for example lines_C, but in many cases the family lines_C is not a minimal cover. Consider the following example. Let $X = \{a,b,c,d\}$, $C = \{(c,d),(d,c),(a,c),(c,a)\}$. In this case, $\text{lines}_C = \{\{a,b\},\{a,d\},\{b,c\}\}$ and $X = \{a,d\} \cup \{b,c\}$, so lines_C is not a minimal cover of X.

A sir-relation $C \subseteq X \times X$ is called regular if the family $lines_C$ is a minimal cover of X.

Regular sir-relations have conveniant properties, among others any regular sir-relation is K-dense (see Petri[11,12], Best[1] and the next section).

Theorem 6.1 (criterion of regularity)
Let $C \subseteq X \times X$ be a sir-relation and let $r: X \mapsto 2^U$ be a main representation of C.
A sir-relation C is regular $\Leftrightarrow (\forall u \in U)(\exists a \in X) \quad \{u\} = r(a)$.

Theorem 6.2. (on common element)
If C is a regular sir-relation then:

$$(\forall A \in lines)(\forall B \in cuts) \qquad |A \cap B| = 1 .$$

The above theorem say that if the sir-relation is regular then every sequential component of a system (process) has one common element with any "case" of that system (process). Petri [11] has postulated that every real process and system has to have that property. This property is called K-density. The postulate of K-density is a generalization of the well known postulate of phisics that every time sequence and every space must have one element in common. Petri require that for every case and for every sequential process it must be well defined how far the process has progressed. This leads to the notion of K-density. For more details, philosophy of K-density the reader is advised to refer to Petri[11,12], Best[1].

7. K-density.

The notion of K-density was introduced as a property of Petri nets, although it can also be considered as a property of every concurrency-like relation. The problem of K-density in the case of Petri nets was precisely considered by Best[1]. We shall deal with that problem in the case of sir-relations. It turns out that K-density can be expressed by means of main representations and by means of covers generated by a sir-relation. It also turns out that, in this general case the properties of K-density are somewhat different than in the case of Petri nets of ocurrences.

A sir-relation $C \subseteq X \times X$ is said to be K-dense iff
$(\forall A \in lines)(\forall B \in cuts) \quad |A \cap B| = 1$.

Lemma 7.1.
A sir-relation $C \subseteq X \times X$ is K-dense if and only if, for every main representation $r: X \mapsto 2^U$ and every $B \in cuts$: $r(B) = U$.

Corollary 7.2.
Every regular sir-relation is K-dense.

The result of Lemma 7.1 might be expected. This is a new formulation of the fact that every case and every sequential component have a common element.

Theorem 7.3.
For every finite sir-relation $C \subseteq X \times X$, if there exists a partial order relation $P \subseteq X \times X$ such that $\overline{C} = P \cup P^{-1}$ then C is K-dense.

The above theorem follows from the well known fact that in the case of finite partial orders, every maximal chain and every maximal antichain have a common element. Using this theorem for nets of occurrences (Petri [11,12]) we obtain the known fact that the concurrency relation of every finite net of occurrences is K-dense.

In the paper [11] Petri has formulated a very useful local property of the concurrency relation, namely so called N-density. This is a necessary condition of K-density. In our terms that condition is the following.

Theorem 7.4 (follows from Petri [11]).
If a sir-relation $C \subseteq X \times X$ is K-dense then:

$$(\forall a,b,c,d \in X) \quad (a,b) \in C \;\&\; (b,c) \in C \;\&\; (c,d) \in C \;\&\; (a,c) \in \overline{C} \;\&\; (a,d) \in \overline{C} \;\&\; (b,d) \in \overline{C} \;\Rightarrow$$
$$(\exists e \in X) \quad (b,e) \in C \;\&\; (e,c) \in C \;\&\; (a,e) \in \overline{C} \;\&\; (e,d) \in \overline{C} .$$

The above theorem is illustrated by the below figure.

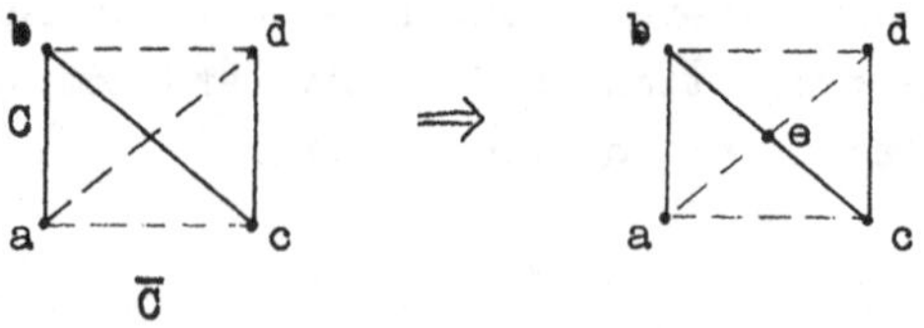

Of course, not every finite sir-relation is K-dense. To prove this fact consider the following construction.

Let T be a set of indeces. Let $X = \bigcup_{t\in T}\{a_t,b_t\}$, and let $C_T = \bigcup_{t\in T}\{(a_t,b_t),(b_t,a_t)\} \cup \{(b_t,b_s) \mid t\neq s \ \&\ t,s\in T\}$.

Of course, C_T is a sir-relation. Note that $\{a_t \mid t\in T\}\in \mathrm{lines}_{C_T}$, $\{b_t \mid t\in T\}\in \mathrm{cuts}_{C_T}$, so if $|T|\geqslant 2$ then the sir-relation C_T is not K-dense.

Now, we shall show the relationship between the notion of K-density and the theory of covers.

Let $C\subseteq X\times X$ be a sir-relation.

Let $\mathrm{COV}_{min}(C)$ (or COV_{min}) be the following family of covers of X:

$$\mathrm{cov}\in \mathrm{COV}_{min} \iff \begin{array}{ll}(1) & \mathrm{cov} \text{ is a minimal cover of } X,\\ (2) & \mathrm{cov}\subseteq \mathrm{lines}_C.\end{array}$$

Lemma 7.5.

For every sir-relation $C\subseteq X\times X$:

$$\bigcup\{\mathrm{cov} \mid \mathrm{cov}\in \mathrm{COV}_{min}\} = \mathrm{lines}_C \iff \bigcap\{\mathrm{cuts}_{C_{\mathrm{cov}}} \mid \mathrm{cov}\in \mathrm{COV}_{min}\} = \mathrm{cuts}_C.$$

The family COV_{min} can be used to characterize the K-density.

Theorem 7.6.

For every sir-relation $C\subseteq X\times X$, if $\bigcup\{\mathrm{cov} \mid \mathrm{cov}\in \mathrm{COV}_{min}\} = \mathrm{lines}_C$ then the relation C is K-dense.

It turns out that for finite sir-relation the above condition is also necessary.

Theorem 7.7.

For every finite sir-relation $C\subseteq X\times X$ the following conditions are equivalent:

1. C is K-dense.
2. $\bigcup\{\mathrm{cov} \mid \mathrm{cov}\in \mathrm{COV}_{min}(C)\} = \mathrm{lines}_C$.

The problem if Theorem 7.7 is true for infinite sir-relations is open. The second condition of Theorem 7.7 means that for every $A\in \mathrm{lines}$ there exists a minimal cover cov of X such that

$$A\in \mathrm{cov}\subseteq \mathrm{lines}.$$

8. Relationship between sir-relation and graphs.

There is a strict connexion between sir-relations and graphs. All results of this paper can be formulated in terms of graph theory. In this section we show some of these formulations.

Let X be a set, and let $V \subseteq 2^X$ be a set such that $(\forall v \in V)\ |v| = 2$ or $V = \emptyset$. Every pair $G = (X,V)$, where X,V are sets of the above form is called an undirect graph (abbr. graph). The set X is called the set of vertexes, the set V is called the set of edges.
A graph $G = (X,V)$ is called full iff: $(\forall a,b \in X)\quad a \neq b \Rightarrow \{a,b\} \in V$.
A graph $G_1 = (X_1,V_1)$ is a subgraph of the graph $G = (X,V)$ iff $X_1 \subseteq X$ and $V_1 \subseteq V$. Every maximal full subgraph of the graph G is called a clique of G. For every graph $G = (X,V)$, let $\overline{G}$ be the following graph: $\overline{G} = (X,\overline{V})$, where $\overline{V} \subseteq 2^X$ and $(\forall a,b \in X)\ \{a,b\} \in \overline{V} \Leftrightarrow \{a,b\} \notin V$ & $a \neq b$. The graph $\overline{G}$ is called a complement of G. For more details the reader is advised to refer to Harrary[3].

For every graph $G = (X,V)$, let $C_G \subseteq X \times X$ be the following relation:

$$(\forall a,b \in X)\quad (a,b) \in C_G \iff \{a,b\} \in V \ .$$

The relation C_G is a sir-relation generated by the graph G.

For every sir-relation $C \subseteq X \times X$, let G_C be the following graph:

$$G = (X,V), \text{ where } \quad (\forall a,b \in X) \quad \{a,b\} \in V \iff (a,b) \in C.$$

The graph G_C is a graph generated by the relation C.

For every graph G, let clq(G) denotes the set of all cliques of the graph G. In terms of graphs the notions of lines, cuts and K-density are the following.

Lemma 8.1.
For every sir-relation $C \subseteq X \times X$:

$$\text{lines}_C = \text{clq}(\overline{G}_C),$$
$$\text{cuts}_C = \text{clq}(G_C),$$
$$C \text{ is K-dense} \iff (\forall Q_1 \in \text{clq}(\overline{G}_C))\ (\forall Q_2 \in \text{clq}(G_C)) \quad |Q_1 \cap Q_2| = 1 \ .$$

The representation of sir-relation in the shape of graph makes the considerations easier.

9. Conclusions.

We proved above that every sir-relation can be represented by a certain, isomarphic with the set of all sequential components set of abstract resources.

It also turned out that the theory of sir-relations and the theory of covers are strictly connected. Every cover describes a sir-relation, but not every element of cover represents an appropriate sequential component. Up till now, the regular sir-relation do not have an interpretation in the Petri nets theory. The property of regularity is stronger than the property of K-density. Every regular sir-relation is K-dense, but not vice versa. An application of the above theory can be found in Janicki [4].

The author wish to thank prof. Antoni Mazurkiewicz and prof. Józef Winkowski for valuable discussions, comments and criticism.

References.

[1] Best E., A Theorem on the Characteristic of Non-Sequential Processes, Technical Report 116, Univ. of Newcastle upon Tyne, Comp. Labor., 1977.

[2] Genrich H.J., A position in panel discussion, MFCS`75 Symposium, Marianskie Laznie, 1975.

[3] Harrary F., Graph Theory, Addison-Wesllay, Mass., 1967.

[4] Janicki R., Synthesis of Concurrent Schemes, Lecture Notes in Comp. Sci., vol. 64, Springer-Verlag, 1978, 298-307.

[5] Knuth E., Petri Nets and Trace Languages, Proc. of the 1st European Conf. on Parallel and Distr. Processing, Toulouse, 1979.

[6] Marczewski E., Sur deux propriétés des classes d`ensembles, Fund. Math., 33(1945), 303-307.

[7] Mazurkiewicz A., Concurrent Program Schemes and Their Interpretations, DAIMI PB-78, Aarhus Univ., Department of Comp. Sci., 1977.

[8] Pawlak Z., On the Notion of a Computer, Logic Meth. and Phil. Sci., 3(1968), 255-267.

[9] Peterson T.L., Petri Nets, ASM Computing Surveys 9, 3(1977), 223-252.

[10] Petri C.A., Concepts of Net Theory, MFCS`73 Proc., Math. Inst. of Slovak Acad. of Sci., 1973, 137-146.

[11] Petri C.A., Non-Sequential Processes, ISF Report 77-01, Gesellshaft für Mathematik und Datenverarbeitung, Bonn, 1977.

[12] Petri C.A., Concurrency as a Basis of Systems Thinking, ISF Report 78-06, Gesellshaft für Mathematik und Datenverarbeitung, Bonn, 1978.

The Analysis of Distributed Systems by Means of Predicate/Transition-Nets

Hartmann J. Genrich, Kurt Lautenbach
Gesellschaft für Mathematik und Datenverarbeitung
Institut für Informationssystemforschung
Schloss Birlinghoven, Postfach 1240
D-5205 St. Augustin 1
West Germany

Abstract

Within the framework of net-semantics of models of dynamic systems, the present paper introduces a new standard interpretation of nets called predicate/transition-nets (Pr/T-nets). These nets are schemes of 'ordinary' Petri nets. The places (circles) of Pr/T-nets represent changing properties of, or relations between, individuals; they are 'predicates' with variable extension. A current case of a system modelled by a Pr/T-net is denoted by marking the places with those tuples of individual symbols for which the respective predicates hold in that case. The transitions (boxes) are schemes of elementary changes of markings constituting the processes carried by the system. Instances of these schemes are generated by means of consistent substitution of individual variables by symbols.

Assuming some familiarity with Petri nets, the paper first introduces the predicate/transition-net model in its most general form, from which some special cases are derived. Then it is shown that the 'dead' transitions of a Pr/T-net represent first-order formulas expressing invariant assertions about the modelled systems. Next the linear-algebraic techniques for finding invariants are transferred to Pr/T-nets. The last part of the paper is devoted to the analysis of a scheme for organizing distributed database systems.

Introduction

It is well known that systems with concurrently working components can be correctly modelled by Petri nets. Originally, Petri nets were introduced by Petri [PE62] as a tool for the conceptual foundation of a new kind of mathematical systems theory capable of treating concurrency in a non-idealizing way. When Petri nets were later seen as powerful instruments for practical systems design, it was also realized rather soon that the user was often forced on too a detailed level of system description. Therefore many extensions and derivatives of Petri nets have been introduced in the meanwhile.

In order to put these attempts into one general framework, Petri [PE73] proposed to interconnect all interpretations of nets by means of net-preserving mappings (netmorphisms) thus integrating the top-down practice of system design and the bottom-up development of the theory. The general principle for that approach is rather simple: Starting with the (axiomatically defined) basic interpretation of nets, the condition/event-systems [PE75], new notions and the semantics of higher level interpretations of nets are formally derived by completion and abstraction from already well defined - and understood - standard interpretations, until the level of practical systems organization is reached.

By means of completion, for example, the enlogic and the synchronic structure of condition/event-systems were discovered by Petri [PE75]. By means of abstraction, the notion of information flow in dynamic systems was explicated; Petri showed that two fundamental forms of distribution of information must be distinguished: flux and influence [PE67,PE77].

Within this framework of net-semantics of models of dynamic systems, the present paper introduces a new standard interpretation of nets called predicate/transition-nets (Pr/T-nets). These nets are schemes of 'ordinary' Petri nets (called place/transition-nets in [GEL78]) which are a generalization of condition/event-nets. They are the result of completing and combining several earlier results: The net calculus of first-order predicate logic given by Genrich and Thieler-Mevissen [GTM76]; transition nets with coloured tokens introduced by Lautenbach and investigated by Schiffers [SC77]; and transition nets with complex conditions introduced by Shapiro [SH79].

The places (circles) of Pr/T-nets represent changing properties of, or relations between, individuals; they are 'predicates' with variable extension. A current case of a system modelled by a Pr/T-net is denoted by marking the places with those tuples of individual symbols for which the respective predicates hold in that case. The transitions (boxes) are schemes of elementary changes of markings constituting the processes carried by the system. Instances of these schemes are generated by means of consistent substitution of individual variables by symbols.

Assuming some familiarity with Petri nets, the paper first introduces the predicate/transition-net model in its most general form, from which some special cases are derived. Then it is shown that the 'dead' transitions of a Pr/T-net represent first-order formulas expressing invariant assertions about the modelled systems. Next the linear-algebraic techniques for finding invariants known from [LA73] and [LAS74] are transferred to Pr/T-nets. The rest of the paper analyses a scheme for organizing distributed database systems taken from [EL77] and [MI78].

1. Predicate/Transition-nets

In the basic interpretation of nets, the condition/event-net model of dynamic systems (C/E-nets), the circles (places) represent conditions which in some cases hold and in others don't. A current case of a modelled system is represented by marking exactly those conditions which hold in this case. The boxes (transitions) represent events; each occurrence of an event is a coincident change in condition holdings: the 'preconditions' of the event cease to hold, the 'postconditions' begin to hold.

In fig.1, a section of a C/E-net is shown which contains two events each having two preconditions and one postcondition. In the case represented by the marking, the upper event may occur since its preconditions hold (may cease to hold) and its postcondition doesn't (may begin to hold).

Conditions of a C/E-net may be viewed as atomic propositions with changing truthvalues. In fig.1, the conditions are named by instances of predicates P, Q, and R, formed by means of individual symbols a, b. In the case represented in fig.1, individual a has the property P, a and b have the property Q, and b is in relation R to a. By an occurrence of the 'enabled' upper event, a looses property P, b looses property Q, and a gets into relation R to b. Thus, P and Q name variable properties and R names a variable relation; P, Q, and R, are predicates with changing extensions.

In fig.2, the properties P and Q and the relation R themselves are represented by places. In order to represent the same case as in fig.1, they are marked by their corresponding extensions: place P carries the set {a}, Q carries {a,b}, and R carries {<b,a>}. The two events of fig.1 are specified in fig.2 by means of individual symbols labelling the arcs. In this way, fig.2 represents exactly the same section of a condition/event-systems as fig.1. The size of the net has been reduced by introducing *condition schemes* (predicates); this is compensated by more complex inscriptions to the net: (tuples of) individual symbols marking the places and labbelling the arcs.

In a next step, the abstraction goes farther by introducing *transition schemes*. The two transitions of fig.2 are 'similar', i.e. except for the arc labels they are connected to the same places in the same way. This allows them to be considered as two instances of a transition scheme which is shown in fig.3. Here the arc labels are tuples of individual *variables*. An instance of the transition scheme is generated by means of consistent substitution of variables by individual symbols. In order to denote the set of valid instances, the list of corresponding value assignments could be inscripted into the box; in our case, for example: (x,y) ← (a,b),(b,a). Instead we have chosen a logical formula which, when interpreted within the given range {a,b}, is true exactly for those assignments belonging to the valid instances. This, in general, yields much more a concise representation.

The schematic representation of 'ordinary' Petri nets for which we have seen a very simple example shall now be completed. Our aim is to create a new type of Petri net model which combines the preciseness of modelling by nets with the power of both first-order predicate logic and linear algebra. Of course these 'generalized' Petri nets shall include the ordinary ones as special cases. The main additions to the elements of fig.3 will be the following:

1. The range of the variables is assumed to be the same for all transitions, a given set of individuals U. U may be structured by functions and relations, named by certain operators (including individual symbols as no-argument operators) and predicate symbols. Then any quantifier-free logical formula using variables, equality, and the operators and predicates associated with U may be inscripted to a transition.
2. The arcs are labelled by formal sums (polynomials) of tuples of variables if the transition is connected to a place by 'multiple' arcs.

3. The places may carry more than one copy of an 'item' (tuple of individual symbols) up to a 'capacity' K.

In this way we get the following

Definition 1: A predicate/transition-net consists of the following constituents:

1. A directed net (S,T;F) where
   - S is the set of predicates ('first-order' places) ○,
   - T is the set of ('first-order') transitions □,
   - F :⊆ S×T ∪ T×S is the set of arcs ⟶.
2. A structured set $\mathbb{U} = (U;op_1,\ldots,op_m;P_1,\ldots,P_n)$
3. A labelling of arcs assigning to all elements of F a formal sum of n-tuples of variables where n is the 'arity' of the predicate connected to the arc. The zero-tuple indicating a no-argument predicate (an ordinary place) is denoted by the special symbol ¢.

   Examples:

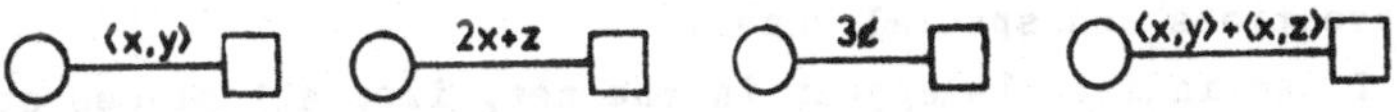

4. An inscription on transitions assigning to some elements of T a quantifier-free logical formula built from equality, operators and predicates given with U, and variables occurring at the surrounding arcs.

   Examples:

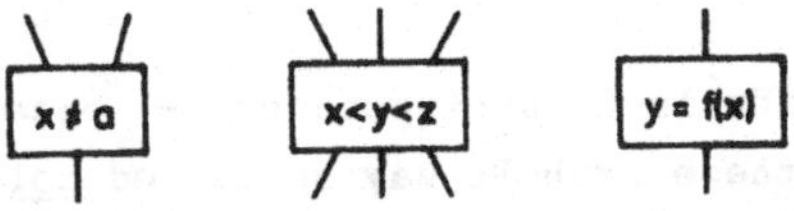

5. A marking of predicates of S with n-tuples of individuals (items).

   Examples:

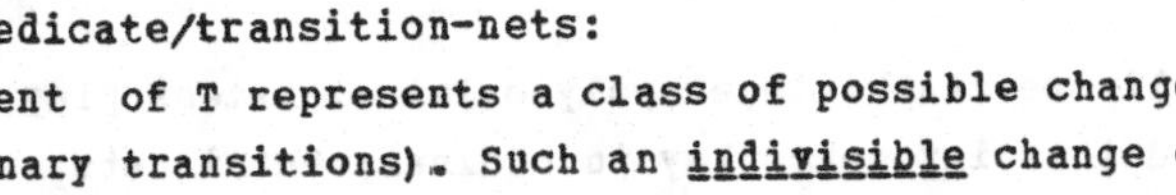

6. A natural number K which is a universal bound for the number of copies of the same item which may occur at a single place (K may be called place capacity).
7. The transition rule "⇝" which expresses the common interpretation of predicate/transition-nets:

   Each element of T represents a class of possible changes of markings (ordinary transitions). Such an indivisible change consists of removing (○→□) and adding (□→○) copies of items from/to places according to the schemes expressed by the arc labels. It may occur whenever, for an assignment of individuals to the variables which satisfies the formula inscripted to the transition, all input places carry enough copies of proper items and for no output place the capacity K is exceeded by adding the respective copies of items.

Example: For a structure ({a,b,c}; < := alphabetical ordering) and K = 3, two of the nine instances of the following transition(scheme) are enabled under the marking shown on the left side. Due to conflict, however, at most one will occur. For the assignment (x,y,z) ← (a,b,c) the resulting marking is shown on the right side.

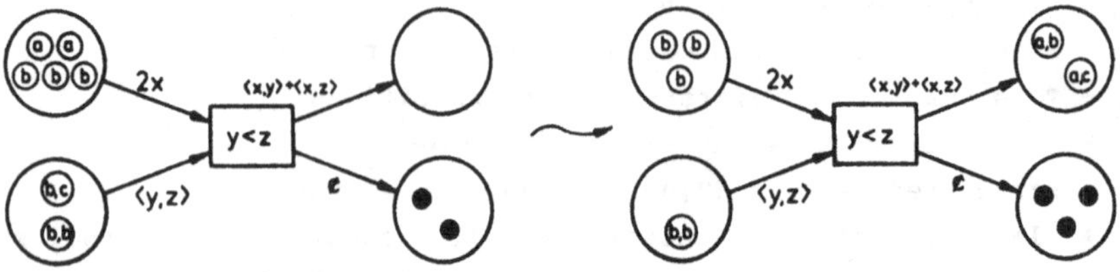

Since we are going to demonstrate the use of Pr/T-nets rather extensively in the next sections, we mention here only some notational conventions and special cases:

1. If no individals appear in the net, i.e. all places are no-argument predicates, we get ordinary Petri nets (P/T-nets).
2. If additionally K = 1 we get C/E-nets.
3. If there are individuals but K = 1, we have first-order predicate schemes of C/E-nets.
4. If the set of individuals is unstructured - except for the individual symbols - these symbols may be called <u>colours</u> of tokens as in the CP-net model of [SC77,SCW78].
5. If a formula at a box has the form $v = t \wedge \dots$ where v is a variable and t a term, all occurrences of v in and around the transition may be replaced by copies of t .
6. Formal sums of items may be also used for denoting the marking of places. They may, and will, be treated as integer polynomials in several variables.

We shall see that integer polynomials in items play the same role in our model as integers play in ordinary Petri nets. In fact, the transfer of the linear-algebraic techniques for Petri nets to predicate/transition-nets is based exactly upon this 'extension' of the integers. Therefore we introduce here a minimum of notation needed in the next sections. The formal apparatus of polynomial rings over commutative rings may be found in any book on algebra, e.g. [HE75].

1. An integer polynomial in n variables $p \equiv p(v_1,\dots,v_n)$ is a sum $\sum_{k_1\geq 0,\dots,k_n\geq 0} p_{k_1\dots k_n} \cdot v_1^{k_1}\dots v_n^{k_n}$ where each $p_{k_1\dots k_n}$ is an integer called the <u>coefficient</u> of the 'object' $v_1^{k_1}\dots v_n^{k_n}$.

2. In our case, the variables are the items, i.e. tuples of individual names. The empty item $\notin$ is the unit element of the ring (the 0th power of any item). The integers are identified with polynomials of degree 0 (in $\notin$ only).
3. For two polynomials $p \equiv p(v_1,\dots,v_n)$ and $q \equiv q(v_1,\dots,v_n)$ we write $p \leq q$ iff $p_{k_1\dots k_n} \leq q_{k_1\dots k_n}$ for all $k_i \geq 0$.
4. For a polynomial $p \equiv p(v_1,\dots,v_n)$ we denote by $|p|$ the <u>(unit) value</u> (sum of coefficients) $p(1,\dots,1)$.
5. For a vector (matrix) of polynomials, its value is defined as the vector (matrix) of the values of its elements.
   If C and D are matrices of polynomials then $|C \bullet D| = |C| \bullet |D|$. In the same way, if x and y are vectors in polynomials then $|x*y| = |x|*|y|$ for the inner product.
6. To a set or, more general, a family of items we assign its <u>characteristic</u> polynomial by means of an operator π:
   $\pi(X) := \sum_{x \in X} x;\ \pi(\{x_i\}_{i \in I}) := \sum_{i \in I} x_i$

2. <u>Facts and Invariants in Pr/T-nets</u>

We have mentioned already that there exists a very close relationship between condition/event-nets and propositional logic. If, for example, the box in fig.4 is a transitional form in conditions then, for a given marking class, the following two statements are equivalent:

- In no marking, the transition is enabled (it is 'dead')
- In all markings, the propostion ($\neg p \vee \neg q \vee r \vee s$) is true.

Hence dead transitions represent <u>invariant assertions</u>, i.e. factually true statements - or <u>facts</u>, for short - about what can be the case in the modelled system. Facts which are denoted by ▭ were discovered by Petri [PE75] as one class of the <u>enlogic structure</u> of condition/event-systems. A corresponding net calculus of propositional logic was extended to a consistent and complete net calculus of first-order predicate logic [GTM76,TM76]. This was mainly based upon well-known techniques ('Skolemization') for representing first-order formulas as sets of quantifier-free disjunctive clauses of instances of predicates.

It follows immediately from the transition rule for Pr/T-nets that each 'dead' transition of a Pr/T-net with place capacity 1 represents a (first-order) fact about the modelled system. For example, fig.5(a) represents the formula

$\forall x,y:[x<y \implies (\neg Px \vee \neg Qx \vee Rx,y)]$

which is a fact about any marking class for which the transition is dead. Of course, this representation is not 'clean' since it still contains a logical formula as an inscription. However, it is easy to find a net representation of the inscription and add it to fig.5(a). We only have to represent the constant predicate < by a place, too, and mark it with its extension when given together with the set of individuals. Fig.5(b) shows the same fact as fig.5(a) together with the laws for < being a strict partial order. (The additional transitions are 'in fact' dead for all (constant) markings of ⓒ which are a strict order relation.)

In this way facts, as being part of the enlogic structure of systems, establish the precise connection between the logic of dynamic systems and classical first-order predicate logic: Exactly the invariant assertions about a system, formulated in terms of atomic assertions with changing truth values, satisfy the laws of logic.

In the same way the notion of facts was extended from condition/event-nets to arbitrary place/transition-nets and a net calculus and an implementation scheme were given for facts as specification elements in [GEL78], facts and their implementation can be extended to Pr/T-nets with place capacity greater than 1. This however, would exceed by far the scope of the present paper. Instead, we use the rest of this section for demonstrating how linear-algebraic techniques can be exploited for <u>determining</u> facts.

Let C be the incidence matrix of a Pr/T-net PN; then any vector x of polynomials is called an <u>S-invariant</u> of the net PN if $C^T \bullet x = 0$ (cf. [LA73,LAS74,GEL78]). If $x(p) \neq 0$ for some place p we call x(p) the <u>weight</u> of p in x, and x an S-invariant <u>through</u> p.

The unit value |C| of C is the incidence matrix of an ordinary Petri net |PN|, the <u>(unit) value of PN</u>. Because of

$|C^T \bullet x| = 0 \implies |C|^T \bullet |x| = 0$

we see that the value of an S-invariant is an S-invariant of the value (of the net).

The concept of an S-invariant is of particular importance because of the 'meta-fact'

(*) $x^T \bullet M = x^T \bullet M_0$, for an S-invariant x and all $M \in [M_0]$

stating that the inner product of an S-invariant with the elements of one marking class is an invariant quantity. (*) is a generalization of the corresponding equation for place/transition-nets and follows from the linear-algebraic representation of the transition rule. It is an equation in the strict sense only if the S-invariant x does not contain an individual variable (like i1,i2 in the following example, given in fig.8). Otherwise it must be viewed as a scheme of a system of equations in a refined representation of the given Pr/T-net PN. Yet it can be easily handled in a formal way when polynomials may be assigned to the variables. We are not going to develop this formalism in detail; rather we shall demonstrate its practical use in the sequel.

By means of the example of fig.6 we will show that S-invariants are a powerful yet easy to handle instrument for finding invariant assertions about a system. The initial marking is M_0, where

$M_0(a) = \pi(U)$, for a finite set U with n elements;

$M_0(d) = \not{c}$;

$M_0(H) = \pi(N)$, for $N = (U \times U) - id$, and $N_s := N \cap (\{s\} \times U)$;

$M_0(p) = 0$ for all other places p.

Fig.7 shows the incidence matrix of the net in fig.6 together with the corresponding vector representation of M_0.

Our interpretation of this net is, that n agents (e.g. database managers whose identifiers the elements of U are) may send messages to each other. The messages are represented by elements of N. We assume that all agents are acting according to the same organization scheme. So we are able to model the behaviour of all agents in a single net. By firing of transition 1 we represent an agent s∈U leaving its idle position a for b, taking all 'its' messages <s,t>, (t∈U,t≠s), from their homeposition H and putting them on R. Coincidently the token $\not{c}$ is taken from d. After firing of transition 1 the marking of R is increased and the marking of H is decreased by $\pi(N_s)$. Let <s,r> be a message on R. This message is sent by s to r as receiver. By firing of transition 3 r takes the message <s,r> from R, puts it on P, and goes itself from state a to c. After performing some reaction (not modelled in the net) r sends <s,r> to A, leaves state c, and goes back to the idle state a by firing of transition 4. If all the receivers t≠s have reacted like r all requests <s,t>, (t∈U,t≠s), can be taken from A back to H by s which by this changes itself from b to the idle state a putting a token $\not{c}$ back to d. All this occurs in one indivisible action by firing of transition 2.

In this description of the dynamic behaviour of the model we have traced the flow of markers which do not change their 'identity', i.e. the tuple of individual symbols carried by them. But, besides this 'natural' flow, there are others to be observed where markers change their identity. For example, repeated firing of transitions 1 and 2 yields an alternating change between a token (trivial marker) $\not{c}$ on d and some $s \in U$ on b (see S-invariant i3 below). It should be noticed that in this flow the identity of the marker is changed 'in' the transitions and not on the places.

In order to find such flows and study their significance for deriving behavioral properties of the system we look for S-invariants. For sake of simplicity we transform the incidence matrix in fig.7 by renaming some variables according to the formulas assigned to the transitions. The result is shown in fig.8; it is the basis for calculating seven S-invariants the vector representations of which are also shown in fig.8.

Applying the equation (*) to the S-invariants i1,...,i7 we get the following (schemes of) invariant assertions, i.e. statements which hold for <u>all</u> follower markings of M_0:

(*') $i^T \bullet M = \underline{constant} = i^T \bullet M_0$

(1) $M(a)+M(b)+M(c) = \pi(U)$

This equation shows that always (under every marking) <u>all</u> agents are in some state. Using the values we get

(1') $|M(a)|+|M(b)|+|M(c)| = |\pi(U)| = n$

(2) $M(H)+M(R)+M(P)+M(A) = \pi(N)$

Similarly, <u>all</u> messages are always somewhere.

(3) $\not{c} \bullet M(b)+s \bullet M(d) = s \bullet \not{c}$

Here we see very clearly that the S-invariants indicate the "metamorphosis" of markers. Consequences of the equation are

(3') $M(b)=0 \iff M(d)=\not{c}$, $M(b)=s \iff M(d)=0$

(4) $\langle q,r\rangle \bullet M(c)-r \bullet M(P) = 0$

Consequently,

(4') $M(c)=0 \iff M(P)=0$, $M(c)=r \iff M(P)=\langle q,r\rangle$

And for the values:

(4") $|M(c)|-|M(P)| = 0$

(5) $\not{c} \bullet \langle q,r\rangle \bullet M(c)+r \bullet \pi(N_S) \bullet M(d)+r \bullet \not{c} \bullet (M(R)+M(A)) = r \bullet \not{c} \bullet \pi(N_S)$

The corresponding equation for the values is interesting, too:

(5') $|M(c)|+(n-1)|M(d)|+|M(R)|+|M(A)| = n-1$

(6) $-\varpi(N_S)\bullet M(d)+\emptyset\bullet M(H) = \emptyset\bullet\varpi(N)-\emptyset\bullet\varpi(N_S)$

Consequently,

(6') $M(d)=0 \iff M(H)=\varpi(N)-\varpi(N_S)$, $M(d)=\emptyset \iff M(H)=\varpi(N)$

(7) $\varpi(N_S)\bullet M(b)+s\bullet M(H) = s\bullet\varpi(N)$

(7') $M(b)=0 \iff M(H)=\varpi(N)$, $M(b)=s \iff M(H)=\varpi(N)-\varpi(N_S)$

These few examples show that S-invariants are a (conceptually) very simple means for finding invariant assertions. Of course one never needs 'all' S-invariants; normally one only looks for S-invariants through special places, which means adding corresponding restrictions (equations or inequalities) to the defining linear equation system.

To finish this section we show how we can use the equations (1) - (7) for completing a marking:

Let M be a marking with $M(c) = u+v+w$. We want to know $M(P)$. From (2) we know that $M(P)$ is a polynomial in pairs ($M(P) \leq \varpi(N)$). So (4) in the form $r\bullet M(P) = (u+v+w)\bullet\langle q,r\rangle$ leads to

$r = u+v+w$ and

$M(P) = \langle q,u+v+w\rangle$ because $u,v,w\in U$ are pairwise different.

Finally we have $|\langle q,u+v+w\rangle| = |u+v+w| = 3$ because of (4").

Even though it is quite easy to write $\langle q,u+v+w\rangle$ as a polynomial $\leq \varpi(N)$ by studying fig.6(a) we are not able to do so only by means of the equations (1) to (7). We need more formal knowledge from the semantics of this net. So we leave fig.6(a) and consider a partial refinement (unfolding) which is shown in fig.6(b). In addition to i4 we find three further S-invariants and consequently three additional equations for $\tilde{M}$ in fig.6(b):

(4u) $q_u\bullet\tilde{M}(c\langle u\rangle)-\emptyset\bullet\tilde{M}(P\langle -,u\rangle) = 0$

(4v) $q_v\bullet\tilde{M}(c\langle v\rangle)-\emptyset\bullet\tilde{M}(P\langle -,v\rangle) = 0$

(4w) $q_w\bullet\tilde{M}(c\langle w\rangle)-\emptyset\bullet\tilde{M}(P\langle -,w\rangle) = 0$

($\tilde{4}$) $\langle q,r\rangle\bullet\tilde{M}(c)-r\bullet\tilde{M}(P) = 0$

(Notice that in this way formula (*') is read as $\tilde{i}^T\bullet\tilde{M} = \tilde{i}^T\bullet\tilde{M}_0$, where $\tilde{i}$ is a matrix with columns i4u, i4v, i4w, and $\tilde{i4}$.)

This now yields

(4u') $\tilde{M}(c\langle u\rangle)=\emptyset \iff \tilde{M}(P\langle -,u\rangle)=q_u$

(4v') $\tilde{M}(c\langle v\rangle)=\emptyset \iff \tilde{M}(P\langle -,v\rangle)=q_v$

(4w') $\tilde{M}(c\langle w\rangle)=\emptyset \iff \tilde{M}(P\langle -,w\rangle)=q_w$

($\tilde{4}$') $\tilde{M}(c)=r \iff \tilde{M}(P)=\langle q,r\rangle$

The relationship between M in fig.6(a) and $\tilde{M}$ in fig.6(b) is

$$M(c) = u\bullet\tilde{M}(c\langle u\rangle) + v\bullet\tilde{M}(c\langle v\rangle) + w\bullet\tilde{M}(c\langle w\rangle) + \tilde{M}(c)$$

$$M(P) = \langle\tilde{M}(P\langle -,u\rangle),u\rangle + \langle\tilde{M}(p\langle -,v\rangle),v\rangle + \langle\tilde{M}(P\langle -,w\rangle),w\rangle + \tilde{M}(P)$$

$$M(c)=u+v+w \iff \tilde{M}(c\langle u\rangle)=\tilde{M}(c\langle v\rangle)=\tilde{M}(c\langle w\rangle)=\emptyset \wedge \tilde{M}(c)=0$$

Consequently,

$$M(c)=u+v+w \iff M(P)=\langle q_u,u\rangle+\langle q_v,v\rangle+\langle q_w,w\rangle$$

$$=\langle q,u+v+w\rangle$$

Because of (5'): $M(c)\neq 0 \Longrightarrow M(d)=0$

Because of (6'): $M(d)=0 \Longrightarrow \exists k\colon M(H)=\pi(N)-\pi(N_k)$

Because of (2): $\Longrightarrow \exists k\colon M(R)+M(P)+M(A) = \pi(N_k)$

$\Longrightarrow \exists k\colon M(P) \leq \pi(N_k)$

$\Longrightarrow \exists k\colon M(P) = \langle k,x\rangle+\langle k,y\rangle+\langle k,z\rangle$

So, using the S-invariants i1,...,i6 we get $M(P)$ up to $k\in U$ exactly.

And from (7') we get $M(b)=s \Longrightarrow M(P)\leq\pi(N_s)$

$\Longrightarrow k = s$

By this example it becomes conceivable how eventually a complete formalism will look like which allows substituting polynomials for variables and by which stepping into the refined representation becomes unnecessary.

3. An Example

Fig.9 shows the Pr/T-net model of the organization scheme of a duplicate database system. It is G. Milne's modification [MI78] of a model by C.A. Ellis [EL76]. There exists another approach for verifying a scheme for organizing duplicate databases by Shapiro and Thiagarajan [SHT78] which is quite different from ours even though it also based on the Petri net theory.

In this example, each of n data base managers is responsible for one copy of the database. We assume that they are equally organized w.r.t. managing their copy (but nothing is assumed, for example, about their relative speeds). Furthermore, we assume that any two requests are in conflict with each other, i.e. only one data item or one resource is under consideration. This restriction focusses on the most difficult part of modelling an organization scheme for duplicate data base systems. Treating the general case of several data items would be beyond the scope of this paper.

In the Pr/T-net of fig.9 the dynamic behaviour of all the n database managers is represented. (For sake of comprehensibility, several places appear more than once; and 'sideconditions' are used to keep the net as small as possible.) The net is the result of folding together n isomorphic transition nets each representing one database manager. Consequently, in fig.9 we have to distinguish between the behaviour of different managers by means of the marking. The initial marking M_0 and its follower markings $M \in [M_0]$ ($M_0 \in [M_0]$ by convention) are defined by means of two finite sets, U and N, where the number of elements of U shall be n and N = (U×U)-id .

U is a set of individual symbols, the identifiers of the database managers. Every $\langle s,r \rangle \in N$ is a request initiated by s (sender) for communication with r (receiver). The initial marking M_0 is given by M_0(passive):=∗(U), M_0(HOME):=∗(N), all other places are unmarked. The transitions b1,b2,b3 serve as representations of the users. When firing, b1 puts $s \in U$ on place INTREQ. This describes that a user of database manager s wants to change (uniformly) all copies of the database. If this 'internal' request has been executed or rejected, the user receives a corresponding message, namely the same $s \in U$ via DONE or REJECT, by firing b2 or b3, respectively. It is reasonable to attach capacities to the places INTREQ, REJECT, and DONE whereby, for every $s \in U$, the number of copies of s on the respective place is limited. So, for $s \in U$, the capacities model the size of the user queues in database s.

We will explain now very briefly how the model works. First we show that always (under every marking) every manager is in some state and every request is at some location:

<u>Proposition 1</u>: Let $M \in [M_0]$; then

(a) M(<u>pass.</u>)+M(<u>act.</u>)+M(<u>soak.</u>)+M(<u>updat.</u>) = M_0(<u>pass.</u>) = ∗(U)

(b) M(HOME)+M(EXTREQ)+M(ACK+)+M(ACK-)+
M(ACKb)+M(UPD)+M(ACKd) = M_0(HOME) = ∗(N)

<u>Proof</u>: There exist two S-invariants I1 and I2 (analogous to i1 and i2 of the previous section) with

I1(<u>pass.</u>)=I1(<u>act.</u>)=I1(<u>soak.</u>)=I1(<u>updat.</u>) = 1 ,

I1(p) = 0 for all other places p.

I2(HOME)=I2(EXTREQ)=I2(ACK+)=I2(ACK-)=I2(ACKb)=(I2(ACKd)=I2(UPD) = 1

I2(q) = 0 for all other places q.

(a) and (b) are evaluations of (*) for I1 and I2. □

To trace an internal request for a manager k we start with the firing of transition 1. By doing so k goes from state *passive* to *active* and its requests <k,i>, ($i \in U, i \neq k$), are put on EXTREQ, which means that they are sent to all other managers i, $i \neq k$, as external requests. Then two possibilities are conceivable:

(1) k gets a positive acknowledgement from all the other managers. Then the corresponding marking M' enables transition 2: $k \leq M'(\textit{active}) \wedge \psi(N_k) \leq M'(ACK+)$. By firing of transition 2 k goes from *active* to *updating* and for every $i \in (U-\{k\})$ the request <k,i> is again sent to i, but now as an update request; furthermore we assume that k performs the update in database k. In database $i \neq k$ the corresponding update is performed by firing of transition 14, 4, 10 or 12, depending on manager i's current state. After all managers have performed this update as requested by k, the requests <k,i>, ($i \in U, i \neq k$), are collected on place ACKd. So transition 13 is enabled and by its firing k changes back to passive and the requests are put back to HOME. Moreover, one copy of k is put on DONE as an acknowledgement for the user that 'its' update is performed in all copies of the database.

(2) In case one manager, say $j \neq k$, is unable or unwilling to perform k's request as soon as possible, he sends a negative acknowledgement back to k; i.e. it fires transition 5 for m=r=j putting <s,r>=<k,j> from EXTREQ to ACK-. Now for k on *active* transition 3 is enabled. By firing it k goes from *active* to *soaking* and its user gets an negative acknowledgement in form of a copy of k on REJECT. In state *soaking* k collects all requests on ACKb by firing transition 8 and/or transition 7 (repeatedly). Then, by firing of transition 9, it goes back to *passive* and the requests <k,i>, ($i \in U, i \neq k$), are put back to their homeposition HOME.

The rest of the model shall be described by viewing from the receivers point. In case a manager j is in state *passive* or *soaking* and receives an external request <k,j> on EXTREQ, it grants by firing transition 15 or 11. In case j is in state *active* there is a conflict between j and k. Firing transition 5 means not granting k's request by putting <k,j> on ACK- as a negative acknowledgement; firing transition 6 means for j abandoning its request in favour of k by changing to *soaking*, putting <k,j> on ACK+, and a copy of j on REJECT to inform the user. If j is in state *updating* it does not take notice of external request <k,j> on EXTREQ until being back in state *passive*. In any state, however, j has to notice an update request <k,j> from k on UPD, to perform the update requested by k, and to put <k,j> on ACKd as an update acknowledgement for k.

We are now prepared to formulate some results about the model. To start with, we state a result about a synchronization of a manager k and the requests <k,i>, (i∈U,i≠k), initiated by k:

__Proposition 2__: Let $M \in [M_0]$; then
$k \le M(\underline{passive}) \iff \pi(N_k) \le M(HOME)$
$k \le M(\underline{active}) + M(\underline{soaking}) \iff \pi(N_k) \le M(EXTREQ) + M(ACK+) + M(ACK-) + M(ACKb)$
$k \le M(\underline{updating}) \iff \pi(N_k) \le M(UPD) + M(ACKd)$

Before we prove this, we interpret it by dividing the places of I1∪I2 into three "request regions": no request region (NR), external request region (ER), update request region (UP).
NR ∩ I1 := {__passive__} , NR ∩ I2 := {HOME}
ER ∩ I1 := {__active__,__soaking__}, ER ∩ I2 := {EXTREQ,ACK+,ACK-,ACKb}
UR ∩ I1 := {__updating__} , UR ∩ I2 := {UPD,ACKd}
(Here we have identified the S-invariants I1, I2 with the sets of places they pass through.)

Proposition 2 then states that a manager k is in one of these request regions if, and only if, all its requests <k,i>, (i∈U,i≠k), are in the same region.
__Proof__: The stated property holds for M_0 (trivial). The property is also __inductive__ since it is preserved by transitions 1,2,9, and 13, which are the only changes from one region into another. □

For applying the organizational scheme it is important to know wether it is __deadlockfree__ and __consistent__.

__Theorem 1__ (liveness): Under any marking $M \in [M_0]$ there exists an enabled transition.

__Proof__: First let us mention that this statement is non-trivial in the case of finite capacities for INTREQ (for every k∈U).
Because of proposition 1 every manager is always in one of four states. Let k be a given manager, and $M \in [M_0]$:

(1) $k \le M(\underline{passive}) \implies \pi(N_k) \le M(HOME)$ because of proposition 2.
Notice now that there is for every s∈U a positive capacity for INTREQ:
$k \le M(INTREQ) \implies$ transition 1 is enabled
$k \le M(INTREQ) \implies$ transition b1 is enabled.

(2) $k \le M(\underline{active}) \implies \pi(N_k) \le M(EXTREQ) + M(ACK+) + M(ACK-) + M(ACKb)$
because of proposition 2.

(2.1) $\neg\exists j: \langle k,j\rangle \leq M(ACKb)$ because putting $\langle k,j\rangle$ on ACKb is only possible for $k \leq M(\underline{soaking})$.

(2.2) $\pi(N_k) \leq M(ACK+) + M(ACK-)$;

$\pi(N_k) \leq M(ACK+)$ ==> transition 2 is enabled,

$\exists j: \langle k,j\rangle \leq M(ACK-)$ ==> transition 3 is enabled.

(2.3) $\exists j: \langle k,j\rangle \leq M((EXTREQ)$;

$j \leq M(\underline{pass.}) + M(\underline{act.}) + M(\underline{soak.})$ ==> one of transitions 15,5,6,11 is enabled;

$j \leq M(\underline{updat.})$ see (4) below.

(3) $k \leq M(\underline{soaking})$ ==> $\pi(N_k) \leq M(ACK+) + M(ACK-) + M(ACKb) + M(EXTREQ)$

(3.1) $\pi(N_k) \leq M(ACKb)$ ==> transition 9 is enabled,

(3.2) $\exists j: \langle k,j\rangle \leq M(ACK+) + M(ACK-)$ ==> transition 7 or 8 is enabled.

(3.3) $\exists j: \langle k,j\rangle \leq M(EXTREQ)$ see (2.3) above.

(4) $k \leq M(\underline{updating})$ ==> $\pi(N_k) \leq M(UPD) + M(ACKd)$

(4.1) $\pi(N_k) \leq M(ACKd)$ ==> transition 13 is enabled,

(4.2) $\exists j: \langle k,j\rangle \leq M(UPD)$ ==> one of the transitions 14,4,10,12 is enabled for j (because of propos.1 applied to j). □

Consistency means for the model under consideration that after every complete update the n copies of the database are identical. Under the assumption that the model is consistent for the initial marking M_0, the next theorem guarantees consistency:

<u>Theorem 2</u> (consistency): For any $M \in [M_0]$ and $k \in U$:

$$k \leq M(\underline{updating}) \implies i \not\leq M(\underline{updating}),\ (i \in U, i \neq k)$$

<u>Proof</u>: Let $k \leq M(\underline{updating})$ and $\langle i,k\rangle \leq M(EXTREQ)$; then $\langle i,k\rangle$ cannot leave EXTREQ for ACK+ because transition 6 is not enabled. So it is impossible to bring first k and then i to place <u>updating</u>. Especially impossible is bringing k and i concurrently to place <u>updating</u>. □

As a consequence of theorem 2, transition 12 turns out to be useless for the model in its present form. Transition 12 would, however, be necessary if the model would be refined by adding further resources, thus granting concurrent updating.

We will finish our analysis of the scheme with some critical remarks using a catalogue of properties of a 'good' solution given by Ellis [EL77]. The model is <u>homogeneous</u> (all managers have essentially identical control programs), <u>speed independent</u>, <u>deadlockfree</u>, <u>consistent</u>, <u>functional</u> (in applications there are no restrictions concerning data and functions).

The model is, however, not free from *critical blocking*. Even for two managers this can be shown easily. Let U:={a,b}, N={<a,b>,<b,a>}. In case both have sent an external request to each other the current marking is M where M(*active*)=a+b, M(EXTREQ)=<a,b>+<b,a>. So we observe a double activation for transitions 5 and 6. If transition 5 fires twice, for the follower marking M' M'(*active*)=a+b, M'(ACK-)=<a,b>+<b,a> holds. No updating can be performed before at least one manager has been back in *passive*. If under M transition 6 fires twice for the follower marking M" M"(*soaking*)=a+b holds. Again, no updating can be performed before a or b has been back to passive. Because this double firing of transition 5 or 6 can be repeated without any intermediate updating, the possibility of critical blocking has to be taken into account. But this drawback can be eliminated by adding mechanisms guaranteeing fair schedules. According to theorem 1 deadlock freeness is guaranteed for any solving of conflicts between competing requests.

As a major drawback the lack of *partial operability* (cf. [EL77]) has to be viewed. Let, again for two managers, M(*active*)=a+b, M(EXTREQ) = <a,b>+<b,a>. Now we assume b abandoning its request in favour of a by firing transition 6. Then the current marking is M"' where M"'(*active*)=a, M"'(*soaking*)=b, M"'(ACK+)=<a,b>, M"'(EXTREQ)=<b,a>. If now a is unable or unwilling to send <b,a> back to b, i.e. firing transition 5 putting <b,a> on ACK-, b starves. In case of a crash of manager a the system dies - a violation of partial operability.

Conclusion

A technique for modelling organizational systems has been presented which adds to the descriptive and analytical power of Petri nets an new level of abstraction. The conceptual and formal relationship between condition/event-nets and propositional logic was extended to the level of first-order predicate logic by introducing individual names, functions, predicates and consistent substitution of variables by terms. Linear-algebraic techniques for finding invariant assertion were transferred to this level by using integer polynomials instead of integers.

The resulting predicate/transition-nets constitute a new standard interpretation of nets which allows many useful Petri net derivatives to be defined as special cases of the general model. By this, the first-order extension of Petri nets may serve as a paradigm for further extension towards the high level notions of the practice of systems organization.

References

[EL77] Ellis, C.A.: Consistency and Correctness of Duplicate Database Systems
Proc. of the 6th Symposium on Operating System Principles, Purdue University, Nov. 1977.
ACM Operating Systems Review Vol.11, Nr. 5 (1977)

[GEL78] Genrich, H.J.; Lautenbach, K.: Facts in Place/Transition-Nets
Mathematical Foundations of Computer Science 1978 / Winkowski, J. (Ed.) - Berlin, Heidelberg, New York : Springer Verlag (1978)

[GTM76] Genrich, H.J.; Thieler-Mevissen, G.: The Calculus of Facts
Mathematical Foundations of Computer Science 1976 / Mazurkiewicz, A. (Ed.) - Berlin, Heidelberg, New York : Springer Verlag (1976)

[HE75] Herstein, I.N.: Topics in Algebra, 2nd Edition
Lexington, Toronto : Xerox College Publishing (1975)

[LA73] Lautenbach, K.: Exakte Bedingungen der Lebendigkeit für eine Klasse von Petri-Netzen
St.Augustin : Gesellschaft für Mathematik und Datenverarbeitung Bonn, Bericht Nr. 82 (1973)

[LAS74] Lautenbach, K.; Schmid, H.A.: Use of Nets for Proving Correctness of Concurrent Process Systems
Proceedings of IFIP Congress 74. - North Holland Publ. Comp. (1974)

[MI78] Milne, G.J.: Modelling Distributed Database Protocolls by Synchronisation Processes (Draft Version, Nov. 1978)
Department of Computer Science, Edinburgh University

[PE62] Petri, C.A.: Kommunikation mit Automaten
Bonn : Institut für Instrumentelle Mathematik, Schriften des IIM Nr. 2 (1962)

[PE67] Petri, C.A.: Grundsätzliches zur Beschreibung diskreter Pozesse
3. Colloquium über Automathentheorie. - Basel : Birkhäuser Verlag (1967)

[PE73] Petri, C.A.: Concepts of Net Theory
Mathematical Foundations of Computer Science -Math. Institute of the Slovak Ac. of Sciences (1973)

[PE75] Petri, C.A.: Interpretations of Net Theory
St.Augustin : Gesellschaft für Mathematik und Datenverarbeitung, Interner Bericht ISF-75-07 (1975)

[PE77] Petri, C.A.: General Net Theory
Computing System Design : Proceedings of the Joint IBM University of Newcastle upon Tyne Seminar, Sept. 1976 / Shaw, B. (Ed.). - University of Newcastle upon Tyne (1977)

[SC77] Schiffers, M.: Behandlung eines Synchronisationsproblems mit gefärbten Petri-Netzen
Universität Bonn, Diplomarbeit (1977)

[SCW78] Schiffers, M; Wedde, H.: Analyzing Program Solutions of Coordination Problems by CP-nets
Mathematical Foundations of Computer Science 1978 / Winkowski, J. (Ed.) - Berlin, Heidelberg, New York : Springer Verlag (1978)

[SH79] Shapiro, R.M.: Towards a Design Methodology for Information Systems
Ansätze einer Organisationstheorie rechnergestützter Informationssysteme 1974 - St.Augustin : Gesellschaft für Mathematik und Datenverarbeitung Bonn, Bericht Nr. 111 (1979)

[SHT78] Shapiro, R.M.; Thiagarajan, P.S.: On the Maitenance of Distributed Copies of a Database
St.Augustin : Gesellschaft für Mathematik und Datenverarbeitung Bonn, Interner Bericht ISF-78-04 (1978)

[TM76] Thieler-Mevissen, G.: The Petri Net Calculus of Predicate Logic
St.Augustin : Gesellschaft für Mathematik und Datenverarbeitung Bonn, Interner Bericht ISF-76-09 (1976)

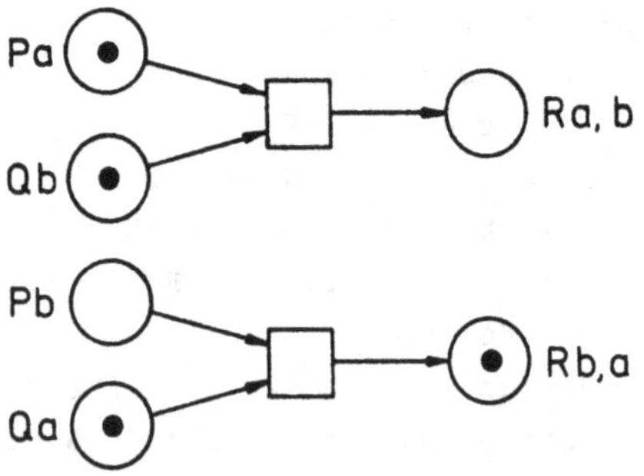

Fig. 1

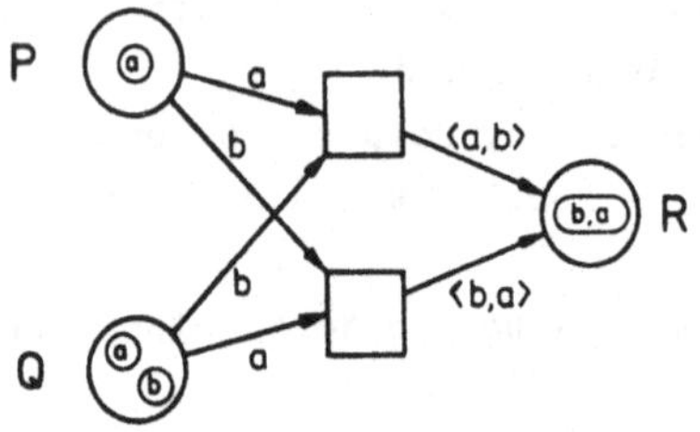

Fig. 2

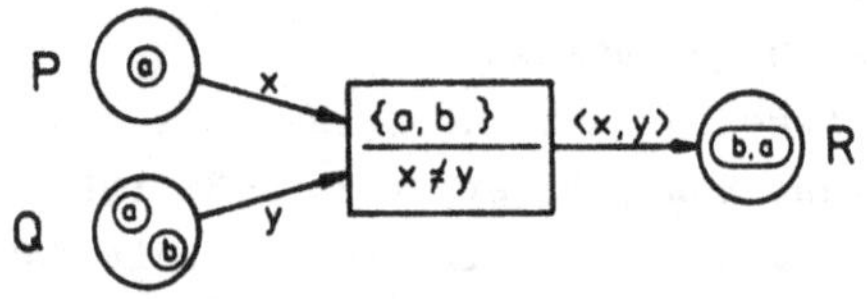

Fig. 3

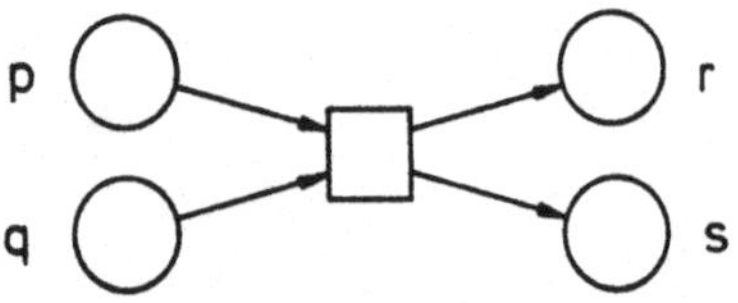

Fig. 4

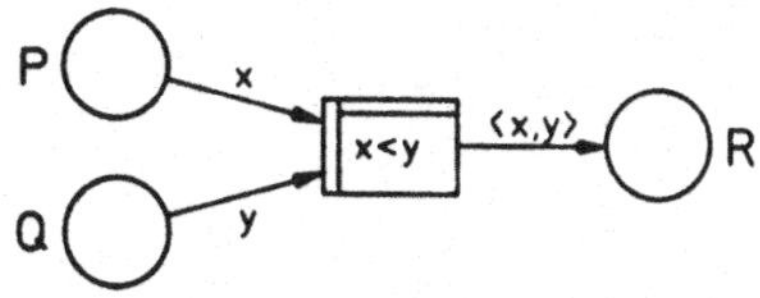

Fig. 5(a)

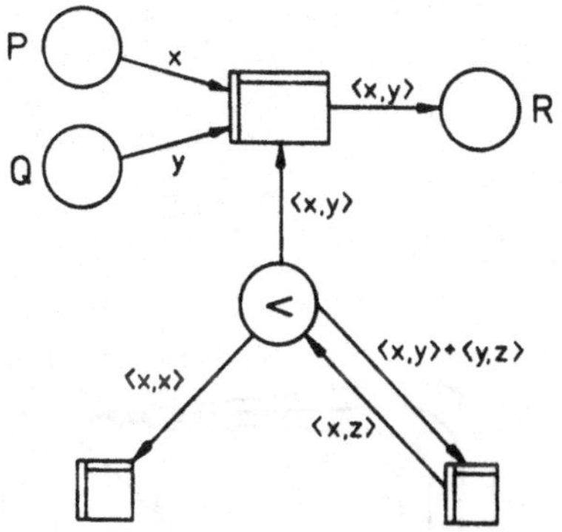

Fig. 5 (b)

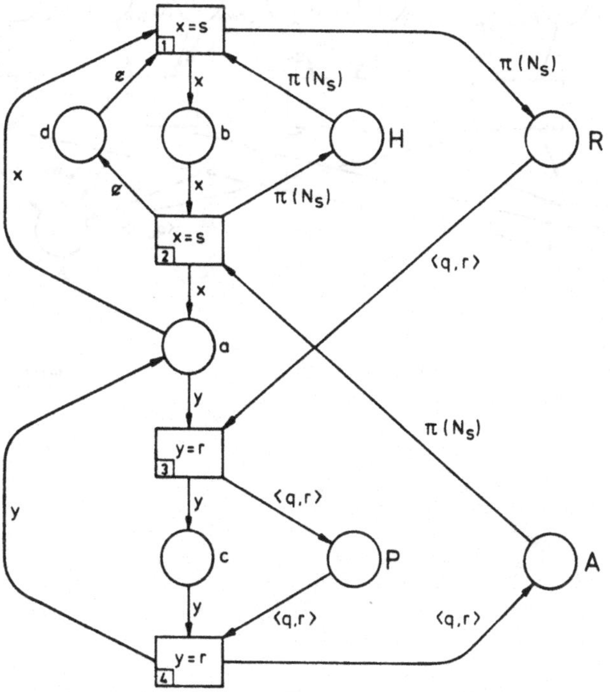

Fig. 6 (a)

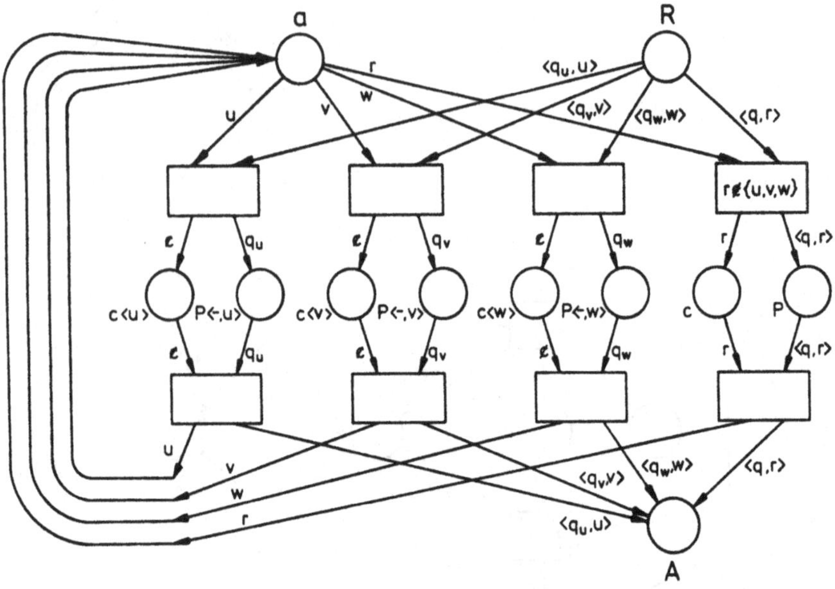

Fig. 6 (b)

	x = s 1	x = s 2	y = r 3	y = r 4	M_0
a	-x	x	-y	y	$\pi(U)$
b	x	-x			
c			y	-y	
d	-¢	¢			¢
H	$-\pi(N_s)$	$\pi(N_s)$			$\pi(N)$
R	$\pi(N_s)$		-<q,r>		
P			<q,r>	-<q,r>	
A		$-\pi(N_s)$		<q,r>	

Fig.7

	1	2	3	4	i1	i2	i3	i4	i5	i6	i7
a	-s	s	-r	r	1						
b	s	-s			1		¢				$\pi(N_s)$
c			r	-r	1			<q,r>	<q,r>•¢		
d	-¢	¢					s		$r\bullet\pi(N_s)$	$-\pi(N_s)$	
H	$-\pi(N_s)$	$\pi(N_s)$				1				¢	s
R	$\pi(N_s)$		-<q,r>			1			r•¢		
P			<q,r>	-<q,r>		1		-r			
A		$-\pi(N_s)$		<q,r>		1			r•¢		

Fig.8

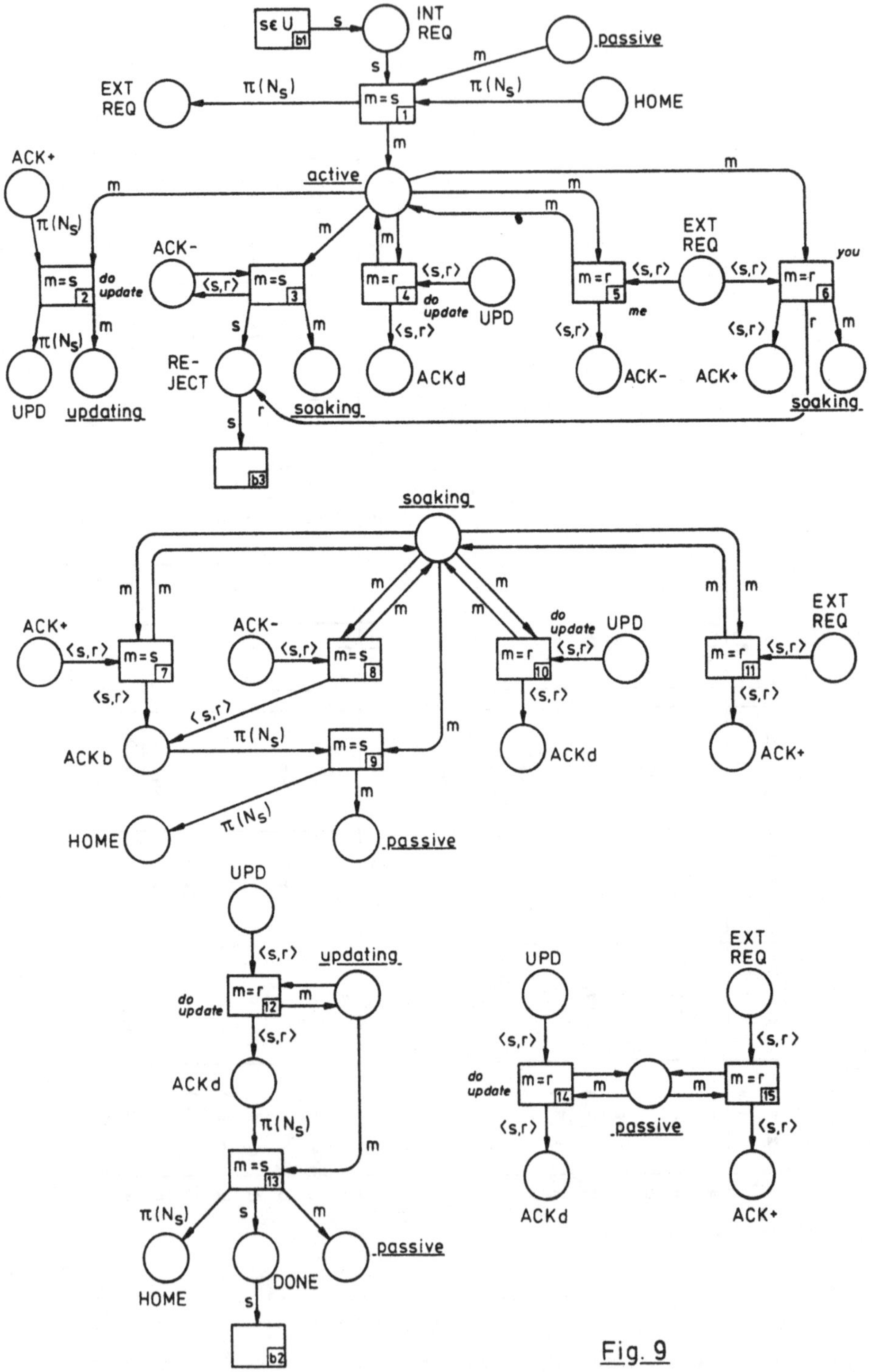

s ε U
b1
s
INT REQ
passive
m
s
EXT REQ
π(N_s)
m=s
1
π(N_s)
HOME
m
ACK+
active
m
m
m
m
π(N_s)
ACK-
m
EXT REQ
m=s
2
do update
⟨s,r⟩
m=s
3
m
m=r
4
⟨s,r⟩
do update
UPD
m=r
5
⟨s,r⟩
⟨s,r⟩
m=r
6
you
me
π(N_s)
m
s
m
⟨s,r⟩
⟨s,r⟩
⟨s,r⟩
r
m
UPD
updating
RE-JECT
soaking
ACKd
ACK-
ACK+
soaking
s
r
b3
soaking
m
m
m
m
m
m
m
m
ACK+
ACK-
do update
UPD
EXT REQ
⟨s,r⟩
m=s
7
⟨s,r⟩
m=s
8
m=r
10
⟨s,r⟩
m=r
11
⟨s,r⟩
⟨s,r⟩
⟨s,r⟩
⟨s,r⟩
⟨s,r⟩
π(N_s)
m
ACKb
m=s
9
ACKd
ACK+
m
HOME
π(N_s)
passive
UPD
⟨s,r⟩
updating
do update
m=r
12
m
⟨s,r⟩
ACKd
π(N_s)
m
m=s
13
π(N_s)
s
m
HOME
DONE
passive
s
b2
UPD
EXT REQ
⟨s,r⟩
⟨s,r⟩
do update
m=r
14
m
m
m=r
15
⟨s,r⟩
passive
⟨s,r⟩
ACKd
ACK+

Fig. 9

On Describing the Behavior and Implementation of Distributed Systems*

Nancy A. Lynch
Georgia Institute of Technology
Atlanta, Georgia 30332/USA

Michael J. Fischer
University of Washington
Seattle, Washington 98195/USA

Abstract: A simple, basic and general model for describing both the (input-output) behavior and the implementation of distributed systems is presented. An important feature of the model is the separation of the machinery used to describe the implementation and the behavior. This feature makes the model potentially useful for design specification of systems and of subsystems.

The implementation model relies on the basic notions of process and variable, assuming indivisibility of variable access. Long-distance communication is modelled by a special process representing a "channel." Process executions are considered to be completely asynchronous; this consideration is reflected in the fairness of the operations for combining processes. The primitivity and generality of the model make it an apparently suitable basis for cost comparison of various message-passing protocols and other higher-level programming constructs, as well as of complex distributed system implementations.

A system's (input-output) behavior is modelled by a set of finite and infinite sequences of actions, each action involving access to a variable.

Basic definitions, examples and characterization results are given. An extended example, involving specification and implementation of an arbiter system, is presented. For this example, equivalent implicit and explicit specifications are given. Several different implementations are described, each of which exhibits the required behavior.

General remarks are made about cost comparison of distributed system implementations.

*This research was supported in part by the National Science Foundation under grants MCS77-02474 and MCS77-15628.

I. Introduction

A distributed computing system consists of a number of distinct and logically separated communicating asynchronous sequential processes. To gain a theoretical understanding of such systems, it is necessary to find simple mathematical models which reflect the essential features of these systems while abstracting away irrelevant details. Such models allow problems to be stated precisely and make them amenable to mathematical analysis.

In this paper, we present a mathematical model of distributed systems and a mathematical model of their input/output behavior. Both are set-theoretic models built from standard mathematical constructs such as set, sequence, function, and relation, rather than axiomatic models consisting of lists of desired properties of systems without a basis for validity or consistency.

In constructing a model, choices must be made regarding which features of actual systems to preserve and which to abstract away, and how these choices are made depends on the intended applications of the model. Our interests are in finding a low-level model that reflects closely many aspects of physical reality and that permits problems of communication and synchronization to be studied. Thus, we do not assume any primitive synchronization mechanism such as is implicit in Petri nets [1] or in the communicating sequential processes of Hoare [2] and of Milne and Milner [3]. We have also chosen to omit from our model any notion of time. Although we realize clocks and time-outs are important mechanisms in real distributed systems, many aspects of distributed computation can nevertheless be modelled without reference to such concepts, and the resulting simplicity and tractability of the model more than compensates for the limitations imposed on it. Eventually, of course, time needs to be introduced into a suitable formal model and studied.

We are concerned with the cooperative behavior of processes, not their internal structure. Hence, we assume simply that each process is an automaton with a possibly infinite number of internal states and an arbitrary set of possible transitions. Each process from time to time takes a step, but we make no assumptions on how long it waits between steps except that the time is finite -- it does not wait forever.

We also permit our processes to exhibit infinitely-branching nondeterminism. This is done because we wish our notion of "process" to encompass not only what a single processor acting alone can do but also what a subsystem of processes or module can do. That will permit us to describe the behavior of a complete system in terms of the behaviors of component modules. Since a system of two deterministic processes can exhibit infinite nondeterminism, we are led to include this capability in our model.

We have chosen the shared variable as our basic (and only) communication mechanism. Because of the popularity of message-based distributed systems and the immediate reaction that a "central" shared memory does not constitute true distribution, some words about this choice are in order.

First of all, at the most primitive level, something must be shared between two processors for them to be able to communicate at all. This something is usually a wire in which, at the very least, one process can inject a voltage which the other process can sense. We can think of the wire as a binary shared variable whose value alternates from time to time between 0 and 1. Note that we are not specifying the protocols to be used by the sending and receiving processes which enable communication to take place -- indeed part of our interest is in modelling and studying such protocols. All we have postulated so far is that the sending process can control the value on the wire and the receiving process can sense it. The setting and sensing correspond to writing and reading, respectively. We contend that shared variables are at the heart of every distributed system.

Because of our decision to leave time out of the model, it is clear that the only way for the receiving process to be sure of seeing a value written by the sending process is for the latter to leave the value there until it gets some sort of acknowledgement from the receiver. Thus, we cannot model the asynchronous serial communication that is commonly used to communicate between terminals and computers, for the success of that method relies on sender and receiver having nearly identical clocks.

We have argued so far that shared variables underlie any timing-independent system, but that certain kinds of communication which depend on time cannot be modelled. Does introducing timing-dependent communication primitives into our otherwise timing-independent system add any new power? Let's consider various possible message primitives. Perhaps the simplest is to assume each process has a "mailbox" [VAX/VMS] or "message buffer" into which another process can place a message. Now, what happens when the sender wants to send a second message before the receiver has seen the first? If the second message simply overwrites the first, then the buffer behaves exactly like a shared variable whose values range over the set of possible messages. If the sender is forced to wait, then there is an implicit built-in synchronization mechanism as in [2,3] which we have already rejected for our model. As a third possibility, the message might go into a queue of waiting messages. If the queue is finite, the same problem reappears when the queue gets full. An infinite queue, on the other hand, seems very non-primitive and can be rejected for that reason alone. In any case, if the needed storage is available, the infinite message queue can be modelled in our system by a process with two shared variables: an input buffer and an output buffer. The process repeatedly polls its two buffers, moving incoming messages to its internal queue, and moving messages from the queue to the output buffer whenever it becomes empty. Of course, the sender must wait until the input buffer becomes empty before writing another message, but it seems to be an essential property of any communication system that there will be a maximum rate at which messages can be sent, and the sender attempting to exceed that rate must necessarily wait if information is not to be lost. (We note also that the delays inherent in long-distance communication between asynchronous processes can also be modelled simply in our framework.)

From the above discussion, we see that various message systems can be modelled naturally using shared variables, provided the variables are not restricted to binary values. Also, there are situations in which it is natural for a variable to have more than one reader or writer. We incorporate such generalized variables in our model. Finally, we generalize our model in one more respect by permitting a variable to be read and updated in a single step. We call such an operation test-and-set. This simplifies the model since both reads and writes are special cases of test-and sets. Moreover, there are situations in which the natural primitive operations are not read and write but are other test-and-set operations such as Dijkstra's P and V [4]. They all become just special cases of our general model. The formal definition of the model appears in Section 2.

A class of interesting and important questions to be addressed by a theory of distributed systems concerns the relative "goodness" of various systems all of which solve the "same" problem. Before these questions can be investigated, one needs appropriate measures of "goodness" (complexity measures) and one needs a precise notion of the "problem" to be solved by a distributed system. We make some brief remarks about complexity measures in Section 5, but a thorough treatment must await another paper. In Section 3, we construct a formal notion of "distributed problem" and define precisely when a given system solves a given problem. Section 4 gives an example of a distributed problem and several radically different systems for solving it.

Several factors contribute to making a satisfactory notion of "distributed problem" considerably more complicated than the simple input-output function which is often identified with the behavior of a sequential program.

1. There is generally more than one site producing inputs and receiving outputs.
2. Infinite, non-terminating computations are the rule rather than the exception.
3. The relative orders of reading inputs and producing outputs is significant as well as the actual values produced.
4. Variations in timing make distributed systems inherently nondeterministic, so one must allow in general for several different possible outputs to a given sequence of inputs, all of which must be considered "correct".

Briefly, we define the behavior of a distributed system to be a set of finite and infinite sequences of interleavings of possible activities at certain external variables (which are assumed to be used for communication with the outside world). Each sequence in the set describes a possible sequence of actions by the system, assuming particular actions affecting the variables by the environment. An action is a triple (u,x,v) consisting of a variable x, the value u read from the variable and the value v written back into the variable. Since the environment can change a variable at any time, it is not true that the system will necessarily see the same value in a variable that it most recently wrote there. We require of the behavior only that it be complete in that it describe at least one possible series of responses by the system for every possible way that the environment might behave.

A problem specification is an arbitrary set of input/output sequences. A particular system is a solution to the problem if its behavior is contained in the problem specification. The problem specification is the set of acceptable computations, while the solution behavior is the set actually realized.

Our definition only requires the solution system to be correct; there is no stipulation that the maximum permitted degree of nondeterminism actually be exhibited. We regard the latter as a performance or complexity issue to be dealt with separately. We remark that the distributed computing paradigm leads one to a very different view of nondeterminism or concurrency than for multiprocessing. In the latter case, the system implementer is presumed to have control of the scheduler, so the greater the possible concurrency among the processes he is trying to schedule, the greater his freedom to do so efficiently. In a truly asynchronous environment, however, one has no direct control over the scheduling, so it is natural to be concerned with the worst case (which might actually occur) rather than the best case. Hence, decreasing the amount of nondeterminism in this situation can never hurt.

We do not address in this paper another important aspect of problem specification, namely, what is an appropriate formal language for describing the sets of sequences that comprise a problem specification? Our example in Section 4 is described informally in standard mathematical notation. We expect the work on path expressions [5, etc.], flow expressions [6], and other formal systems of expressions might be applicable here.

2. A Model for Distributed Systems

Processes and Shared Variables

The primitive notions in our model are that of "process" and variable". A process can be thought of as a sequence of changes of state; likewise, a variable is a sequence of changes of value. The interaction among system components occurs at the process-variable interface.

Each variable x has an associated set of values, values(x), which the variable can assume. A variable action for x is a triple (u, x, v) with u, v ε values(x); intuitively, it represents the action of changing the value of x from u (its old value) to v (its new value). (u and v are not required to be distinct.) Act(x) is the set of all variable actions for x. If X is a set of variables, we let $act(X) = \bigcup_{x \varepsilon X} act(x)$.

A process p has an associated set (finite or infinite) of process states, states(p), which it can assume. Start(p) is a nonempty set of starting states, and final(p) a set of final or halting states. We let nonfinal(p) = states(p) - final(p).

A process action for p is a triple (s, p, t) with s ε nonfinal(p), t ε states(p); it represents intuitively the action of p going from state s to state t in a single step. (s and t are not required to be distinct.) Act(p) is the set of all process actions for p. If P is a set of processes, we let act(P) $\stackrel{df}{=} \bigcup_{p \varepsilon P}$ act(p).

Every process action occurs in conjunction with a variable action; the pair forms a complete execution step. If P is a set of processes and X a set of variables, we let steps(P,X)$\stackrel{df}{=}$ act(P) $\times$ act(X) be the set of execution steps. To specify which steps are permitted in a computation, a process has two other components in its description. Variables(p) is a set of variables which the process can access. Oksteps(p) is a subset of steps(p, variables(p)) describing the permissible steps of p. Oksteps(p) is subject to three restrictions:

(a) For any s ε nonfinal(p), there exist t, u, x, v with ((s, p, t), (u, x, v)) ε oksteps(p).

(b) (Read Anything): If ((s, p, t), (u, x, v)) ε oksteps(p) and u' ε values(x), then there exist t', v' with ((s, p, t'), (u', x, v')) ε oksteps(p).

(c) (Countable Nondeterminism): Start(p) is countable, and also for any s ε nonfinal(p), x ε variables(p) and u ε values(x), there are only countably many pairs t, v with ((s, p, t), (u, x, v)) ε oksteps(p).

Some intuitive remarks are in order. Oksteps(p) represents the allowable steps of p. A particular step ((s, p, t), (u, x, v)) ε oksteps(p) is applicable in a given situation only if p is in state s and x has value u. (a) indicates that some step is applicable from every nonfinal state. In general, more than one step might be applicable; hence, we are considering non-deterministic processes. However, restriction (c) limits the number of applicable steps to being countable, a technical restriction we need later for some of our results. The effect of taking the step is to put p into state t and to write v into x. A step is considered an atomic, indivisible action in our model. With respect to the variable x, a step involves a read followed by a write -- the read to verify that the transition is applicable and the write to update its value. We term such an action a "test-and-set". This is a generalization of the familiar Boolean semaphores or test-and-set instructions found on many computers.

Restriction (b) formalizes an important assumption that a process be able to respond in some way to anything that might be given to it as input. In other words, if it is possible for a process in state s to access variable x, then there must be a transition from s accessing x for every u ε values(x).

A process is not required to be finite-state, nor to have a finite number of transitions from any state. Later (Theorem 3.7), we will see that countable nondeterminism arises from application of natural combination operations to even deterministic processes. Since we wish to treat single processes and groups of processes uniformly, we allow the greater generality from the beginning.

Systems of Processes

The way in which processes communicate with other processes and with their environment is by means of their variables. A value placed in a variable is available to anybody who happens to read that variable until it is replaced by a new value. Unlike message-based communication mechanisms, there is no guarantee that anyone will ever read the value, nor is there any primitive mechanism to inform the writer that the value has been read. Thus, for meaningful communication to take place, both parties must adhere to previously-agreed-upon protocols, though we place no restrictions on what kinds of protocols are allowed. Indeed, part of our motivation in defining systems in this way is to give us a formal model in which to study such protocols.

We wish to consider variables accessed by a process or system of processes to be either internal or external. Internal variables are to be used only by the given process or system; thus, some consistency of the values of those variables must be hypothesized, and an initial value must be provided. External variables will not have such consistency requirements. That is, a process or system of processes is to be able to respond to values of these variables other than the ones it most recently left there. Intuitively, the external variables may be accessible to other processes (or other external agents) which could change the values between steps of the given process or system.

More formally, if X is a set of variables, a partial assignment for X is any partial function $f : X \to \bigcup_{x \in X} \text{values}(x)$ with $f(x) \in \text{values}(x)$ whenever f(x) is defined. If f is defined for all $x \in X$, it is called a total assignment for X. The full specification of a system of processes S has four components: proc(S) is a finite set of processes, ext(S) is a set of external variables, int(S) is a set of internal variables, and init(S) is a total assignment for int(S). S is subject to certain restrictions:

(a) $\text{Ext}(S) \cap \text{int}(S) = \emptyset$.

(b) For each $p \in \text{proc}(S)$, $\text{variables}(p) \subseteq \text{ext}(S) \cup \text{int}(S)$.

If P is a set of processes and X a set of variables, we let $\mathcal{S}(P,X) \overset{df}{=} \{S : S$ is a system of processes with $\text{proc}(S) \subseteq P$ and $\text{int}(S) \cup \text{ext}(S) \subseteq X\}$.

Execution Sequences

The execution of a system of processes is described by a set of execution sequences. Each sequence is a list of steps which the system could perform when interleaved with appropriate actions by the external agent.

If A is any set, A^* (A^ω) denotes the set of finite (infinite) sequences of A-elements. $\underline{A^{count}}$ denotes $A^* \cup A^\omega$, the set of finite or infinite sequences of elements of A. Length: $A^{count} \to N \cup \{\infty\}$ denotes the number of elements in a given sequence.

Let P be a set of processes and X a set of variables. $\underline{E(P,X)} \overset{df}{=} (steps(P,X))^{count}$ is the domain of sequences used to describe executions of processes and sets of processes over P and X.

To define the allowable execution sequences of a system, we first define the execution sequences for processes and sets of processes.

Let p be a process. An execution sequence for p is a sequence $e \in (oksteps(p,variables(p)))^{count} \subseteq E(p,variables(p))$ for which four conditions hold.

Let $e = ((s_i, p, t_i), (u_i, x_i, v_i))_{i=1}^{length(e)}$.

(a) If length(e) = 0, then $start(p) \cap final(p) \neq \emptyset$.
(b) If length(e) $\neq$ 0, then $s_1 \in start(p)$.
(c) If e is finite, then $t_{length(e)} \in final(p)$.
(d) $t_j = s_{j+1}$ for $1 \leq j < length(e)$.

Finally, exec(p) is the set of execution sequences for p. (Note, for example, that this set is nonempty.) Thus, an execution sequence for a process exhibits consistency for state changes, but not necessarily for variable value changes.

Next we describe the execution of a set of processes. We wish the execution to be fair in the sense that each process either reaches a final state or continues to execute infinitely often; it cannot be "locked out" forever by other processes when it is able to execute. In other words, processes are completely asynchronous and thus cannot influence each other's ability to execute a step. Since no consistency of values of variables will yet be assumed, a simple "shuffle" operation will suffice.

Let A be any set and $b = (b_k)_{k \in K}$ be an indexed set of elements of A^{count}. Shuffle(b) is the set of sequences obtained by taking all of the sequences in b and "merging" them together in all possible ways to form new sequences. Formally, if $n \in N$, then define $\underline{[n]} = \{1,\ldots,n\}$. If $n = \infty$, then $\underline{[n]} = N$. Now a sequence $c \in A^{count}$ is in shuffle(b) iff there is a 1-1, onto, partial map $\pi : K \times N \to [length(c)]$ such that (a)-(c) hold.

(a) π is defined for (k,n) iff $n \in [length(b_k)]$.

(b) π is monotone increasing in its second argument.

(c) If $\pi(k,i) = j$, then c_j = the ith element in the sequence b_k.

The shuffle operator is easily extended to an indexed set of subsets of A^{count}, viz. if $B = (B_k)_{k \in K}$, where $B_k \subseteq A^{count}$, then $\underline{shuffle(B)} \overset{df}{=} \bigcup \{shuffle(b) : b = (b_k)_{k \in K}$ and $b_k \in B_k, k \in K\}$.

If P is a set of processes, define exec(P) $\stackrel{df}{=}$ shuffle($(\text{exec}(p))_{p\varepsilon P}$).

We now extend our notions of execution sequences to systems of processes.

If X is a set of variables, let $\mathcal{B}(X) \stackrel{df}{=} (\text{act}(X))^{\text{count}}$. Let b ε $\mathcal{B}(X)$, x ε X, and f be a partial assignment for X. Latest(b, x, f) is the value left in x after performing the actions in b, assuming x had initial value f(x). We define it recursively on the length of b. If length(b) = 0 then

$$\text{latest}(b, x, f) = \begin{cases} f(x) \text{ if } f(x) \text{ is defined;} \\ \text{undefined otherwise.} \end{cases}$$

Now assume length(b) $\geq$ 1, and b = b' • (u, y, v) for some (u, y, v)ε act(X).

$$\text{Then latest}(b, x, f) = \begin{cases} v \text{ if } x=y; \\ \text{latest}(b', f, x) \text{ if } x\neq y \text{ and latest}(b', f, x) \text{ is defined;} \\ \text{undefined otherwise.} \end{cases}$$

Let X, K be sets of variables, b ε $\mathcal{B}(X)$, and f a total assignment for K. We say b is (K,f)-consistent if for every prefix b' • (u, y, v) of b with y ε K, then u = latest(b', y, f). For sets of action sequences B $\subseteq$ $\mathcal{B}(X)$, define

$$\text{consist}_{K,f}(B) \stackrel{df}{=} \{b \,\varepsilon\, B : b \text{ is } (K,f)\text{-consistent}\}.$$

Let P be a set of processes. A sequence of steps e ε E(P,X) is (K,f)-consistent provided erase(e) is (K,f)-consistent, where erase : E(P,X) → $\mathcal{B}$(X) is a homomorphism mapping each pair (a,b) ε steps(P,X) to its second member b. For sets of execution sequences E $\subseteq$ E(P,X), define $\text{consist}_{K,f}(E) \stackrel{df}{=} \{e \,\varepsilon\, E : e \text{ is } (K,f)\text{-consistent}\}$. Now let S be a system of processes. Exec(S) $\stackrel{df}{=}$ $\text{consist}_{\text{int}(S),\text{init}(S)}(\text{exec}(\text{proc}(S))) \subseteq$ E(proc(S), ext(S) ∪ int(S)). Thus, exec(S) consists of those execution sequences of the system's processes in which the internal variables are consistent across the sequence.

Behavior Sequences

Exec(P) gives complete information on how a set of processes might execute in any given environment. Often, however, one is not interested in how the processes execute but only in their effect on the environment, that is, the way they change the variables. We obtain this information from the execution sequences by extracting the variable actions.

If S is a system of processes, we define the behavior of S, beh(S) $\stackrel{df}{=}$ erase(exec(S)) $\subseteq$ $\mathcal{B}$(ext(S) ∪ int(S)).

Similarly, we define the behavior for a process p and a set of processes P.

$\underline{Beh(p)} \overset{df}{=} erase(exec(p))$.

$\underline{Beh(P)} \overset{df}{=} erase(exec(P))$.

One might be interested in only these actions involving the external variables. Let X, K be sets of variables, $b \in \mathcal{B}(X)$, then $\underline{elim_K(b)}$ is the subsequence of b consisting of the actions not involving variables in K. ($Elim_K(b)$ might be finite even if b is infinite.) We define the external behavior of S,

$\underline{extbeh(S)} \overset{df}{=} elim_{int(S)}(beh(S))$.

The following proposition demonstrates the use of some of the preceding notation, and shows an elementary implication of the read-anything property ((b) in the definition of a process).

Proposition 2.1:

Let p be a process, $x \in$ variables(p), $(v_i)_{i=1}^{\infty}$ any infinite sequence of elements of values(x). Then for some $(w_i)_{i=1}^{\infty}$, it is the case that

$$b = (v_i, x, w_i)_{i=1}^{length(b)}$$

is in $elim_{variables(p)-\{x\}}(beh(p))$. (That is, there is some possible execution of p for which the sequence of values read from x is given by $(v_i)_{i=1}^{\infty}$ or some prefix thereof.)

Proof sketch. By repeated use of the read-anything property.

□

Operations on Systems

One goal of our formalism is to permit complex systems to be understood in terms of simpler ones. For this, we need some operations for building larger systems from smaller ones. Corresponding to these operations will be operations on execution sequences and behaviors. This approach is similar to that of Milne and Milner [3].

The first operation joins a finite collection of systems into a single one. Let $(S_i)_{i \in I}$ be a finite indexed family of systems such that

(a) $i \neq j$ implies $proc(S_i) \cap proc(S_j) = \emptyset$.

(b) $i \neq j$ implies $int(S_j) \cap (int(S_j) \cup ext(S_j)) = \emptyset$.

Then $\oplus (S_i)_{i \in I}$ is the system S such that

$$proc(S) = \bigcup_{i \in I} proc(S_i),$$

$$ext(S) = \bigcup_{i \in I} ext(S_i),$$

$$\text{int}(S) = \bigcup_{i \in I} \text{int}(S_i),$$

$$\text{init}(S) = \bigcup_{i \in I} \text{init}(S_i).$$

We define $\oplus$ for finite indexed families of execution sets and indexed families of behaviors to be simply the shuffle operation.

The second operation on systems is the one of turning selected external variables into internal ones. Let S be a system, K a set of variables and f a total assignment for K such that $K \cap \text{int}(S) = \emptyset$. We define $\underline{\text{consist}_{K,f}(S)}$ to be the system S' such that proc(S') = proc(S), ext(S') = ext(S) - K, int(S') = int(S) $\cup$ K, and init(S') = init(S) $\cup$ f. $\text{Consist}_{K,f}$ has already been defined for execution sets and behaviors.

That these definitions all make sense together is shown by the following.

Theorem 2.2. The following diagram commutes. ($\mathcal{P}$ denotes the power set operator.)

$$\begin{array}{ccccc}
\mathcal{S}^* & \xrightarrow{\text{exec}} & (\mathcal{P}(\mathcal{E}))^* & \xrightarrow{\text{erase}} & (\mathcal{P}(\mathcal{B}))^* \\
\downarrow \oplus & & \downarrow \oplus & & \downarrow \oplus \\
\mathcal{S} & \xrightarrow{\text{exec}} & \mathcal{P}(\mathcal{E}) & \xrightarrow{\text{erase}} & \mathcal{P}(\mathcal{B}) \\
\downarrow \text{consist}_{K,f} & & \downarrow \text{consist}_{K,f} & & \downarrow \text{consist}_{K,f} \\
\mathcal{S} & \xrightarrow{\text{exec}} & \mathcal{P}(\mathcal{E}) & \xrightarrow{\text{erase}} & \mathcal{P}(\mathcal{B})
\end{array}$$

Here we assume a fixed set P of processes and X of variables, and we let $\mathcal{S} = \mathcal{S}(P,X)$, $\mathcal{E} = \mathcal{E}(P,X)$, and $\mathcal{B} = \mathcal{B}(X)$.

We omit the straightforward but tedious proof.

Modules

The two operations of $\oplus$ and $\text{consist}_{K,f}$ are sufficient to build any system from one-process systems in a simple way.

Let S, S' be systems. S' is a module of S if proc(S') $\subseteq$ proc(S), ext(S') $\subseteq$ ext(S) $\cup$ int(S), int(S') $\subseteq$ int(S), and init(S') = init(S)/int(S') (the restriction of the function init(S) to domain int(S')). Thus, a module is a subsystem whose internal variables are private to it and whose external variables form the interface between the module and the remaining system and/or the external world.

S is partitioned into modules $(S_m)_{m \in M}$ if M is finite, S_m is a module of S for each $m \in M$, $(\text{proc}(S_m))_{m \in M}$ is a partition of proc(S), and for all m, n $\in$ M, if $m \neq n$, then $\text{int}(S_m) \cap (\text{int}(S_n) \cup \text{ext}(S_n)) = \emptyset$.

A system S is atomic if it consists of a single process with no internal variables, i.e. if $|\text{proc}(S)| = 1$ and int(S) = init(S) = $\emptyset$.

The following propositions are immediate from the definitions.

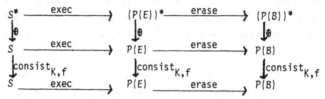

Proposition 2.3. Every system can be partitioned into a finite number of atomic modules.

Proposition 2.4. Every system can be obtained from an arbitrary partition into modules by one application of ⊕ followed by one application of $\text{consist}_{K,f}$ for appropriate K,f.

Remarks on Communication Mechanisms

The basic communication mechanism in our model is the availability of the last written value. We work at a "primitive" level, not basing communication on "messages" as do Hoare [2], Feldman [7] and Milne and Milner [3]. Some message models involve an implicit queuing mechanism or implicit process synchronization, neither of which we wish to assume as basic. Both of these mechanisms involve significant implementation cost and require cost analysis in terms of a more primitive common basis. Neither mechanism seems to be universal in the sense that the most efficient programs for arbitrary tasks would always be written using it. Moreover, the abstraction of automatic process synchronization serves to hide the asynchrony of the basic model. Since we wish to understand asynchronous behavior, we prefer not to mask it at the primitive levels of our theory.

The generality of our process and execution sequence definitions assumes possible indivisibility of a fairly powerful form of variable access. In particular, processes that can both read and change variables in one indivisible step (such as the "test-and set" processes of Cremers-Hibbard [8] and Burns et al [9] are included in the general definitions. Some readers may consider this general access mechanism to be unreasonably powerful, arguing that a process model based on indivisibility of "reads" and "writes" only is more realistic. Such a process model can be defined by certain restrictions on our general model (as we describe below). Thus, our development not only specializes to include consideration of a read-write model, but also allows comparison of the power of the read-write model with that of the more general access model. The specialization can be carried out as follows.

A process p is called a read-write process provided for each s ε states(p) and each x ε variables(p), the set

oksteps(p) ∩ {((s,p,t),(u,x,v)) : t ε states(p), u, v ε values(x)}

can be partitioned into a collection of subsets T, with each *T* ε *T* satisfying (at least) one of the following.

(a) (T describes a "read".)
For all ((s,p,t),(u,x,v)) in T, it is the case that u = v. Moreover, for each u ε values(x) there exists t with ((s,p,t),(u,x,u)) in T.

(b) (T describes a "write".)
For some t,v, T = {((s,p,t),(u,x,v)) : u ε values(x)}.

Two very simple examples follow.

<u>Example 2.5</u>. Let states(p) = start(p) = {s}, final(p) = ∅, variables(p) = {x}, values(x) = {0,1}, and oksteps(p) = {((s,p,s),(0,x,1)), ((s,p,s),(1,x,0))}. Process p simply examines x repeatedly, changing its value at each access. The change is clearly an activity that involves both reading and writing, so that, intuitively, p is not a read-write process. Formally, if p were a read-write process, oksteps(p) would be partitionable as above. No T can describe a read since it is never the case that u = v. So ((s,p,s),(0,x,1)) is in T for some T which describes a write. But then ((s,p,s),(1,x,1)) is in T $\subseteq$ oksteps(p) as well, a contradiction.

<u>Example 2.6</u>. Let states(p) = start(p) = {s}, final(p) = ∅, variables(p) = {x}, and oksteps(p) = {((s,p,s),(0,x,1)), ((s,p,s),(1,x,1))}. Process p simply examines x repeatedly, writing "1" every time. It is easy to see that p is a read-write process.

So far, our model describes asynchronous processes communicating by shared variables, a situation which suggests that the processes are physically located sufficiently near to each other to share memory without delay. We also wish to model more general "distributed" systems of asynchronous processes, in which communication is done by means of a channel with significant transmission delay. No new primitives are required in order to extend the present model to handle such communication. A one-way channel is simply modelled by a special "channel process" p, as detailed below.

<u>Example 2.7</u>. Let V be any set, states(p) = {write} × V ∪ {read}, start(p) = {read}, final(p) = ∅, variables(p) = {x,y}, values(x) = values(y) = V, and oksteps(p) = {((read,p,(write,v)),(v,x,v)) : u,v ε V} ∪ {(((write,u),p,read),(v,y,u)) : u,v ε V}. Process p is thought of as sharing a variable with each of two other processes. It alternately reads from one of the variables and writes the value read in the other variable. (p is obviously a read-write process.) When p is combined with two processes at its ends in the manner already described in this section, the consistent execution sequences exactly describe the effect of an arbitrary-delay channel used for communication between the two original processes.

<u>3. Characterizations and Elementary Examples of Behaviors</u>

The principal justification for a formalism for describing distributed systems is that techniques can thereby be developed for specifying requirements for their operation. It should be possible to determine whether a particular system is a satisfactory realization of the specified requirements. Typical requirements might involve exclusion, fairness, synchronization and other logical correctness properties; they can also involve performance and efficiency.

Requiring that a system exhibit <u>exactly</u> a specified set of execution sequences is generally too strong. For instance, if p_1 and p_2 are processes with exec(p_1) $\subseteq$ exec(p_2), then p_1 is always an adequate replacement for p_2. In contrast to the usual assumptions about nondeterminism, in the case of asynchronous systems all possible nondeterministic choices should be "correct". Thus, a system exhibiting any subset of the specified execution sequences should be acceptable. (Recall that a process cannot have an empty set of execution sequences.)

The subset requirement above is still stronger than one would necessarily want. We are not generally interested in requiring that the complete detail of the specified execution sequences be exhibited by an implementing system, but rather only certain abstracted aspects. Such aspects might be of two different types. One possibility is to specify state reachability requirements as in Cremers-Hibbard [8] and Burns et al [9]. A second possibility, appropriate for specifying processes or groups of processes to be used as modules in larger systems, is to specify external behavior. That is the type of specification we emphasize in this paper.

Monotonicity and the Adequate Replacement Property

Let S_1, S_2 be systems. Define $S_1 \sqsubseteq S_2$ iff $\mathrm{extbeh}(S_1) \subseteq \mathrm{extbeh}(S_2)$. We call the partial order "$\sqsubseteq$" on systems the adequate replacement order, for we argue that S_1 should always be an adequate replacement for S_2, at least for the purpose of determining logical correctness of input-output behavior.

Proposition 3.1. $\oplus$, $\mathrm{consist}_{K,f}$, and elim_K as operations on $\mathcal{P}(\mathcal{B})$ preserve inclusion of subsets of $\mathcal{B}$.

Proof: Immediate.

□

Proposition 3.2.

(a) Let $(B_i)_{i\in I}$ be an indexed family of sets, where each $B_i \subseteq \mathcal{B}(X)$, K any set of variables.
Then $\mathrm{Elim}_K(\oplus(B_i)_{i\in I}) = \oplus\,(\mathrm{Elim}_K(B_i))_{i\in I}$.

(b) If K, K' are disjoint sets of variables, f a total assignment for K, $B \subseteq \mathcal{B}(X)$; then $\mathrm{Elim}_{K'}(\mathrm{Consist}_{K,f}(B)) = \mathrm{Consist}_{K,f}(\mathrm{Elim}_{K'}(B))$.

Proof: Immediate.

□

Proposition 3.3.

$\oplus$ and $\mathrm{Consist}_{k,f}$ as operations on $\mathcal{S}$ preserve $\sqsubseteq$.

Proof: By Theorem 2.2 and Propositions 3.1 and 3.2.

□

It follows that if a module S_1 of a system S is replaced by an adequate replacement S_1', then the resulting system S' is an adequate replacement for S.

Equivalence of Systems

We can also define an equivalence among systems based only on their input-output behaviors. While this equivalence is still too strong for many purposes, it nevertheless is not so strong as notions of equivalence based on simulation.

Let S_1, S_2 be systems. Define $S_1 \equiv S_2$ iff $\text{extbeh}(S_1) = \text{extbeh}(S_2)$. (Thus, $S_1 \equiv S_2$ iff $S_1 \sqsubseteq S_2$ and $S_2 \sqsubseteq S_1$.)

We now proceed to show that any system is equivalent to an atomic system. Thus, groups of processes and single processes can be treated uniformly, an indication of the usefulness of our model for modular design of systems.

We give the construction in two parts. First we show how to reduce the number of processes to one, then we show how to eliminate the internal variables.

Lemma 3.4. For any system S, there is a system S' with the same external and internal variables such that $|\text{proc}(S')| = 1$ and $\text{beh}(S') = \text{beh}(S)$.

Proof Sketch. By induction on $|\text{proc}(S)|$. For instance, given a system of two processes p_1 and p_2, we must define a single process p whose behavior is exactly the shuffle of those of p_1 and p_2. The first obvious idea might be to allow states of p to represent pairs consisting of states of p_1 and p_2. Transitions could be composed naturally from the transitions of p_1 and p_2, essentially allowing either one. The only problem is that nothing prevents the nondeterministic choice from always choosing to simulate one process over the other, violating the fairness of the shuffle operation. However, the countable branching capability of processes can be used to enforce fairness. When p begins simulating one of p_1, p_2, it nondeterministically chooses an integer ≥ 1 representing the number of steps p will simulate for that process before shifting to the other process.

□

A process p is called treelike provided (a) and (b) hold.

(a) For all $t_0 \in \text{states}(p)$, $|\{((s,p,t),(u,x,v)) \in \text{oksteps}(p) : t = t_0\}| \leq 1$.

(b) For all $t_0 \in \text{start}(p)$, $|\{((s,p,t),(u,x,v)) \in \text{oksteps}(p) : t = t_0\}| = 0$.

Lemma 3.5. If p is a process, there exists a treelike process q with $\text{Beh}(p) = \text{Beh}(q)$.

Proof Sketch. Process p can be "opened up into a tree" by replicating states; process q has states corresponding to finite paths in p.

□

Theorem 3.6. For any system S, there is an atomic system S' such that $S' \equiv S$.

Proof Sketch. By Lemma 3.4, we can assume $\text{proc}(S) = \{p\}$. By Lemma 3.5, we can assume p is treelike. A process transformation is carried out in two steps, the intermediate result of which need not be a process. First, p_1 is constructed from p by "pruning" p's tree so that only (K,f)-consistent paths remain, where K = int(S) and f = init(S). Since p is treelike, there will be no ambiguity involved in deciding when to prune. Now p_2 is constructed from p_1 by condensing paths involving variables in K. This construction is not carried out in stages because of the possible condensation of infinite paths to finite paths. The possibility that p_1 could continue forever on branches involving only variables in K involves transition to a final state of p_2. Finally, S' is the atomic system such that proc(S') = $\{p_2\}$ and ext(S') = ext(S).

□

Unbounded Nondeterminism

We argue that it is natural to use countable nondeterminism for the basic process model. Restriction to finitely many states would surely be unnatural, ruling out processes which resemble natural sequential computation models such as Turing machines. But the usual models, though having infinitely many states, are restricted to finite nondeterminism. This restriction does not seem overly strong in more conventional settings, since it is preserved by natural sequential combination operations. But for the asynchronous parallel case, the finite-branching property would not be preserved by our combination and internalizing constructions. The next result implies that any behavior of a process can be realized as the external behavior of a pair of communicating finite-branching processes. Since behaviors realizable by finite-branching processes form a proper subset of those realizable by all processes (as we show by Example 3.9), uniformity requires at least countable nondeterminism.

More precisely, a process p is finite branching provided start(p) is finite, and also for any s ε nonfinal(p), x ε variables(p), u ε values(x), there are only finitely many t, v with ((s,p,t),(u,x,v)) ε oksteps(p). A system S is finite branching if every process in proc(S) is finite branching. In the following theorem, let p denote the process of Example 2.6. Process p is finite branching and finite state. Assume variables(p) = {x}, and f(x) = 0.

Theorem 3.7. Let S be a system of processes, p $\notin$ proc(S). Then there exists an atomic finite branching system S_1 such that S $\equiv$ $\text{consist}_{\{x\},f}(S_1 \oplus S_p)$, where S_p is the fixed atomic system with proc(S_p) = {p}, ext(S_p) = {x}, and int(S_p) = init(S_p) = $\emptyset$.

Proof Sketch. By Theorem 3.6, we can assume that S is atomic. Let proc(S) = {q}. For each s ε states(q), y ε variables(q), u ε values(y), there are only countably many pairs (v,t) such that ((s,q,t),(u,y,v)) ε oksteps(q). Some ordering is fixed for each such set of pairs. An ordering is also fixed for the elements of start(q). Process q_1 simulates a step of process q as follows. Process q_1 alternately tests x and increments a counter until it sees that x has been set to 1. It then uses the value of its counter to select one of the possible alternatives of q to simulate and resets the counter and variable x to 0 in preparation for the next step of simulation. S_1

then is the system with $\text{proc}(S_1) = \{q_1\}$, $\text{ext}(S_1) = \text{ext}(S) \cup \{x\}$, $\text{int}(S_1) = \text{init}(S_1) = \emptyset$. □

We conclude this section with an example of a set of sequences which can be obtained as the behavior of a process, but not of any finite-branching process.

Lemma 3.8. Let p be a finite-branching process, $x \in \text{variables}(p)$, $b \in (\text{act}(x))^{\omega}$. If $\text{beh}(p)$ contains infinitely many prefixes of b, then $b \in \text{beh}(p)$.

Proof Sketch. By a König's Lemma-style argument. □

Example 3.9: Intuitively, we consider the specification to "write a value any finite number of times."

Let x be a variable, $v \in \text{values}(x)$, $A = \{(u,x,v) : u \in \text{values}(x)\}$. A* is the set of all finite sequences of actions, each of which "writes v" into x. A* can easily be realized as beh(p) for a process p which uses countable nondeterminism to choose an element of N for a counter initialization. Process p alternately decrements the counter and writes v, halting when the counter is 0.

On the other hand, Lemma 3.8 implies that A* is not beh(p) for any finite-branching process p, since $b = (v,x,v)^{\omega}$ has all of its finite prefixes in A*.

4. Examples

In this section, we discuss behavior specification for a typical distributed system - an arbiter. (A similar treatment has been worked out for a ticket distribution system, but space limitations preclude inclusion of the details of this second example.) We also describe particular and diverse implementations within our model that realize this behavior. We do not espouse any particular formal specification language, but rather express behavior restrictions in general mathematical terminology.

The specification example follows a pattern which has more general applicability, so we first describe that pattern. A finite set X of variables is accessed by a "user" and by a "system". The user is required to follow a simple and restrictive behavior pattern; formally, a set $U \subseteq \mathcal{B}(X)$ of "correct user sequences" is defined. The system is to be designed so that when it is combined with a user exhibiting correct behavior, with correct initialization of variables, certain conditions (on the values of variables) hold. Formally, a set $M \subseteq (\{\text{user},\text{system}\} \times \text{act}(X))^{\text{count}}$ is defined in order to describe the desired conditions. A total assignment f for X is defined in order to describe correct initialization of variables.

In a sense, U, M and f may together be regarded as a specification for the behavior of the desired system: any $b \in \mathcal{B}(X)$ can be considered "acceptable" if whenever it is combined consistently with a sequence in U, the resulting combination is in M. A system of processes is a correct implementation if all of its external behavior sequences are acceptable.

More formally, if A is any set, $t \in A^{count}$, L any set, x any element of L, then $\underline{t^x}$ denotes that element of $(\{x\} \times A)^{count}$ whose i^{th} element is (s,t_i), where t_i is the ith element of t. (That is, the entire sequence is labelled by x.) This superscript operator is extended to subsets of A^{count} in the obvious way.

For X, K sets of variables, L any set, $t \in (L \times act(X))^{count}$, f a total assignment for K, we say that t is (K,f)-consistent provided the sequence of second components of t is (K,f)-consistent.

In the present examples, L is taken to be {user,system}, a set of identifying labels for the modules of interest.

A sequence $b \in \mathcal{B}(X)$ is called <u>(U,M,f)-acceptable</u> provided $\{c \in shuffle(U^{user}, b^{system}) : c \text{ is } (X,f)\text{-consistent}\} \subseteq M$. Then a system of processes S would be considered to be a correct implementation provided every sequence in extbeh(S) is (U,M,f)-acceptable.

However, this type of description may be somewhat difficult for a system designer to use as a specification, so that it may be helpful to define explicitly a set B of (U,M,f)-acceptable sequences. Any system of processes S with extbeh(S) $\subseteq$ B is then considered correct. B should be as large as possible so as not to constrain the system designer unnecessarily. In the following example, we are able to obtain B exactly equal to the set of (U,M,f)-acceptable sequences, thus providing an explicit correctness characterization. We do not yet have a general equivalence theorem for specifications, however.

<u>Example 4.1: Arbiter</u>

Values(x) = {E,A,G} for each $x \in X$. Intuitively, E indicates "empty", A indicates "ask" and G indicates "grant" of a resource. The user is restricted simply to initiating requests and returning granted resources. More precisely, $U \subseteq \mathcal{B}(X)$ is defined as follows.

(Let $a \in shuffle(\{a_x : x \in X\})$, where each $a_x \in \mathcal{B}(x)$.

<u>$a \in U$</u> iff for each $x \in X$, (a)-(c) hold

(Let $a_x = (u_i,x,v_i)_{i=1}^{length(a_x)}$.)

<u>(a) Correct Transitions</u>

For all i, $1 \leq i \leq length(a_x)$, if u_i = E then $v_i \neq G$, and if u_i = A then $v_i = u_i$.

(The user cannot grant a request, and once he has initiated a request he cannot retract it.)

(b) Stopping

If a_x is finite and nonempty, then $v_{length(a_x)} = E$. (The user cannot leave the system when a request is pending or granted.)

(c) Return of Resource

For all i, if $u_i = G$ then there exists $j \geq i$ with $v_j \neq G$.

(If the user sees that his request has been granted, he must eventually return the resource.)

■

Thus, user correctness is defined locally at each variable. In particular, the user can consist of separate processes, one for each variable, with no communication between them. It is easy to design various sets of processes with behavior a subset of U.

Correct operation for our arbiter system will require that all requests eventually be granted, and that no two requests be granted simultaneously. Of course, variants on these conditions could be specified instead.

Let $f = \lambda x[E]$, $L = \{user, system\}$. $M \subseteq (L \times act(X))^{count}$ is defined as follows. $c \in M$ iff c is (X,f)-consistent and both (a) and (b) hold.

(a) Local Conditions

(Let $c \in shuffle(\{c_x : x \in X\})$, each $c_x \in (L \times act(x))^{count}$.)

For each $x \in X$, both (a1) and (a2) hold.

(Let $c_x = (\ell_i,(u_i,x,v_i))_{i=1}^{length(c_x)}$.)

(a1) Correct Transitions

For all i, $1 \leq i \leq length(c_x)$, either $u_i = v_i$ or else one of (a11)-(a13) holds.

(a11) ℓ_i = user, $u_i = E$ and $v_i = A$.

(a12) ℓ_i = user and $u_i = G$.

(a13) ℓ_i = system, $u_i = A$, $v_i = G$.

(The allowed transitions are depicted at right.)

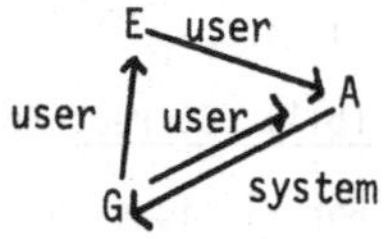

(a2) Progress

For all i, if $v_i \neq E$ then there exists $j \geq i$ with $v_j \neq v_i$.

(Any value other than E is eventually changed.)

(b) Global Conditions

(Let $c = (\ell_i,(u_i,x_i,v_i))_{i=1}^{length(c)}$, $d = (u_i,x_i,v_i)_{i=1}^{length(c)}$.)

(b1) Mutual Exclusion

For no $x_1,x_2 \in X$, $x_1 \neq x_2$ and no prefix e of d is it the case that $latest(e,x_1,f) = latest(e,x_2,f) = G$.

∎

Next, we define B.

$b \in B$ iff either (a) or (b) holds.

(a) Initialization or User Observed to be Incorrect

(Let $b \in shuffle(\{b_x : x \in X\})$ as before.)

For some $x \in X$, one of (a1)-(a3) holds.

(Let $b_x = (u_i,x,v_i)_{i=1}^{length(b_x)}$.)

(a1) $u_1 = G$.

(a2) For some i, $v_i = E$ and $u_{i+1} = G$, or else $v_i = A$ and $u_{i+1} \neq A$.

(a3) length $(b_x) = \infty$, and $u_i = G$ for all sufficiently large i.

(Thus, a sequence is "correct" if it involves incorrect action on the part of the user or an incorrect initialization of the variables. It is the job of the system designer to discover how such errors can be detected during system operation. It is easy to program a system to check for errors such as those represented in (a1) and (a2), but (a3) errors could not be detected at any finite point during the computation. However, the system is required to obey some conditions involving infinite execution sequences. It is possible to allow some of the system's "eventual" behavior to wait for the user's "eventual" behavior. An example will be seen in Implementation 1.)

(b) Correctness Conditions

Both (b1) and (b2) hold.

(b1) Local Conditions

(Let $b \in shuffle(\{b_x : x \in X\})$ as before.)

For each $x \in X$, (b11)-(b13) all hold.

($b_x = (u_i,x,v_i)_{i=1}^{length(b_x)}$.)

(b11) Correct Transitions

For all i, if $u_i = E$ or G, then $v_i = u_i$, and if $u_i = A$, then $v_i = A$ or G.

(b12) Infinite Examination

b_x is infinite

(b13) Response

For all i, if $u_i = A$, then for some $j \geq i$ it is the case that $v_j \neq A$.

(b2) Global Conditions

(Let $b = (u_i,x_i,v_i)_{i=1}^{length(b)}$.)

(b21) Mutual Exclusion

For no $x_1,x_2 \in X$, $x_1 \neq x_2$, and no prefix d of b it is the case that

latest(d,x_1,f) = latest(d,x_2,f) = G. ∎

The following theorem shows that our explicit characterization for system behavior is as general as possible.

Theorem 4.2: For U,M,f,B of this example, B = {b : b is (U,M,f)-acceptable}.

Proof: $\subseteq$: Let $b \in B$, $a \in U$, $c \in$ shuffle(a^{user},b^{system}), c (X,f)-consistent. We must show $c \in M$.

Since $a \in U$ and c is (X,f)-consistent, we can show that b fails to satisfy (a) of (the definition of) B. Thus, b satisfies (b) of B.

We check that c satisfies each condition of M. c satisfies (a1) of M because of (a) of U and (b11) of B. To verify (a2) of M, write $c \in$ shuffle$(\{c_x : x \in X\})$, and for fixed x, write $c_x = (\ell_i,(u_i,x,v_i))_{i=1}^{length(c_x)}$. If $(\ell_i,(u_i,x,A))$ is an element of c, then (b12) and (b13) of B together imply that for some $j > i$, $v_i \neq A$. If $(\ell_i,(u_i,x,G))$ is an element of c, then let j be the largest number $\leq i$ with ℓ_j = user. By (b11) of B, j exists and v_j = A or G. Then by (b) of U, there exists $k > i$ with ℓ_k = user. If $u_k \neq G$ we are done. Otherwise, (c) of U implies that for some $m \geq k$, $v_m \neq G$.

(b1) of M follows easily from (b21) of B and (a) of U.

$\supseteq$: Let $b \notin B$. We must produce $a \in U$, $c \in$ shuffle(a^{user},b^{system}), c (X,f)-consistent, and $c \notin M$. Clearly, b fails to satisfy (a) of B. In addition, b will fail to satisfy at least one of (b11), (b12), (b13) and (b21) of B.

We consider four cases.

(b11) fails: Any $a \in U$, $c \in$ shuffle(a^{user},b^{system}) which is (X,f)-consistent will fail to satisfy (a1) of M. One such c can be constructed by immediately preceding each element (system,(u,x,v)) of c which is derived from an action of b by an element (user,(y,x,u)). The value of y is uniquely determined by the consistency requirements on c; since b fails to satisfy (a) of B, this determination produces $a \in U$.

(b12) fails: Consider x such that actions (u,x,v) only appear finitely often in b.

Construct a ε U, c ε shuffle(a^{user}, b^{system}), c (X,f)-consistent, with the following property. In c, following all elements of the form (system, (u,x,v)) (for any u,v), there is an element of the form (user,(u,x,A)) (for some u), and following that element there are infinitely many elements of the form (user,(A,x,A)). Such a, c can be constructed by a slight addition to the construction for the preceding case. The resulting c fails to satisfy (a2) of M.

(b13) fails: Consider x such that (A,x,A) occurs in b and moreover for all following actions in b of the form (u,x,v), we have v = A.

Then any a ε U, c ε shuffle(a^{user}, b^{system}) which is (X,f)-consistent will fail to satisfy (a2) of M. Such a, c can be constructed as before.

(b21) fails: Let $b = (u_i, x_i, v_i)_{i=1}^{length(b)}$, where (u_j, x_j, G) and (u_k, x_k, G) are actions witnessing the contradiction to (b21) of B. We can assume that $j < k$, $x_j \neq x_k$ and for no m, $j < m < k$ it is the case that $x_m = x_j$.

Construct a ε U, c ε shuffle(a^{user}, b^{system}), c (X,f)-consistent, with the following property. In c, the elements derived from b's actions (u_j, x_j, G) and (u_k, x_k, G) have no intervening elements of the form (user, (u, x_j, v)) for any u, v. Such a, c fail to satisfy (b1) of M.

Such a, c can be constructed as before.

□

The given description of B seems sufficiently manageable to be used to specify system behavior. B is also sufficiently general to admit many different implementations - i.e. processes or communicating groups of processes with behavior a subset of B but with very different internal structure and execution behavior. Outlines of three such examples follow.

Implementation 1: The simplest implementation is a single process p which polls each variable in circular sequence. When A is read, p changes it to G and then repeatedly reads that variable until its value reverts either to E or A. When this occurs, p resumes polling with the next variable.

Note that p may fail to examine some variable after some time, contradicting (b12) of the definition of B. But the only way this can occur is if the user acts incorrectly, failing, for example, to change G to E or A. Then the execution will satisfy, for example, (a3) of the definition of B. Thus, although p does not actually detect certain incorrect user behavior, it nevertheless can cause its own correct eventual behavior to depend on the eventual correctness of user behavior.

Checking that beh(p) $\subseteq$ B is straightforward.

Implementation 2: The idea of Implementation 1 can be extended to allow "more concurrency" using a binary tree of polling processes, with the leaves accessing the interface variables $x \in X$.

Each non-root process p alternately polls its left and right son variables. When A is seen, p changes its own father variable to A. When the father variable changes to G, p grants its pending son's request by changing the appropriate A to G. p then waits for that son variable to revert to either E or A. When this occurs, p changes its father variable to E and then resumes polling its sons with the other son being polled next.

The root process acts just like p of Implementation 1 for $|X| = 2$.

One must do a little work to convince oneself that the alternating strategy guarantees eventual granting of all requests. All other properties in the definition of B are easy to check, if all father variables are assumed to be initialized at E.

Implementation 3: The third implementation is based on the state-model algorithms used in Burns et al [9], (see also Cremers-Hibbard [8]). This time, the implementing system consists of identical processes p_x, each of which has access to exactly one of the interface variables. In addition, there is a common variable x* to which all the processes p_x have access. One of the algorithms from [9], such as algorithm A, is used. This algorithm enables asynchronous processes requiring mutual exclusion synchronization to communicate using x* to achieve the needed synchronization, with good bounds on the number of times any single process might be bypassed by any other (and with a very small number of values for x*). The processes themselves must be willing, however, to execute a complicated protocol. In the present development, we have defined a very simple arbiter protocol and do not require a user to learn the more complicated protocol of the earlier algorithm. We can still use the earlier ideas, however, by isolating the earlier protocol in the system processes and allowing a user to communicate with one of those processes.

In outline, and referring to some ideas from algorithm A, the p_x accessing x examines x until A is detected. Then p_x enters the trying protocol using x*. When p_x is allowed (in algorithm A) to enter its critical region, it passes the permission on by changing the value of x to G. p_x then examines x until it reverts to E or A, and then p_x enters the exit protocol using x*. When p_x has completed its exit protocol, it is ready to begin once again, examining x for further requests.

Correctness of the resulting system of communicating processes is easy to understand based on that of Algorithm A.

□

The main point to be made by this example is that there are many different processes and systems of processes which can meaningfully be said to realize the same input-output behavior. In the three implementations above, the systems vary both in process configuration and in execution. There is no realistic sense in which the internal states and transitions (i.e. the execution sequences) of the different implementations could be thought to simulate each other. And yet, they are all solutions to the problem of constructing an arbiter.

A technical question which may be of interest for the purpose of obtaining a sequence-based characterization for behaviors in whether B in the above example is exactly equal to extbeh(S) for some system S. It is not hard to show that U can be so obtained.

5. Complexity Measures

Separation of behavior and implementation opens the way for comparison of different implementations of the same behavior, a fundamental subject of study for any theory of computation. Intuitively, comparisons might be made on the basis of process configuration, local process space requirements, communication space requirements, number of local process steps executed, number of changes made to variables, and possible "amount of concurrency". Tradeoffs would be expected.

Configuration and space measures seem easy to formalize. For instance, the three implementations in Example 4.1 use 1, n-1 and n processes, 0, n-2 and 1 auxiliary communication variables, and 0, 3 and n+5 values for each communication variable, respectively.

In contrast, time and concurrency measures are not so straightforward. For instance, "response time" might be expected (sometimes) to be better for Implementations 2 and 3 than for Implementation 1 of Example 4.1, because of "use of concurrency". But much work remains to be done in quantifying such time comparisons.

In order to state time bounds, one must meet several requirements. First, one must decide what actions to count during execution. Second, in order to state time bounds as closed-form functions (e.g. "runtime = $2n^2$"), one requires an appropriate notion of the "size of the task being accomplished", (i.e. an appropriate parameter n on which to base complexity analysis). Finally, one needs to establish appropriate quantification over alternatives in the present nondeterministic setting. We believe that partial orders of the type studied by Greif [11] and Hewitt [12] will provide useful ways of satisfying the first requirement but do not yet know how best to satisfy the remaining requirements.

In some detail, let X be a set of variables, p a set of processes, $a = ((s_i,p_i,t_i), (u_i,x_i,v_i))_{i=1}^{\text{length }(a)}$ be a sequence of elements of steps(P,X). For i, j ε N, define i P' j iff i < j and either $x_i = x_j$ or $p_i = p_j$. Let P be the transitive closure of P'. In words, P formalizes the ordering of steps of a imposed by the sequentiality of each individual process and each variable. P seems to provide much useful information about the "running time" and "possible concurrency" in a, including some seemingly natural formal measures. An important remaining task is the use of these measures to obtain clean statements of upper and lower complexity bounds, both for particular systems and for the collection of systems realizing particular specified behavior.

REFERENCES

[1] Petri, C.A., "Kommunikation mit Automaten," Schriften des Reinish Westfalischen Inst. Instrumentelle Mathematik, Bonn. 1962.

[2] Hoare, C.A.R., "Communicating Sequential Processes," Technical Report, Department of Computer Science, the Queen's University, Belfast, Northern Ireland, December, 1976.

[3] Milne, G. and R. Milner, "Concurrent Processes and Their Syntax," Internal Report CSR-2-77, Department of Computer Science, Edinburg, May, 1977.

[4] Dijkstra, E.W., "Co-operating Sequential Processes," Programming Languages, NATA Advanced Study Institute, Academic Press, 1968.

[5] Campbell, R. and A. Habermann, "The Specification of Process Synchronization Using Path Expressions," Lecture Notes in Computer Science, 16, Springer-Verlag, 1974.

[6] Shaw, A.C., "Software Descriptions with Flow Expressions," IEEE Trans. on Software Engineering SE-4, 3 (1978), 242-254.

[7] Feldman, J., "Synchronizing Distant Cooperating Processes," Technical Report 26, Department of Computer Sciences, University of Rochester, October, 1977.

[8] Cremers, A. and T. N. Hibbard, "Mutual Exclusion of N Processes Using an O(N) - Valued Message Variable," USC Department of Computer Science Manuscript, 1975.

[9] Burns, J.E., M. J. Fischer, P. Jackson, N.A. Lynch, and G. L. Peterson, "Shared Data Requirements for Implementation of Mutual Exclusion Using a Test-and-Set Primitive," Proceedings of 1978 International Conference on Parallel Processing (1978).

[10] Chandra, A.K., "Computable Nondeterministic Functions," Proceedings of 19th Annual Symposium on Foundations of Computer Science, 1978.

[11] Greif, Irene, "A Language for Formal Problem Specification," Comm. ACM, 20, 12 (1977), 931-935.

[12] Atkinson, R. and C. Hewitt, "Specification and Proof Techniques for Serializers," AI Memo 438, Massachusetts Institute of Technology, August, 1977.

ON THE ABSENCE OF LIVELOCKS IN PARALLEL PROGRAMS

Y.S. Kwong
Unit for Computer Science
McMaster University
Hamilton, Ontario, Canada

Abstract

We explore in this paper the subtle correctness criterion of the absence of livelocks in parallel programs. The basic concepts underlying livelocks are formalized. A classification of livelocks into two types according to their causes of formation is introduced. Two techniques for proving the absence of livelocks are also presented. One is based on the notion of problem reduction; the other is an extension of the well-founded set method for proving termination in sequential programs.

1. Introduction

In this paper we investigate what is probably one of the least explored correctness criteria in asynchronous parallel computation, namely, the absence of livelocks. Deadlock-freedom has long been recognized as an important correctness property in concurrent systems. Informally speaking, a process is said to have a deadlock if there exists a reachable state in which no matter what the system does, it is impossible for the process to be executed any further. However, livelock is a very different notion. It refers to the phenomenon in which a process is never executed along an infinite computation even though it is not deadlocked. Until recently, livelocks have always been discussed informally in the literature as "starvation" or "permanent blocking." As we shall show in later sections, these notions are only special cases of livelocks. A formal investigation is obviously desirable.

First, we review what had appeared in the literature. In [3], Dijkstra proposed a solution to the critical section problem, which guarantees mutual exclusion and if several processes are competing for entry, at least one of them succeeds. The solution is not deadlocked in the sense that it is possible for all processes to gain entry. However, as observed by Knuth [11], some process may have to wait until eternity while others are executing their critical sections. Holt [6] called it "permanent blocking" in his investigation of resource allocation. A very elegant example of livelocks is Dijkstra's Five Dining Philosophers in [4], where he pointed out the danger of "individual starvation" due to the conspiracy of neighbors. In [1], Ashcroft observed that in an airline reservation system, a booking process may be permanently stopped by a "continuously changing pattern of constraints," and he coined the term "livelock" which is adopted in this paper. He also noted that even with the finite delay property and in the absence of all deadlocks, livelocks may still occur. More recent works include, for example, Lamport's extension of Floyd's assertion method to verifying "liveness" properties [15], and also van Lamsweerde and Sintzoff's treatment of the absence of starvation through fixed point theory [16].

We believe that an important first step towards a better understanding of the topic of livelocks is to put it on a precise setting to facilitate investigations. In this paper we attempt to present a formal treatment. Section 2 describes our model for representing parallel programs. We then address the question: What constitutes a livelock? To start with, we first examine in Section 3 a number of simple examples that lead very naturally to the concepts of the finite delay property, computations, and their validity. Hopefully, they will provide an intuitive understanding of the livelock concept which will then be formalized in Section 4. Also presented is a classification of livelocks in accordance with their causes of formation. In Section 5 we discuss techniques for proving the absence of livelocks.

In a subsequent paper we shall investigate how scheduling disciplines for process queuing would affect livelocks in parallel programs. A parallel program is considered to have two system representations: an abstraction and an implementation. The latter has queuing disciplines being represented explicitly, whereas the former has not. We may envision that abstractions of parallel programs are obtained from their corresponding implementations by reductions or by masking out all details of scheduling. We shall show that the behaviour of livelocks in abstractions and implementations of parallel programs is not always the same, even if some fair scheduling disciplines are employed. The interactions between the two types of livelocks and the crucial role of the so-called "finite-delay property" in livelock investigations will be examined. The implications of our results on verification of livelock-freedom will also be discussed.

2. Model of Parallel Programs

An <u>asynchronous parallel program</u>, or simply a <u>parallel program</u>, is represented graphically by a labeled Petri net, where <u>tokens</u> denote instruction pointers of processes, <u>place nodes</u> (or simply <u>places</u>)

correspond to locations where instruction pointers may dwell, and transition nodes represent classes of transitions. We attach to each transition node an instruction of the form:

t : when $P(\xi)$ do $\xi \longleftarrow F(\xi)$

where t is a label, ξ denotes program variables, and P, F are the enabling predicate and action function of t, respectively. We usually omit the "when part" if P is identically true, and the "do part" if F is an identity function. We allow action functions to be multi-valued, which means that a parallel program may be non-deterministic. We also assume that each transition node has at most one input place and one output place.

Let Π be an indexing set and assume that each process has a unique process index $\pi \in \Pi$, which is assigned on its creation or initialization and destroyed on its deletion or exit. For convenience, we sometimes write process π instead of process with index π.

Semantically, we envision a parallel program to be a state transition system or simply a system $(Q,\Sigma,\longrightarrow,Q_0)$, where Q is a set of states, Σ is a set of transitions, $\longrightarrow \subseteq Q \times \Sigma \times Q$ is the state transition relation, and $Q_0 \subseteq Q$ is a set of initial states.

A state q in Q has two components – the program state ξ and the control state c, which consist of all program variables and instruction pointer variables, respectively. We use $i(\pi)$ to denote the instruction pointer variable of process π and v_i the number of instruction pointers residing at place p_i. v_i's are sometimes called place variables. We define Q_0 by assigning initial values to ξ and c. An unspecified variable can have any arbitrary value initially. For an expression E and a state q, we let q.E be the value of E in q. For example, $q.i(\pi)$ denotes the place where the instruction pointer of process π is dwelling in state q. If P is a predicate, we write q.P if the variables in q satisfy P.

To emphasize the importance of instructions and processes, we let $\tilde{\Sigma}$ be the set of instructions and represent Σ by $\tilde{\Sigma}\times\Pi$. Any transition t in Σ can then be written as $\tilde{t}(\pi)$ where $\tilde{t}$ is an instruction and π is a process. Let q, q' be any state in Q, π be a process, and $\tilde{t}$ be a transition node. We say that transition $\tilde{t}(\pi)$ is enabled or firable in q if $q.i(\pi)$ is the input place of $\tilde{t}$ and q.P holds. We also say that $\begin{Bmatrix}\pi\\ \tilde{t}\end{Bmatrix}$ is enabled or firable in q if there exists some

$\left\{\begin{matrix}\tilde{t} \in \tilde{\Sigma} \\ \pi \in \Pi\end{matrix}\right\}$ such that $\tilde{t}(\pi)$ is enabled in q. Otherwise, $\overset{\pi}{\tilde{t}}$ is <u>disabled</u> in q. We write $q \xrightarrow{\tilde{t}(\pi)} q'$, saying that π <u>executes</u> or <u>fires</u> $\tilde{t}$ in progressing from q to q', if $\tilde{t}(\pi)$ is enabled in q, $q'.\xi = F(q.\xi)$, $q'.i(\pi)$ is the output place of $\tilde{t}$, and $q'.i(\sigma) = q.i(\sigma)$ for all other processes $\sigma \neq \pi$. If $F(q.\xi)$ is a set then $q'.\xi$ is assigned any element in $F(q.\xi)$. Note that all instruction pointer variables are <u>local</u>, i.e. they can be modified only by the processes owning them, whereas the program variables in ξ can be either local or <u>global</u>.

It should be noted that parallelism is introduced into the model through the relation $\longrightarrow$: For any state q in Q, there may be many t in Σ and q' in Q such that $q \xrightarrow{t} q'$. The firing of a transition represents an <u>indivisible action</u> which takes the system from one state into another. We assume that each such action denotes a single <u>event</u> in the system, and any simultaneous event occurrences can be represented by a sequence of events in some arbitrary order.

Let Σ^+ be the set of all finite, nonempty sequences of transitions, and $\Sigma^* = \Sigma^+ \cup \{\Lambda\}$ where Λ is the empty sequence. We usually use t_i's to represent individual transitions, and w, x, y, etc. to denote transition sequences. The firing of transition sequences can be defined as follows:

(1) $(\forall q \in Q)\ q \xrightarrow{\Lambda} q$

and (2) $(\forall q, q' \in Q)\ (\forall x \in \Sigma^*)\ (\forall t \in \Sigma)$

if $(\exists q'' \in Q)\ (q \xrightarrow{x} q'' \wedge q'' \xrightarrow{t} q')$ then $q \xrightarrow{xt} q'$.

We write $q \longrightarrow q'$ if there exists some t in Σ such that $q \xrightarrow{t} q'$, and denote the reflexive and irreflexive transitive closures of $\longrightarrow$ by $\xrightarrow{*}$ and $\xrightarrow{+}$, respectively. For any x in Σ^*, we say that x is <u>enabled</u> or <u>firable</u> in a state q if there exists q' in Q such that $q \xrightarrow{x} q'$. Otherwise, x is disabled in q. If $q \xrightarrow{*} q'$ then we say that q' is <u>reachable</u> from q. The set of all states reachable from some initial state is denoted by Q_r, i.e., $Q_r = \{ q \in Q \mid (\exists q_0 \in Q_0)\ q_0 \xrightarrow{*} q \}$. We sometimes call Q_r the <u>reachability set</u> and any state in it a <u>reachable state</u> of the system.

We also let Σ^ω be the set of all infinite transition sequences. For any x in Σ^*, x^ω denotes the sequence xx..... which consists of infinite repetitions of x. The sets of finite and infinite sequences of states are denoted by Q^* and Q^ω, respectively.

P, V operations on "semaphore" can be represented as shown in Figure 2.1. If P and V are the only types of operations allowed for synchronization, then we call such parallel programs *PV systems of processes*.

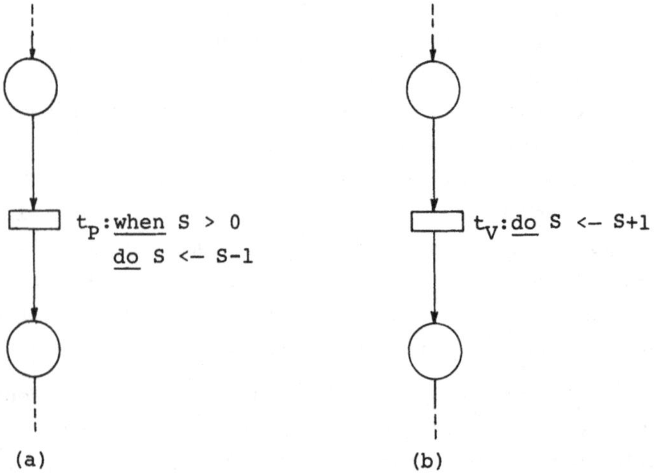
t_P: *when* S > 0
do S <– S-1
t_V: *do* S <– S+1
(a)
(b)

Figure 2.1 P- and V- operations on semaphore S.

3. *Examples of Livelocks*

To illustrate the basic concepts behind livelocks, we shall examine in this section some simple examples. In the following, we let q be a state and π be any process.

Definition 3.1 We say that a predicate $J : Q \longrightarrow \{T,F\}$ is q-*invariant*, if

$$(\forall q' \in Q) \text{ if } q \xrightarrow{*} q' \text{ then } J(q')$$

q-*reachable*, if

$$(\exists q' \in Q) \quad (q \xrightarrow{*} q' \wedge J(q')).$$

Observation 3.1 Let $J : Q \longrightarrow \{T,F\}$ be a predicate. Then

J is q-invariant iff $\neg J$ is not q-reachable. □

Definition 3.2 We say that a process π

has not exited in q, if

$q.i(\pi) = p$ for some place node p

is *dead* in q, or write $dead_\pi(q)$ if

π has not exited in q and there exists no state q'
such that $q \xrightarrow{*} q'$ and π is enabled in q'

is deadlockable in q, or write $\text{deadlockable}_\pi(q)$, if
dead_π is q-reachable.

We also say that the system is not deadlockable, or deadlock-free if for any process π and any initial state q_0, $\neg\, \text{deadlockable}_\pi(q_0)$.

Example 3.1 Consider the parallel program P_1 in Figure 3.1. After firing $t_1(\pi_1)t_5(\pi_2)$, the system reaches a state q in which both π_1 and π_2 are dead. Although there is an infinite computation $(t_9(\pi_3)t_{10}(\pi_3))^\omega$ for state q along which π_1 and π_2 are never executed, however, we do not regard these processes as being livelocked because their permanent blocking is due to deadlock. Livelocks are not particular instances of deadlocks. □

initially $S_1 = S_2 = S_3 = 1$

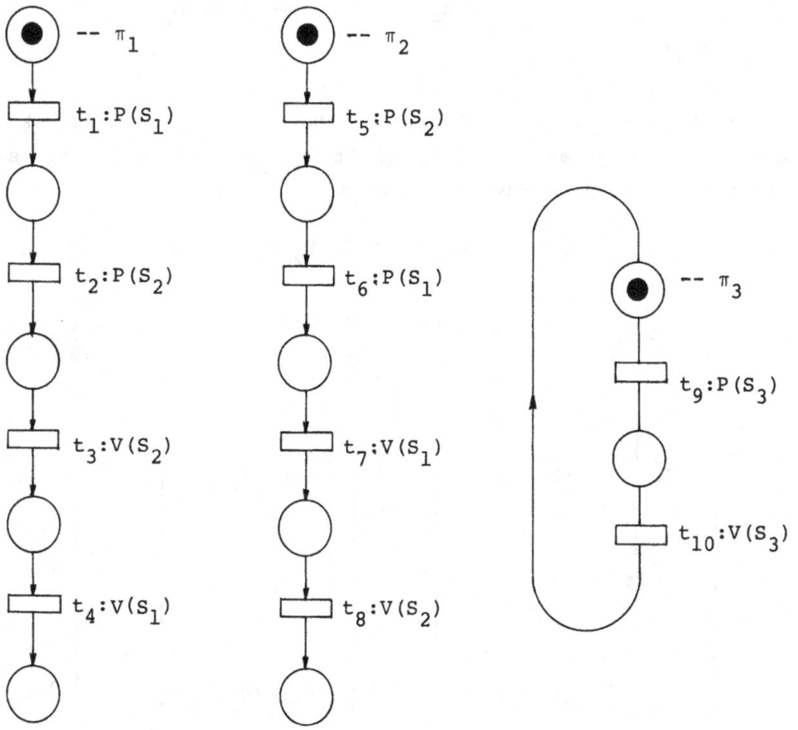

Figure 3.1 P_1 : Illustration of deadlock.

Note that the absence of deadlocks, or deadlock-freedom, guarantees that no matter which state the system is in, it is always possible for a process to advance provided that it has not yet exited from the system. However, the possibility for a process to be executed does not imply that it will be executed; it all depends on which transitions the system chooses to fire. Hence, it is possible for a process to be permanently blocked even though it is not deadlockable. Many interesting examples of livelocks which have been observed are exhibited by deadlock-free systems. For instance, the PV system in [2] which solves the first reader/writer problem has a peculiar feature: a writer may be livelocked by an infinite stream of readers, and this livelock is not removable even with FIFO queues for semaphores. It should be noted that there are limitations to what scheduling disciplines can do in removing livelocks.

Example 3.2 Consider the deadlock-free parallel program P_2 in Figure 3.2. We let $P(S_1,S_2)$ be

$$\underline{\text{when}}\ S_1 > 0 \wedge S_2 > 0\ \underline{\text{do}}\ (S_1,S_2) \longleftarrow (S_1-1,S_2-1)$$

and $V(S_1,S_2)$ be

$$\underline{\text{do}}\ (S_1,S_2) \longleftarrow (S_1+1,S_2+1).$$

P_2 is a PV multiple (or PV_m) system. Note that π_2 is livelocked because of the computation $(t_5(\pi_3)t_2(\pi_1)t_1(\pi_1)t_6(\pi_3))^{\omega}$ in which π_2 is never enabled due to conspiracy of π_1 and π_3. □

initially $S_1 = 0;\ S_2 = 1;$

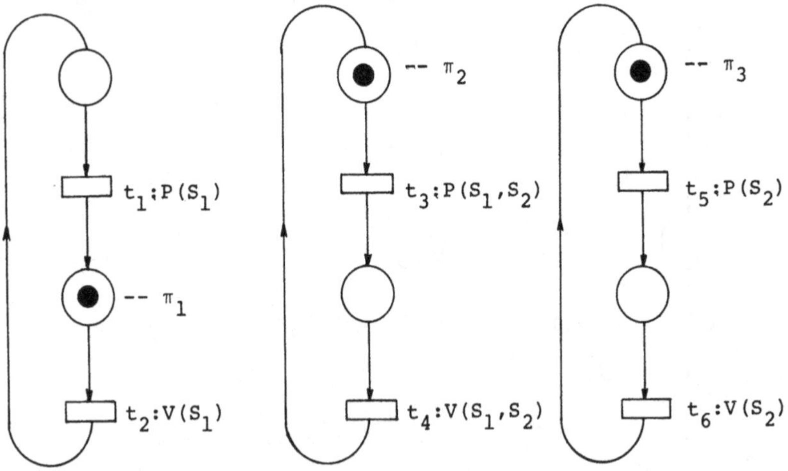

Figure 3.2 P_2 : Illustration of type 1 livelock.

Example 3.3 In P_3 (Figure 3.3) transition nodes t_1 and t_4 are used to create and delete processes dynamically, and are called entry and exit operations, respectively. We assume that processes created are assigned the indices $\pi_1, \pi_2, \ldots, \pi_i, \ldots$ according to their order of creation. Although deadlocks are absent in P_3, however, π_1 is live-locked due to the computation

$t_1(\pi_1)(t_1(\pi_2)t_2(\pi_2)t_3(\pi_2)t_4(\pi_2))\ldots(t_1(\pi_i)t_2(\pi_i)t_3(\pi_i)t_4(\pi_i))\ldots$

Note that $t_2(\pi_1)$ is enabled and disabled infinitely often. □

initially S = 1;

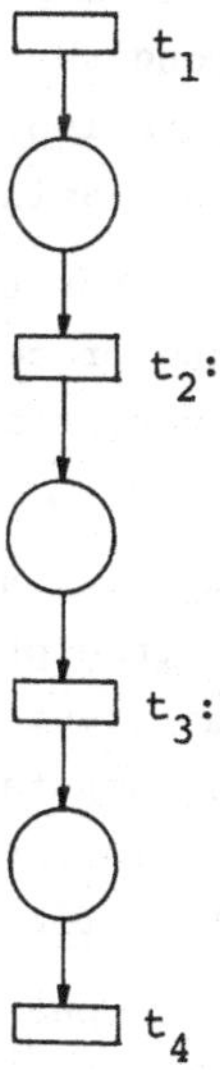

Figure 3.3 P_3 : Illustration of type 2 livelock.

We now proceed to define precisely the intuitive notions of computations, finite delay property and validity.

Definition 3.3 We say that x in $\Sigma^* \cup \Sigma^\omega$ is a computation for q (or simply a computation if q is understood) provided that

(1) For any prefix y of x, there exists some q' in Q such that $q \xrightarrow{y} q'$.

(2) If x is finite then any state reachable from q by firing x must be dead.

For a computation $x = t_1 \ldots. t_i \ldots.$ for q, we say that $s = q_1 \ldots. q_i \ldots.$ is a <u>state sequence</u> for (q,x) if for all $i \geq 1$, $q_i \xrightarrow{t_i} q_{i+1}$ and $q_1 = q$.

Informally, a computation is a sequence of transitions which can be fired one after another, and if it is finite then its execution must lead to a dead state. A state sequence is simply a sequence in $Q^* \cup Q^\omega$ which the system goes through in the execution of a computation. The reader may notice that there are some computations which allow a process to dwell at a place forever, even though it is always enabled.

<u>Example 3.4</u> Consider systems P_2 and P_3 in Figures 3.2 and 3.3. In P_2, $(t_2(\pi_1)t_1(\pi_1))^\omega$ is an infinite computation for the initial state. Although π_3 is always enabled along the associated state sequence, it is never executed in such a computation. In P_3, let $x_i = t_1(\pi_i)t_2(\pi_i)t_3(\pi_i)t_4(\pi_i)$ and examine the infinite computation $(t_1(\pi_1)t_2(\pi_1)t_3(\pi_1))x_2x_3 \ldots. x_i \ldots.$ for the initial state. After the firing of t_1, t_2 and t_3 by π_1, the process is never executed again although it remains enabled in every state of the state sequence associated with $x_2x_3 \ldots. x_i \ldots.$. □

Undoubtedly many such computations can be found in parallel programs, and there are deadlock-free processes which are never executed in them. However, we do not regard these processes as being livelocked. We claim that these computations are not "realistic" in the sense that they would be ruled out by any reasonable schedulers. Next we shall examine the so-called <u>finite delay property</u>:

FDP_0: Let $x = t_1 \ldots. t_i \ldots.$ be a computation for a state q_1. For any state sequence $s = q_1 \ldots. q_i \ldots.$ for (q_1,x), any state q_i $(i \geq 1)$ and any set of transitions $T \subseteq \Sigma$, if for all $j \geq i$, there exists $t \in T$ such that t is enabled in q_j, then there exists some $k \geq i$ such that $t_k \in T$.

Informally, FDP_0 says that if a "set of transitions" is enabled persistently, then the set will be executed infinitely often. Although this is very general and applicable to any transition system, however, it only deals with the enabling of a process in an implicit manner. Since we are concerned mainly with parallel programs and "process" is a key entity, the following is conceptually more appealing:

FDP: Let $x = t_1 \ldots t_i \ldots$ be a computation for a state q_1. For any state sequence $s = q_1 \ldots q_i \ldots$ for (q_1, x), any state q_i $(i \geq 1)$ and a process π, if π is enabled in q_j for all $j \geq i$ then there exists some $k \geq i$ such that $t_k = \tilde{t}(\pi)$ for some instruction $\tilde{t} \in \tilde{\Sigma}$.

Convention In the sequel we shall adopt FDP as the finite delay property unless stated otherwise. □

Observation 3.2 FDP_0 implies FDP. □

Definition 3.4 A computation for a state is valid provided that it satisfies the finite delay property.

It is obvious that all computations examined in Examples 3.1, 3.2 and 3.3 are valid, whereas those in Example 3.4 are not. In words, FDP means that:

If a process is enabled persistently,
then it must be executed infinitely often.

This notion is similar to the finite delay property in [7,8], but different from that in [19], which corresponds to the following:

If a process is enabled infinitely often,
then it must be executed infinitely often.

In a subsequent paper it is shown that this slightly different assumption has a drastic effect on our investigation of livelocks.

Observation 3.3 All finite computations are valid. □

4. Definitions and Classification

In the previous section, we have examined a number of examples to illustrate what constitutes a livelock. Informally it can be regarded as a phenomenon in which a process is never executed in some valid infinite computation even though it is not deadlocked. In verification of system correctness, we are concerned not only about livelocks in particular computations, but also about the possibility of livelock occurrences in all reachable states. Note that livelocks are associated with computations whereas the possibility of occurrences of livelocks is a property of a system state.

Before proceeding to formalize livelocks, let us introduce some preliminaries. Let N denote the set of all natural numbers. Adding a top element ω to N, we have a complete lattice $N \cup \{\omega\}$ with the usual ordering by magnitude. We define the firing counter

$$\psi : (\tilde{\Sigma} \cup \Pi) \times (\Sigma^* \cup \Sigma^\omega) \longrightarrow N \cup \{\omega\}$$

as follows: For any element a in $\tilde{\Sigma} \cup \Pi$ and any x in $\Sigma^* \cup \Sigma^\omega$, let $\psi(a,x)$ be the number of occurrences of a in x. For example, $\psi(\tilde{t},x) = 0$ for some $\tilde{t}$ in $\tilde{\Sigma}$ means that the instruction $\tilde{t}$ is not executed by any process in x; $\psi(\pi,x) = \omega$ means that process π is executed infinitely often in x.

Let P be the set of all enabling predicates. Define the enabling counter

$$e : (\Pi \cup P) \times (Q^* \cup Q^\omega) \longrightarrow N \cup \{\omega\}$$

to count the number of states in a state sequence in which a $\left\{ \begin{matrix} \text{process} \\ \text{predicate} \end{matrix} \right\}$ is $\left\{ \begin{matrix} \text{enabled} \\ \text{true} \end{matrix} \right\}$. $e(\pi,s) = 0$ denotes that process π is never enabled in s whereas $e(\pi,s) = \omega$ means that π is enabled infinitely often in s.

We also define the continuity predicate c as a binary relation on $(\Pi \cup P) \times Q^\omega$: for a $\begin{matrix} \text{process} \\ \text{predicate} \end{matrix}$ p and an infinite state sequence $s = q_1 \ldots q_i \ldots$, we write c(p,s) if there exists $i \geq 1$ such that p is $\left\{ \begin{matrix} \text{enabled} \\ \text{true} \end{matrix} \right\}$ in q_j for all $j \geq i$. Intuitively this means that p is $\left\{ \begin{matrix} \text{enabled} \\ \text{true} \end{matrix} \right\}$ continuously after a finite number of states in s.

Definition 4.1 We say that a process π is
starvable in q, or write $\text{starvable}_\pi(q)$, if
π has not exited in q and there is a valid infinite computation x for q such that $\psi(\pi,x) = 0$
livelockable in q, or write $\text{livelockable}_\pi(q)$, if

a) $\neg\,\text{deadlockable}_\pi(q)$

and b) starvable_π is q-reachable.

We also say that the system is not livelockable, or livelock-free if for any process π and any initial state q_0, $\neg\,\text{livelockable}_\pi(q_0)$.

It should be noted that in the predicate "livelockable," the main concern is whether it is possible for a deadlock-free process being not executed in some valid infinite computation. We usually do not care in which computation the process actually demonstrates this phenomenon. However, references to the particular computation are sometimes desirable e.g. in the presentation of examples. Instead of writing $\text{livelockable}_\pi(q)$, we then say that process π has a livelock, or is livelocked in a computation x for some state reachable from q.

In the following, we shall show that livelocks can be classified into two different types according to their causes of formation. Let us assume that a process π is livelockable in some state q in Q. Then π is not deadlockable in q and there exists a state q_1 such that $q \xrightarrow{*} q_1$ and $\text{starvable}_\pi(q_1)$, i.e. π has not exited in q_1 and there is a valid infinite computation x for q_1 such that $\psi(\pi,x) = 0$. Let $s = q_1 \ldots q_i \ldots$ be a state sequence for (q_1,x) and consider the following cases:

■ (1) $e(\pi,s) \neq \omega$: We call this a type 1 livelock.

■ (2) $e(\pi,s) = \omega \wedge \neg c(\pi,s)$: We call this a type 2 livelock.

Definition 4.2 Let π be a process and q be a state in Q. For i = 1 or 2, we write

$\text{starvable}^i_\pi(q)$, if

π has not exited in q, and there exists a valid infinite computation x for q and a state sequence s for (q,x) such that $\psi(\pi,x) = 0$ and

if i = 1 then $e(\pi,s) \neq \omega$

if i = 2 then $e(\pi,s) = \omega \wedge \neg c(\pi,s)$;

$\text{livelockable}^i_\pi(q)$, if

a) $\neg\,\text{deadlockable}_\pi(q)$

and b) starvable^i_π is q-reachable.

To emphasize the computation x and the state sequence s involved, instead of simply writing $\text{livelockable}^i_\pi(q)$, we sometimes say that process π has a type i livelock in x along s. We also say that the system is free of type i livelocks if for any process π and any initial state q_0, $\neg\,\text{livelockable}^i_\pi(q_0)$.

In words, livelocks of types 1 and 2 correspond, respectively, to the cases in which a process is either enabled only a finite number of times, or enabled infinitely often but not continuously, along some state sequence of a valid infinite computation in which the process is never executed. Livelocks in Examples 3.2 and 3.3 are of types 1 and 2, respectively.

Proposition 4.1 All livelocks are of the two types defined above. □

Observation 4.2 For a given state q, a process π may have livelocks of both types, i.e., $\text{livelockable}^1_\pi(q)$ and $\text{livelockable}^2_\pi(q)$. □

This is of course not surprising because there are usually many valid computations for a given state.

Example 4.1 In P_2 (Figure 3.2), process π_2 has livelocks of types 1 and 2 in the initial state because of the valid computation $(t_5(\pi_3)t_2(\pi_1)t_1(\pi_1)t_6(\pi_3))^\omega$ and $(t_2(\pi_1)t_1(\pi_1)t_5(\pi_3)t_6(\pi_3))^\omega$, respectively. □

It should be noted that type 1 livelocks with $e(\pi,s) = 0$ are of particular interest because they form a subclass to which all type 1 livelocks can be reduced. Consider $e(\pi,s) = n$ for some nonzero n. This implies that there must be some $k \geq n$ such that $s = q_1 \cdots q_k s'$ and $e(\pi,s') = 0$. The reader may have noticed that "starvation" in [4,16], "waiting until eternity" in [11], and "livelock" in [1] are actually type 1 livelocks in our formalism. "Permanent blocking" in [6] includes both deadlocks and type 1 livelocks. To our knowledge, type 2 livelocks have never been identified explicitly in the literature.

5. Proving the Absence of Livelocks

In verification of system correctness, we are obviously interested in showing a system to be free of all livelocks. However, not much has been published on proving the absence of livelocks in a general system. The recent work of van Lamsweerde and Sintzoff [16] introduced a method which guarantees "strong correctness" of parallel programs by strengthening the synchronization conditions. Although "strong correctness" implies the absence of starvation, their method is constructive in nature and not applicable for verification purposes. Lamport's paper [15] is the only work we are aware of which presents a technique that can be applied to prove the absence of starvation, i.e., type 1 livelocks. In proving that "something must happen," he assumed that it cannot happen on all computations and arrived at a contradiction for each computation by extending Floyd's assertion method [5].

To prove that a parallel program is correct, it is generally helpful to reduce the interleaving of actions involved, thereby making the program more transparent and correctness proofs more tractable. Such reduction techniques have been investigated by Lipton [17] and Kwong [12]. The notions of "D-routines" and "D-reductions" are due to Lipton [17]. In [12] Kwong presents a general class of reductions under which many interesting correctness properties are preserved, including, for example, the absence of deadlocks, determinacy, homing, and the Church-Rosser property. The term "preserved" is used in the sense that any conclusions obtained about the correctness of the reduced parallel program with respect to these properties are also valid for the original program. A natural question to ask is whether these reductions can be used in proving the absence of livelocks. The reader unfamiliar with reduction is referred to [12,17].

Observation 5.1 Livelocks are not preserved under reductions as defined in [12]. □

Example 5.1 Consider the parallel programs P_4 and P_4' in Figure 5.1. Note that P_4' is obtained from P_4 by reduction of the D-routines R_1 and R_2. In the initial state, P_4' is not livelockable whereas process π_2 in P_4 has a type 2 livelock along the infinite computation $(t_1(\pi_1)t_2(\pi_1))^{\omega}$. □

initially S = 1;

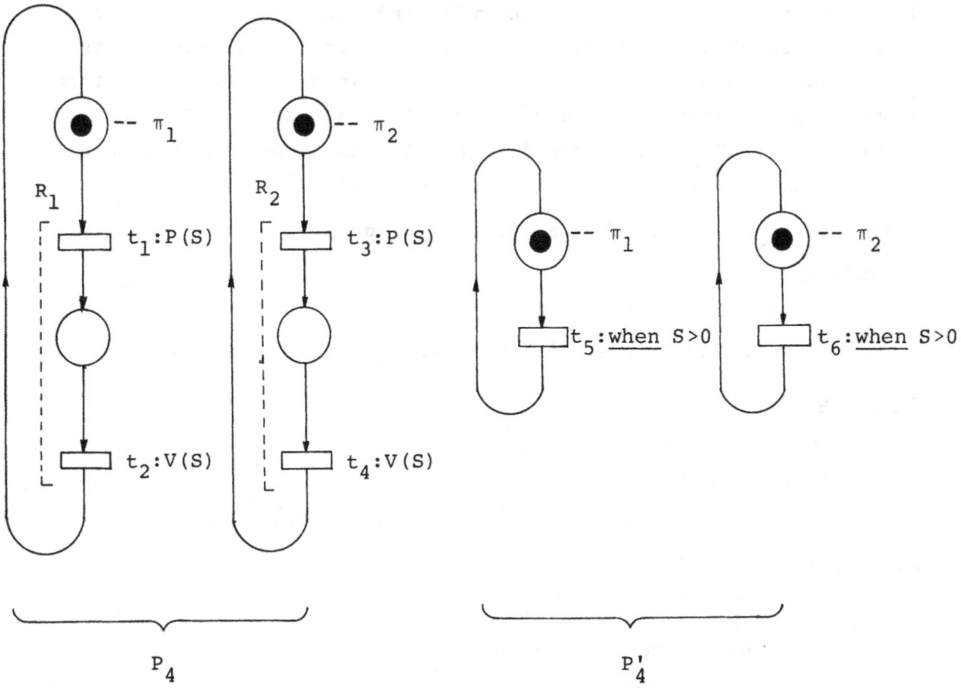

Figure 5.1 Livelocks and reductions.

In the following, we shall present two techniques for proving the absence of livelocks. One is based on the notion of problem reduction; the other is an extension of the well-founded set method for proving termination [5] and homing discussed in [10,13].

5.1 Problem Reduction Method

We shall investigate conditions for parallel programs under which the absence of deadlocks implies the absence of livelocks. For such parallel programs, the task of proving livelock-freedom is then reduced to verifying the absence of deadlocks. Various known techniques for proving deadlock-freedom, including, for example, reduction in [12,17], and homing in [10,13], can be applied directly.

Let us consider the concepts of determinism, commutativity and persistence in the study of parallel program schemata [7,8]. In our model a parallel program is deterministic if all its action functions are single-valued. Many parallel programs of interest are indeed deterministic. However, commutativity and persistence are quite severe restrictions although they play some important roles in the investigation of determinacy. Keller [9] has shown that these three properties are sufficient to guarantee that a system is Church-Rosser. We claim that they are also sufficient to guarantee that the absence of deadlocks implies the absence of livelocks.

Definition 5.1 We say that a parallel program is deterministic, if

$(\forall q, q', q'' \varepsilon Q) \quad (\forall t \ \varepsilon \ \Sigma)$

if $q \xrightarrow{t} q' \wedge q \xrightarrow{t} q''$ then $q' = q''$

commutative, if

$(\forall \ q \ \varepsilon \ Q) \quad (\forall \ t, \ t' \ \varepsilon \ \Sigma)$

if tt' and $t't$ are enabled in q

then $(\exists \ q' \ \varepsilon \ Q) \quad (q \xrightarrow{tt'} q' \wedge q \xrightarrow{t't} q')$

persistent, if

$(\forall \ q \ \varepsilon \ Q) \quad (\forall \ t, \ t' \ \varepsilon \ \Sigma)$

if t and t' are enabled in q

then tt' is enabled in q

Church-Rosser, or has the Church-Rosser property, if

$(\forall \ q, \ q'$ and $q'' \ \varepsilon \ Q)$

if $q \xrightarrow{*} q' \wedge q \xrightarrow{*} q''$

then $(\exists \ \tilde{q} \ \varepsilon \ Q) \quad (q' \xrightarrow{*} \tilde{q} \wedge q' \xrightarrow{*} \tilde{q})$.

Theorem 5.2 For a deterministic, commutative and persistent parallel program, let q be a state and π be any process. If $\neg$deadlockable$_\pi$(q) then $\neg$ livelockable$_\pi$(q). □

initially ms = mr = 0;
s = r = 0;

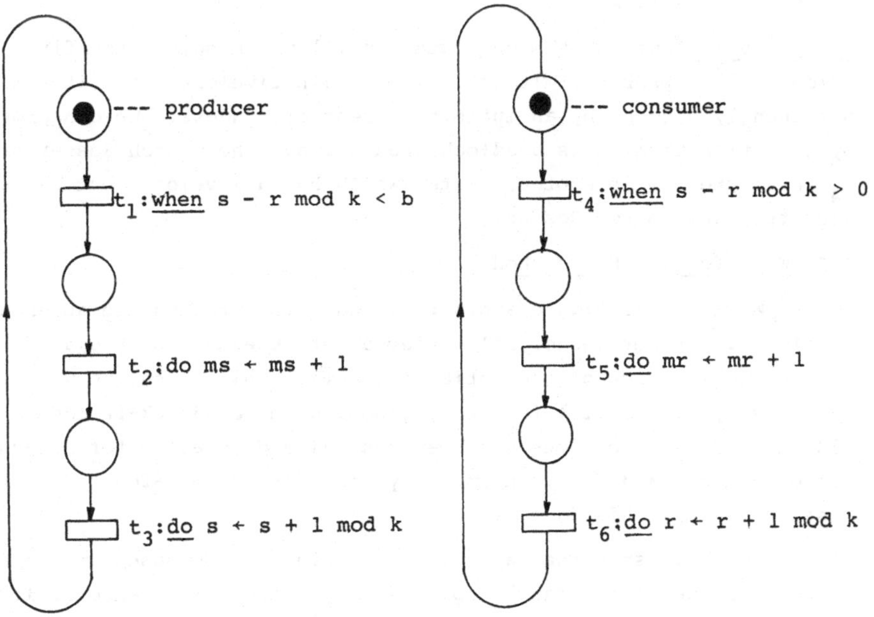

Figure 5.2 Single producer/consumer system with k > b.

Example 5.3 Consider the single producer/consumer program in Figure 5.2. The system is essentially the same as the one in [15]. We claim that it is deterministic, commutative, and persistent. The proof is fairly straightforward.

(a) Determinism is immediate since all action functions are single-valued.

(b) Commutativity is a direct consequence of the disjointness of the sets of variables which the processes can modify.

(c) Persistence can be verified by simple case analysis.

To prove that the system is free of livelocks, it suffices to verify only the absence of deadlocks because of Theorem 5.2. Note that $t_1t_2t_3$ and $t_4t_5t_6$ are D-routines. After reduction, it is obvious that the system is deadlock-free. □

Observation 5.8 Although the Church-Rosser property follows directly from determinism, commutativity, and persistence, however, it is not sufficient to guarantee that the absence of deadlocks implies the absence of livelocks. □

Example 5.3 Consider the PV system in [2] which solves the first reader/writer problem. It has a well-known livelock: a writer may be permanently blocked by an infinite stream of readers. We can prove by reduction that it is deadlock-free and has the Church-Rosser property. P_4 in Figure 5.1 is another system which has a livelock, but is deadlock-free and Church-Rosser.

5.2 Well-founded Set Method

We now investigate another approach for proving the absence of livelocks. Properties of well-ordered set were used by Floyd [5] for proving termination of sequential programs. This technique was later extended by Keller [10] for proving homing and deadlock-freedom. In [13] the homing technique has been generalized to allow for non-unique "zero states" and "zero norms" by considering well-founded sets instead of well-ordered sets.

We shall show that a similar technique, also based on properties of well-founded sets, can be applied to proving the absence of livelocks. The main idea is: if a process is in a zero state, it has to be enabled after a finite delay and remains enabled until being fired; if the norm is non-zero, then it must subsequently reach a zero state, independent of which computation it may follow.

Definition 5.2 A set of instructions C in $\tilde{\Sigma}$ is a cut set if every valid infinite computation has an infinite number of occurrences of instructions in C.

Definition 5.3 A place node is a synchronizing place if the disjunction of the enabling predicates of all its output transitions is not identically true.

Definition 5.4 Let $(W, \prec)$ be a well-founded set, C be a cut set, q be a state and π be any process. We say that a function

$$m : Q \longrightarrow W$$

is a firing norm for (q,π) provided that for any state q' reachable from q such that $q'.i(\pi)$ is a synchronizing place, the following conditions hold:

Let $\tilde{0}$ be any minimal element in W.

(1) If $m(q') = \tilde{0}$ then for any valid computation x for q' and any state sequence s for (q',x), $\psi(\pi,x) = 0$ implies $c(\pi,s)$.

(2) If $m(q') > \tilde{0}$ then for any x in Σ^+ and any state q" such that $q' \xrightarrow{x} q''$ and $\psi(\pi,x) = 0$, if x contains elements in C then $m(q') > m(q'')$.

Theorem 5.3 Let q be a state and π be any process. If there exists a firing norm for (q,π) then $\neg$ livelockable$_\pi$(q). □

6. Concluding Remarks

In this paper we have attempted

i) to illustrate, through simple examples, what constitutes a livelock in parallel programs;

ii) to present a formalization of the correctness criterion of the absence of livelocks;

iii) to introduce a classification of livelocks according to their causes of formation, and

iv) to provide two techniques for verifying livelock-freedom.

We feel that this work presents a sound foundation for studying the absence of livelocks in a manner more formal than what we usually find in the literature. Moreover, it provides the groundwork for our investigation of the effects of "fair" scheduling and the finite delay property on livelocks in abstractions and implementations of parallel programs.

Acknowledgements

The author would like to thank Robert Keller for many invaluable discussions. This paper was prepared with the financial support from the Natural Sciences and Engineering Research Council of Canada under grant A-3042.

References

[1] Ashcroft, E. A.: Proving assertions about parallel programs. J. Comp. Sys. Sci., 10, 1(Jan., 1975), 110-135.

[2] Courtois, P. J., Heymans, F. and Parnas, D. L.: Concurrent control with "readers" and "writers." Comm. ACM, 14, 10(Oct., 1971), 667-668.

[3] Dijkstra, E. W.: Solution of a problem in concurrent programming control. Comm. ACM, 8, 9(Sept., 1965), 569.

[4] Dijkstra, E. W.: Hierarchical ordering of sequential processes. Acta Informatica, 1, 2(Oct., 1971), 115-138.

[5] Floyd, R. W.: Assigning meanings to programs. Proc. Symp. in Applied Math., 19, American Math. Society (1967), 19-32.

[6] Holt, R. C.: Comments on prevention of system deadlocks. Comm. ACM, 14, 1(Jan., 1971), 36-38.

[7] Karp, R. M. and Miller R. E.: Parallel program schemata. J. Comp. Sys. Sci., 3(May, 1969), 147-195.

[8] Keller, R. M.: Parallel program schemata and maximal parallelism. J. ACM, 20, 3(July, 1973), 514-537; and J. ACM, 20, 4(Oct., 1973), 696-710.

[9] Keller, R. M.: A fundamental theorem of asynchronous parallel computation. Parallel Processing, T. Y. Feng (ed.), Springer-Verlag, Berlin (1975).

[10] Keller R. M.: Formal verification of parallel programs. Comm. ACM, 19, 7(July, 1976), 371-384.

[11] Knuth, D. E.: Additional comments on a problem in concurrent programming control. Comm. ACM, 9, 5(May, 1966), 321-322.

[12] Kwong, Y. S.: On reduction of asynchronous systems. Theoretical Computer Science, 5(1977), 25-50.

[13] Kwong, Y. S.: On reductions and livelocks in asynchronous parallel computation. Ph.D. Dissertation, Dept. of Electrical Engineering and Computer Science, Princeton University, Princeton, N. J. 08540 (1978).

[14] Kwong, Y. S.: Livelocks in parallel programs. Parts I and II. Technical reports 78-CS-15 & 16. Dept. of Applied Math., McMaster University (August, 1978).

[15] Lamport, L.: Proving the correctness of multiprocess program. IEEE Trans. Software Engineering, SE-3, 2(March, 1977), 125-143.

[16] van Lamsweerde, A. and Sintzoff, M.: Formal derivation of strongly correct parallel programs. Report R338, M.B.L.E. Research Laboratory, Brussel, Belgium (Oct., 1976).

[17] Lipton, R. J.: Reduction: A method of proving properties of parallel programs. Comm. ACM, 18, 12(Dec., 1975), 717-721.

[18] Rosen, B. K.: Correctness of parallel programs: The Church-Rosser approach. Theoretical Computer Science, 2(1976), 183-207.

[19] Slutz, D.: The flow graph schemata model of parallel computation. Rep. MAC-TR-53 (Thesis), MIT project MAC (Sept., 1968).

Denotational Semantics of Parallelism

Jerald S. Schwarz

University of Michigan
Dept. of Computer and Communication Sciences
Ann Arbor, Michigan 48109

Abstract.

This paper studies the denotational semantics of programming language constructs whose operational semantics require interleaving of computations. In particular a semantics is given for recursion equations with a convergence test. A convergence test is a nondeterministic construct which selects among expressions according to which one converges (i.e. takes on a value) first. This denotational semantics is shown to be equivalent to an operational semantics.

This paper uses the powerdomain construction to handle nondeterminism. The new idea is the treatment of parallelism. It is neccessary to add new elements to the domains in order to be able to distinguish between nonterminating computations and partial values. This distinction cannot be used in writing semantic equations. It is only used in interpreting the meaning of complete computations in which case partial values can be ignored.

1. Introduction

In this paper I examine programming language contructs which "require parallelism" in their implementation and present a denotational semantics for one such contruct. I distinguish between requiring parallelism and permitting it. Chandra[78] has considered several different nondeterministic constructs and distinguishes between those with "finite delay" and those without. Requiring parallelism corresponds to nondeterminism with finite delay. Nondeterminism in a programming language means that certain choices are not specified by the language's definition and an implementation may make arbitrary decisions. Parallelism is not as well defined a concept as nondeterminism. Roughly, a programming language permits parallelism if an implementation is allowed to interleave the evaluation of two or more expressions or statements. The simplest form of parallel construct is a statement ($S_1 \backslash\backslash S_2$) which permits execution of S_1 and S_2 to be interleaved. If an implementation is allowed to proceed by first evaluating S_1, and only when S_1 terminatesbeginning evauluation of S_2, I say that the construct permits but does not require parallelism.

In expression languages (those without assignment) parallelism is usually permitted because there is no means for evaluation of different expressions to interact and thus the potential parallelism does not lead to nondeterminism. Nondeterminism can be added to an expression language with a choice construct (see e.g. Hennesy[77] or Friedman and Wise[78]). The expression (E_1 or E_2) may have a value taken on by E_1 or a value taken on by E_2. (In the presence of nondeterminism E_1 and E_2 do not posess unique values.) This construct does not require paralellism. An implementation is allowed to always select E_1 for evaluation and ignore E_2. If it does so and evaluation of E_1 does not terminate (I will say E_1 does not converge) then evaluation of the entire expression does not terminate. Parallelism would be required if the semantics required selection of E_2 whenever E_1 did not converge and E_1 if E_2 did not converge. Such a definition would require the evaluation of E_1 and E_2 to be interleaved and selection of whichever expression converged first. A construct like this one is the main concern of this paper.

The denotational semantics of nondeterminism and parallelism has attracted much interest lately. See for example Hennesey[77], Plotkin[76], Francez et. al. [78], Milner[78]. However, to my knowledge, this paper is the first to attempt to deal with constructs which require parallelism rather than merely permitting it.

Some authors have made a distinction between fair and unfair execution (e.g. Hoare[78]) which is related to the distinction between requiring and permitting parallelism. I prefer my terminology because it indicates something about allowed implementations of a programming language. An operational semantics must indicate (i.e. make it possible to enumerate) all possible outcomes of a program. An implementation is only required to produce a single allowable result.

2. Domains

Denotational semantics invlolves finding meanings for programs in certain kinds of domains. The reader is assumed to be reasonably familiar with denotational semantics. (See, for example, Tennent[76] or Stoy[77]) In this section I will briefly describe the domains and operations required for this paper.

A domain is a partially ordered set with a least element in which increasing chains have limits. There are constructions which allow one to build new domains from old ones, and there is a method for solving recursive domain definitions involving these constructions. In order to accomplish this it is neccessary to consider a subset of partially ordered sets which meet certain further conditions but these additional requirements are not relevant to this paper. The operations required by this paper are product, function and powerdomain. Given domains A and B define:

Definition: $A \times B$ is the set of pairs (I write a pair $a \times b$) with $a \in A$ and $b \in B$. The order is given by $a_0 \times b_0 \sqsubseteq a_1 \times b_1$ iff $a_0 \sqsubseteq a_1$ and $b_0 \sqsubseteq b_1$.

Definition: $A \to B$ is the set of continuous functions from A to B with the order $f_0 \sqsubseteq f_1$ iff $(\forall a \in A)\ f_0(a) \sqsubseteq f_1(a)$.

Definition: $\mathcal{P}[A]$ is the powerdomain of A as defined by Plotkin[76]. $\mathcal{P}[A]$ consists of certain nonempty subsets of A taken modulo a certain equivalence relation. The order is related to (although not identical to) the Milner order

$$a_0 \sqsubseteq_M a_1 \text{ iff } (\forall x_0 \in a_0)(\exists x_1 \in a_1)\ x_0 \sqsubseteq x_1 \text{ and}$$
$$(\forall x_1 \in a_1)(\exists x_0 \in a_0)\ x_0 \sqsubseteq x_1$$

In fact $a_0 \sqsubseteq a_1$ can be defined by $a_0^+ \sqsubseteq_M a_1^+$ where a_0^+ and a_1^+ are appropriate members of the equivalance classes of a_0 and a_1. For more details the reader should consult Plotkin[76] or the more readable Smyth[78].

The key facts about powerdomains for this paper are:

1. There is a membership relation (written ε) between A and the powerdomain of A. This is actually defined in terms of the functions given below by $x\varepsilon a$ iff $\{\!|\, x \,|\!\} \cup a = a$.

2. Function extension. Given $f{:}A\to B$ there is an $\hat{f}{:}\ \mathcal{P}[A]\to \mathcal{P}[B]$. This will usually be written $\{\!|\ \beta : x\varepsilon\alpha\ |\!\}$ for $\widehat{(\lambda x.\beta)}\alpha$. The key fact about function extension is that if $y\varepsilon\hat{f}(a)$ there are x_0,x_1 a such that $f(x_0) \sqsubseteq y \sqsubseteq f(x_1)$.

3. There is a union function $\cup : \mathcal{P}[A] \times \mathcal{P}[A] \to \mathcal{P}[A]$ satisfying

$$x \in a_0 \cup a_1 \text{ iff}$$
$$(\exists x_0 \varepsilon a_0)(\exists x_1 \varepsilon a_1)\ x{=}x_0 \text{ or } x{=}x_1 \text{ or } x_0 \sqsubseteq x \sqsubseteq x_1 \text{ or } x_1 \sqsubseteq x \sqsubseteq x_0$$

The last two disjuncts are slightly unexpected and care is required in certain argu ments because of them.

4. Singleton. $\{\!|\ \ |\!\}{:}A \to \mathcal{P}[A]$. $x\varepsilon\{\!|\, y \,|\!\}$ iff $x{=}y$. I will write $\{\!|\, x_0, x_1, \ldots x_n \,|\!\}$ for $\{\!|\, x_0 \,|\!\} \cup \{\!|\, x_1 \,|\!\} \cup \ldots \cup \{\!|\, x_n \,|\!\}$.

5. Big-union: $\mathcal{P}[\mathcal{P}[A]]\to A$. This will always be used in expressions of the form <u>union</u> α <u>suchtthat</u> $x\varepsilon\beta$, which abbreviates big-union($\{\!|\ \alpha : x\varepsilon\beta\ |\!\}$).

We have $x\varepsilon$big-union(a) iff there are sequences $x_0 \sqsubseteq x_1 \sqsubseteq \ldots$ and $x^0 \sqsubseteq x^1 \sqsubseteq \ldots$ with $\bigsqcup x_i \sqsubseteq x \sqsubseteq \bigsqcup x^i$ and each x_i and x^i are members of some member of a.

Certain obvious extensions of there notations will also be used.

In writing semantic equations I will use $\to$ as a conditional. That is, if β is an arbitrary condition then $\beta\to\alpha_0,\alpha_1$ is α_0 if β holds and α_1 otherwise. Such a term is not neccessarily continuous in its free variables. I will limit myself to conditions which are conjunctions of terms "variable"$=\bot$ and "variable"$\sqsupset\bot$. In that case the conditional is continuous in its free variables providing it is monotonic and each α_i is continuous in its free variables.

The vertical domain of natural number $\mathbb{N}$ plays an important role in the development. It is $\{0,1,\ldots\}\cup\{\infty\}$ with the ordering $i \leq j$ iff $j{=}\infty$ or i and j are natural numbers with $i \leq j$. There is an operation + defined by

$$i + j = \begin{cases} \infty & \text{if } i{=}\infty \text{ or } j{=}\infty \\ \text{the sum of i and j} & \text{otherwise} \end{cases}$$

$\mathbb{N}$ will often be a factor in products of domains. In that case I will write $(x * i)+j$ for $x * (i+j)$. I also let + be extended (according to function extension as defined above) so that if $s\varepsilon\mathcal{P}[A\times\mathbb{N}]$, $s+j=\{\!|\ x+j : x\varepsilon s\ |\!\}$.

I will write $\bot_A$ for the least element of the domain A.

3. Recursion Equations

I now return to constructs requiring parallelism and in particular to convergence tests in recursion equations. The use of such constructs has recently been advocated by Friedman and Wise[78] who do not give any formal semantics.

The construct I use here has the syntax $(T_0 \rightarrow S_0 \,||\, T_1 \rightarrow S_1)$ where T_0, T_1, S_0 and S_1 are arbitrary expressions. The intended operational meaning of this expression is that T_0 and T_1 are evaluated in parallel at unrelated rates but with both evaluations guaranteed to make progress. If one of these evaluations terminates then the evaluation of the other is halted and a value for the original expression is obtained by evaluating the corresponding S_i. The values of the T_i are not relevant for determining the value of the expression. By appropriate choice of T's the convergence test can serve as an if-then-else. Nondeterminism is introduced because if both T's converge the selection of an S depends on the arbitrarily determined relative rates of evaluation of the T's.

The convergence test is included in a simple recursion equation language. For simplicity all defined functions are unary. I assume that we are given.

1. A flat domain A of basic values. (A domain is flat if all elements are unrelated by $\sqsubseteq$ except that $\perp_A \sqsubseteq x$ for all x.)

2. A set of primitive function symbols $\{ g, g', \ldots \}$ and an interpretation map $\mathfrak{I}$ from primitive function symbols to basic functions. A basic function is a continuous function from lists of A's to A. $\mathfrak{I}$ is extended in an obvious way to expressions made up entirely of primitive function symbols.

3. A set of defined function symbols $Fct = \{ f, f', \ldots \}$, and for each defined symbol an expression rhs(f) the right hand side of the defining equation.

Expressions are defined by the following recursive definition in which S's and T's are expressions. An expression is either:

a) The variable <u>var</u> (only one is needed because of the restriction to unary defined function symbols.)

b) An application of a primitive function symbol, $g(T_0, \ldots, T_n)$.

c) An application of a defined function symbol, f(T).

d) A convergence test, $(T_0 \rightarrow S_0 \,||\, T_1 \rightarrow S_1)$.

The set of all expressions is EXP. If T_0 and T_1 are expressions I will write $T_0 \langle T_1 \rangle$ for T_0 with T_1 substituted for the variable. The angled brackets indicate that this is a syntactic operation.

A <u>basic expression</u> is one built up from applications of primitive function symbols. A <u>ground expression</u> is one not containing <u>var</u>.

The semantics of a program will have the following pattern. The domains involved are:

A = the given domain of basic values

V = values = an extended version of A. For the moment the reader may take this as A itself.

NDV = nondeterministic values = the domain for the meaning of expressions. For the moment the reader may assume NDV= $\mathcal{P}$[V].

F = V→NDV = function meanings.

Functions take their meanings in V→NDV rather than NDV→NDV for two reasons. Firstly it slightly simplifies the technical development. Secondly, and more importantly it is more in keeping with the informal discussion. An implementation is only required to produce a single result in evaluating the argument of a function symbol and should not be required to search the entire space of all possible values.

I will give a semantics for a call-by-value interpretation of recursion equations and will assume that $\mathcal{I}$[| g |] is strict in all arguments. That is, $\mathcal{I}$[| g |] applied to any list containing $\bot_A$ is $\bot_A$.

The meaning of expressions is given by the following semantic functions which will be defined below via a mutual recursion.

$\mathcal{M}$: Fct → F

$\mathcal{E}$: EXP → V → NDV

(V as an argument of $\mathcal{E}$ gives the value for the unique variable, i.e. it is the environment.

A useful auxillary function is $\mathcal{V}$:EXP→NDV defined by $\mathcal{V}$[| T |] = $\mathcal{E}$[| T |]$\bot_V$. Given a ground expression we can take $\mathcal{V}$[| T |] as its meaning. This is a value in NDV. But an implementation will evaluate T to yield an element of A (possibly $\bot_A$ if evaluation does not terminate). Thus is order to relate the denotational semantics to permissible implementations a relation between A and NDV is needed. I call the relation possible result. If NDV is the powerdomain of A we can take membership as this relation. Since in general this will not be the case "possible result" will have to be defined when the domains are specified.

Notation. For xεA, sεNDV, x$\lessdot$s means x is a possible result of s. s:PA is the set { x : x$\lessdot$s }. PA stands for powerset of A.

4. Choosing V and NDV

The natural development within the framework of the previous section would be to take V=A, NDV= $\mathcal{P}$[A]. In this section I will show why this cannot be done. Indeed I will show that if V=A any choice of NDV such that a unique element of NDV is determined by the set of possible results is unsatisfactory. I will do this by showing that this assumption forces us to identify expressions which should be distinguished according to our operational semantics.

Assume that subsets of A determine unique elements of NDV. That is if s$\subset$A there is a unique s:NDV such that s=(S:NDV):PA. If we take NDV= $\mathcal{P}$[A] the general theory of powerdomains will force us to identify certain sets and exclude certain others. This does not affect the following discussion because any additional identifications beyond those developed below can only strengthen the argument.

If we have an expression which takes on certain values as possible results when $\underline{var}=\bot_A$ and other values when $\underline{var}\neq\bot_A$ then the element of NDV corresponding to the first set of values must be less (in the domain ordering of NDV) than the set corresponding to the second. This is a consequence of the monotonicity of $\mathcal{E}$. The set of possible results will be determined from the informal interpretation of the meaning of expressions. Consider

(I) $\quad g() \rightarrow g() \;||\; \underline{var} \rightarrow \text{LOOP}$

where LOOP is an expression whose evaluation never terminates. Let $\mathcal{R}[\![g()]\!] = gg$. If $\underline{var}=\bot_A$ the only possible result is gg. If $\underline{var}\neq\bot_A$ another possible result is $\bot_A$. Thus $\{gg\}:\text{NDV} \sqsubseteq \{gg, \bot_A\}:\text{NDV}$.

Consider next

(II) $\quad g() \rightarrow g() \;||\; g() \rightarrow \underline{var}$

Taking $\underline{var}=\bot_A$ yields $\{gg, \bot_A\}:\text{NDV} \sqsubseteq \{gg\}:\text{NDV}$. Taken together (I) and (II) show that we must identify $\{gg,\bot_A\}:\text{NDV}$ and $\{gg\}:\text{NDV}$. Thus (I) is equivalent to the expression g(). There expressions are not equivalent in the informal semantics of the language and therefore some of the assumptions which were made in the development must be abandoned.

It may be possible to give a satisfactory treatment outside the framework of the previous section but the solution I have found is to abandon the particular choice of V and NDV and the assumption that the set of possible results determines a unique element of NDV. Thus an element of NDV carries information not only about the possible results but also about how these results are obtained. This is not desirable but it seems to be necessary.

5. Semantic Equations

The previous section indicated that V and NDV must be made more complicated without indicating how this should be done. The justification of the domains given here is that they work. There may be other alternatives which work and are improvements in some way on what follows.

Recall that $\mathbb{N}$ is the vertical domain of natural numbers. Let

$$V = A \times \mathbb{N}$$

$$\text{NDV} = \mathcal{P}[V]$$

Informally $x \ast i$ is "x produced after i steps of the computation". Except for the case $x = \bot_A$ in a denotational semantics it should not matter how many steps are required to obtain a result. In that case however, $\bot_A \ast i$ for a finite i represents a partial result, a value that has not been determined after i steps, while $\bot_A \ast \infty$ represents an evaluation which does not converge. And the convergence test treats there differently. These considerations lead to the definition of $\leqslant$

$$x \lessdot a \text{ iff } \begin{cases} (\exists i \in \mathbb{N})\ x * i \in a & \text{if } x \neq \bot_A \\ \bot_A * \infty \in a & \text{if } x = \bot_A \end{cases}$$

Notice that $\lessdot$ is not continuous and cannot be used in semantic equations. This is acceptable because the sole role of $\lessdot$ is to relate the results of operational and denotational semantics.

The defining equations for $\mathcal{E}$ and $\mathcal{M}$ are

$\mathcal{E}[\![\ \underline{\text{var}}\ ]\!]v = \{\!|\ v\ |\!\}$

$\mathcal{E}[\![\ g(T_1,\ldots,T_n)\ ]\!]v$

$= \{\!|\ \mathcal{I}[\![\ g\ ]\!][a_1,\ \ldots,\ a_n] * (1 + \Sigma i_k)\ :\ a_k * i_k \in \mathcal{E}[\![\ T_k\ ]\!]v\ |\!\}$

(if n=0 the sum is 0)

$\mathcal{E}[\![\ f(T)\ ]\!]v = \underline{\text{union}}\ \mathcal{M}[\![\ f\ ]\!]u\ \underline{\text{suchthat}}\ u \in \mathcal{E}[\![\ T\ ]\!]v$

$\mathcal{E}[\![\ T_0 \to S_0\ ||\ T_1 \to S_1\ ]\!]v$

$= \underline{\text{let}}\ t_0 = \mathcal{E}[\![\ T_0\ ]\!]v\ \underline{\text{and}}\ t_1 = \mathcal{E}[\![\ T_1\ ]\!]v$

$\underline{\text{and}}\ s_0 = \mathcal{E}[\![\ S_0\ ]\!]v\ \underline{\text{and}}\ s_1 = \mathcal{E}[\![\ S_1\ ]\!]v$

$\underline{\text{in}}\ \underline{\text{union}}$

$x_0 = \bot_A\ \&\ x_1 = \bot_A \to \{\!|\ \bot_A * m\ |\!\},$

$x_0 = \bot_A\ \&\ x_1 \sqsupset \bot_A \to \{\!|\ \bot_A * m\ |\!\} \cup s_1 + m,$

$x_0 \sqsupset \bot_A\ \&\ x_1 = \bot_A \to s_0 + m \cup \{\!|\ \bot_A * m\ |\!\},$

$x_0 \sqsupset \bot_A\ \&\ x_1 \sqsupset \bot_A \to (s_0 \cup s_1) + m,$

$\underline{\text{where}}\ m = \min(i_0, i_1)$

$\underline{\text{suchthat}}\ x_0 * i_0 \in t_0\ \underline{\text{and}}\ x_1 * i_1 \in t_1$

$\mathcal{M}[\![\ f\ ]\!](a * i) = a = \bot_A \to \{\!|\ a * i\ |\!\} + 1,\ \ (\mathcal{E}[\![\ \text{rhs}(f)\ ]\!](a * 0)) + i + 1$

Notice the use of min in the clause for the convergence test. Its use means that the presence of $\bot_A * \infty$ in $\mathcal{E}[\![\ t_0\ ]\!]v$ does not in itself cause the presence of $\bot_A * \infty$ in the value of the expression. It does so only in conjunction with the presence of $\bot_A * \infty$ in $\mathcal{E}[\![\ t_1\ ]\!]v$. In other words the convergence test converges if either of its T's does.

Certain aspects of this definition are relatively arbitrary. In particular the way the steps are counted (i.e. the way the second component of V is computed) could be changed. The actual definition has been made in order to have the proofs of some theorems go through smoothly. Also the form of $\mathcal{M}$ is written to make it easy to verify that it is monotonic, i.e. that the conditional has been used properly.

It will be useful to have a notation for certain approximations of and . Define

$\mathcal{E}^0[\![\ T\ ]\!]v = \{\!|\ \bot_A * 0\ |\!\} = {}_{\text{NDV}}$

$\mathcal{E}^{n+1}[\![\ T\ ]\!]v = \ldots\ \mathcal{E}^n\ \ldots\ \mathcal{M}^n\ \ldots$

$\mathcal{M}^n[\![\ f\ ]\!]v = \ldots\ \mathcal{E}^n\ \ldots$

That is, $\mathcal{E}^{n+1}$ and $\mathcal{M}^n$ are defined using the equations for $\mathcal{E}$ and $\mathcal{M}$ with appropriate substitutions. $\mathcal{E}$ and $\mathcal{M}$ are the limits of these approximations. An important fact is

Lemma: (finiteness of approximants) $\mathcal{E}^n[\![T]\!]v$ is a finite set and if $v=a\times i$ for finite i then all members of $\mathcal{E}^n[T]v$ have the form $x\times j$ for finite j.

Proof: A simple induction on n. ∎

6. Implications and Examples.

To aid in understanding the definition of $\mathcal{E}$ it is useful to consider some examples.

Example 1. Suppose rhs(f)=f(var). We expect that f should have result $\perp_A$ for any input. In fact

$$\mathcal{M}[\![f]\!](a\times i) = a=\perp_A \rightarrow \{ a\times i \}+1,\ \mathcal{E}[\![f(\underline{var})]\!](a\times 0) + i + 1$$
$$= a=\perp_A \rightarrow \{ a\times i \}+1,\ \mathcal{M}[\![f]\!](a\times 0) + i + 1$$

It is not hard to see that the least fixed point of this equation is

$$\mathcal{M}[\![f]\!](a\times i) = \{\!|\ \perp_A\times\infty\ |\!\}$$

Thus $(\mathcal{M}[\![f]\!](a\times i) : PA) = \{\perp_A\}$.

Example 2. Assume f as in example 1. Consider T=(g() → g() || $\underline{var}$ → f($\underline{var}$)). This is essentially (I) of section 4. Let $\mathcal{R}[\![g()]\!]$=gg. Using the definition of $\mathcal{E}$ we get $\mathcal{E}[\![T]\!](\perp_A\times i) : PA = \{gg\}$. This does not depend on whether i is finite or not. For $x\neq\perp_A$, $v=x\times i$ we get

$$\mathcal{E}[\![g()]\!]v = \{\!|\ gg\times 0\ |\!\}$$
$$\mathcal{E}[\![\underline{var}]\!]v = \{\!|\ x\times i\ |\!\}$$
$$\mathcal{E}[\![T]\!]v = (\mathcal{E}[\![g()]\!]v + 0)\cup(\mathcal{E}[\![f(var)]\!]v +1)$$
$$= \{\!|\ gg\times 0,\ \perp_A\times\infty\ |\!\}$$

Thus $\mathcal{E}[\![T]\!]v : PA = \{gg, \perp_A\}$.

Example 3. Consider f with rhs(f)=(g() → g() || f(var) → g()). Note that $\mathcal{E}^n[\![g()]\!]v = \{\!|\ gg\times 0\ |\!\}$ for all n > 0 and $\mathcal{E}^0[\![rhs(f)]\!]v = \{\!|\ \perp_A\times 0\ |\!\}$ for all v. Using these facts we can determine for all $a\neq\perp_A$

$$\mathcal{E}^{n+2}[\![rhs(f)]\!](a\times i)$$
$$= \underline{let}\ t_0=s_0=s_1=\{\!|\ gg\times 0\ |\!\}\ \underline{and}\ t_1=\mathcal{E}^n[\![rhs(f)]\!](a\times 0) + 1$$
$$\underline{in}\ \ldots$$
$$= \underline{union}\ x_1=\perp_A \rightarrow \{\!|\ gg\times 0\ |\!\}\cup\{\!|\ \perp_A\times 0\ |\!\},$$
$$x_1\sqsupset\perp_A \rightarrow \{\!|\ gg\times 0\ |\!\}\cup\{\!|\ gg\ \ 1\ |\!\}$$
$$\underline{suchthat}\ x_1\times i_1 \in \mathcal{E}^n[\![rhs(g)]\!](a\times 0)$$

Thus

$$\mathcal{E}^2[\![rhs(f)]\!](a\times i) = \{\!|\ gg\times 0,\ \perp_A\times 0\ |\!\}$$
$$\mathcal{E}^4[\![rhs(f)]\!](a\times i) = \mathcal{E}^6[\![rhs(f)]\!](a\times i) = \ldots = \{\!|\ gg\times 0,\ gg\times 1,\ \perp_A\times 0\ |\!\}$$

Example 4. Let rhs(f)=(g() → g() || f($\underline{var}$) → f($\underline{var}$)). Proceeding as in example 3 we find for $a\neq\perp_A$

$\mathcal{E}^{n+2}[\![\text{rhs}(f)]\!](a \times i)$

$= \underline{\text{let}}\ t_0=s_0= \{\!| gg \times 0 |\!\}$

$\underline{\text{and}}\ t_1=s_1= \mathcal{E}^{n}[\![\text{rhs}(f)]\!](a \times 0) + i + 1$

$\underline{\text{in}} \ldots$

$= \underline{\text{union}}\ t_1=\bot_A \rightarrow \{\!| gg \times 0,\ \bot_A \times 0 |\!\}$,

$t_1 \sqsupset \bot_A \rightarrow \{\!| gg \times 0 |\!\} \cup \mathcal{E}^{n}[\![\text{rhs}(f)]\!](a \times 0) + i + 1 + 1$

$\underline{\text{suchthat}}\ t_1 \times i_1 \in \mathcal{E}^{n}[\![\text{rhs}(f)]\!](a \times 0) = i + 1$

Thus $\mathcal{E}^{0}[\![\text{rhs}(f)]\!](a \times i) = \{\!| \bot_A \times 0 |\!\}$

$\mathcal{E}^{2}[\![\text{rhs}(f)]\!](a \times i) = \{\!| gg \times 0,\ \bot_A \times 0 |\!\}$

$\mathcal{E}^{4}[\![\text{rhs}(f)]\!](a \times i) = \{\!| gg \times 0,\ \bot_A \times 0,\ gg \times i+2,\ \bot_A \times i+2 |\!\}$

etc.

When n is increased to infinity and the limit taken $\bot_A \times \infty$ and $gg \times \infty$ are added in.

7. Bounded choice

NDV contains some elements which represent an unbounded choice. For example if there were a T with $\mathcal{V}[\![T]\!] = \{\!| \bot_A \times 0,\ a_1 \times 0,\ a_2 \times 0,\ \ldots |\!\}$ that T would be an expression which could take on any of an infinite number of values and whose evaluation would be guaranteed to terminate. It is not obvious whether such a T can exist. In this section I will show that it can not.

Lemma: a) If $\mathcal{E}^{n+1}[\![T]\!]v_1$ contains more members than $\mathcal{E}^{n}[\![T]\!]v_0$ then $\bot_A \times i \in \mathcal{E}^{n}[\![T]\!]v_0$ for some $i \geq n$. (Note that v_0 and v_1 can be different.)

b) If $\mathcal{M}^{n+1}[\![f]\!]v_1$ contains more members than $\mathcal{M}^{n}[\![f]\!]\, v_0$ then $\bot_A \times i \in \mathcal{M}^{n+1}[\![f]\!]v_0$

Proof: An induction on n. Within each n a structural induction on T. The details are left to the reader. The case for application of primitive function symbols relies on the assumption that $\mathcal{J}[\![g]\!]$ is strict. ∎

Lemma(Bounded Choice) : If $\mathcal{V}[\![T]\!]$:PA contains infinitely many members then $\bot_A \in \mathcal{V}[\![T]\!]$.

Proof:immediate from the previous lemma. ∎

8. Operational Semantics

Examples such as those in section 7 can give some confidence in the reasonableness of the denotational semantics. In this section that confidence is strengthened by showing that the denotational and a certain operational semantics are equivalent.

The operational semantics is based on expressions and reductions in the usual manner (see e.g. Manna[74]) with a special reduction rule for the convergence test. Let T be a ground expression (recall this means it does not contain var) containing the expression U. The possible reductions are:

AP. U=f(B) and B is a basic expression. (Recall this means B is built from primitive function symbols.) Replace the occurance of U in T by rhs(f)$\langle G \rangle$.

TST. $U = (T_0 \to S_0 \,||\, T_1 \to S_1)$

TST_0. If T_0 is a basic expression replace the occurance of U by S_0.

TST_1. If T_1 is a basic expression replace the occurance of U by S_1.

Proposition: A ground expression is reducible (i.e. can be reduced) iff it is not a basic expression.

Proof: Immediate. ∎

This reduction system is not Church-Rosser because both TST_0 and TST_1 can be applicable to the same expression and there is no connection between S_0 and S_1.

Definition: $T_0 \Rightarrow T_1$ means that T_1 is obtainable from T_0 by performing 0, 1 or more reductions.

Definition: A potential value (note the distinction between possible and potential) of a ground expression T is $\mathcal{I}[\![B]\!]$ where B is a basic expression such that $T \Rightarrow B$.

Definition: A ground expression T can diverge if there is an infinite sequence of expressions $T=T_0 \Rightarrow T_1 \Rightarrow T_2 \Rightarrow \cdots$ such that if a subexpression of T_i is reducible it is either reduced or eliminated (by TST or AP with var not on the rhs) in going to T_{i+1}. This is not completely formal but it should be clear. A completely formal definition requires residuals or some other method of relating subexpression between the T_i's.

I am now ready to give the operational semantics.

Definition: Let T be a ground expression. Let R = { a : a is a potential value of T} .

$$\mathcal{O}[\![T]\!] = \begin{cases} R \cup \{\bot_A\} & \text{if T can diverge} \\ R & \text{otherwise} \end{cases}$$

Before stating the main result of this section and the paper I state

Lemma(Substitution): If B is a basic expression then for all v

$\mathcal{E}[\![T\langle B\rangle]\!]v = \mathcal{E}[\![T]\!](\mathcal{I}[\![B]\!] \times i)$ for some finite i. (The same i for all v)

Proof: Structural induction on T. Details left to the reader.

The main result of this paper is that the operational and denotation semantics are equivalent.

Theorem: For all ground expressions T, $\mathcal{O}[\![T]\!] = \mathcal{V}[\![T]\!]:PA$

Proof: I will only sketch the main ideas of the proof. There are four cases to be considered.

Case 1. $a \neq \bot_A$, $a \in \mathcal{O}[\![T]\!]$. I must how that $a \triangleleft \mathcal{V}[\![T]\!]$. Since a is a potential value of T there is a sequence of reductions which reaches a basic expression which is interpreted as a. The proof of this case is by induction on the number of steps in this sequence.

Case 2. $\bot_A \in \mathcal{O}[\![T]\!]$. I must show that $\bot_A{*}\,\infty \in \mathcal{V}[\![T]\!]$. The proof shows that if T can diverge then for each n there is an $m \geq n$ with $\bot_A{*}\,m \in \mathcal{V}^n[\![T]\!]$.

Case 3. $a \neq \bot_A$, $a \triangleleft \mathcal{V}[\![T]\!]$. I must show that a is a potential value of T. By induction on n I show that if $a \triangleleft \mathcal{V}^n[\![T]\!]$ there is a basic expression B with $\mathcal{I}[\![B]\!]=a$ such that $T \Rightarrow B$. The proof of this case uses the flatness of A.

Case 4. $\bot_A \triangleleft \mathcal{V}[\![T]\!]$. I must show that T can diverge. There is an algorithm which given a T with $\bot_A \leq \mathcal{V}[\![T]\!]$ gives another expression T' such that $T \Rightarrow T'$ and $\bot_A \leq \mathcal{V}[\![T']\!]$. Further if this algorithm is repeatedly applied the reduction sequence satisfies the requirement that all reducible subexpressions are eventually reduced or eliminated. The correctness of this algorithm depends on the bounded choice lemma.

This completes the proof of the equivalence of operational and denotational semantics of recursion equations. ∎

9. Conclusion

I have shown how to give a semantics to some constructs which require parallelism for their implementation. In particular I have given a semantics for a version of recursion equations containing a convergence test. The main idea of this semantics is to restructure the domains involved so that a distinction can be made between a value representing an infinite computation and a partial value. In the usual kinds of denotational semantics bottom is used for both these purposes. Making these distinctions leads to certain technical problemswhich have been solved for the particular language considered here.

The reader may wonder whether the techniques of this paper are more generally applicable. I believe they are and that similar semantics can be found for other such constructs. In particular with regard to recursion equations it would be useful to be able to remove the requirement that primitive functions be strict and that the domain A be flat. Unfortunately the strictness of the primitive functions plays a critical role in the proof of the bounded choice lemma which in turn is needed for the proof of the equivalance of operational and denotational semantics.

10. References

Chandra, A. [78] Computable nondeterministic functions, 19th Symp. on Foundations of Computer Science, Ann Arbor

Francez, N. & Hoare, C.A.R. & Lehmann, D & de Roever, W. P. [78] Semantics of nondeterminism, concurrency and communication

Friedman, D. & Wise, D. [78] A Note on conditional expressions, CACM 21, pp. 931-933

Hennessy, M. C. B. [77] The semantics of call-by-value and call-by-name in a nondeterministic environment, Computer Science Dept. Univ. of Waterloo CS-77-13

Hoare, C. A. R. [78] Communciating sequential processes, CACM 21, pp. 666-677

Manna, Zohar [74] Mathematical Theory of Computation, McGraw-Hill

Milner, Robin [78] Synthesis of communicating behavior, in Mathematical foundations of computer science 1978, Springer-Verlag Lecture Notes in Computer Science No. 64

Plotkin, G. [76] A powerdomain construction, SIAM Journal of Computing 5

Smyth, M. B. [78] Power domains, Jour. of Comp. and System Sciences 16, pp. 23-36

Stoy, J. [77] Denotational semantics of Programming Languages, MIT press

Tennent, R. D. [76] The denotational semantics of programming languages, CACM 19 pp. 437-453

An Approach to Fair Applicative Multiprogramming

Daniel P. Friedman
David S. Wise
Computer Science Department
Indiana University
Bloomington, IN 47405/USA

Abstract

This paper presents a brief formal semantics of constructors for ordered sequences (*cons*) and for unordered multisets (*frons*) followed by a detailed operational semantics for both. A multiset is a generalization of a list structure which lacks order *a priori*; its order is determined by the *a posteriori* migration of computationally convergent elements to the front. The introductory material includes an example which demonstrates that a multiset of yet-unconverged values and a timing primitive may be used to implement the scheduler for an operating system in an applicative style. The operational semantics, given in PASCAL-like code, is described in two detailed steps: first a uniprocessor implementation of the *cons*/*frons* constructors and the *first*/*rest* probes, followed by an extension to a multiprocessor implementation. The center of either implementation is the EUREKA structure transformation, which brings convergent elements to the fore while preserving order of shared structures. The multiprocessor version is designed to run on an arbitrary number of processors with only one semaphore but makes heavy use of the **sting** memory store primitive. **Stinging** is a conditional store operation which is carried out independently of its dispatching processor so that shared nodes may be somewhat altered without interfering with other processors. An appendix presents the extension of this code to a "fair" implementation of multisets.

Introduction

This paper is directly motivated by a practical implementation of a constructor function for applicative multiprogramming [2]. The new constructor, dubbed *frons*, offers a new perspective on the problem of synchronizing inherently asynchronous computation, by allowing asynchronous processes to be assembled into an unordered structure which behaves like an ordered structure upon access. The order is determined by their relative order of convergence.

The demands of a fair implementation (presented only as the appendix) for an environment of asynchronous processors have been difficult to master. The solution has prompted the invention of new synchronization primitives for imperative (von Neumann-style) programming, so that this implementation is not even practical on current hardware. In particular, we present here the programs which prompted the invention of the **sting** conditional store instruction [3], whose implementation is tractable.

What follows, then, is an operational introduction to the *frons* (and *cons*) constructor using the **sting** primitive for PASCAL-like languages. There are six sections: Formal Semantics; Examples (which presents a scheduler for an operating system); a section on implementing the constructors and the probing functions, *first* and *rest*, which depend on EUREKA. EUREKA is the centerpiece of the operational semantics, because *it* is responsible for uniformly evaluating several suspended evaluations and transforming the unordered structures into "slightly ordered" ones while preserving the formal semantics. The bulk of the paper appears in the last three sections: a uniprocessor EUREKA; an extension of that to a multiprocessor EUREKA; and finally some conclusions.

Formal Semantics

The *frons* constructor is introduced elsewhere [2] where its semantics and use are developed in greater detail. (The Latin word "frons" means "leafy branch" and is motivated by the definition of *Fern* there.) We present its definition in a form similar to LISP's axioms [6] before proceeding to a formal structure semantics.

$$\text{first:NIL} = \bot = \text{rest:NIL}. \qquad (1)$$

Let z = cons:<x y> then

$$\text{atom:z} = \mathit{false} = \text{null:z}; \qquad (2)$$
$$\text{first:z} = \text{x}; \qquad (3)$$
$$\text{rest:z} = \text{y}. \qquad (4)$$

Let z = frons:<x y> then we define the same primitives

$$\text{atom:z} = \mathit{false} = \text{null:z}; \qquad (5)$$

$$\text{first:z} = \begin{cases} \text{x, if } x \neq \bot \text{ ;} \\ \text{first:y, if first:y} \neq \bot \text{ ;} \\ \text{x, if y = NIL ;} \end{cases} \quad \left\{ \begin{array}{l} \text{where the choice made} \\ \text{must be the same as} \\ \text{that made for } \mathit{rest}. \end{array} \right. \qquad (6)$$

$$\text{rest:z} = \begin{cases} \text{y, if } x \neq \bot \text{ ;} \\ \text{frons:}\langle \text{x rest:y} \rangle\text{, if first:y} \neq \bot\text{;} \\ \text{y, if y = NIL ;} \end{cases} \quad \left\{ \begin{array}{l} \text{where the choice made} \\ \text{must be the same as} \\ \text{that made for } \mathit{first}. \end{array} \right. \qquad (7)$$

The binding of z to a particular structure requires that the choices made in (6) and (7) must be the same when both x and first:y converge. This semantics is slightly different from [2] because we have included a third alternative; its effect is that cons:<x NIL> = frons:<x NIL>; singleton unordered structures evaluate to singleton lists.

Just as the purpose of *cons* is to construct ordered structures, so also does *frons* construct unordered structures. Since the content of either form of data structure may be suspended, we may use behavior of these postponed evaluations to advantage in case one or more of them might diverge. In the definitions above we allow that the convergent elements make their way to the front of the unordered structures, or *multisets*, and once they arrive they stay! The structure therefore behaves like a sequence upon probing.

Definition: $\text{STRICTIFY}(X,Y) = Y \text{ if } X \neq \bot;$

$$\text{AMB}(X,Y) = \begin{cases} X, & \text{if } X \neq \bot; \\ Y, & \text{if } Y \neq \bot. \end{cases}$$

The function AMB is from McCarthy [6] where it is introduced as a non-deterministic choice operation. We shall only use it embedded *within* a structure to determine order, so that we only calculate AMB once--as in called-by-delayed value [8]---for any structure.

We define the set $\mathcal{D}$ of all computational structures to include the set of atomic items $\mathcal{A}$ (and whatever semantics one likes for them) and the set of structures $\mathcal{S}$ which are quadruples (or trivially NIL).

$$\mathcal{D} = \mathcal{A} \cup \mathcal{S};$$

$$\mathcal{S} = \{\text{NIL}\} \cup (\mathcal{D}^{+} \times \mathcal{S}^{+} \times \{\text{TRUE},\text{FALSE}\}^{+} \times \omega) ;$$

where ω is the set of natural numbers; the fourth element is only used as an index on the quadruple whose effect on semantics is to guarantee uniqueness of structure. In any implementation no two quadruples will have the same index (analogous to memory address). Thus, the domain equations for our primitives follow:

null: $\mathcal{S} \to \{\mathit{true}, \mathit{false}\}$;

cons: $\mathcal{D}^{+} \times \mathcal{S}^{+} \to \mathcal{S}$;

frons: $\mathcal{D}^{+} \times \mathcal{S}^{+} \to \mathcal{S}$;

first: $\mathcal{S} \to \mathcal{D}^{+}$;

rest: $\mathcal{S} \to \mathcal{S}^{+}$;

strictify: $\mathcal{D} \times \mathcal{D}^{+} \to \mathcal{D}^{+}$.

In the following definition the occurrence of "$i \in \omega$" denotes a new integer which has not occurred in any other quadruple. As mentioned above, for any structures indexed by such an i as a fourth element, an AMB expression as the third element is evaluated *at most once* and its evaluation is delayed until accessed [1] (i.e. call-by-need, call-by-delayed value or lazy evaluation is implied [9,8,4]).

Definition:

$$I[\![\text{null:f}]\!] = \begin{cases} \text{TRUE, if } I[\![\text{f}]\!] = \text{NIL, the trivial element of } S; \\ \text{FALSE, if } I[\![\text{f}]\!] \text{ is a quadruple in } S. \end{cases}$$

```
I⟦cons:pair⟧ = (I⟦1:pair⟧, I⟦2:pair⟧, TRUE, i) where i ε ω.

I⟦frons:pair⟧ = (I⟦1:pair⟧,
                 I⟦2:pair⟧,
                 AMB (STRICTIFY(I⟦1:pair⟧, TRUE),
                      STRICTIFY(I⟦first:2:pair⟧, FALSE)),
                 i) where i ε ω.

I⟦first:f⟧ = FIRST(I⟦f⟧) where
               FIRST(NIL) = ⊥;
               FIRST((u, v, TRUE, j)) = u;
               FIRST((u, v, FALSE, j)) = FIRST(v); and
               FIRST((u, NIL, b, j)) = u.

I⟦rest:f⟧ = REST(I⟦f⟧) where
               REST(NIL) = ⊥;
               REST((u, v, TRUE, j)) = v;
               REST((u, v, FALSE, j)) =
                 (u,
                  REST(v),
                  AMB(STRICTIFY(u, TRUE),
                      STRICTIFY(FIRST(REST(v)), FALSE)),
                  i) where i ε ω; and
               REST((u, NIL, b, j)) = NIL.

I⟦strictify:pair⟧ = I⟦2:pair⟧, if I⟦1:pair⟧ ≠ ⊥.
```

Notation:

$$I[\![1\text{:f}]\!] = I[\![\text{first:f}]\!];$$

$$I[\![2\text{:f}]\!] = I[\![\text{first:rest:f}]\!];$$

$$I[\![\langle\rangle]\!] = \text{NIL} = I[\![\{\}]\!];$$

$$I[\![\langle x_1\ x_2\ \ldots\ x_k\rangle]\!] = I[\![\text{cons:}\langle x_1\ \langle x_2\ \ldots\ x_k\rangle\rangle]\!];$$

$$I[\![\{x_1\ x_2\ \ldots\ x_k\}]\!] = I[\![\text{frons:}\langle x_1\ \{x_2\ \ldots\ x_k\}\rangle]\!];$$

$$I[\![\{x_1 \mid x_2\ \ldots\ x_k\}]\!] = I[\![\text{cons:}\langle x_1\ \{x_2\ \ldots\ x_k\}\rangle]\!].$$

Examples

Two examples will help explain the applications of *frons* and multisets. In both cases correctness proofs will follow known recursion-induction techniques; a stronger correctness will follow when fairness is established.

The first example demonstrates the power of encapsulating the choice (or AMB operator) within the structure, because a familiar function definition does not change from its traditional form in order to introduce nondeterminism. The conventional operator for taking the disjunction of arbitrarily many arguments is *or*.

```
or:disjuncts ≡
  if null:disjuncts then false
  elseif first:disjuncts then true
  else or:rest:disjuncts   .
```

If *or* is applied to the sequence of truth values $\langle b_1\ b_2 \ldots b_k \rangle$ where $B = \{$*true*,*false*$\}$ and $b_i \in B^+$ then its value is the desired value in B unless $\bot$ precedes *true* in that list. If *or* is applied to the multiset of values $\{b_1\ b_2 \ldots b_k\}$, however, its result will be in B whenever *true* is in that list of values or whenever $\bot$ is not, regardless of the order. Thus the multiset as an argument structure implements the *symmetric or* [7] without redefinition of the function.

As an intermediate example we consider the conversion of a sequence of (perhaps not yet converged) elements into a multiset. In the scheduler example below the need arises for the function *scramble* which introduces disorder into the structure of potential solutions of (what is stated as) a sequence of jobs.

```
scramble:seq ≡
  if null:seq then {}
  else frons:<first:seq scramble:rest:seq>.
```

The second example is the timing of independent simultaneous processes as a distributed processor might do for scheduling purposes. The problem is to take a sequence of (unevaluated) expressions as an argument and to return those (still not completely evaluated) which do not converge after t units of "time". We shall develop its solution as a series of functions, the proof of which would establish the validity of the entire solution. With the intermediate example we may anticipate that the input argument, *exprlist*, may as well be a multiset.

The "function" *clock* is a constant-valued function whose implementation, like *strictify* (in our call-by-need environment) cannot be optimized; we require it to consume t units of "time" before it converges:

```
clock:t ≡
  if zerop:t then ALARM
  else clock:pred:t .
```

(zerop:n = *true* if n = 0; pred:n = n-1 if n > 0.)

We do not suggest that the *clock* function need be perfectly accurate any more than the peripheral hardware clock on actual computers will interrupt at future, predictable machine cycles. We do assume that for relatively larger settings of its argument, it will converge in times asymtotically proportional to those settings. Such a *clock* will be added to the multiset of unconverged values.

We partition the resulting multiset by separating all elements up to the occurrence of ALARM from the remainder. If the implementation of multisets is fair then we may be assured that its prefix consists of the values of the expressions which converged within the time-limit set.

```
partition:M ≡
  if same:<first:M ALARM> then < <> rest:M >
  else buildup:<first:M  partition:rest:M>;
buildup:<value pair> ≡ < cons:<value 1:pair>  2:pair>.
```

Finally, if *exprlist* is the sequence of (suspended or perhaps already evaluated) expressions, the invocation

```
partition:frons:<clock:t scramble:exprlist>
```

returns a sequence of two items which we shall call "done-pending". The first item in the pair is the list of values which converged within *t* units of time; the second item is the multiset of those which *might* not converge. The accuracy of the timing partition is somewhat dependent on the size of *exprlist* compared to *t*, the clock setting. We must take care to use sufficiently large values of *t* compared to its size in order to ensure equitable timing (just as one shouldn't clock processors with just a few nanoseconds).

The solution to the originally stated problem is then 2:done-pending which may be viewed as a sequence. If viewed as a multiset,

```
frons:<clock:t'  2:done-pending>
```

provides resumption of the unconverged computations for *t'* more units of time, just as a scheduler might resume these processes.

Implementing construction

In this section we present the code for the constructors, *cons* and *frons*. The implementation is temporarily incomplete, because we say little about the implementation of the probing functions, *first* and *rest*. We can implement *null*, however, as a predicate which tests a

```
type
  pointer = ↑node;
  field = packed record
             exists : Boolean;
             value : pointer
           end;
  more = packed record
            sinker : Boolean;
            d : field
          end;
  node = packed record
            case atom : Boolean of
              true : (pname : packed array[1..6] of char);
              false : (a : field;
                     [ birthdate : smallint; ]
                       next : more)
          end
```

Figure 1. Type Declarations.

```
function cons(X,Y : pointer) : pointer;
var Q : pointer;
    NQ : node;
begin
  NQ.a := SUSPEND(X);
  NQ.d := SUSPEND(Y);
  NQ.sinker := true;
[ NQ.birthdate := TIME; ]
  NQ.atom := false;
  NEW(Q);
  sting Q with NQ;
  cons := Q
end
```

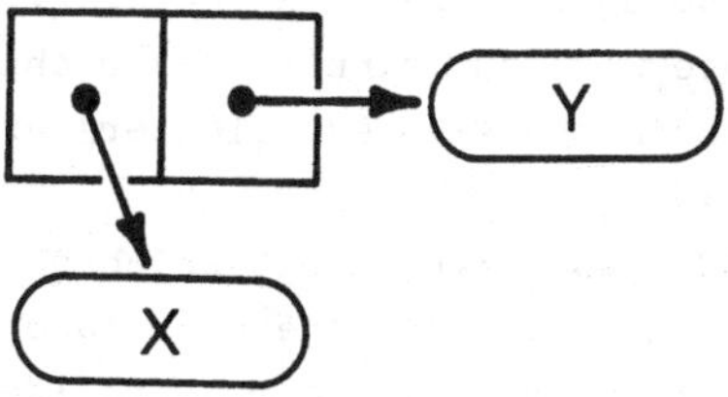


```
function frons(X,Y : pointer) : pointer;
var Q : pointer;
    NQ : node;
begin
  NQ.a := SUSPEND(X);
  NQ.d := SUSPEND(Y);
  NQ.sinker := false;
[ NQ.birthdate := TIME; ]
  NQ.atom := false;
  NEW(Q);
  sting Q with NQ;
  frons := Q
end
```

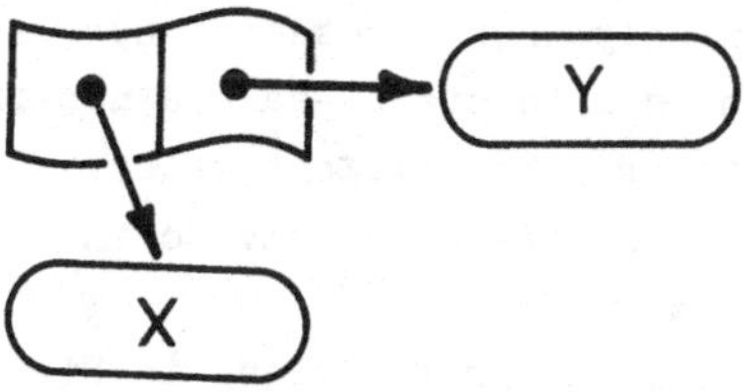

Figure 2. The Constructors.

pointer to see that it does *not* refer to a node allocated by these constructors.

We use the notation of PASCAL for the declarations and most control structures. A major exception is the **sting** operation [3] which we shall explain in two steps. For the moment we define **sting** as the only memory store operation; later it will be extended to be a conditional store operation. That is, if P is a pointer (or a memory reference) then the operation "**sting** P **with** value" is synonomous with PASCAL's "P↑ := value" assignment. Also the form "**sting** P **in** field **with** value" is synonomous with PASCAL's field assignment "P↑.field := value". All memory store operations are implemented with **sting** so that the only variable which appears to the left of the ":=" operator is a local register/variable. (As we move toward a multiprocessing environment this distinction becomes important.) The only use of the "↑" operator is, therefore, as a memory fetch. Thus, all memory operations are flagged either by "**sting**" or by "↑".

The data *type* declaration in Figure 1 prescribes the sort of node which will represent sequences and multisets. A node is either an *atom* or it is *constructed*: constructed nodes are either *sinkers* (allocated by *cons*) or *floaters* (allocated by *frons*). Floaters may eventually be *promoted* to be sinkers when necessary and when certain convergence properties are met, but sinkers never change. Sinkers are represented by rectangles in the figures; floaters are drawn as ripples (i.e. wavy rectangles).

A node has a *sinker* bit which characterizes its "shape". It also has two pointer fields, the *a-field* and the *d-field* (corresponding to *car* and *cdr*) which may refer to *exist*ent values or to *suspensions* [1]. An *exists* bit on *each* field determines whether it refers to a value or to a suspension. (In the original definition of a suspension we described it as a computation which would be coerced through complete evaluation only when necessary; here we envision that such an evaluation be fragmented into steps--each a non-trivial but finite advance from the last toward the *exist*ent value.) A node also contains a *birthdate* field which is necessary only to the fair implementation presented in the appendix.

The constructor functions in Figure 2 each allocates a fresh node, using PASCAL's *NEW* primitive, and fills all its fields appropriately. Since both the a-field and the d-field are initially filled with suspensions of the two parameters, X and Y, both these functions necessarily converge upon the successful allocation by NEW. (The fact that there is but one memory **sting** in order to fill this node is of interest in

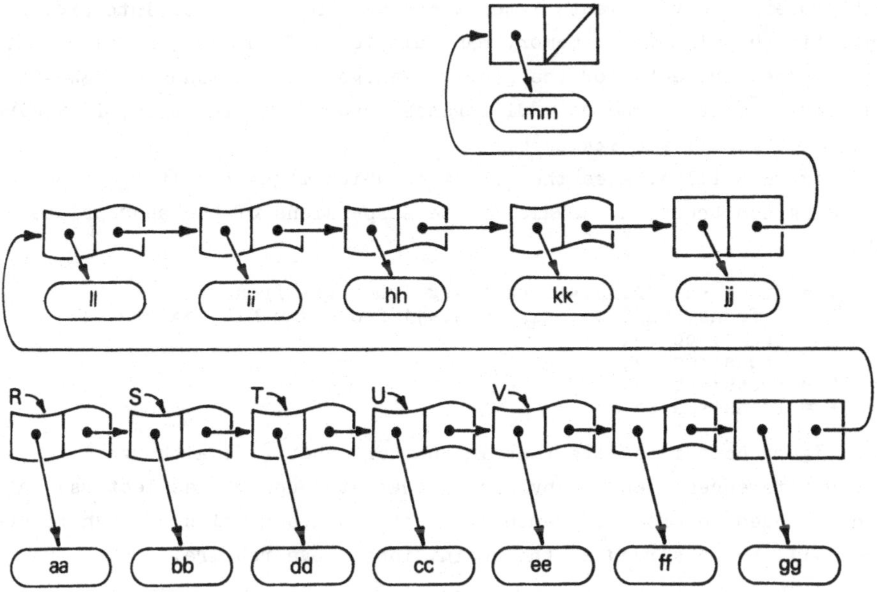

Figure 3. A fern structure referenced by R, with shared references by S, T, U, and V.

```
function first(F : pointer) : pointer;
var NF : node;
begin
  NF := EUREKA(F);
  if NF.a.exists
    then first := NF.a.value
    else NF.a := COERCE(NF.a);
         sting F [ unless a.exists ] in a with NF.a;
         first := F↑.a.value
  fi
end

function rest(F : pointer) : pointer;
var NF : node;
begin
  NF := EUREKA(F);
  if NF.d.exists
    then rest := NF.d.value
    else NF.d := COERCE(NF.d);
         sting F [ unless d.exists ] in d with NF.d;
         rest := F↑.d.value
  fi
end
```

Figure 4. Probing Functions for a Uniprocessor [or Multiprocessor].

multiprocessor environments later where we want to reduce **interprocessor** contention by minimizing memory manipulation. We do not, however, anticipate the requirements for the storage manager--the demands of NEW--in that environment.) The only difference between the functions in Figure 2 is the setting of the *sinker* bit.

Figure 3 illustrates the structure which might result from the following construction. Ovals denote suspensions of the appropriate values.

```
V = frons:<ee frons:<ff cons:<gg frons:<ℓℓ frons:<ii
       frons:<hh frons:<kk cons:<jj frons:<mm NIL>>>> >>>>>;
U = frons:<cc V>;
T = frons:<dd U>;
S = frons:<bb T>;
R = frons:<aa S>.
```

This figure coincides with that in another paper [2], although more shared references (denoted by single-character upper case letters) have been included in order to demonstrate that the semantics of such references will be preserved as the definitions above require.

Observation 1: The functions *cons* and *frons* always return a value, a pointer to an unshared node.

Observation 2: The function *cons* allocates a sinker, and the function *frons* allocates a floater.

The definitions of the (uniprocessor) user functions *first* and *rest* in Figure 4 [without bracketed code] are straightforward except for the function EUREKA. EUREKA is a system function upon which *all* the semantic problems fall and--in the case of concurrent processors--which will bear the responsibility for synchronization; the remainder of this paper is devoted to it. Briefly, EUREKA will search all floaters up to and including the first sinker (if there is one) accessible through successive d-fields. If there is more than one such node, it finds one which has a convergent a-field and then alters the data structure (consistently with Equations 3, 4, 6 and 7) so that the node at the front of the structure *is* a sinker; its value is the content of that node. EUREKA amounts to a simple memory fetch if that node is already a sinker. After EUREKA has returned the contents of the first node, it only remains to *coerce* any suspension which might remain in the a-field (d-field) which *first* (*rest*) must return. That coerced value must be stung into the node in memory so that further probes of that field will find the exact same value.

Observation 3: *First* and *rest* return values stored in memory.

Observation 4: (Uniprocessor) In any sinker (node) at most one

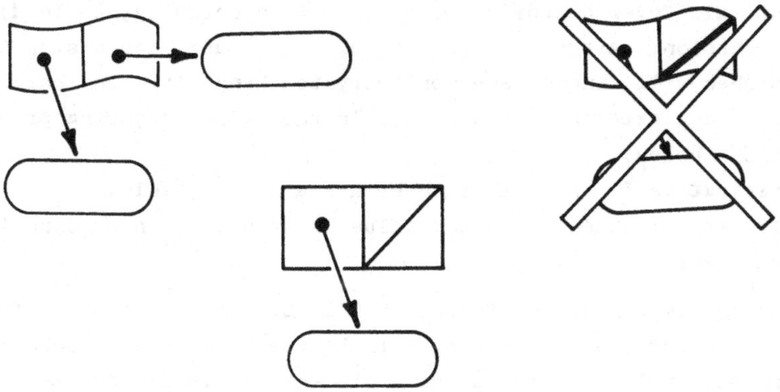

Figure 5. Floaters never have null *d*-fields.

```
function COERCE(AFIELD : field) : field;
begin
  repeat
      AFIELD := COAX(AFIELD);
    until AFIELD.exists
  taeper;
  COERCE := AFIELD
end

function COAXA(AFIELD : field, Q : pointer) : Boolean;
begin
  if not AFIELD.exists
    then AFIELD := COAX(AFIELD);
         sting Q [ unless a.exists ] in a with AFIELD
  fi;
  COAXA := AFIELD.exists
end

procedure COAXD(NEXTFIELD : more, Q : pointer);
begin
  NEXTFIELD.d := COAX(NEXTFIELD.d);
  if NEXTFIELD.value = nil
    then NEXTFIELD.sinker := true;
         sting Q in next with NEXTFIELD
    else sting Q [ unless d.exists ] in d with NEXTFIELD.d
  fi
end
```

Figure 6. Evaluation by COAXing on a Uniprocessor [or Multiprocessor].

*exist*ent value ever occupies the d-field (respectively, a-field).

Discussion: After an *exist*ent value is stung into a sinker all other probes will find it and won't try to change it. The only potential changes to *any* *exist*ent field occurs in the d-fields during promotion (see EUREKA below).

Observation 5: A floater never has a null d-field.

Discussion: Whenever a *nil* value is stung, the node type is stung with it (Figure 5).

The system evaluation functions COERCE, COAXA, and COAXD for a single processor are all displayed in Figure 6 [without bracketed code]. They are all built upon the assumed elementary evaluation step, COAX, which is defined according to whatever language semantics is desired, including, of course, those presented here [2]. COAX is a function which takes a suspension as an argument and returns a field as a value; that field may have its *exists* bit *true* and its pointer referring to an *exist*ent value, or it may have its *exists* bit *false* and its pointer referring to another suspension. Such a new suspension must represent a proper advance in the computation (or process) represented by the initial suspension; the exact amount may be presumed to be random yet finite. It is sufficient that COAX iterate a few times through the innermost loop of the evaluator and then put the (suspended) process back to sleep. COERCE is nothing more than a repeated COAXing until the *exist*ent value appears. The code uses a generalized form of the *repeat* loop which allows for two distinguishable kinds of exits. (D.S. Wise D.P. Friedman, S.C. Shapiro, and M. Wand. Boolean valued loops. *BIT 15*, 4 (December, 1975), 431-451.)

Postulate: COAX makes non-trivial progress in advancing a suspended computation.

Observation 6: COAXA and COAXD properly advance the suspended computation known to some processor.

Discussion: (Uniprocessor) Each fetches a suspension, coaxes it, and restores the result if an *exist*ent value is not present. Progress depends on the postulate.

COAXA is declared as a function whose Boolean value tells whether its one application of COAX was the one which yielded an *exist*ent value. In any event, the coaxed field must be delivered to memory at Q. Of course, if the value already *exist*ed there, COAXA trivially returns *true*. COAXD, similar in effect but different in form is defined as a procedure since we never need to know if it uncovers a value, and it is only invoked when a suspension is known to be in the d-field so it need

UNIPROCESSOR

```
function EUREKA(F : pointer) : node;
var Q, W, FNEXT : pointer;
    SUFFIX : more;
    NQ, NW : node;
begin
  NQ := F↑;
  Q := F;
  repeat
      if NQ.sinker
        then if Q = F then return(EUREKA := NQ) else Q := F fi
        else if NQ.d.exists
               then Q := NQ.d.value
               else COAXD(NQ.next,Q); Q := F
             fi
      fi;
      NQ := Q↑;
    until COAXA(NQ.a,Q)
  taeper;
  NQ := Q↑;
  W := Q; NW := NQ;
  NW.sinker := true; sting W in sinker with true;
  if W = F then
            return(EUREKA := NW)
  fi;
  SUFFIX := NW.next; NW.d.exists := true;
  NQ := F↑; FNEXT := NQ.d.value;
  NEW(Q);
  sting Q with NQ;
  NW.d.value := Q; sting F with NW;
  EUREKA := NW;
  repeat
    until FNEXT = W;
      F := FNEXT;
      NQ := F↑; FNEXT := NQ.d.value;
      NEW(Q);
      sting Q with NQ;
      sting NW.d.value in d.value with Q;
      NW.d.value := Q; sting F with NW
  taeper;
  if SUFFIX.exists
    then if SUFFIX.value = nil
           then sting Q in next with SUFFIX
           else sting Q in d with SUFFIX.d
         fi
    else sting Q in d with SUSPEND("rest(W)")
  fi
end
```

Fiqure 7. Uniprocessor EUREKA.

not test the *exists* bit. In the event, however, that the result of coaxing in the d-field is the *exist*ent value *nil*, then COAXD must **sting** this value in such a way that the stung node becomes a sinker. Observation 5 is sustained in COAXD (as in all code which changes the d-field of a floater) because there is again a special test (after the value to be stung is available) which determines the way it is to be stung. If that value happens to be *nil*, then the field stung will include the *sinker* bit so that the node must become a sinker as the *nil* is stung. Observation 5 motivated the declaration of the d-field in Figure 1 to be associated with the *sinker* bit in the *more*-field. This declaration provides the more-field which is the target of the **sting** when the d-field is receiving the value *nil*.

Uniprocessor EUREKA

All implementation problems are now placed upon EUREKA. We present the code for the uniprocessor EUREKA in Figure 7 and then argue for its correctness. The reader is referred to the examples in Figure 3 and Figure 8 as this code is introduced; Figure 8 illustrates EUREKA's effect upon Figure 3 when the suspension cc is found to converge to CC. The appendix completes a full 83 line version of EUREKA which we claim is a "fair" implementation for arbitrarily many processors. We cannot justify that claim in this paper, which is only an approach to that argument, but we do use the line numbering convention from the full blown version here and in the following sections. Here we present a multiprocessor and a uniprocessor version of that EUREKA operator which are each more severe abbreviations of the code in the appendix. We develop the final version by introducing a simple version and then by adding more lines in the later one; with a few exceptions (denoted by daggers), once a line occurs in EUREKA, it is identical in all following versions. Once the uniprocessor version is verified we need only show that the additional lines do not destroy its validity under the new operating requirements.

All the local variables denote register-variables in a sophisticated system. Associated with the pointers Q and W are the node registers, NQ and NW which reflect their recent content. Memory operations, as mentioned earlier, are explicitly denoted by **sting**. EUREKA is divided into two phases: Lines 6 through 32 are the *coaxing strategy* and Lines 33 through 82 are the *promotion*. The coaxing strategy must traverse all floaters up-to-and-including the first sinker accessible through successive d-fields, and COAX all a-fields so encountered. The loop in Lines 16 through 26 performs this function on a single processor. Whenever

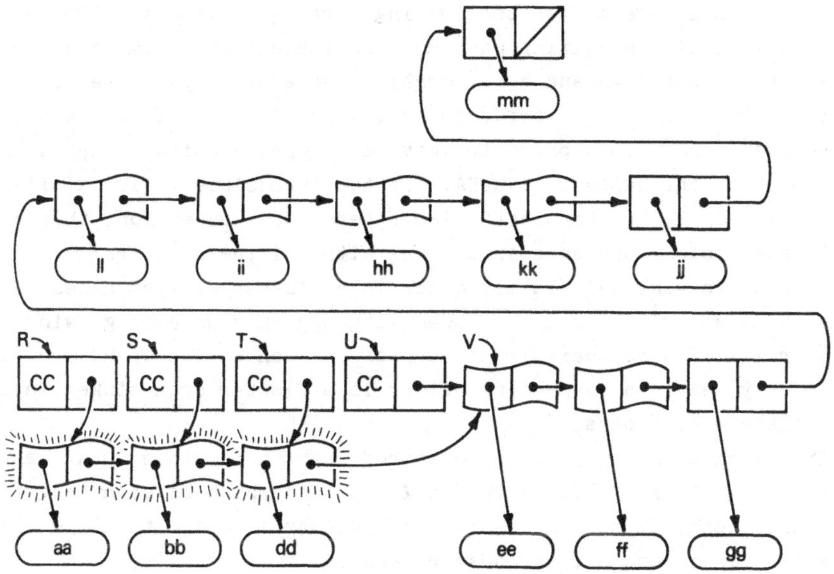

Figure 8. *first*:R = CC; shared references, as well, see CC as their *first*. If there were no shared references then no new nodes need be allocated.

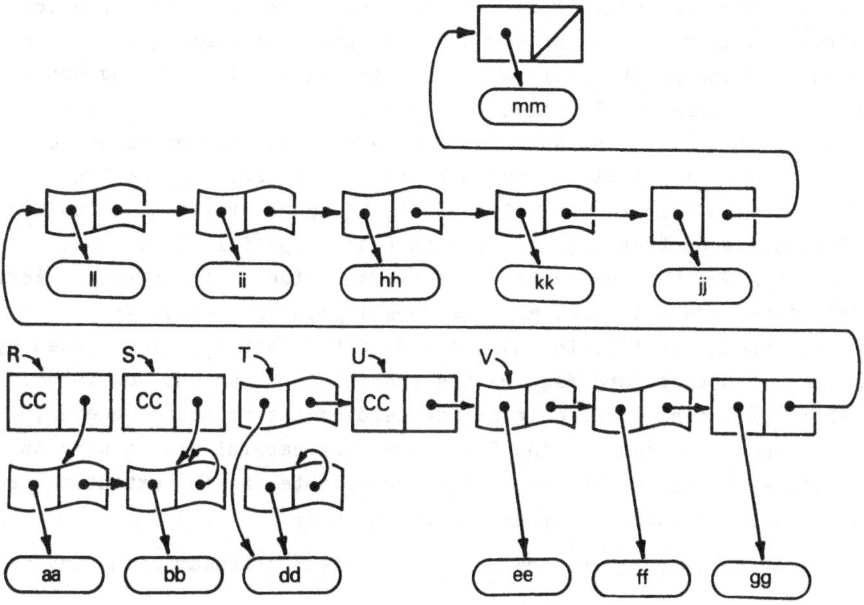

Figure 10. Reflexive pointers *during* promotion on a multiprocessor.

any a-field is *exist*ent then the coaxing strategy may cease. There are several ways that one coaxing pass may terminate; some terminate the entire coaxing strategy and some merely cause another pass over the data structure from the top, referred to by the pointer F. If F, itself, refers to a sinker, then promotion may be skipped and its contents may be returned as the value of EUREKA. If the accessible d-fields all refer to floaters, but the last which refers to a suspension, then that d-field suspension must be coaxed along with all the floaters' a-fields because a convergent a-field may occur in a floater not yet accessible. (Thus unbounded multisets are allowed although only an ever growing finite prefix will be coaxed. Because of the convention on null d-fields, we need only detect a suspended d-field in a floater or a sinker in order to terminate a coax pass).

The fetch at Line 35 is somewhat redundant here since COAXA has the contents of Q at Line 25. As in *first* and *rest* which refetch an *exist*ent value just stung, we tolerate this inefficiency in order to allow easy generalization to the multiprocessor version.

At Line 39 the pointer W refers to a node which has an *exist*ent a-field and NW is a copy of its content. That value will be moved to the head of all structures accessible by references to nodes between F and W (along the chain of d-fields). The necessary transformation requires the introduction of new nodes to hold intervening a-field suspensions and the planting of NQ.a.value in all the intervening nodes as shown in Figure 8. In Lines 49 through 55 NW is set up as a prototype node to be stung at R, S, and T in Figure 8 except for different d-fields. (We know that all d-fields between F and W do *exist*.) Promotion is performed in the loop from Line 64 to 73, part of which is duplicated as Lines 56 to 60 treating the node at F as a special first case. After that first node, the new contents of F--*the value of the EUREKA function*--is determined and F is used as a traversal pointer thereafter. Lines 74 through 79 fill in the d-field of the last node introduced by promotion, and therefore require the special test for null d-fields. SUFFIX is essentially the original d-field of the promoted node NW; if that is suspended then at Line 79 we are very careful not to copy that suspension-- rather we create an indirect pointer to the extant one so that it will eventually only be evaluated once!

Observation 7: There are no (non-trivial) circular paths in the system.

Observation 8: The coaxing strategy will find a convergent candidate for promotion if one exists.

Discussion: It coaxes on all suspensions up through the first sinker uniformly.

Observation 9: Promotion makes the *first* node in a structure into a sinker containing an *existent* value.

Observation 10: Promotion preserves the structure semantics.

Discussion: The proof is by induction on the distance from the node pointed to by F and the node pointed to by W. Each sharing causes a new node to be created as the d-value of a sinker.

Theorem 1: The uniprocessor implementation is correct.

Multiprocessor EUREKA

The modification of EUREKA to run on arbitrarily many processors is the centerpiece of this paper (Figure 9). The coaxing strategy proceeds on many processors *without* synchronization of the *processors*. Promotion may proceed simultaneously with coaxing, but only one promotion may be active at a time. Thus, we introduce a binary semaphore, MUTEX, at Lines 33, 52, and 81 to protect that part of the program which distorts the data structure in order to effect promotion.

The fact that coaxing, which is the more expensive computation, may proceed without processor synchronization is due to the **sting** primitive which we now extend to its conditional form. We introduce this primitive separately in another paper [3], but this example is a better demonstration of its power. The operation "**sting** P **unless** bit **in** field **with** value" dispatches a description of a bit location and a field location within a memory word, and a value to the location at P. There (not *in* the dispatching processor) an uninterruptible test-and-store operation proceeds; if the *bit* in that word is already *true* then nothing happens; if the *bit* is *false* then the *value* is stored in the *field*. The dispatching processor receives no feedback on what actually happens!! Because there is no feedback the dispatching processor is free to proceed immediately. Because there is no waiting for feedback (as there is with a *test-and-set*) no processor may monopolize a path to memory during an uninterruptible memory operation, and there will be fewer instances of one processor blocking another's access to memory during the storing of sensitive data. Viewed another way, the **sting-unless** primitive avoids implementing every *exists* bit as a semaphore.

The major problem with multiprocessor coaxing under EUREKA is that we do not allow a second *existent* value to be stored over an earlier one in any field. This might occur, for instance, if two processors picked up the same suspension at about the same time, coaxed it to an *existent* value, and then stored two different incarnations of that value back at two separate times. (If that *existent* value were a floater then Equations (6) and (7) might be violated through duplication of what ought to be a single floater.) Thus in Figures 4 and 6 whenever a **sting** is directed *in* an a-field (d-field), the sting must be conditional--**unless** a.exists (d.exists) as indicated by the bracketed code.

Coaxing may run on many processors at once, but not without a benign sort of interference called *regression*. If several processors are coaxing the same suspension, then all might make the same progress. If one of those processors were inordinately slow, then the remainder might have made considerable coaxing progress on that same field--far beyond just one coax, but not yet *exist*ent-- before the sloth processor delivers its duplicate (now stale) effort. Since none of these processors have stung an *exist*ent value, anyone may yet sting this field. When the sloth processor delivers its suspension, all future coaxes will begin from there--even those coaxes by the speedy processors which had already coaxed the value much further along. These processors may appear to be dragged backwards, but this backward progress or regression is limited by the number of active processors in the system. In the worst case, all processors are coaxing at one field, and the time to coerce will be no worse than the slowest processor. Thus the coaxing strategy in Figure 9 is sufficient for one, two, or two hundred simultaneous incarnations of EUREKA.

We modify the discussion of a previous observation:

Observations 6's discussion (Multiprocessor): In this case the COAXing advances the suspension known to the coaxing processor. If stinging the result is *un*successful, then there is a value in that field, so no further advancement is necessary.

Promotion is a different story because it alters the *exist*ent d-fields. Only one promotion may proceed at a time; promotion is a critical region protected by the binary semaphore MUTEX, but it is a very fast transformation because it involves no coaxing and only two traversals of the structure from F to W. (**Sting-unless** is also sufficient to implement a binary semaphore if we do not require fairness from it [3].) Because of the probable wait at Line 33 when the structure might change, the value to be promoted must be relocated by a pre-pass through the structure at Lines 34-38. If a change did occur as a result of another promotion during the wait, it can only simplify the waiting promotion.

Observation 4: (Multiprocessor) In any sinker at most one *exist*ent value ever occupies either field.

Discussion: The only change from the uniprocessor version of this invariant is that the a-fields of floaters may change. That might occur

MULTIPROCESSOR

```
  1.    function EUREKA(F : pointer) : node;
  2.    var Q, W, FNEXT : pointer;
  3.        SUFFIX : more;
  4.        NQ, NW : node;
  5.    begin
  6.      NQ := F↑;
  8.      Q := F;
 16.      repeat
 17.          if NQ.sinker
 18.            then if Q = F then return(EUREKA := NQ) else Q := F fi
 19.            else if NQ.d.exists
 20.                   then Q := NQ.d.value
 21.                   else COAXD(NQ.next,Q); Q := F
 22.                 fi
 23.          fi;
 24.          NQ := Q↑;
 25.        until COAXA(NQ.a,Q)
 26.      taeper;
*29.      Q := F;
*33.      P(MUTEX);
*34.      repeat
 35.          NQ := Q↑;
*36.        until NQ.a.exists;
*37.          Q := NQ.d.value
*38.      taeper;
 39.      W := Q; NW := NQ;
 49.      NW.sinker := true; sting W in sinker with true;
 51.      if W = F then
*52.                V(MUTEX);
 53.                return(EUREKA := NW)
 54.      fi;
 55.      SUFFIX := NW.next; NW.d.exists := true;
 56.      NQ := F↑; FNEXT := NQ.d.value;
 57.      NEW(Q);
*58.      NQ.d.value := Q;
 59.      sting Q with NQ;
 60.      NW.d.value := Q; sting F with NW;
 62.      EUREKA := NW;
 64.      repeat
 65.        until FNEXT = W;
 66.          F := FNEXT;
 67.          NQ := F↑; FNEXT := NQ.d.value;
 68.          NEW(Q);
*69.          NQ.d.value := Q;
 70.          sting Q with NQ;
 71.†         sting NW.d.value in d with NQ.d;
 72.          NW.d.value := Q; sting F with NW
 73.      taeper;
 74.      if SUFFIX.exists
 75.        then if SUFFIX.value = nil
 76.               then sting Q in next with SUFFIX
 77.               else sting Q in d with SUFFIX.d
 78.             fi
 79.        else sting Q in d with SUSPEND("rest(W)")
 80.      fi;
*81.      V(MUTEX)
 83.    end
```

Figure 9. Multiprocessor EUREKA.

when coaxing proceeds to create an *existent* value (say, BB in Figure 3) after/while an active promotion has already selected a deeper value (say, CC in Figure 3) to promote at Line 39 of EUREKA. The promotion proceeds, moving the *existent* value into one of the NEW nodes.

This semaphore would be sufficient to assure that promotion still works correctly if we had some control over coaxing. But coaxing is unrestricted and so we must consider conflicts between coaxing and promotion. Because promotion plants sinkers with *existent* a-fields whenever it alters accessible structure, one might think that it blocks coaxing implicitly. That is true directly, but indirectly coaxing may be resumed upon the *rest* of those new sinkers. If coaxing were fast and promotion were slow, then coaxing might proceed into the floaters newly allocated by an incomplete promotion. The problem is that the d-field of one such floater (at most one at any time) contains temporarily spurious information (in Figure 7) which might cause this secondary coaxing to terminate prematurely.

The solution is illustrated in Figure 10 and is effected by Lines 58 and 69 (duplicates) in EUREKA.† Instead of tolerating a spurious pointer in the d-fields of newly created floaters, those fields are initially filled with a reflexive pointer. That diverts any local coaxing strategy (temporarily at worst since the critical process will overwrite it at Line 71 or one of 76, 77, or 79) onto a valid candidate suspension rather than allowing it to wander off to a spurious value which will become inaccessible when the current promotion is complete. With the temporary reflexive link, the worst that could happen is that coaxing by another instance of EUREKA might succeed as a result of an unanticipated strategy, and it would then queue up at the semaphore and wait for this instance of EUREKA to finish.

The following summarizes the previous discussion:

Observation 11: Coaxing does not inhibit other simultaneous coaxing permanently.

Discussion: Any regression is finite.

Observation 12: Coaxing does not inhibit simultaneous promotion.

Discussion: If coaxing is active at an accessible node while promotion altered it, then necessarily that node will have an *existent* a-field and d-field after promotion affects it. Thus the coaxing process

---

†The addition of Lines 58 and 69 allow a simplification at Line 71. Since the proper d-field is available as a leftover from the reflexive link, Line 71 may be refined to sting an entire d-field like *rest* and COAXD. (Thus hardware designers need not provide a "d.value-field sting".)

must **sting** unsuccessfully.

Observation 13: Only one promotion proceeds at a time.

Observation 14: Promotion does not interfere with coaxing.

Discussion: If coaxing occurred at the promotion site, either it would find a promoted value and quit, or proceed (perhaps circularly) oblivious to the promotion thereabouts.

Observation 15: Lockup is impossible.

Discussion: EUREKA cannot be invoked directly or indirectly during promotion. Once promotion begins, it will find an *exist*ent value and eventually execute the V operation (Lines 52 or 81) terminating promotion.

Theorem 2: The multiprocessor version is correct.

Conclusion

We have briefly introduced a new constructor for multiprogramming, which allows a facile expression of complicated order interdependencies with a familiar programming style. The proof techniques for such programs, although not treated directly here, promise to be as straightforward as one can hope for since the language has an applicative style which yields nicely to inductive proofs.

The emphasis in this paper has been on the uniprocessor and multiprocessor implementations of the semantics for this language. The problems of efficient implementation have motivated new control structures, notably the **sting-unless** (Others are suggested in the appendix) which has simplified the interprocessor protocol. We have argued informally that the implementations of the constructors, *cons* and *frons*, are correct for this semantics, but these implementations are not the ultimate goal of this work.

In order to establish *frons* as a constructor truly suitable for applicative multiprogramming we must address the problem of fairness proofs. For nondeterminism, such fairness might imply that any convergent value in a multiset could not be ignored forever. (One might make a more precise statement, but this will do.) A scheduler may be correct without being fair if it loses a job it's supposed to be timing, because the output from the other processes might be correct. That doesn't mean that such an operating system is useful, however; good systems don't lose processes.

The uniprocessor system is implemented, and a multiprocessor version can be simulated on a single processor. A good implementation of the fair version is an exciting prospect for machines with a high degree of parallelism (e.g. a hundred processors).

Acknowledgement

We thank several colleagues who helped in the development of EUREKA, especially by sitting still while the problem *and* this solution were described. Particular thanks are due to Mitchell Wand who raised important questions that redirected early attempts to "find it." The research reported herein was supported (in part) by the National Science Foundation under grants numbered MCS75-06678 A01 and MCS77-22325.

References

1. D.P. Friedman and D.S. Wise. CONS should not evaluate its arguments. In *Automata, Languages and Programming*, S. Michaelson and R. Milner (eds.), Edinburgh, Edinburgh University Press (1976), 257-284.
2. D.P. Friedman and D.S. Wise. Applicative multiprogramming. Technical Rept. No. 72, Computer Science Dept., Indiana University (December, 1978).
3. D.P. Friedman and D.S. Wise. A conditional, interlock-free store instruction. Preliminary version in M.P. Pursley and J.B. Cruz, Jr. (eds.), *Proc. 16th Allerton Conf. on Communication, Control, and Computing*, Univ. of Ill., Urbana (1978), 578-584.
4. P. Henderson and J.H. Morris, Jr. A lazy evaluator. *Proc. 3rd ACM Symp. on Principles of Programming Languages* (1976), 95-103.
5. L. Lamport. Time, clocks, and the ordering of events in a distributed system. *Comm. ACM 21*, 7 (July, 1978), 558-565.
6. J. McCarthy. A basis for a mathematical theory of computation. In *Computer Programming and Formal Systems*, P. Braffort and D. Hirschberg (eds.), Amsterdam, North-Holland (1963), 33-70.
7. Z. Manna. *Mathematical Theory of Computation*, New York, McGraw-Hill (1974), 418.
8. J. Vuillemin. Correct and optimal implementation of recursion in a simple programming language. *J. Comp. Sys. Sci. 9*, 3 (June, 1974), 332-354.
9. C. Wadsworth. *Semantics and Pragmatics of Lambda-calculus*, Ph.D. dissertation, Oxford (1971).

Appendix

We present a complete version of EUREKA which represents the unattained goal of this paper. We intend that it run in the same processor-rich environment as the multiprocessor version, but that it be "fair". Fairness includes the guarantee that no accessible suspension ever go uncoaxed; the procedure COAXSUFFIX serves this purpose:

```
procedure COAXSUFFIX(NQ : node, Q : pointer);
begin
  if not repeat
           until NQ.sinker;
           while NQ.d.exists;
             Q := NQ.d.value; NQ := Q↑;
             COAXA(NQ.a,Q)
         taeper
     then COAXD(NQ.next,Q)
  fi
end
```

Moreover, we must guarantee that no converged value ever go unpromoted. The solution is a system clocking mechanism like Lamport's [5] used to referee the choice of which value gets promoted. The time when a node is created is installed in that node by *cons* or *frons* and it remains with that node and its copies forever; given a choice, we always promote the "oldest" value. (Rather than providing one field in every node for an unbounded birthdate, Guy Steele, Jr., has suggested that a pointer field would suffice for linking the finite number of accessible nodes together in order of their creation. The storage requirements would then be quite tractable, but the determination of the relative age of two arbitrary nodes at Line 44 becomes a computation whose time is linear in the number of nodes; here that determination takes only constant time.)

The code below only includes lines which are new to or changed in the fair version of EUREKA. As before a dagger (†) denotes a line slightly changed by additions. The new lines which assure fairness are noted by asterisks (*). Several new lines are included to assure efficiency, particularly to avoid the critical region (promotion) as much as possible; these are noted by dollar signs ($). The process creation suggested by **spawn** at Lines 15 and 61 may be ignored; these lines may be read here simply as procedure invocations and Line 82 (related to Line 61) may also be ignored.

FAIR

```
$ 7.     if NQ.sinker then return(EUREKA := NQ) fi;
* 9.     if repeat
*10.          until COAXA(NQ.a,Q);
*11.          while not NQ.sinker;
*12.          while NQ.d.exists;
*13.             Q := NQ.d.value; NQ := Q↑
*14.       taeper
*15.       then spawncall(COAXSUFFIX(NQ,Q))
 16.†      else repeat
*27.     fi;
$28.     if Q = F then sting F unless d.exists in sinker with true
 29.†      else Q := F
$30.     fi;
$31.     NQ := Q↑;
$32.     if NQ.sinker then return(EUREKA := NQ) fi;
*40.     repeat
*41.       until NQ.sinker;
*42.       while NQ.d.exists;
*43.         Q := NQ.d.value; NQ := Q↑;
*44.         if NQ.a.exists andif NQ.birthdate < NW.birthdate
*45.           then W := Q; NW := NQ
*46.         fi
*47.     taeper;
$48.     if not NW.sinker
 49.†      then NW.sinker := true; sting W in sinker with true
$50.     fi;
$61.     spawnreturn(
$63.                 );
$82.     quit
```

MODELING A SOLUTION FOR A CONTROL PROBLEM IN DISTRIBUTED SYSTEMS BY RESTRICTIONS

Andrea Maggiolo-Schettini

Unità di Ricerca del C.N.R.-G.N.I.M.
Istituto di Scienze dell'Informazione
Università di Pisa
56100 Pisa/Italy

Horst Wedde

Gesellschaft für Mathematik und
Datenverarbeitung
Postfach 1240
D-5205 St.Augustin 1/Germany

Jozef Winkowski

Instytut Podstaw Informatyki PAN
P.O.Box 22
00-901 Warszawa/Poland

Abstract

For an independent representation of the constraints on processes in distributed system parts the formalism of Loosely Coupled Systems is introduced. The event structure is derived only from prespecified restrictions of behaviour,concurrency of events is described in elementary and local terms. Formal construction methods (constraint module and slack phase techniques) are defined and used to model a solution for a control problem under various constraints (fairness). The correctness of the solution is proved using a general and new formal procedure: A restricted case graph is evaluated which is minimal with respect to the needed information. For the sake of evaluation the system is reduced to another one by a simple and efficient algorithm. It is proved that the wanted restricted case graph is an invariant under the algorithm. In the reduced system the restricted case graph is very simple to compute.

0. Introduction

Restrictions have been widely used as independent tools for specifying systems of concurrent processes sharing distributed systems of resources. We mention here PATIL's constraint modules [5],facts in place/transition nets [2],also programming concepts like path expressions [3] or distributed processes [1]. In order to prove correctness of system descriptions which contain restriction elements these restrictions are given a semantics which is expressed in terms of the remaining specification elements of the given formal approach. So the effect of PATIL's constraint modules is described by P-net structures. Facts in place/ transition nets correspond to dead subnets. The semantics of path expressions is described by Petri nets. This makes the restrictions un-

derstandable as a shorthand description of structures which are often enough very complicated and consequently of limited usefulness for practical proofs.
We are here concerned with a new formalism of restrictions on processes in distributed system parts,called Loosely Coupled Systems.This is a model which syntactically is based only on mutual exclusion of states. But different from the approaches mentioned above the semantics of this formal language is derived from the restrictions themselves: Roughly spoken,the event structure in our systems essentially describes the slack of behaviour which system parts have under the prespecified restrictions. Also concurrency of events is definable in elementary and local terms,and it is to be canonically understood as causal independence.

This paper is a conceptual study. After a short formal introduction into Loosely Coupled Systems - for a more detailed and well-motivated description see [4],[6],[7] - we construct two classes of compound restrictional forms,so-called elementary and conditional elementary restrictions,by which a large class of synchronization constraints is covered ([4]). These constructions serve as abstract constraint modules which admit all events which do not infringe on the represented constraint. We introduce a slack phase technique by means of which we are able to manipulate the effect of the constraint modules,especially the slack which they leave with respect to special subsystems. In order to demonstrate the power of our modelling tools we formulate a problem of asymmetrical interaction of processes in distributed system parts. We do not refer to any implementation detail. The six problem conditions are partially restrictive and easy to understand - e.g. a fairness condition is included - but it is very hard to see directly how they influence possible runs of the interacting processes. Starting with a "partial" solution and using the formal tools which were introduced before we refine this "solution" stepwise such that the system so far constructed is essentially not changed by the next step and that the imposed conditions are successively satisfied.

The correctness of our solution is proved only on the basis of restrictions. All the information which we need for this purpose is contained in a restricted case graph (with respect to a subsystem). We define a reduction algorithm which reduces a subsystem of the solution but which leaves this restricted case graph invariant (up to an isomorphism). It finally turns out that with respect to the properties to be proved the evaluated restricted case graph is minimal. The algorithm is simple and efficient. It is needed in order to make the evaluation of the restricted case graph practically efficient. The results are discussed in some detail.

1. Loosely Coupled Systems

In order to formalize the interdependence between the components of a real system we do not assume anything about the system parts except that they are in exactly one state or section of activity at any time. We call these states phases. Let B be the (finite) set of parts, P the set of all phases. Our assumption then has the following form:

$$1.1 \quad \forall_{b \in B}\ b \subseteq P\ ; \quad \bigcup_{b \in B} b = P\ ; \quad \forall_{b_1, b_2 \in B}\ b_1 \neq b_2 \implies b_1 \cap b_2 = \emptyset\ .$$

The interdependence between parts is reduced to the mutual exclusion of some of their states. The binary relation which describes the mutual exclusion of phases in b_1 and b_2 is called coupling relation between b_1 and b_2 and denoted by $K\langle b_1\ b_2\rangle$. So we have:

$$1.2 \quad K\langle b_1 b_2\rangle \subseteq b_1 \times b_2 \quad ; \quad K\langle b_1 b_2\rangle = K\langle b_2 b_1\rangle^{-1}\ .$$

For the matter of convenience we define

$$1.3 \quad K\langle bb\rangle = (b \times b) - id\langle b\rangle\ ; \quad K := \bigcup_{b_1, b_2 \in B} K\langle b_1 b_2\rangle\ .$$

1.3 is motivated by the character of the phases.

1.4 Definition : Let $c \subseteq P$.

a) c is a maximal configuration iff: $\forall_{b \in B}\ |c \cap b| = 1$;

b) c is a case $c \in C$ iff : c is a maximal configuration and

$$\forall_{p_1, p_2 \in c}\ (p_1, p_2) \notin K\ .$$

The system situations are represented by cases, i.e. by maximal subsets of pairwise "compatible" phases. A Loosely Coupled System (LCS) is a quadruple (P,B,C,K) where P,B,C,K are defined and related to one another by 1.1 to 1.4.

1.5 Definition: Let $c_1, c_2 \in C$ be two cases. The pair (c_1, c_2) represents an elementary event iff $|c_1 - c_2| = |c_2 - c_1| = 1$.

Let $\{p\} := c_1 - c_2$; $\{q\} := c_2 - c_1$. (Obviously p and q belong to the same part.) Then (c_1, c_2) describes the phase transition $p \to q$ in c_1. In fig.1 we have three parts b_1, b_2, b_3. The coupling relations are represented by undirected arcs between phases.

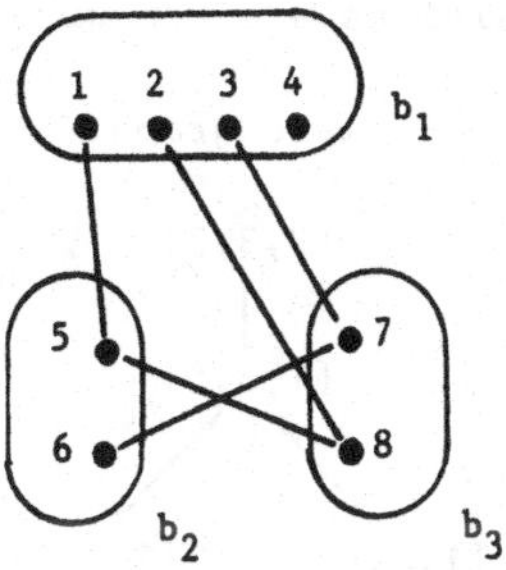

Fig.1

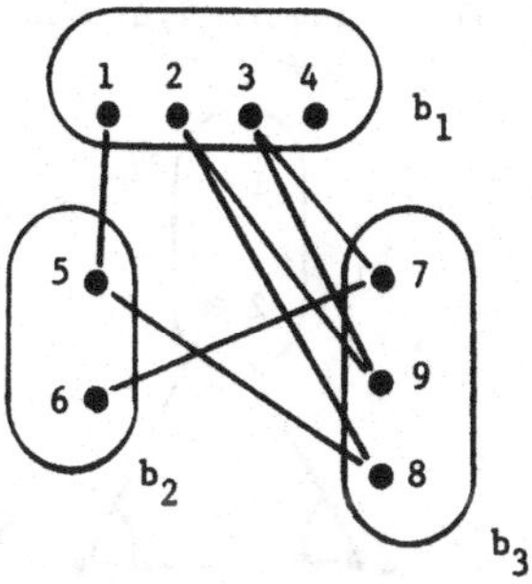

Fig.2

One can see that there is a phase transition $1 \to 3$ from $\{1,6,8\}$ but $5 \to 6$ is no elementary event: A case which contains 5 must contain 7, and a case which contains 6 necessarily 8. A pair (c_1, c_2) of cases such that $|c_1 - c_2| > 1$ does not represent a system case transformation unless it is decomposable into a sequence of elementary events. So the coincident jump $5 \to 6$ and $7 \to 8$ which would lead from $\{4,5,7\}$ to 4,6, 8} is excluded. (The special character of cases and elementary events is directly derivable from a formal understanding of infringements (on constraints). For more details see [6] and [7].)

1.6 Definition: Let $c, c_1, c_2 \in C$ and $c - c_1 =: \{p_1\}$; $c_1 - c =: \{q_1\}$; $c - c_2 =: \{p_2\}$; $c_2 - c =: \{q_2\}$. The elementary events $p_1 \to q_1$ and $p_2 \to q_2$ are concurrent in c iff $(q_1, q_2) \notin K$.

The case graph of an LCS has the cases as nodes and an (undirected) edge between any two iff there is a phase transition from one case to the other one. With this notation we formulate:

1.7 Theorem: Under the assumptions of 1.6 $p_1 \to q_1$ and $p_2 \to q_2$ are concurrent in c iff there is $c_3 \in C$ which completes the following part of the case graph as indicated by the dotted lines:

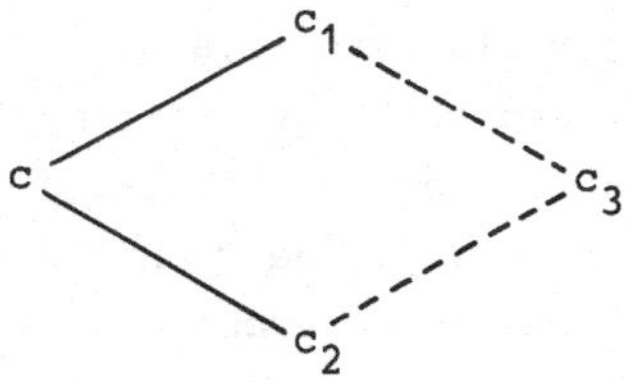

In fig.3 both $3 \to 4$ and $5 \to 6$ may happen starting from $\{1,3,5\}$ but after each of them the other one is blocked. They are in conflict. In fig.4

only (4,6) is removed, and now both transitions are concurrent in {1,3,5}.

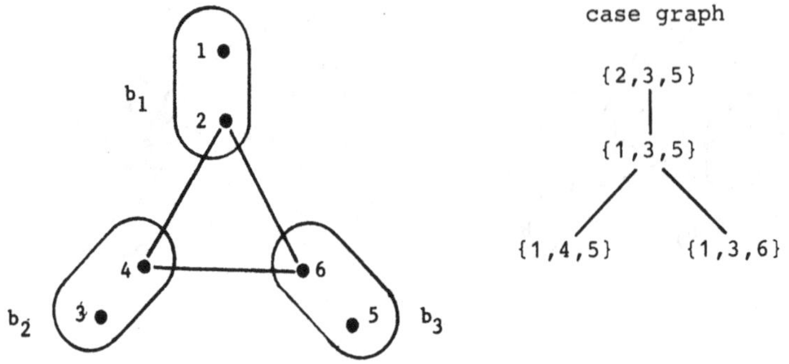

Fig.3

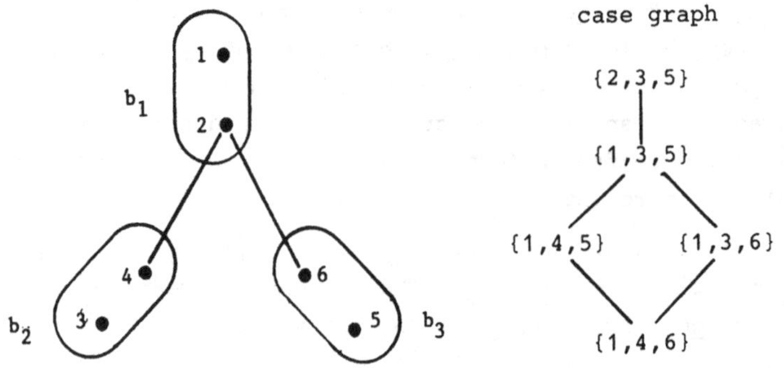

Fig.4

In such a situation there is no restriction which prevents us to execute 3 → 4 and 5 → 6 simultaneosly. Such a restriction (bottleneck) would be represented by adding a part b_4 as shown in fig.5. Here 3 and 5 belong to a common case (as they did before), e.g. to {1,3,5,7} and to {1,3,5,8} . One can switch between both, but starting from each of these cases only one transition can be executed, then, after a change in b_4, the other one. (By the necessary step in b_4 between 3 → 4 and 5 → 6 we establish a causal dependence between these events.)

Let $I := \{1,\ldots,k,k+1,\ldots,l,l+1,\ldots,n\}$. Let $b_i \in B$; $i \in I$ and $p_i \in b_i$ such that:

a) $p_i \neq p_j$; $i \neq j$ and $1 \leq i,j \leq n$;

b) $b_i \neq b_j$; $i \neq j$ and ($1 \leq i,j \leq k$ or $k+1 \leq i,j \leq l$ or $l+1 \leq i,j \leq n$) .

If $A_1(i,c)$, $A_2(i,c)$, $A_3(i,c)$ are formulas of the type $p_i \in c$ or $p_i \notin c$ and if #,#',#" represent one of the quantifiers $\forall, \exists$ we have the following general scheme for logical formulas about an LCS:

1.8 $\forall_{c \in C} \left(\left(\#_{1 \leq i \leq k} A_1(i,c) \wedge \#'_{k+1 \leq j \leq l} A_2(j,c) \right) \Longrightarrow \#''_{l+1 \leq m \leq n} A_3(m,c) \right)$

They are called <u>conditional elementary restrictions</u>, in case k=l we call them <u>elementary restrictions</u>.

There is a general method to realize these restrictions by adding exactly one part, the <u>control part</u>, to the given b_i and by only coupling the control part to the b_i (see [4]). If we specialize 1.8 to $k = l = 2$; $n = 4$; $\# = \forall$; $\#'' = \exists$; $A_1(i,c) = p_i \in c$; $A_3(m,c) = p_m \notin c$ then fig.6 gives the representation of this restriction. It means that not all elements $p_1,\ldots,p_4$ can hold at the same time. A conditional elementary restriction is used in 3..

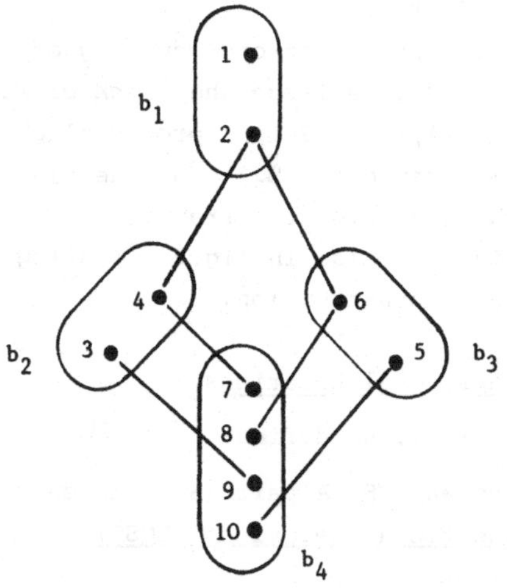

Fig.5

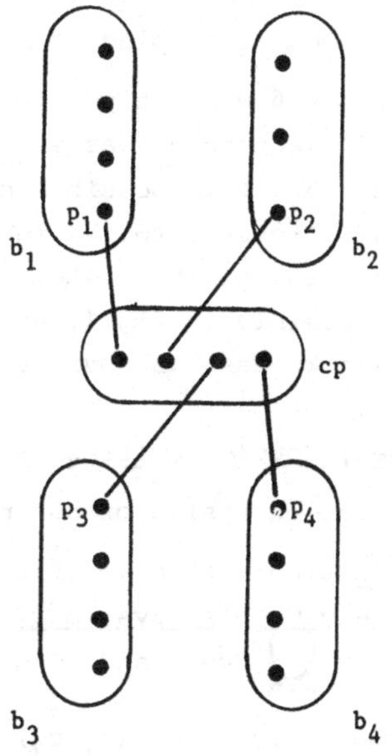

Fig.6

It can be shown that for restrictions of the type 1.8 the following holds ([4]):

1.9 Theorem:

a) If the premise of 1.8 does not hold for $c \in C$ all phase transitions are admitted which do not change the truth value of the premise.

b) Let neither the premise nor the conclusion of 1.8 hold for $c_1 \in C$; let the premise hold for $c_2 \in C$. Then c_2 cannot be reached from c_1 before the conclusion begins to hold.

c) If nothing is prescribed about the validity of the conclusion of 1.8 in case that the premise does not hold all situations and operations described in a) and b) may occur in the LCS representation of the restriction.

Except pathological formulas we see that the realization of a formula of the type 1.8 restricts the behaviour in the b_i in an easily understandable way and only insofar as it is specified by the formula.

1.10 Definition: Let, for an LCS (P,B,C,K), $B:=\{b_1,\ldots,b_k,b_{k+1},\ldots,b_n\}$ and let S' be the subsystem which is covered by $b_1,\ldots,b_k$. If $p \in b_l$; $k+1 \le l \le n$ we call p a slack phase (with respect to S') iff p is not coupled to any phase in S'. A slack phase p (with respect to S') is called proper iff it is coupled to every phase q outside of S' which is coupled to a phase in b_l.

In fig.1 5 → 6 was not possible because of the strong coupling of b_2 and b_3. If we create 9 as shown in fig.2 we enlarge the slack between b_1 and b_2. 5 → 6 is possible now from {4,5,9}. 9 is a proper slack phase (with respect to the subsystem covered by $\{b_2\}$). So the slack of b_3 to the rest of the system is unchanged: E.g. the transition 2 → 3 was not possible in fig.1, and this is true also in fig.2. Creating a proper slack phase is obviously a basic construction.

2. Loosely Coupled Systems with Transitional Relations

As a slight extension of our notions in 1. we define:

2.1 Definition: Let $S := (P,B,C,K)$ be an LCS. A pair (S,T) is called a Loosely Coupled System with Transitional Relations (LCST) iff:

1) $T = \bigcup_{b \in B} T\langle b\rangle$ and $T\langle b\rangle \subseteq b \times b$;

2) Let $c_1, c_2 \in C$. (c_1,c_2) represents a phase transition iff $|c_1-c_2| = |c_2-c_1| = 1$ and for $\{p\} := c_1-c_2$; $\{q\} := c_2-c_1$: $(p,q) \in T$.

2.2 Remark: Except some small occasion in 3. we shall only consider symmetrical relations $T(b)$. So, instead of writing $\{(p,q),(q,p)\} \in T$

we introduce the more convenient notation : $p \leftrightarrow q$. We mention without proof that there are some standard constructions by which some parts are added to the LCS structure S such that a symmetrical relation T is realized in terms of an LCS structure. Note e.g. that in fig.1 the addition of the two phase part b_3 to the subsystem covered by b_1 (if we forget $K\langle b_1 b_2\rangle$) excludes $2 \to 3$ (and $3 \to 2$) in b_1 and so realizes the transitional relation $T\langle b_1\rangle := (b_1 \times b_1) - \{(2,3),(3,2)\}$. In other words, in the special case where $T = T^{-1}$ LCSTs are only a shorthand description of LCSs.

<u>2.3</u> We shall now define a reduction algorithm for LCSTs. It will have two different types of operations,called <u>step1</u> and <u>step2</u>,corresponding to the merging of parts and of phases in a part,respectively. Let (S,T) be an LCST with $S := (P,B,C,K)$.

<u>step1</u>

Let b_1, b_2 be two different parts. We replace them by only one part which is denoted by $b_1 * b_2$. It is defined by:

$$b_1 * b_2 := \{\{(p,q),(q,p)\} \mid p \in b_1 \ , \ q \in b_2 \ ; \ (p,q) \notin K\} \ .$$

For short we shall write (p,q) instead of $\{(p,q),(q,p)\}$ when we refer to <u>phases</u> of $b_1 * b_2$. For $j \notin \{1,2\}$ we define:

$$K\langle b_j (b_1 * b_2)\rangle (p) := \{(p_1,p_2) \mid (p,p_1) \in K\langle b_j b_1\rangle \text{ or } (p,p_2) \in K\langle b_j b_2\rangle\} \ .$$

Let $(p_1,p_2),(p_3,p_4) \in b_1 * b_2$. Then

$(p_1,p_2) \leftrightarrow (p_3,p_4)$: <==> 1) $p_1 = p_3$ or $p_2 = p_4$;

2) If $p_1 \neq p_3$ or $p_2 \neq p_4$ then $p_1 \leftrightarrow p_3$ or $p_2 \leftrightarrow p_4$, respectively .

<u>step2</u>

Let $b \in B$ and $p_1, p_2 \in b$ such that :

1) $\forall_{b_i \neq b} \quad K\langle bb_i\rangle(p_1) = K\langle bb_i\rangle(p_2)$;

2) $p_1 \leftrightarrow p_2$.

Then we replace b by b' where $b' := (b - \{p_1,p_2\}) \cup \{\{p_1,p_2\}\}$. The coupling in $b' - \{\{p_1,p_2\}\}$ is as before. In addition to that we define:

$$b_i \neq b' \Longrightarrow K\langle b'b_i\rangle(\{p_1,p_2\}) := K\langle bb_i\rangle(p_1) \ .$$

Finally,let $p,q \in b' - \{\{p_1,p_2\}\}$. Then $p \leftrightarrow q$ iff it was true before,and

$$p \leftrightarrow \{p_1,p_2\} \ :\Longleftrightarrow \ p \leftrightarrow p_1 \text{ or } p \leftrightarrow p_2 \text{ in } b \ .$$

The algorithm works as follows: Given $b_1, b_2 \in B$ one applies step1 , afterwards one applies step2 as often as possible. The result is again denoted by $b_1 * b_2$ if there is no misunderstanding. The rest of the system is unchanged. Let (S',T') be the resulting LCST.

2.4 Theorem: With the notation of 2.3 the mapping $(b_1, b_2) \mapsto b_1 * b_2$ (application of step1 and step2) is a commutative and associative operation.

Due to space limitations we do not give a formal proof. (The commutativity is obvious.) As it is easy to see that multiple application of step1 (and also of step2 alone if that is possible) is associative (up to notational differences which we are not interested in) the idea is simply to show that if step2 was applicable for two phases then it will still be applicable after application of step1 and if it was not applied at once.

The algorithm will be used in 3. to reduce the computational complexity of a restricted case graph.

2.5 Definition: Let (S,T) be an LCST where S := (P,B,C,K) . Let $B := \{b_1, \ldots, b_n\}$ and $B' := \{b_1, \ldots, b_k\}$; $k<n$. Let (C,N) be the case graph of (S,T) with C as node set and N as the arc set which describes the transition between cases (see 2.2) .

1) For $c_1, c_2 \in C$ we define:

$c_1 \underset{B'}{\sim} c_2 \;:\Longleftrightarrow\; \underset{1 \le i \le k}{\forall}\; c_1 \cap b_i = c_2 \cap b_i$, and for $c_1 \neq c_2$ there is a path in (C,N) from c_1 to c_2 which describes only transitions in B - B' .

2) The restriction of the case graph to B' (or the restricted case graph if we do not explicitely refer to B') is denoted by G((S,T)|B') and defined to be the following graph (C|B',N|B') : $C|B' := C/\underset{B'}{\sim}$; $(\tilde{c}_1, \tilde{c}_2) \in N|B'$ iff there are $c_1' \in \tilde{c}_1$, $c_2' \in \tilde{c}_2$ such that $(c_1', c_2') \in N$ and $c_1' - c_2'$ is in a part of B'.

As an example let us take the LCST which is given by the subsystem S in fig.5 which is covered by $\{b_2, b_3, b_4\}$. T is trivial and therefore omitted. $G(S|\{b_2, b_3\})$ is drawn in fig.7 . For the matter of convenience we have written {3,[7 8],5} instead of {{3,7,5},{3,8,5}} .

The restricted case graph G((S,T)|B') shows all transitional details in B' which can be found in the case graph (C,N) but the transitional structure in the rest of the system is preserved only insofar as it is needed to understand the behaviour of the subsystem covered by B' .

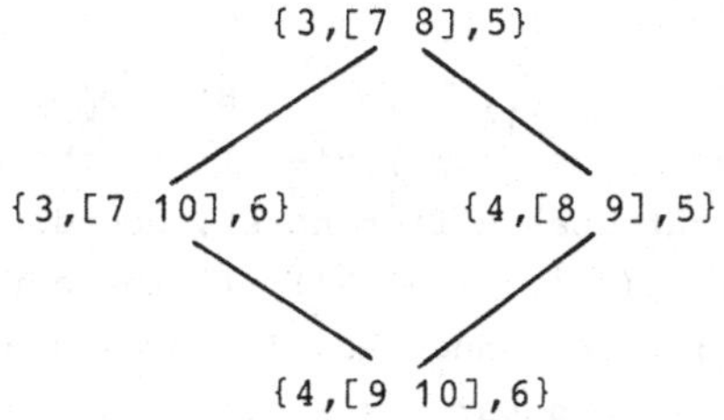

Fig.7

In fig.7 one sees that 3 → 4 and 5 → 6 are possible in an arbitrary order and that they cannot occur at the same time because the classes [7 10] and [8 9] are disjoint. But it is not shown how one comes from one class in the restricted case graph to the other one. This corresponds to the practical situation where a user of a computer system uses service programs to manipulate his data sets: He must know how these facilities can be combined in order to work for his purpose but he will not be interested at this level (and maybe we cannot explain it to him) by which internal procedures these programs are made available for him.

The formal motivation for the algorithm defined in 2.3 and at the same time the key result of our paper is the following:

2.6 Theorem: Let (S,T) be an LCST; S:= (P,B,C,K);

$B := \{b_1,\dots,b_k,b_{k+1},\dots,b_n\}$; $2\le k<n$; $B_k := \{b_1,\dots,b_k\}$.
With the notations of 2.3 let (S',T') be the resulting LCST after a single application of the algorithm. So we have S':=(P',B',C',K') with $B' = (B-\{b_1,b_2\}) \cup \{b_1 * b_2\}$. Let finally $B_k' := \{b_1 * b_2,\dots,b_k\}$.
Then the following holds: The following diagram has the dotted commutative completion where f is an isomorphism of graphs:

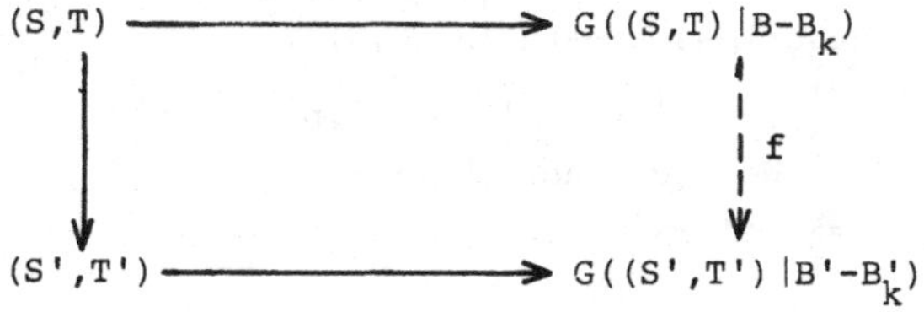

As a consequence of 2.4 we derive:

2.7 Corollary: Multiple application of the algorithm in order to reduce the number of elements in B_k leaves the corresponding restricted case graph <u>invariant</u>.

<u>Proof of 2.6</u>: We have $B - B_k = \{b_{k+1}, \ldots, b_n\} = B' - B'_k$. It is to show firstly that the classes in $G((S',T') \mid B'-B'_k)$ are the same as in $G((S,T) \mid B-B_k)$ (up to notational differences), secondly that two classes are connected in $G((S',T') \mid B'-B'_k)$ iff the corresponding classes in $G((S,T) \mid B-B_k)$ were connected. If we assume that the first part has been shown the second part is an obvious consequence of the definition of connection (see 2.5).

Let $c_1, c_2 \in C$; $c_1 := \{p_1^1, p_2^1, \ldots, p_n^1\}$; $c_2 := \{p_1^2, p_2^2, \ldots, p_n^2\}$.
By the transformation from (S,T) to (S',T') the pairs (p_1^1, p_2^1) and (p_1^2, p_2^2) are occasionally elements of subsets P^1 and P^2 of phase pairs which were merged by multiple application of <u>step2</u> .

$P^1 := \{(p_1,q_1),(p_2,q_2),\ldots,(p_r,q_r)\}$;
$P^2 := \{(s_1,t_1),(s_2,t_2),\ldots,(s_v,t_v)\}$ where $p_i, s_i \in b_1$; $q_j, t_j \in b_2$.
Without loss of generality assume that P^1 and P^2 were formed by successive adding of phase pairs in the listed order. So we know:

(*) 1) All pairs in P^1 (in P^2) are coupled with the same phases in $b_3, \ldots, b_n$ (see 2.3) ;

2) The (p_i, q_i) ; $1 \le i \le r$ are connected with respect to "$\leftrightarrow$" ; the (s_j, t_j) ; $1 \le j \le v$ are connected with respect to "$\leftrightarrow$" .

Because of 2.3 we assume without loss of generality:

$$(p_i = p_{i+1} \;\vee\; q_i = q_{i+1}) \;\wedge\; (p_i \neq p_{i+1} \Longrightarrow p_i \leftrightarrow p_{i+1} \;;\; q_i \neq q_{i+1} \Longrightarrow q_i \leftrightarrow q_{i+1})$$

for $1 \le i \le r-1$, and a similar relation holds for pairs in P^2 .

(**) Because of 1) in (*) we derive that the sequence with elements $c_i^1 := \{p_i, q_i, p_3^1, \ldots, p_n^1\}$; $1 \le i \le r$ describes a path in (C,N) , and c_1 is contained in this sequence.

(***) The sequence with elements $c_j^2 := \{s_j, t_j, p_3^2, \ldots, p_n^2\}$; $1 \le j \le v$ contains c_2 and describes a path in (C,N) .

Let $c'_1 := \{P^1, p_3^1, \ldots, p_n^1\}$; $c'_2 := \{P^2, p_3^2, \ldots, p_n^2\}$. Of course we have $c'_1, c'_2 \in C'$. We then show that:

($\square$) $c_1 \underset{B-B_k}{\sim} c_2 \iff c'_1 \underset{B'-B'_k}{\sim} c'_2$.

<u>Proof of ($\square$)</u>: Because of 2.5 it remains to show that c_1 is reachable from c_2 in (C,N) by transitions from $\{b_1, \ldots, b_k\}$ iff c'_1 is reachable from c'_2 in (C',N') by transitions from $\{b_1 * b_2, \ldots, b_k\}$.

"==>" : It is sufficient to show that if $(c_1, c_2) \in N$ and

$c_1 - c_2 \subseteq b_1 \cup b_2$, say $c_1 - c_2 \subseteq b_1$, then $(c_1', c_2') \in N'$. (The sufficiency results from the fact that e.g. for $c_3 \in C$ with $(c_1, c_3) \in N$ and $c_1 - c_3 \subset b_1 \cup b_2$ obviously $(c_1', c_3') \in N'$.) But following the argumentation from (*) to (***) this is at once verified because we see that $P^1 \leftrightarrow P^2$.

"<==": It is sufficient to show that if $(c_1', c_2') \in N'$ and $c_1' - c_2' \subseteq b_1 * b_2$ then c_1 is reachable from c_2. With the notation above we have: $P^1 \neq P^2$; $P^1 \leftrightarrow P^2$. Therefore we derive from (*) to (***) that there is a "bridge" in (C,N) between the paths $\{c_i^1 \mid 1 \leq i \leq r\}$ and $\{c_j^2 \mid 1 \leq j \leq v\}$,and these sequences contain c_1 and c_2,respectively.

We define for $c \in C$: $f(c) := [c']_{\underset{B'-B_k'}{\sim}}$ where c' is constructed as in (***). Because of (□) f is one-to-one , and this completes the proof.

3. A Problem of Fair Interruption

We assume that in a complex system with many interacting parts there are two parts named C1 and C2 . The processes in C1 and C2 be mainly independent with the only exception that processes in C1 may interrupt processes in C2 at certain conditions . For descriptional simplicity we assume that the processes in C2 run along a cycle of states. We do not want to make use of any further structural detail of the processes involved. We even do not postulate a special direction of the processes in C2 along the specified cycle. As an example take the data transmission in a data bus,e.g. in a minicomputer network.

A cyclic process in C1 is allowed to interrupt the processes in C2 under the following requirements (which we shall take as constraints for the construction of a solution):

1) We do not make any assumption on the geographical or timely distance between C1 and C2 or on the relative speeds of the processes in C1 and C2.

2) There is a special section of activity in C1 (and only one) called the <u>interrupting section</u> during which the processes of C2 may be interrupted after at most one cycle,e.g. after sending an interrupt signal. There is another section in C1 during which C2 is completely free from C1. It may be called the <u>free section</u> of C1.

3) There is one and only one section in C2 (called the <u>halting</u> or <u>inter-</u>

ruptible section) in which the cyclic processes can be stopped.

According to 1) the distance between C1 and C2 may be very large. So the information transmission from C1 to C2 may need some functionally non-trivial facilities. We formulate as a requirement:

4) In case of a conflict in the information transmission facility the events which were activated by C1 will have priority.

5) The process in C1 cannot be prevented by C2 from doing its next step.

Let us assume that the process in C1 is very fast compared to those in C2 (see 1)). So it may happen that a cyclic process in C2 was free while he began to prepare himself to leave the interruptible section (see 2)). During this time the process in C1 might go to the interrupting section (see 2)). As a requirement of fairness (with respect to C1) we therefore formulate:

6) If one of the cyclic processes in C2 was left free by C1 (see 2)) while he prepared himself to leave the interruptible section he will be allowed to do so (but will halt as soon as he enters the interruptible section because of 3)).

Altogether the influence of the interruption is not in force immediately,and the structure of the constraints given in 1) to 6) seems not very lucid. We shall construct a suitable LCST in several steps. The first one is found in fig.8. (In those parts in which the transitional relation is not drawn it is regarded to be the full relation.) The interruptible section in C2 consists only of the phase 1 . In phase 2 or 4 a process which is to go to 1 is warned when he may be interrupted in 1. 2 and 4 are therefore called warning phases. Phase 3 represents the remainder sections of activity of the involved processes. The information transmission facility consists of the parts A and B, C2 has only the two phases 12 and 15. If C2 is in 15 and is kept there the following will happen:

a) If a process of the form 1 → 2 → 3 → 4 → 1 ... is running in C2 then after at most one cycle - more precisely: after 4 → 1 - the parts A and B had been forced to come to 7 and 11,respectively. But from the case {1,7,11,15} there cannot be a transition 1 → 2. Consequently these processes are interrupted in 1.

b) If a process of the form 1 → 4 → 3 → 2 → 1 ... is running in C2 then A and B are enforced to go to 8 and 10,respectively, before 2 → 1 can be done. But then 1 → 4 cannot happen,and therefore these processes are also interrupted in 1.

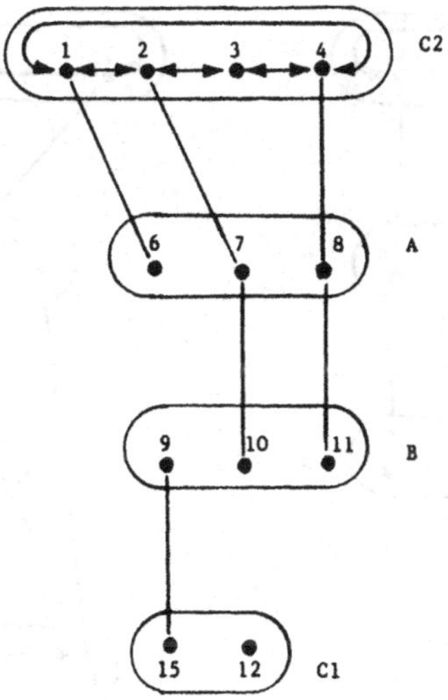

Fig.8

In both cases the processes are not interrupted outside of phase 1. Furthermore 15 → 12 can occur in any case, and then the processes in C2 may run arbitrarily. We see that this "solution" already satisfies the requirements 1),3),5) and - partially - 2). (15 represents the interrupting section.) On the other hand: If C1 is in 12 the processes in C2 are not completely free because they have to enforce some changes in A during their runs. In order to cut these mutual influences between C1 and A if required we introduce a slack phase 5 in A (with respect to C2 and B) as shown in fig.9 (see 1.10). Nearly everything remains true what was said about the system in fig.8 . The only exception is that if C1 is in 12 the processes in C2 now have the chance to be completely free, namely if A comes to 5 and remains there once C1 has been moved to 12. We enforce this by extending our "solution" again (see fig.10): First we split 12 into two phases 12 and 14, then we change the previous transitional relation in the indicated manner. This does not at all change the validity of the requirements. 12 plays the same role as before. Now we couple 12 to 6,7,8. Consequently A is forced to go to 5 (thus C2 is left free) before C1 enters 12. In order to come from 15 to 12 we need the slack phase 14 (with respect to A). Requirement 2) is satisfied now: 12 represents the free section.-

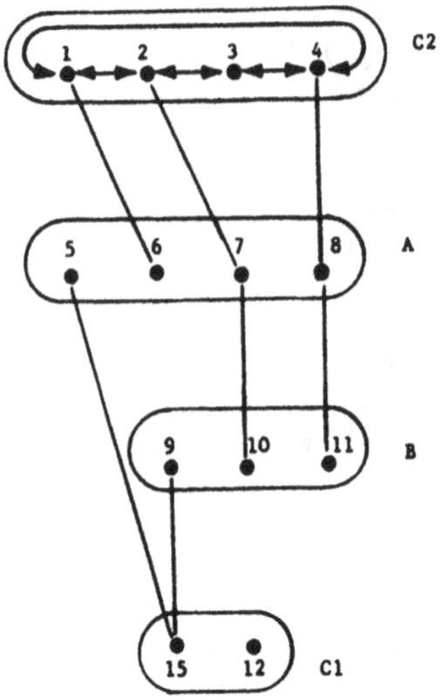

Fig.9

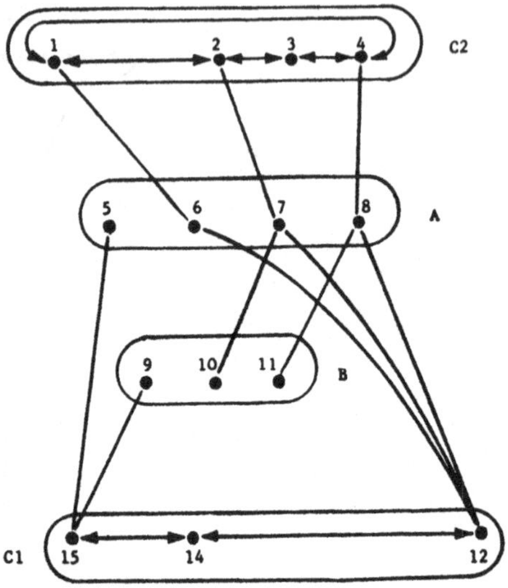

Fig.10

The idea for the construction here is that the processes in C2 are enforced to strangulate themselves - i.e. they decrease their slack of behaviour by their own power up to zero - once C1 has come to 15. A is pushed to 5 if C1 goes to 12. Although this procedure is not explicitly used in the field of programming and our argumentation is in abstract terms there is a well-known technical realization: The combination of a free-wheeling installation and the back-pedaling brake which is found in every bicycle.-

Our "solution" is not yet fair (compare 6)): Starting from {1,5,9,12} we may have - due to certain relative speeds in C1 and C2 - the following transition sequence: $12 \to 14$, $9 \to 11$, $5 \to 7$, $14 \to 15$. Consequently $1 \to 2$ cannot occur any more although a process like $1 \to 2 \to 3 \to 4 \to 1 \to \ldots$ was free initially. Another sequence would be: $12 \to 14$, $9 \to 10$, $5 \to 8$, $14 \to 15$,and then $1 \to 4$ could no longer occur although a process like $1 \to 4 \to 3 \to 2 \to 1 \to \ldots$ was free initially.

Now we split the interruptible phase 1 into three phases 1(4),1(0),1(2) (see fig.11). They play the same role with respect to A,B,C1 as 1 did before. The transitional relation is extended in the indicated manner. So a process which wants to go to 2 (4) has first to go to the immediate predecessor 1(2) (1(4)) . Next we want to exclude the first of the two bad transition sequences above. Therefore we require that as long as 14 and 1(2) hold A cannot go to 7: The coupling of part D to A,C1,C2 realizes the <u>elementary restriction</u>

$$\forall_{c \in C} \quad : \quad 14 \in c \wedge 1(2) \in c \implies 7 \notin c \qquad \text{(see 1.8)} .$$

By 1.9 we know that from every case every transition is possible which does not violate this restriction.- A similar construction would guarantee that during 14 and 1(4) A cannot go to 8. We combine both steps

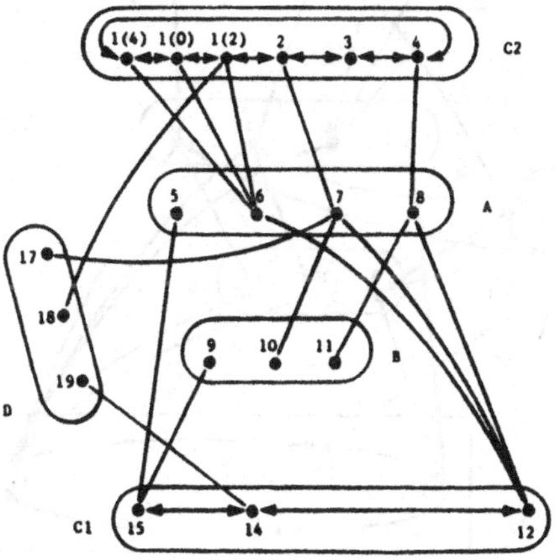

Fig.11

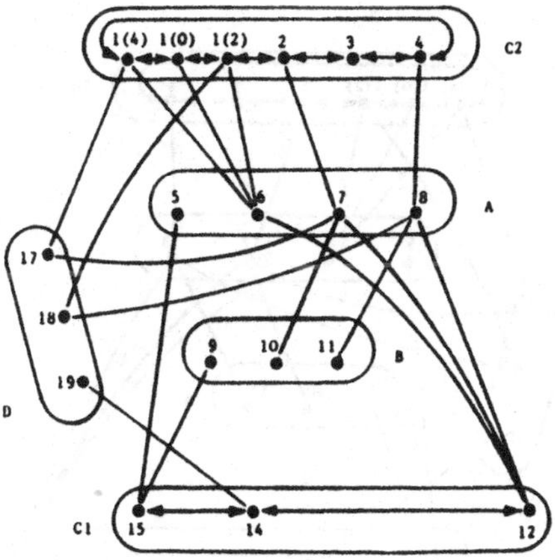

Fig.12

as shown in fig.12 : Instead of two elementary restrictions we have a single <u>conditional elementary restriction</u> (see 1.8 and specialize as follows: $k=1; l=3; n=5;$ $\# = \forall$; $\#' = \exists$; $\#'' = \forall$; $A_1(i,c) = p_i \in c$; $A_2(j,c) = p_j \in c$; $A_3(m,c) = p_m \notin c$):

$$\forall_{c \in C} \quad : \quad (14 \in c \wedge (1(2) \in c \vee 8 \in c)) \implies 1(4) \notin c \wedge 7 \notin c \quad ;$$

Let us assume that the LCST in fig.12 came to the case {1(2),5,9,12,19}. The processes in C2 are free-running, and we may have the following sequence of transitions:

19 → 17, 12 → 14, 5 → 8, 9 → 10, 14 → 15, 1(2) → 2, 2 → 3, 8 → 6,
3 → 4, 10 → 11, 6 → 7, 17 → 19, 4 → 1(4), 1(4) → 1(0), 1(0) → 1(2) .

Then 1(2) → 2 is not possible. But at the same time we cannot go from 15 to 14 unless we move C2 from 1(2) back to 1(0). This deadlock strongly violates requirement 5) because the process in C1 would depend here on C2. The crucial point is that we pass phase 14 both along the way from 12 to 15 and from 15 to 12. In order to differ between these functions of 14 we split it into two phases,named 14 and 16 (see fig.13). The transitional relation of fig.12 is transformed into the precedence relation as indicated (compare 2.2!). The role of 14 is that of the previous phase 14 while 16 is a slack phase with respect to D.- In order to satisfy requirement 2) again we couple 12 to 10 and 11 and 9 to 17 and 18 (see fig.14). If C1 is now in 12,D must be in 19 (which is a slack phase with respect to C2). Phase 12 represents the free section of C1.

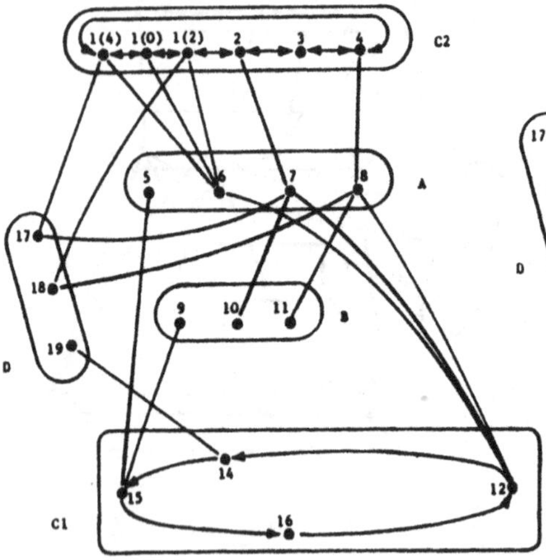

Fig.13

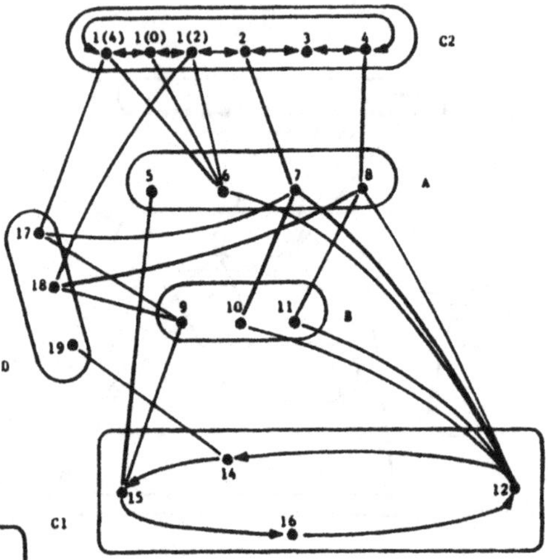

Fig.14

Assume that C1 is in 12 and therefore D in 19. Then C1 cannot go to 14 because D would have to leave phase 19 before,and this would be impossible because B cannot leave phase 9. Again requirement 5) would be violated. We overcome this difficulty by splitting 12 into two phases, named 12 and 13. 12 plays the same role as the previous phase 12,and 13 acts as phase 12 did in fig.13 (see fig.15). The precedence relation is extended as shown. We now claim that the LCST in fig.15 is a solution of our problem.

By our construction method certain restrictive properties were preserved. So we know that processes like

1(2) → 2 → 3 → 4 → 1(4) → 1(0) → 1(2) → ... are interrupted in 1(2) after at most one cycle if C1 is in 15. Similarly processes like

1(4) → 4 → 3 → 2 → 1(2) → 1(0) → 1(4) → ... are interrupted in 1(4).

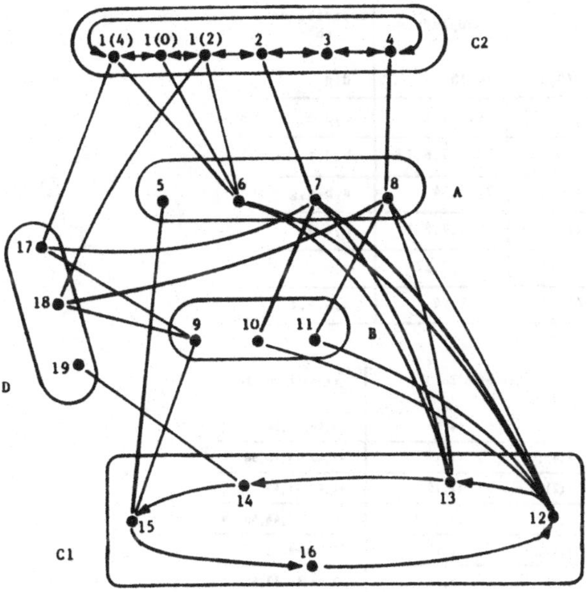

Fig.15

The interruptible section is {1(4),1(0),1(2)} .

Inorder to show that all requirements are satisfied we are interested in phase configurations {p,q} with p ϵ C1 , q ϵ C2 and their relations to one another. Therefore it is sufficient to evaluate the case graph restricted to {C1,C2} (see 2.5). We first"compress",by applying the algorithm defined in 2.3,the system covered by {A,B,D} to a single part. Merging D and B leads to D*B for which we listed the information in fig.16. Step2 does not apply here because any two phases in D*B are coupled with different sets of phases.- Next we merge A and D*B according to step1. The resulting part A*D*B is listed in fig.17. (Except the coupling of phases in A the list is only computed from that in fig.16.- From the second column of the list in fig.17 we see that e.g. 41 and 44 are both coupled to 1(4),12,15. From the third column we learn that there is a transition between them. So they can be merged according to step2. The list which results from the full application of step2 is in fig.18. A graphical representation of A*D*B is in fig.19.

In the reduced LCST we have B' =: {C1,C2,A*D*B} as the set of parts,and K<C1 C2> = ∅ . From this simple structure we compute the case graph restricted to B' - {A*D*B} by elementary checks in the list in fig.18. The result is found in fig.20. By corollary 2.7 we know that this graph

phases	coupled to	transitions to
a = (9,19)	14,15	d,g
b = (10,17)	1(4),7,12	c,d,e
c = (10,18)	1(2),7,8,12	b,d,f
d = (10,19)	7,12,14	a,b,c,g
e = (11,17)	1(4),7,8,12	b,f,g
f = (11,18)	1(2),8,12	c,e,g
g = (11,19)	8,12,14	a,d,e,f

Fig.16

phases	coupled to	transitions to
40 = (5,a)	14,15	43,46,47,54,57
41 = (5,b)	1(4), 12,15	42,43,44,48,58
42 = (5,c)	1(2), 12,15	41,43,45,49
43 = (5,d)	12,14,15	40,41,42,46,50,59
44 = (5,e)	1(4), 12,15	41,45,46,51
45 = (5,f)	1(2), 12,15	42,44,46,52,55
46 = (5,g)	12,14,15	40,43,44,45,56
47 = (6,a)	1(4),1(0),1(2),12,13,14,15	40,50,53,54,57
48 = (6,b)	1(4),1(0),1(2),12,13	41,49,50,51,58
49 = (6,c)	1(4),1(0),1(2),12,13	42,48,50,52
50 = (6,d)	1(4),1(0),1(2),12,13,14	43,47,48,49,53,59
51 = (6,e)	1(4),1(0),1(2),12,13	44,48,52,53
52 = (6,f)	1(4),1(0),1(2),12,13	45,49,51,53,55
53 = (6,g)	1(4),1(0),1(2),12,13,14	46,47,50,51,52,56
54 = (7,a)	2, 12,13,14,15	40,47,56,57
55 = (7,f)	1(2),2, 12,13	45,52,56
56 = (7,g)	2, 12,13,14	46,53,54,55
57 = (8,a)	4, 12,13,14,15	40,47,54,59
58 = (8,b)	1(4),4, 12,13	41,48,59
59 = (8,d)	4, 12,13,14	43,50,57,58

Fig.17

is isomorphic to the case graph restricted to B - {A,D,B} of the LCST in fig.15. So we have an explicit representation of the information which we need for our correctness proof. The columns in the scheme correspond to phases of C2, the rows to phases of C1. One finds especially that starting from {1(2),[E],12} a process in C2 cannot be prevented from 1(2) → 2 even if the process in C1 goes very quickly to 15 and therefore the system comes to the class {1(2),[QR],15} . (The solution is <u>fair</u>.) On the other hand, when the same process was interrupted (in a case belonging to {1(2),[O],15}) it is necessary (and possible) first to go from 15 to 16 before 1(2) → 2 can occur. It is also obvious that the process in C1 is not influenced by those in C2 (see requirement 5)).

phases	coupled to	transitions to
E = {40}	14,15	H,I,M,P
F = {41,44}	1(4), 12,15	G,H,L,Q
G = {42,45}	1(2), 12,15	F,H,L,N
H = {43,46}	12,14,15	E,F,G,K,O,R
I = {47}	1(4),1(0),1(2),12,13,14,15	E,K,M,P
K = {50,53}	1(4),1(0),1(2),12,13,14	H,I,L,O,R
L = {48,49,51,52}	1(4),1(0),1(2),12,13	F,G,K,N,Q
M = {54}	2, 12,13,14,15	E,I,O,P
N = {55}	1(2),2, 12,13	G,L,O
O = {56}	2, 12,13,14	H,K,M,N
P = {57}	4, 12,13,14,15	E,I,M,R
Q = {58}	1(4),4, 12,13	F,L,R
R = {59}	4, 12,13,14	H,K,P,Q

Fig.18

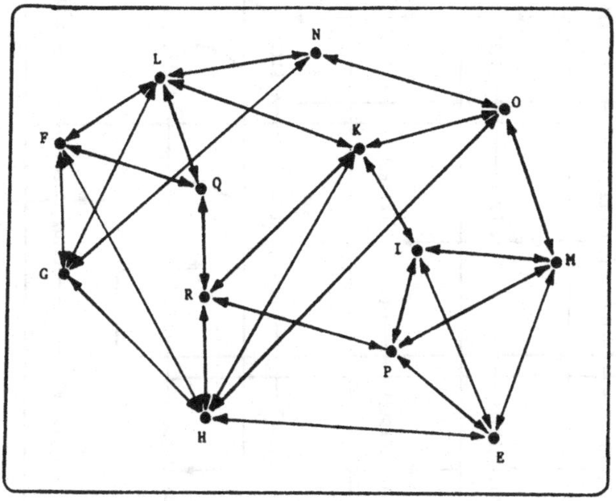

A * D * B

Fig.19

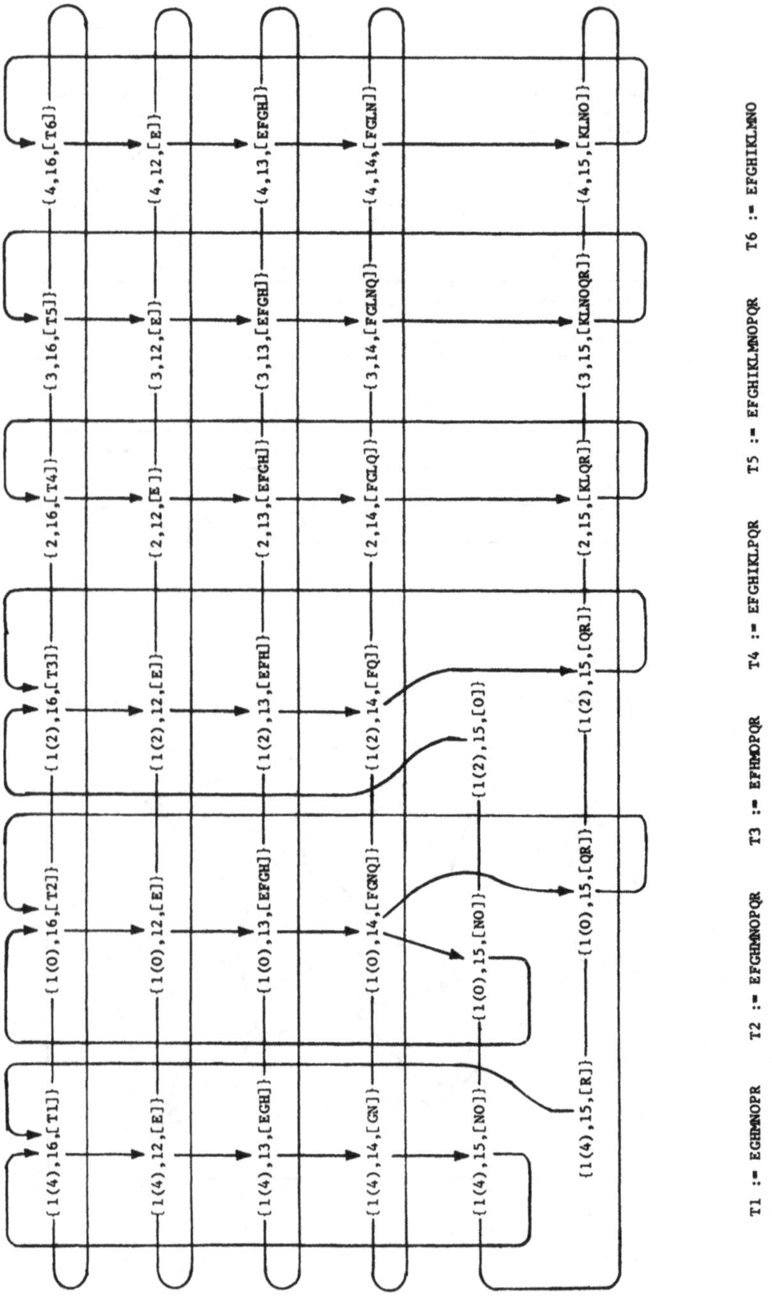
{1(4),16,[T1]}
{1(0),16,[T2]}
{1(2),16,[T3]}
{2,16,[T4]}
{3,16,[T5]}
{4,16,[T6]}
{1(4),12,[E]}
{1(0),12,[E]}
{1(2),12,[E]}
{2,12,[E]}
{3,12,[E]}
{4,12,[E]}
{1(4),13,[EGH]}
{1(0),13,[EFGH]}
{1(2),13,[EFH]}
{2,13,[EFGH]}
{3,13,[EFGH]}
{4,13,[EFGH]}
{1(4),14,[GN]}
{1(0),14,[FGNQ]}
{1(2),14,[FQ]}
{2,14,[FGLQ]}
{3,14,[FGLNQ]}
{4,14,[FGLN]}
{1(4),15,[NO]}
{1(0),15,[NO]}
{1(2),15,[O]}
{1(4),15,[R]}
{1(0),15,[QR]}
{1(2),15,[QR]}
{2,15,[KLQR]}
{3,15,[KLNOQR]}
{4,15,[KLNO]}
T1 := EGHMNOPR
T2 := EFGHMNOPQR
T3 := EFHMOPQR
T4 := EFGHIKLPQR
T5 := EFGHIKLMNOPQR
T6 := EFGHIKLMNO

Fig.20

4. Discussion of results and conclusions

The subsystem U in fig.15 which is covered by A,D,B was mainly understood (in terms of our construction) to describe the function of the information transmission between C1 and C2. But our language of parts, phases and coupling edges is general enough to regard A,D,B at the same time as representations of real objects which realize these functions by their interaction.

U was compressed by the algorithm to a single part and a non-trivial transition structure (see fig.19). This structure corresponds to the case graph of U! Thus it is worth mentioning that A*D*B has nearly the same number of phases - 13 - as altogether are in U which has 10.

The evaluation of the case graph restricted to B - {A,D,B} = {C1,C2} was very simple,a consequence of 2.7 . The original system has 1080 configurations and 207 cases,and therefore a direct computation of this restricted case graph would have been terribly laborious. Compared with the number of cases in the reduced system (132) the restricted case graph in fig.20 looks conveniently small. Furthermore: As we required that there should be no influence from C2 to C1 and that C2 be not disturbed except that C1 would be in 15 we could expect that every configuration {p,q} with $p \in C1$; $q \in C2$ should occur in some class. For the interruptible section {1(4),1(0),1(2)} in C2 there should be at least two classes for each of the involved phases in order to reflect the different status of this section concerning interrupts from C1. Therefore we would need at least 33 reduced cases for a correctness proof. But this is exactly the number to be found in fig.20. We conclude that the case graph restricted to {C1,C2} was shown to be a minimal invariant (under the algorithm). The algorithm is very simple. For our problem, but also in many other examples it worked practically efficient. So first steps were made here to settle a principle of invariance (and derived methods) also for the formal manipulation of restrictions which is introduced by Loosely Coupled Systems.

Our solution is not "minimal" but by the stepwise construction (in terms of symmetrical relations) it could be shown how flexible our modelling tools can be. Especially we could in a systematic way increase or decrease the slack of behaviour which system parts have with respect to other parts. When we used (conditional) elementary restrictions the given slack was decreased only as far as it was required by the constraint which was to be realized.-

As we solely used restrictions as specification elements we established the constraints on the behaviour of system parts as an independent aspect of a system description. This is especially useful in case that the interconnection between parts is very complex,e.g. in computer networks.

Our formal techniques introduce new construction ideas into the field of programming which are close to (informal) working principles in technical mechanics. Although the application of our formalism is therefore not restricted to systems which are implemented by computer it is conceivable, with our results above, to provide, for a compiler, additional and independent information which is based only on a restrictional structure (constraint modules) and its derived semantics.

Acknowledgement

The idea of a reduction algorithm comparable to ours was suggested by Ugo Montanari and then discussed during the visit of one of the authors in Pisa in March, 1978. Hereby the development of our algorithm was highly stimulated.

The results of this paper were worked out during a guest researcher's stay of two of the authors in May, 1978 at the Institut für Informationssystemforschung of the Gesellschaft für Mathematik und Datenverarbeitung, St. Augustin. They thank Prof. Petri for the invitation.

References

1. Brinch Hansen, P.: Distributed Processes: A Concurrent Programming Concept; CACM; Vol. 21,11(1978)
2. Genrich,H.J. and Lautenbach,K.: Facts in Place/Transition Nets; Proc. of the MFCS'78 Symp., in: Springer Lecture Notes in Computer Science; Vol. 64(1978)
3. Lauer,P.E., Best,E. and Shields,M.W.: On the Problem of Achieving Adequacy of Concurrent Programs; in: Formal Description of Programming Concepts; E.J. Neuhold (ed.); North Holland Publ. Comp., Amsterdam (1978)
4. Lautenbach,K. and Wedde,H.: Generating Control Mechanisms by Restrictions; Proc. of the MFCS'76 Symp.; in: Springer Lecture Notes in Computer Science; Vol. 45(1976)
5. Patil,S.S.: Coordination of Asynchronous Events; MAC TR-72; MIT(1970)
6. Wedde,H. and Winkowski,J.: Determining Processes by Violations; Proc. of the MFCS'77 Symp.; in: Springer Lecture Notes in Comp.Sc.;53(1977)
7. Wedde,H.: Fundamentals of a Theory of Infringements; in: Progress in Cybernetics and Systems Research; Hemisphere; Washington D.C.(inpress)

Adequate Path Expressions

M. W. Shields

Computing Laboratory, University of Newcastle-upon-Tyne,
Claremont Tower, Claremont Road, Newcastle-upon-Tyne,
NE1 7RU. England.
Tel. Newcastle-upon-Tyne 29233.

Abstract

The object of this paper is to present some results in the formal study of path expressions. Path expressions, or GR-paths, are syntactic objects, that is, terminals strings of a grammar. GR-paths themselves may also be regarded as grammars; each GR-path determines a trace language, in the sense of [M_{az}77]. In this sense, GR-paths may be thought of as a defining systems, in that each is associated with a set of possible histories of concurrent behaviour, represented formally by traces. In this exposition, traces are represented as n-tuples of strings and it is briefly shown how such n-tuples determine labelled, partially ordered sets, a popular way of modelling concurrent histories.

A general problem in the study of path expressions is that of being able to deduce dynamic properties of paths from their static properties, that is to deduce properties of a set of traces from combinatorial properties of a string, the GR-path which generates this set. In this paper we show that the formalism associated with path expressions supports rigorous mathematical analysis of paths with respect to a dynamic property called adequacy, a notion related to freedom from deadlock and to the internal consistency of a specification. Several theorems are proved about this property, including a generalisation of the well-known liveness theorem for 1-safe marked graphs (3.3) and a number of results on adequacy-preserving transformations, which may, in some cases, be used to reduce large programs to smaller and more manageable ones with the same adequacy properties. These results are illustrated with examples.

1 Introduction

This paper is concerned with the analysis of certain mathematical objects called GR-paths or less formally path expressions. Path expressions were invented by R.H. Campbell and A.N. Habermann as a formalism for specifying process synchronization [CH74]. They were later incorporated into the path-process notation described in [LC75] and there equipped with a formal semantics in terms of marked, labelled transition nets. An object in this notation, a program, is associated with such a net and the program is to be considered as formally specifying the concurrent behaviour of the net under the usual firing rule. This semantics also allowed the authors of the quoted paper to give formal definitions of dynamic properties of the systems notionally specified by the notation; one such dynamic property is that of adequacy, a property akin to liveness in token mathematics, which is the property with which we are concerned in this paper, in fact.

The path-process notation has now been incorporated into the COSY (concurrent system) notation [LTS78] which essentially provides facilities for the iterative definition of large path-process programs and program fragments. However, it may be shown that any COSY program is in some sense equivalent to a path expression and that it is sufficient, in order to develop a theory of adequacy of COSY programs, merely to study path expressions. This is what we are doing here.

There are two different points of view from which a GR-path may be considered as specifying a system. Informally, a GR-path consists of a set of objects called R-paths (or just paths) each one of which may be thought of as a formal definition of some (sequential) constraint on the way in which occurrences of events in a system are to relate. Thus, to write a path expression to describe a system, take a description of the system in a natural language in which each sentence defines some sequential constraint on occurrences of some of the events generated to the system. (For example: don't try to read from a buffer frame until something has been deposited into it, put in the milk before you pour in the tea; don't cross the road until the green man starts flashing).

Translate each sentence into a R-path and concatenate these paths; the resulting object a GR-path may be considered to be an abstract description of the system. The second point of view from which one may consider path expressions as specifying concurrent systems is from the point of view of analysing a path expression. Here, a path expression P may be regarded as a grammatical object, generating, in fact, a trace language in the sense of [Maz77]. Each element of this trace language, VFS(P), which in fact consists of n-tuples of strings, may be considered as formally representing some possible history of concurrent behaviour. In this sense a path expression P may be considered as formally representing a system in that it is 'something with a certain kind of behaviour', the 'kind of behaviour' possessed by all the elements of VFS(P) .

One may here formally define systems properties in terms of properties of trace languages, or any equivalent formalism such as, in this case, occurrence graphs or causal nets, and hope that one is in the possession of enough mathematics to successfully determine, in any particular case, whether a system has such a property or not. It is with the development of such a mathematical superstructure that we are here concerned.

There is a third aspect to the use of paths (or indeed the full COSY notation) as a formalism for modelling and analysing systems that needs mentioning. This is the business of convincing oneself that the path expression one has written to describe a system actually does what one wants it to, the vindication of a path model. There is no space to go into this here, but essentially, it involves interpreting events contained in the path model as functions and showing that certain invariants hold for all the elements of the corresponding language. For example, in [SL79], it was shown that programs using Agerwala's extended semaphore primitives as their only means of synchronization could be 'translated' into COSY programs. This translation was vindicated by showing that the functional properties of the primitives were implicit in the synchronization properties of the corresponding COSY program.

Of these three aspects of modelling, writing, vindication and analysis, we shall only be dealing with the latter. The writing of - in fact of COSY programs is dealt with in [LTS78,TL77] and in [LS77] where a certain amount of informal analysis is done. As another example of vindication, [S79] deals with the modelling and analysis of a toy train set with trains run asynchronously.

2 Preliminaries

An n-tuple semantics for GR-paths

An R-path is any string of terminal symbols generated by the following production rules. Non-terminals are written between the symbols '<' and '>'.

<path>= path <sequence> end

<sequence>= <orelement>|<orelement>;<sequence>

<orelement>= <element>,<orelement>

<element>=<operation>|(<sequence>)|<element>*

'<operation>' may be replaced from some set of operation names; we shall usually use subscripted algol-like identifiers.

If P is an R-path, we shall denote by Ops(P) the set of operations belonging to P. If op is an operation and elem, orelem, and seq are, respectively, terminal strings generated from non-terminals, respectively, <element>, <orelement> and <sequence>, then we define:

Cyc(op) = {op}

Cyc((seq)) = Cyc(seq)

Cyc(elem*) = Cyc(elem)*

Cyc(elem,orelem) = Cyc(elem)$\cup$Cyc(orelem)

Cyc(orelem;seq) = Cyc(orelem)Cyc(seq)

Cyc(path seq end) = Cyc(seq)

Here juxtaposition denotes concatenation of strings and for two sets of strings A and B, AB is the set $\{xy|x\in A \wedge y\in B\}$. A* denotes the set $\bigcup_{0}^{\infty} A^n$, where $A^0 = \{\varepsilon\}$ and ε is the null string.

If P is an R-path, the set Cyc(P) is called the set of cycles of P. The reason for this name is that each element of Cyc(P) corresponds to a simple cycle in the simulating net of P according to the net semantics for path expressions, or equivalently to a firing sequence of this net, which is a labelled state machine, which takes the token of this net round the net and back to the initially marked place exactly once.

This remark motivates the definition of the set of firing sequences of an R-path P,FS(P). We define

FS(P) = Pref(Cyc(p)*).

Pref(A) here denotes the set of string prefaces of the stringset A.

Pref(A) = {x| y such that xy$\in$A}.

FS(P) may be thought of as representing the set of possible histories of behaviour of a system obeying constraints enshrined in the path P. For example, if P = path deposit; remove end, then Cyc(P) = {deposit remove} and FS(P) = {deposit remove}*{deposit,ε}.

Thus, a history of a system described by this path consists of a sequence of alternate deposits and removes beginning with a deposit. This is intuitively the behaviour of a buffer frame which is initially empty.

The behaviours associated with individual paths are sequential. If we wish to generate non-sequential behaviour, we must use several paths. A GR-path is a string $P=P_1 \ldots P_n$ where each P_i is an R-path. Informally, if we think of P_i as describing a constraint c_i then P describes a constraint c_1 and c_2 and ... and c_n. For example 'do a then b' and 'do a then c' will mean the same thing as 'do a then do b and c concurrently'.

There are several ways in which we could define behaviours of a GR-path. For example, we might use labelled partially ordered sets or occurrence graphs. We shall however represent histories of a GR-path by n-tuples of strings. These allow us to represent concurrency and have the advantage that they may be manipulated in the same manner as strings.

So, let $P = P_1 \ldots P_n$, where each P_i is an R-path, and define Ops(P) = $\bigcup_{i=1}^{n}$Ops(P_i). If a$\in$Ops(P), let $\underline{a}_p = (a_1,\ldots,a_n)$, where a_i is a if a$\in$Ops(P) and ε otherwise. We define the vector operations of P, Vops(P), to be the elements of the set $\{\underline{a}_p | a \in Ops(P)\}$. The elements of Vops(P) may be concatenated, where concatenation is defined componentwise

$$(x_1,\ldots,x_n)(y_1,\ldots,y_n) = (x_1y_1,\ldots,x_ny_n)$$

and with this definition of composition we may, as in the string case, generate from Vops(P) a semigroup with identity $\underline{\varepsilon}_p = (\varepsilon,\ldots,\varepsilon)$. We call this semigroup Vops(P)*. Note that Vops(P)* is not necessarily a free semigroup since, for example, if $a,b \in Ops(P)$ and $a \in Ops(P_i) \Rightarrow b \notin Ops(P_i)$ for each i then $\underline{a}_p\underline{b}_p = \underline{b}_p\underline{a}_p$. Commutativity here is to be equivalent to concurrency, as we shall explain shortly. First let us define the set of histories of a GR-path.

Let P be as above, then we define $VFS(P) = \{\underline{x} \in Vops(P)^* | [\underline{x}]_i \in FS(P_i)$ for each $i\}$. Here we are using $[\underline{x}]_i$ to denote the i'th coordinate of the n-tuple $\underline{x}$, $\underline{x} = ([\underline{x}]_1,\ldots,[\underline{x}]_n)$.

Intuitively, we may regard elements of VFS(P) as describing histories as follows. There are two kinds of constraint on a system specified by P; firstly, in any history of the system, the operations mentioned in P_i <u>must</u> occur in an order permitted by P_i, each P_i, and that the P_i together define the only sequential constraints on the members of Ops(P). A history, may then be completely described by listing the sequences, one for each P_i, of occurrences of events from $Ops(P_i)$, that is, may be completely described by some element of $FS(P_1)\times\ldots\times FS(P_n)$. Secondly, the sequences must be consistent with each other. Thus if $a,b \in Ops(P_1) \cap Ops(P_2)$ and $(x_1,\ldots,x_n)$ is a history, then the i'th occurrence of a in x_1 preceeds the j'th occurrence of b in x_1 if and only if the i'th occurrence of a in x_2 preceeds the j'th occurrence of b in x_2. It may be shown that the set of all such n-tuples is Vops(P)*. the set of all histories of P may thus be modelled by $(FS(P_1)\times\ldots\times FS(P_n)) \cap Vops(P)^* = VFS(P)$.

VFS(P) is called the set of vector firing sequences of P. It may be regarded as a trace language with independence relation $\{(a,b) | \underline{a}_p\underline{b}_p = \underline{b}_p\underline{a}_p\}$ over the string language $FS(P) = \{a^1\ldots a^m \in Ops(P)^* | \underline{a}^1_p\ldots\underline{a}^m_p \in VFS(P)\}$. Alternatively, we may construct from each element of VFS(P) a labelled poset as follows; if $\underline{a}^1_p\ldots\underline{a}^m_p \in VFS(P)$, let X be a set $\{p_1,\ldots,p_m\}$ and define a relation on X,R, by $(p_i,p_j) \in R$ if and only if $i \leq j$ and for some $k, a^i, a^j \in Ops(P_k)$. Let $\leq$ be the transitive closure of R, then $(X,\leq)$ may be shown to be a poset. Define $lab(p_i) = a^i$. Intuitively, each p_i represents the occurrence of some event $lab(p_i)$ and $p_i \leq p_j$ and $i \neq j$ may be interpreted as meaning that the occurrence p_i of $lab(p_i)$ has strictly preceeded occurrence p_j of $lab(p_j)$. If p_i and p_j are not comparable under $\leq$ then they may be thought of as being concurrent occurrences. This will be the case iff $\underline{a}^i_p\underline{a}^j_p = \underline{a}^j_p\underline{a}^i_p$.

Our concern here is not, however, with concurrency but with a property called <u>adequacy</u>. A GR-path will be said to be adequate if and only if for all $\underline{x} \in VFS(P)$ for all $\underline{a}_p \in Vops(P)$ there exists $\underline{y} \in Vops(P)^*$ such that $\underline{x}\underline{y}\underline{a}_p \in VFS(P)$.

Thus adequacy is a strengthening of the notion of freedom from deadlock. In an adequate path, no operation ever becomes 'dead', that is, incapable of ever occurring again without infringing the constraints enshrined in the path. It is to the presentation of results to support the analysis of the adequacy properties of GR-paths that this paper is devoted.

A relationship between GR-paths and transition nets

The problem of dtermining whether a given path is adequate was first proposed, along with a definition of adequacy, in [LC75], where the 'meaning' of the notation was defined in terms of a mapping from programs to marked labelled transition nets. We have shown that it is not necessary, in order to say what a path expression means, to map it to anything else; P 'means' what it potentially does, that is VFS(P). However, it is necessary to clarify the relationship between the work of the previous section and the net semantics of [LC75], while a connection between paths and transition nets is at least of some technical importance. For example, the problem of finding general necessary and sufficient criteria for adequacy may be shown to be equivalent to the liveness problem for 1-safe transition nets, while results on liveness may give rise to results on adequacy. For example, and adequacy criterion for a class of paths called GE_0-paths was given in [LC75]; this was an almost direct translation of the liveness theorem for 1-safe marked graphs. In fact, we shall later derive this latter result as a corollary of a theorem on another class of paths, the GR_0-paths.

We shall give here a mapping of paths into marked labelled nets. A marked labelled net is a quintuple $N=(S,T,F,M,L)$, where $S\neq\emptyset$ is a finite set of places, $T\neq\emptyset$ is a finite set of transitions, $F\subseteq S\times T\cup T\times S$ is the flow relation, where $S\cup T=$ Field(F), that is, there are no isolated places or transitions. $M:S\rightarrow\mathbb{N}$, $\mathbb{N}$ the natural numbers, is the initial marking and $L:T\rightarrow Ops$, is the labelling function, where Ops is some set. We shall assume that the reader is familiar with the notions of firing rule and firing sequence. The firing sequences of N from the initial marking M will be denoted by $FS(N)\subseteq T^*$. L may clearly be extended to a mapping $L^*:T^*\rightarrow Ops^*$, by $L^*(a_1\ldots a_m)=L(a_1)\ldots L(a_m)$, $a_i\in T$ and $L^*(\varepsilon)=\varepsilon$.

Suppose first that P is an R-path. We shall construct a marked, labelled net $N_P=(S_P,T_P,F_P,M_P,L_P)$ such that $L^*(FS(N_P))=FS(P)$. This, in the terminology of [LC75] will be a simulating net of P.

'I am in state so-and-so' means 'certain options are opten to me'; accepting that, we may conclude that two firing sequences $x,y\in FS(P)$ give rise to the same state (and we shall denote this by writing $x\equiv_P y$) if and only if

$\forall_z\in Ops(P)^*: xz\in FS(P)$ iff $yz\in FS(P)$.

$\equiv_P$ is an equivalence relation, if nothing else. Let us denote by $(x)_P$ the $\equiv$ P-equivalence class of $x\in FS(P)$, then $x\equiv_P y$ iff $(x)_P=(y)_P$. It should not seem arbitrary to identify states with equivalence classes. Indeed, we shall now define $S_P=\{(x)_P \mid x\in FS(P)\}$. Transitions will be associated with state changes: formally,

$T_P = \{((x)_P, a, (y)_P) | x,y \in FS(P) \wedge xa \equiv y\}$. $t \in T_P$ is associated with an input state $(x)_P$ and an output state $(y)_P$ such that an occurrence of event a takes the former into the latter. This intimates to us how to construct the flow relation;

$F_P = \{([t]_1, t) | t \in T_P\} \cup \{(t, [t]_3) | t \in R_P\}$ where $[t]_i$ denotes the i'th coordinate of the triple t. Similarly, the state that holds before anything has happened must be $(\varepsilon)_P$; we define M_P so that it maps $(\varepsilon)_P$ to 1 and everything else to 0. Finally, $L_P(t)$ can be nothing other than $[t]_2$. The energetic reader may easily check that N_P is well defined and that it is a simulating net of P, that is $FS(P) = L_P^*(FS(N_P))$.

This construction differs from that in [LC75] in a number of ways; first, it makes no distinction between paths if they have the same set of firing sequences: thus, path a end in this semantics means the same as path a;a end - as it should, given the informal explanations of the language in, for example, [LTS79] - contrary to the semantic in [LC75]. Also, the path path(a;b),(a;c) end is to mean the same as path a;b,c end. This corresponds to an observation in [Ha75] that ',' distributes over ';'. Finally, we do not use the 'multiple transition' construction of [LC75]. These are, however, the only essential differences; the paths path a;a end and path (a;b),(a;c) end typify the paths for which the semantics is really different and they are both 'pathological cases', the first of 'redundancy' and the second of 'ambiguity'.

Now suppose we have R-paths $P_1, \ldots, P_n$ and let $P = P_1 \ldots P_n$. We construct nets $N_{P_i} = (S_i, T_i, F_i, M_i, L_i)$ and combine them to give a marked labelled net N_P. We assume that the sets are pairwise disjoint. The places of N_P, S_P, are simply the elements of the set $S_1 \cup \ldots \cup S_n$. To form the transitions T_P one identifies all transitions of the N_{P_i} with the same labels in all possible ways. Formally, for each $a \in Ops(P)$ and each i, we define T_i^a to be $\{\varepsilon\}$ if $a \notin Ops(P_i)$ and $\{t \in T_i | L_i(t) = a\}$ otherwise. We define $T^a = T_1^a \times \ldots \times T_n^a$ and $T_P = \bigcup_{a \in Ops(P)} T^a$. The flow relation of N_P, F_P, is determined as follows. For all $s \in S_P$, $t = (t_1, \ldots, t_n) \in T_P$, if $s \in S_i$, then $(s,t) \in F_P$ iff $(s, t_i) \in F_i$ and $(t,s) \in F_P$ iff $(t_i, s) \in F_i$. (S_P, T_P, F_P) is a state machine decomposable net with as state machine components, the subnets generated by the sets S_i. The marking function M_P of N_P is simply $M_1 \cup \ldots \cup M_n$ and the labelling function L_P is defined by $L_P(T^a) = \underline{a}_P$. For simplicity, we shall assume that the elements of T_P do not commute, unlike the n-tuples in Vops(P), that is, we shall suppose that $FS(N_P)$ is a subset of the free semigroup on T_P, T_P^*. Again, $L_P^*: T_P^* \to Vops(P)^*$ is well defined. Consider $x \in FS(N_P)$, $x = t^1 \ldots t^m$ and $t^j = (t_1^j, \ldots, t_n^j)$. By construction for each i, $t_i^1 \ldots t_i^m \in FS(N_i)$ and $[L_P^*(x)]_i = L_i^*(t_i^1 \ldots t_i^m)$. From this it follows that $L_P^*(x) \in VFS(P)$. The argument may be reversed to show that $L_P^*(FS(N_P)) = VFS(P)$. N_P is thus indeed a simulating net of P.

We may now reformulate the definition of adequacy in terms of simulating nets. P is adequate iff $\forall x \in FS(N_P)\ \forall a \in Ops(P)\ \exists y \in T_P^* \exists t \in T_P : xyt \in FS(N_P) \wedge L_P(t) = \underline{a}_P$. If none of the component R-paths of P contain more than one instance of any o peration, that is if P is composed of E-paths, then the above equivalence reduced to :P is adequate iff N_P is live-5.

This is because for such paths P there is a one-to-one correspondence between transitions and labels. It should be remarked that the original definition of adequacy in [LC75] was that P is adequate iff N_P is live-5. This had some rather unfortunate consequences however, both in terms of the present construction and that of the cited paper. For example, if P = <u>path</u> a;b;a <u>end</u> <u>path</u> a;b;a <u>end</u>, then N_P is not live-5 in either case, although it is live-1. We have therefore adopted the slightly weeker form above.

We remark that the elements of T_P <u>may</u> be regarded as tuples and concatenated componentwise as in the case of elements of Vops(P)*. In this case we may form the set of vector firing sequences of N_P, VFS(N_P), simply by forming FS(N_P) and then 'remembering' that some of the transitions commute. (Formally we are factoring through by an independence relation in the sense of [Maz77]). Using a construction similar to that sketched in the previous section, it may be shown that each element of VFS(N_P) gives rise to a <u>casual net</u> [Pe76]. In fact, the set VFS(N_P) is equivalent to the set of all casual nets representing possible histories of N_P under the usual firing rule but taking into account all possible concurrency.

<u>Elementary results on adequacy: case graphs</u>

For small path programs, the case graph construction provides a direct means of checking adequacy. This graph may be built in two ways, either via the simulating net or directly. The first is more straightforward, the latter has certain direct technical advantages.

If (S,T,F,M,L) = N is a marked labelled net, its case graph G_N is a rooted labelled directed graph whose nodes are the markings of N reachable from M via the usual firing rule, with initial node or root M, and such that there is an arc from M_1 to M_2 labelled $a \in L(T)$ iff there is a transition $t \in T$ enabled by M_1 whose firing transforms M_1 to M_2 and such that L(t) = a. Clearly, any sequence of labels corresponding to some directed path through G_N rooted at M will belong to L*(FS(N)) and vice versa.

Alternatively, let P be a GR-path and define a relation $\equiv_P$ on VFS(P) as follows. If $\underline{x},\underline{y} \in$ VFS(P), then $\underline{x} \equiv_P \underline{y}$ iff $\forall_{\underline{z}} \in$ Vops(P)*: ($\underline{xz} \in$ VFS(P) iff $\underline{yz} \in$ VFS(P)). It may easily be seen that $\equiv_P$ is an equivalence relation on VFS(P). If P is an R-path, this is the relation discussed in the previous section. As in the previous section, we may construct a rooted labelled directed graph G_P with nodes $(\underline{x})_P$, $\underline{x} \in$ VFS(P), where $(\underline{x})_P$ the $\equiv_P$ equivalence class of $\underline{x}$, with initial node $(\underline{\varepsilon})_P$ and an arc from $(\underline{x})_P$ to $(\underline{y})_P$ labelled $\underline{a}_P \in$ Vops(P) iff $\underline{xa}_P \in$ VFS(P) and $\underline{xa}_P \equiv_P \underline{y}$. The reader is invited to assure himself that this construction is well defined.

If P is a GR-path and N_P is its simulating net as constructed in the previous section, then we may set up a bijection between the nodes of G_{N_P} and G_P. Suppose $(\underline{x})_P$ is a node of G_P, then it is easy to check that for any $\underline{y},\underline{z} \in (\underline{x})_P$, for any i, $[\underline{y}]_i \equiv_{P_i} [\underline{z}]_i$, where P_i is some component R-path of P.

Thus, $(\underline{x})_P$ determines a set of places $([\underline{x}]_i)_{P_i}$ in N_P. We define $f((\underline{x})_P)$ to be the marking of N_P which places one token on each of the places $([\underline{x}]_i)_{P_i}$ and leaves the other places of N_P unmarked. It may be shown that (a) $f((\underline{\varepsilon})_P) = M_P$ (b) if $f((\underline{x})_P)$ is a marking of N_P, $\underline{x} \in VFS(P)$, and $\underline{xa_P} \in VFS(P)$, $a \in Ops(P)$, then there exists $t \in T_P$ fireable at $f((\underline{x})_P)$ and labelled by $\underline{a}_P$, which transforms $f((\underline{x})_P)$ to $f((\underline{xa_P})_P)$ (c) if $x \in FS(N_P)$ transforms M_P to a marking M, then $f((L_P{*}(x))_P)=M$. These three facts establish that f determines an isomorphism of rooted labelled directed graphs taking G_P to G_{N_P}.

We remark that for any R-path, P, its simulating net N_P is finite. Since, for a GR-path the net N_P is decomposable into 1-safe finite state machines it follows that both G_{N_P} are finite.

Now let $DP(G_P)$ be the set of all sequences of directed arcs rooted at $(\underline{\varepsilon})_P$ in G_P. Thus, $(e_1,\dots,e_m)$ belongs to $DP(G_P)$ if (a) $(\underline{\varepsilon})_P$ is the input node of e_1(b) for each $i\in\{2,\dots,m\}$, the output node of e_{i-1} is the input node of e_i. If $lab(e_i)$ denotes the vector operation labelling the arc e_i in G_P, then we shall define for $(e_1,\dots,e_m) = p\in DP(P)$, $lab^*(p) = lab(e_1)\dots lab(e_m)$. We may now quote the following easy result

2.1 Proposition

Let P be a GR-path, then

(a) $\{lab^*(p) \mid p\in DP(G_P)\}=VFS(P)$

(b) P is adequate iff

(i) For every node in G_P, there is a directed path from this node into some strongly connected subgraph of G_P

(ii) Suppose G is a subgraph of G_P such that for every node n in G arc e with input node n, then the output node of e belongs to G. In this case, every element of Vops(P) labels some arc in G.

Since G_P is finite, this results shows that in particular, adequacy is decideable.

This result may sometimes be useful in verifying the adequacy of small programs, at least, the author has found it so, although it is not to be recommended in general, as even 'small' programs may have prohibitively large case graphs. Anyone wishing to build a case graph is advised to go via the net semantics, as constructing G_P directly can be somewhat messy. Indeed, the reader is advised to use the net semantics of [LC75] whenever possible, as for example in the case of GE-paths, as the construction of the net is more straightforward than in the case of the semantics given in the previous section. Remember that the two constructions only differ, apart for the merging rule, in pathological cases, where it is arguable that the [LC75] semantics allows one to 'mean nonsense'.

We now give an alternative formulation of 2.1, which is of technical use.

2.2 Lemma

Let P be a GR-path, then the following are equivalent:

(a) P is adequate

(b) Let $\underline{x}$ be any member of VFS(P), then there exist $\underline{y},\underline{z} \in$ Vops(P)* such that

(i) $\underline{xy} \in$ VFS(P) and $\underline{xyz} \in$ VFS(P)

(ii) $\underline{xy} \equiv_P \underline{xyz}$

(iii) $\underline{z}$ contains every element of Vops(P)

Note that (iii) implies that every coordinate of $\underline{z}$ is non-null.

The usefulness of this lemma is that it allows us to derive a necessary condition for adequacy of a particular class of paths the GR_0 or comma-free paths. We shall be looking at this result in the next section.

3 GR_0-paths

In this section, we present our most general result on the adequacy of a given class of paths, the GR_0-or comma-free-paths. As the name suggests, a GR_0-path is anything of the form $P = P_1 \ldots P_n$, where each P_i is an R-path of the form path $a_1;\ldots;a_m$ end. Such R-paths are called R_0-paths.

GR_0-paths have rather agreeable properties. Suppose $P = P_1 \ldots P_n$ is GR_0 and adequate. By 2.2, there exists $\underline{x},\underline{xy} \in$ VFS(P) such that $\underline{y}$ contains every member of Vops(P). Suppose $\underline{x} \neq \underline{\varepsilon}_P$ and that for some $\underline{a}_P \in$ Vops(P), $\underline{x}=\underline{x}'\underline{a}_P$. There may of course be several such a's but we do know that if $a \in Ops(P_i)$ then $[\underline{x}]_i = [\underline{x}']_i a$. Also, we may write $[\underline{xy}]_i$ as $[x']_i\ a\ [y']b$ for some $b \in Ops(P), y_i' \in Ops(P_i)^*$. We now use one of the agreeable properties of R_0-paths.

3.1 Lemma

Let P' be an R_0-paths and suppose that $xa,yb \in FS(P')$, $a,b \in Ops(P)$, then $xa \equiv_P yb \Rightarrow a=b \wedge x \equiv_P y$.

We thus have that if $a \in Ops(P_i)$, then $[\underline{y}]_i = [y']_i\ a$ for some $y_i' \in Ops(P_i)^*$. In terms of n-tuples, $\underline{xy} = \underline{x}'\underline{a}_P\underline{y}'\ \underline{a}_P \equiv_P \underline{x}'\ \underline{a}_P$. We now appeal to a second easy

3.2 Lemma

Suppose P is a GR_0-path, and suppose for $\underline{x},\underline{y} \in$ VFS(P) and $a \in Ops(P)$ that $\underline{xa}_P,\underline{ya}_P \in$ VFS(P) and $\underline{xa}_P \equiv_P \underline{ya}_P$, then $\underline{x} \equiv_P \underline{y}$.

Applying this lemma to our argument, we see that $\underline{x}' \equiv_P \underline{x}'\ \underline{a}_P\underline{y}'$. Furthermore, if $\underline{y} = \underline{y}'\underline{a}_P$ contains every element of Vops(P), then surely $\underline{a}_P\underline{y}'$ does.

We may repeat this argument for $\underline{x}'$. Ultimately, we may conclude that there is an element $\underline{z} \in$ Vops(P)* such that $\underline{\varepsilon}_P\underline{z} \in$ VFS(P), $\underline{\varepsilon}_P\underline{z} \equiv_P \underline{\varepsilon}_P$ and that $\underline{z}$ contains every element of Vops(P). Obviously $\underline{z} \in$ VFS(P). In fact $\underline{z}$ belongs to a special subset of VFS(P) defined in general as follows:

$$RVFS(P) = \{\underline{x} \in VFS(P) \mid \forall_i \in \{1,\ldots,n\}: [\underline{x}]_i \neq \varepsilon \wedge [\underline{x}]_i \in Cyc(P_i)^*\}$$

We have shown that if P is adequate then $RVFS(P) \neq \emptyset$. On the other hand if $RVFS(P) \neq \emptyset$, then it is faitly easy to show that VFS(P) = Pref(RVFS(P)*), where Pref is defined for subsets of Vops(P)* as follows:

$$Pref(X) = \{\underline{x} \in Vops(P)^* \mid \exists \underline{y} \in Vops(P)^* : \underline{xy} \in X\}.$$

Note, it is practically trivial that if VFS(P)=Pref(RVFS(P)*) then P is adequate. We have derived, albeit sketchily:

3.3 Theorem

Let P be a GR_0-path, then P is adequate iff $RVFS(P) \neq \emptyset$.

A GR_0-path is said to be a GE_0-path if no operation appears more than once in any of its constituent R-paths. For GE_0-paths, we have the following

3.4 Corollory

Suppose $P=P_1 \ldots P_n$ is a GE_0-path and $Cyc(P_i)=\{x_i\}$ for each i, then P is adequate $\Leftrightarrow$ $(x_1, \ldots, x_n) \in VFS(P)$. We remark that there is an algorithm, a modification by E. Best of an algorith, due to R. Devillers, for checking whether $RVFS(P) \neq \emptyset$ for any GR_0-path P. The algorithm may be found in [LSB78]. The following may be shown to be equivalent to 3.4.

3.5 Corollary

Let N be a 1-safe marked graph, then N is live-5 if and only if it is a disjoint union of strongly connected marked graphs and every simple cycle in N contains a token.

Let us now look at a simple application of these results. Define F_i = **path** $deposit_i$;$remove_i$ **end** D_n = **path** $deposit_1$;...;$deposit_n$ **end** R_n=**path** $remove_1$;..., $remove_n$ **end** $P_n = F_1 \ldots F_n D_n R_n$

P_n is the n frame ring buffer. We shall show that P_n is adequate for each n. Let $\underline{x}_n = \underline{deposit_1 deposit_2 \ldots deposit_n remove_1 remove_2 \ldots remove_n} \in Vops(P_n)^*$

Observe that $[\underline{x}_n]_i$ = $deposit_i remove_i \in Cyc(F_i)$ $1 \leq i \leq n$

$deposit_1 \ldots deposit_n \in Cyc(D_n)$ $i = n+1$

$remove_1 \ldots remove_n \in Cyc(R_n)$ $i = n+2$

We have thus shown that $\underline{x}_n \in RVFS(P_n)$ and that hence, by 3.3, that P_n is adequate for each n.

4 Some Substitution and Reduction Theorems

The string approach to the analysis of path expressions presented here, or at least a sequential form of it, was developed by the author in 1977 in order to demonstrate that a certain class of GR-paths, generated syntactically, consisted entirely of adequate paths. Before that, the net semantic of [LC75] had been used for analysis. In this section, we present a number of results which generalise the proof of adequacy of the aforementioned class; the class referred to in proposition 7 of [LBS77].

The essence of the matter is this; we have a GR-path $P = P_1 \ldots P_n$, the P_i, R-paths. P contains some operation a. We consider an n-tuple $S = (S_1, \ldots, S_n)$ of simple substitutions $S_i = (a, e_i)$, written $a \to e_i$, where e_i is some expression derived from one of the non-terminals element, orelement or sequence. S(P) is defined to be $S_1(P_1) \ldots S_n(P_n)$, where $S_i(P_i)$ is defined to be the path obtained from P_i by replacing each a in P_i by e_i. (The reader is invited to reassure himself that $S_i(P_i)$ is indeed a path whatever e_i is). Of course, if a does not belong to P_i then $S_i(P_i) = P_i$. We are interested in the question, under what circumstances may we conclude that S(P) is adequate if (or if and only if) P is adequate. The utility of such a result is clear; if we may show that a path Q is obtainedable from an adequate path P via the application of a sequence of adequacy-preserving substitutions, then we may conclude that Q is adequate.

For the rest of this section, we shall consider a GR-path $Q=Q_1 \ldots Q_n$, Q_i a R-path and a compound substitution $S = (S_1, \ldots, S_n)$, where each S_i is a simple substitution $a \to e_i$, and where each e_i is a terminal string derived from a non-terminal of type element. We shall also assume, which we may do without loss of generality, that for some m, $1 < m \le n$, $a \in Ops(Q_i)$ if $1 \le i \le m$ and $a \notin Ops(Q_i)$ if $i > m$.

Whether S preserves adequacy or not depends very much on the relationships between the e_i. We shall find it convenient to place the e_i between parenthetical 'path' and 'end' s; we are then in a position to use notation already developed for describing GR-paths. Let us therefore define P_{S_i} to be path e_i end and $P_S^Q = P_{S_1} \ldots P_{S_m}$. We shall drop the superscript Q for the rest of this section where it is clear from context what path is being substituted into. In general P_S^Q may not be the same as $P_S^{Q'}$ if the sets of R-paths in each case which contain 'a' are different.

There are two restrictions we shall impose on all the substitutions considered in this section. The first is that $Ops(Q) \cap Ops(P_S) = \emptyset$ and the second is that P be pseudo-cyclic.

A GR-path $P=P_1 \ldots P_m$ will be said to be pseudo-cyclic if and only if there is a set $R_P \subseteq VFS(P)$ such that (a) for every $\underline{x} \in R_P$ and for each i $[\underline{x}]_i \in Cyc(P_i)$ and (b) $VFS(P) = Pref(R_P{}^*)$. If P_S is pseudo-cyclic, then we define $R_S = \{(x_1, \ldots, x_m, \varepsilon, \ldots, \varepsilon) \in Vops(S(Q))^* \mid (x_1, \ldots, x_m) \in R_{P_S}\}$.

If $\underline{x} \in Vops(Q)^*$, we define $S(\underline{x})$ to be the set of n-tuples obtained from $\underline{x}$ by replacing each $\underline{a}$ in $\underline{x}$ by some element of R_S. We have

4.1 Lemma

Under the above assumptions

(a) $S(VFS(Q)) \subset VFS(S(Q))$

(b) For every $\underline{x}, \underline{y} \in Vops(Q)$, $S(\underline{x})S(\underline{y}) = S(\underline{xy})$

(c) For $\underline{x} \in Vops(Q)$, $\underline{x}$ contains every element of Vops(Q) if and only if $S(\underline{x})$ contains every element of Vops(S(Q)),

A substitution may be thought of as introducing grammatical 'structure' (it operates on the path Q; it has to do with Q's combinatorial properties, the *static* properties of the system) which has consequences in terms of *dynamic* structure, the properties of VFS(Q). The case in which VFS(S(Q)) is equal to Pref(S(VFS(Q))) is of particular interest. We have

4.2 *Lemma* (*Substitution Lemma*)

With the above terminology and assumptions, if VFS(S(Q)) = Pref(S(VFS(Q))), then (Q is adequate $\wedge P_S$ is adequate) iff S(Q) is adequate.

We shall now construct a number of kinds of substitution to which 4.2 applies.

We first define a property of S, or P_S, or indeed any GR-path $P=P_1\ldots P_n$. P will be said to be *connected* if for no partition A,B of $\{1,\ldots,n\}$ is it the case that $\{a\in Ops(P_i)\mid i\in A\}\cap\{b\in Ops(P_j)\mid j\in B\}=\emptyset$. P is connected iff N_P is connected, hence the terminology. Connectedness makes R_S (see above) 'hang together properly'. Next we defin a local property of Q about a, the notion of *properness*. Properness about a will be an essential hypothesis in two of the substitution theorems which follow, but properness is also useful for a certain simple but very useful kind of reduction, the proof of correctness of which is rather similar to that of 4.2, so we shall digress briefly to describe it.

An R-path P will be said to be proper for an element a∈Ops(P) if and only a appears in P only in substrings of the form

*path*a;...   ...;a;...   ...;a)   ...;a *end*

and P/a is defined to be the R-path obtained from P by deleting from it every a and one semicolon adjacent to a. If Ops(P)={a} then we shall make the convention that P/a is the empty path. In the sequel, however, we shall assume that Ops(P)≠{a}. Otherwise P means the same as *path* a *end*, and we may apply 4.4.

If $P=P_1\ldots P_n$ is a GR-path, then we shall say that P is *G-proper* for a∈Ops(P) if and only if $a\in Ops(P_i)$ implies that P_i is proper for a. If in addition a belongs to only one of the sets $Ops(P_i)$, then we shall say that P is *proper* for a. P/a is defined analagously.

4.3 *Proposition*

Suppose $P=P_1\ldots P_n$ is a GR-path which is proper for a∈Ops(P) and such that $a\in Ops(P_i)\Rightarrow P_i$ is an E-path, then P is adequate (respectively, pseudo-cyclic) if and only if P/a is adequate (respectively, pseudo-cyclic).

To see that the hypothesis that a belong to an E-path is necessary, consider the path P=*path* (b;c;a),(c;b) *end* *path* c;b *end*. P is proper for a, which is contained in a path which is not an E-path. We have VFS(P)=VFS(P/a)=Pref({c,c)(b,b)}*). Thus P/a is adequate but P is not. Another very useful result is

4.4 *Fact*

Suppose P is a GR-path and $A=\{op_1,\ldots,op_m\}$ is any set of operations. Define P_A= *path* $op_1,\ldots,op_m$ *end*, then P is adequate (respectively, pseudo-cyclic) if and only if P_AP is adequate (respectively, pseudo-cycluc).

To illustrate these two excision results, consider the following path program, which we shall call P(k,i), where i and k are some integers > 0.

R_1 { <u>path</u> $deposit_{1i}$; $remove_{1i}$ <u>end</u>
<u>path</u> $deposit_{2i}$; $remove_{2i}$ <u>end</u>
. . .
<u>path</u> $deposit_{ki}$; $remove_{ki}$ <u>end</u>
<u>path</u> $deposit_{1i}$; $deposit_{2i}$;...;$deposit_{ki}$ <u>end</u>
<u>path</u> $remove_{1i}$; $remove_{2i}$;...;$remove_{ki}$ <u>end</u> }

R_2 <u>path</u> $skip_i$,($remove_{1i}$,...,$remove_{ki}$;critical-$section_i$) <u>end</u>

R_3 <u>path</u> ($skip_i$;v_i), critical-$section_i$ <u>end</u>

Let us provisionally say that a GR-path is <u>nice</u> if it is both adequate and pseudo-cyclic. We shall show that P(i,k) is nice for all i,k. Note that P(k,i) is a GE-path.

(i) P(k,i) is proper for v_i, which appears only in the E-path R_3 and in a substring of the form ...;v_i). Thus P(k,i) is nice iffP(k,i)/v_i is nice, by 4.3. Call P(k.i)/v_i P'(k,i).

(ii) P'(k,i) has a component R-path <u>path</u> ($skip_i$), critical-$section_i$ <u>end</u>. Removing parentheses, which makes no differences to the set of firing sequences of this path, we see that P'(k,i) is of the form $R_1R_2P_A$, where A = {$skip_i$,critical-$section_i$}. By 4.4, P'(k,i) is nice iff R_1R_2 is nice.

(iii) We may now repeat this procedure with R_2.R_1R_2 is proper for critical-$section_i$, which may accordingly be deleted giving a GE-path R_1R_2' which is nice iff R_1R_2 is nice. Removing superfluous parantheses from R_2' gives a path of the form $P_{A'}$, where A'={$skip_i$,$remove_{1i}$,...,$remove_{ki}$}. We may again apply 4.4 to conclude that $R_1R_2' = R_1P_{A'}$ is nice iff R_1 is nice.

(iv) Putting the chain of equivalences together, we see that P(k,i) is nice iff R_1 is nice. But R_1 is a k-frame ring buffer. As we have already seen R_1 is adequate. 3.4 and the observation that for an adequate GE_0-path, P, VFS(P)=Pref(RVFS(P)*) shows that R_1 is also pseudo-cyclic. R_1 is therefore nice. We may accordingly conclude that P(k,i) is nice.

Note that P(k,i) is also connected.

S will be said to be a <u>substitution</u> <u>of</u> <u>type</u> 1 if and only if (a)$Ops(P_S) \cap Ops(Q) = \emptyset$ (b)P_S is pseudo cyclic and connected (c) Q is G-proper for a, where Q, a and S are as were fixed at the beginning of this section.

(1) Let $P=P_1...P_n$ be a GR-path. P will be said to be <u>initially</u> <u>connected</u> if and only if there exist $a_1,...,a_m \in Ops(P)$ such that (a) for every i, for every cycle of $c \in Cyc(P_i)$ there exists j such that $c=a_jc'$, $c' \in Ops(P_i)^*$(b) for every i,j there is a cycle $c \in Cyc(P_i)$ such that $c=a_jc'$,$c' \in Ops(P_i)^*$.

S will be said to be a <u>substitution of type</u> 2 if and only if

(a) $Ops(P_S) \cap Ops(Q) = \emptyset$ (b)P_S is pseudo-cyclic and initially connected.

(2) Let $P=P_1 \ldots P_n$ be a GR-path. P will be said to be <u>loosely connected</u> if and only if for each $i, P_i=$<u>path</u> b, b_i <u>end</u>, where the b and b_i are all distinct operations.

S will be said to be a <u>substitution of type</u> 3 if and only if

(a) $Ops(P_S) \cap Ops(Q) = \emptyset$ (b) P_S is loosely connected (c) Q is G-proper for a.

Let us go straight into an explanation of the properties of these substitutions.

4.5 <u>Theorem</u> (<u>First substitution theorem</u>)

Let S be a substitution of type 1 for a in Q, then Q is adequate^P is adequate if and only if S(Q) is adequate.

4.6 <u>Theorem</u> (<u>Second substitution theorem</u>)

Let S be a substitution of type 2 for a in Q, then Q is adequate^ P is adequate if and only if S(Q) is adequate.

5.7 <u>Theorem</u> (<u>Third substitution theorem</u>)

Let S be a substitution of type 3 for a in Q, the Q is adequate only if S(Q) is adequate.

We conclude this section with an example. The following program is taken from [LTS79]. We shall refer to it as PM(k,m).

<u>path</u> $deposit_{1m}$;$remove_{1m}$ <u>end</u> ... <u>path</u> $deposit_{km}$;$remove_{km}$ <u>end</u>
<u>path</u> $deposit_{1m}$;$deposit_{2m}$;...;$deposit_{km}$ <u>end</u> <u>path</u> $remove_{1m}$;...;$remove_{km}$ <u>end</u>
<u>path</u> $skip_m$,($remove_{1m}$,$remove_{2m}$,...,$remove_{km}$; critical-$section_m$)<u>end</u>

. . . .

<u>path</u> $deposit_{11}$;$remove_{11}$ <u>end</u> ... <u>path</u> $deposit_{k1}$;$remove_{k1}$ <u>end</u>
<u>path</u> $deposit_{11}$;$deposit_{21}$;...;$deposit_{k1}$ <u>end</u> <u>path</u> $remove_{11}$;...;$remove_{k1}$ <u>end</u>
<u>path</u> $skip_1$,($remove_{11}$,$remove_{21}$,...,$remove_{k1}$; critical-$section_1$) <u>end</u>
<u>path</u> ($skip_1$;($skip_2$;(...),critical-$section_3$), critical-$section_2$), critical-$section_1$ <u>end</u>

We shall prove that PM(k,m) is adequate for all k.m.

First, recall the GR-paths P(k,i) that we analysed earlier. We showed that it was adequate, pseudo-cyclic and connected. We are going to use the paths P(k,i) to define type-1 substitutions and prove adequacy by appealing to theorem 4.5.

Define paths P(i) and Q(i) and substitutions S^i as follows:

$P(1)=P(k,1)$ $Q(i)=$<u>path</u> v_i <u>end</u>,..<u>path</u> v_i <u>end</u>$^{P(i)}$ (k+3 times)

$P(i+1) = S^i(Q(i))$ $S^i=(S^i_1,\ldots,S^i_{(i+1)(k+3)+1})$ where $S^i_j = (v_i \to e^i_j)$ for each j and:

$e^{i-1}_j =$ $deposit_{ji}$;$remove_{ji}$, j=1,...,k;
$deposit_{1i}$;...;$deposit_{ki}$ j=k+1
$remove_{1i}$;...;$remove_{ki}$ j=k+2

$skip_i$, ($remove_{1i}$, ..., $remove_{ki}$; critical-section$_i$) j=k+3
($skip_i$; v_i), critical-section$_i$ j=i(k+3)+1
anything else otherwise.

Now let us proceed to the proof, which will be by induction. First remark that P(k,m)=P(k)/v_k. Since P(k) is proper for v_k, 4.4 entails that it suffices to show that P(k) is adequate.

(i) P(1) is adequate- we have already proved this previously.

Suppose P(i) is adequate. By 4.4, P(i) is adequate iff Q(i) is adequate. Now, Q(i) is G-proper for v_i and $P_S i$ = P(k,i+1). We have shown that P(k,i+1) is adequate, pseudo-cyclic and connected. It is also apparent that $Ops(Q(i)) \cap Ops(P_S i) = \emptyset$. S^i is therefore a type-1 substitution and we may apply 4.5 to conclude that P(i+1) is adequate.

The proof now follows from induction on i.

Note that we have proved here the adequacy of an infinite class of paths.

Acknowledgements

The work presented in this paper was supported by a grant from the Science Research Council of Great Britain. The author would like to thank Dr. P. E. Lauer for his helpful comments and suggestions and Mrs. Diane Pelley for her patience and persistence in preparing this typescript.

References

CH74 **Campbell, R.H., Habermann, A.N. : The specification of process synchronisation by path expressions. Lecture Notes in Computer Science (ed. G. Goos and J. Hartmanis), pp.89-102, Vol. 16, Springer Verlag 1974.**

Ha75 **Habermann, A.N. : Path expressions, Carnegie Mellon University, 1975.**

Maz77 **Mazurkiewicz, A. : Concurrent program schemes and their interpretations. Proc. Aarhus Workshop on Verification of Parallel Processes, June 13-24, Aarhus, Denmark, 1977.**

LC75 **Lauer, P.E., Campbell, R.H. : Formal semantics for a class of high level primitives for co-ordinating concurrent processes. Acta Informatica 5, pp.297-332, 1975.**

LBS77 **Lauer, P.E., Best, E., Shields, M.W. : On the problem of acheiving adequacy of concurrent programs. Proc. of a working conference on formal description of programming concepts, 1977, North Holland.**

LSB78 **Lauer, P.E., Shields, M.W., Best, E. : On the design and analysis of asynchronous systems of processes. Final Report, period 1976-77. University of Newcastle-upon-Tyne Asynchronous Systems Memoranda ASM/49 and ASM/45. To appear as a technical report. 1978**

LS77 Lauer, P.E., Shields, M.W. : Abstract specification of resource accessing disciplines: adequacy, starvation, priority and interrupts. Tech. Report 117, University of Newcastle-upon-Tyne, 1977.

LTS78 Lauer, P.E., Torrigiani, P.R., Shields, M.W. : COSY, a system specification language based on paths and processes. Tech. Report 136, University of Newcastle-upon-Tyne, 1978. To appear in Acta Informatica.

Pe76 Petri, C.A. : Non-sequential processes, GMD internal report, Bonn, 1976.

S79 Shields, M.W. : COSY train journeys: an analysis of deadlock in a toy train set. University of Newcastle-upon-Tyne ASM series. To appear. 1979.

SL79 Shields, M.W., Lauer, P.E. : A formal semantics for concurrent systems. ICALP79 : 6-th International Colloquium on Automata, Languages and Programming, July 16-20, Graz, Austria, 1979. To appear in Springer Lecture Notes.

TL77 Torrigiani, P.R., Lauer, P.E. : An object oriented notation for path expressions. AICA 1977, Annual Conference 3rd volume. Software Methodologies, pp.349-371, 12-14 October, 1977.

PETRI NETS, EVENT STRUCTURES AND DOMAINS

Mogens Nielsen,
Computer Science Department,
University of Aarhus,
8000 Aarhus C,
Denmark

Gordon Plotkin,
Dept. of Artificial Intelligence,
University of Edinburgh,
Hope Park Square, Meadow Lane,
Edinburgh EH8 9NW, Scotland

Glynn Winskel,
Dept. of Artificial Intelligence,
University of Edinburgh,
Hope Park Square,
Meadow Lane,
Edinburgh, Scotland.

0. Introduction

The general aim of the paper is to find a theory of concurrency combining the approaches of Petri and Scott (and other workers) [Pet 1,2],[Sco 1,3],[Sto]. To connect the abstract ideas of events and domains of information, we show how causal nets induce certain kinds of domains where the information points are certain sets of events. This allows translations between the languages of net theory and domain theory. Following the idea that events of causal nets are occurrences we generalise causal nets to occurrence nets, by adding forwards conflict; just as infinite flow charts unfold finite ones [Sco 2], so transition nets can be unfolded into occurrence nets. Next we extend the above connections between nets and domains to these new nets. Event structures, which are intermediate between nets and domains play an important part in all our work.

We consider the discreteness and initiality restrictions which are assumptions on how nets describe processes or computations. This leads to the definition of observers (runs of the computation) and states (of the computation) and a discussion of K-density. Finally we connect up Petri's notion of confusion with Kahn and Plotkin's concrete domains [Kah].

1. Causal Nets

We start off with an explanation of our computational interpretation of causal nets - the process level of net theory. To define these nets, we follow the axiomatic approach of Petri [Pet 1] and Best [Bes]:

Definition 1.1 A Petri net is a triple $N = (B,E,F)$, where:

B is a set of conditions,

E is a set of events,

$F \subseteq (B \times E) \cup (E \times B)$ is the causal dependency relation,

satisfying:

A1. $B \cap E = \emptyset$.

A2. $F \neq \emptyset$.

A3. $B \cup E = \text{Field}(F) \quad (=_{def}\{x \in B \cup E \mid \exists y: (xFy) \vee (yFx)\})$.

We call N a causal net iff further:

A4. $\forall b \in B: |b^{\bullet}| \leq 1$ (where $b^{\bullet} =_{def} \{e \in E \mid bFe\}$).

A5. $\forall b \in B: |{}^{\bullet}b| \leq 1$ (where ${}^{\bullet}b =_{def} \{e \in E \mid eFb\}$).

A6. F^+ is irreflexive.

A7. $\forall b_1, b_2 \in B: ({}^{\bullet}b_1 = {}^{\bullet}b_2) \wedge (b_1^{\bullet} = b_2^{\bullet}) \Rightarrow b_1 = b_2$.

There is a well-known standard graphical representation of Petri nets, which we shall use throughout this paper. Conditions are represented by circles: ○ , and events by boxes: □ . The relation F is represented by oriented arcs between circles and boxes, so that there is an arc from x to y iff xFy.

Example 1.2

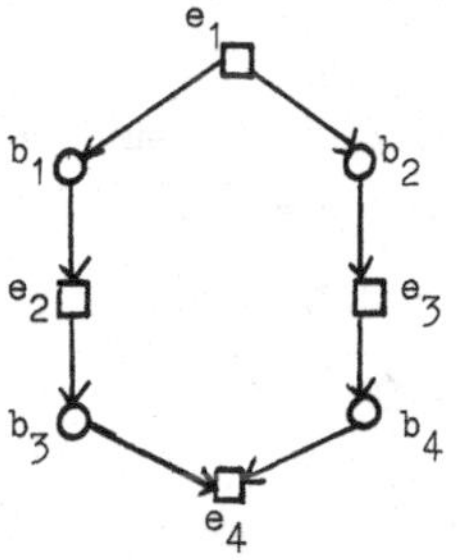

Here the causal net $N = (B,E,F)$ where $B = \{b_1,b_2,b_3,b_4\}$ and $E = \{e_1,e_2,e_3,e_4\}$.

In [Pet 1] Petri gives a deeply considered discussion of causal nets and how they provide the foundation for general net theory. The notion of concurrency plays an important role in this analysis, and, as noted by Petri himself, is easily defined in the context of causal nets.

Definition 1.3 For a causal net $N = (B,E,F)$ the concurrency relation $co_N \subseteq (B \cup E) \times (B \cup E)$ is defined by

$$co_N = ((B \cup E) \times (B \cup E)) \setminus (F^+ \cup (F^+)^{-1}).$$

It follows that co_N is symmetrical and reflexive (from A6). It also follows that in causal nets any two elements of $B \cup E$ are either causally dependent or concurrent. We shall not go into Petri's careful arguments for the axioms for causal nets (based on the ideas behind general net theory), but only briefly outline our intuition behind causal nets as representing computations.

The events of causal nets represent occurrences of certain "atomic" events, and a state of a computation is represented by holdings of certain conditions. An occurrence of an event e is associated with a state in which all its preconditions (${}^{\bullet}e$) hold, and the effect of its occurrence is that all its preconditions cease to hold, and all its postconditions ($e^{\bullet}$) begin to hold. Furthermore, each event e is "caused by" a unique subprocess ($\{x \in B \cup E \mid xF^+e\}$), and "causes" a unique subprocess ($\{x \in B \cup E \mid eF^+x\}$). (Causality is probably not the right English word in this context - necessity may be better.) This is not necessarily true in higher level nets, in which events (and conditions) may be repeatable, and (forwards or backwards) conflict may be present.

We now focus on the pattern of occurrences of events of causal nets. The relation F specifies a certain dependency, in the sense that if eF^+e', for $e,e' \in E$, then in the process described by the net, e' cannot occur without e having already occurred. This leads to the following definition of a "causality" structure on events:

Definition 1.4 An elementary event structure is just a partial order $S = (E,\leq)$, where E is a set of events, and $\leq$, the partial order over E, is called the causality relation.

Theorem 1.5 Let $N = (B,E,F)$ be a causal net. Then $\mathcal{E}[N] =_{def} (E, F^* \restriction E^2)$ is an elementary event structure.

Theorem 1.6 Let $S = (E,\leq)$ be an elementary event structure (with $E \neq \emptyset$). Then there is a causal net $\mathcal{N}[S]$ such that $S = \mathcal{E}[\mathcal{N}[S]]$.

Proof We construct $\mathcal{N}[S]$ as $N = (B,E,F)$, where

$$B = \{\langle e,e'\rangle \mid e,e' \in E, e \neq e', e \leq e'\}$$
$$\cup \{\langle o,e\rangle, \langle e,1\rangle \mid e \in E\},$$
$$F = \{(\langle e,e'\rangle,e'),(e,\langle e,e'\rangle) \mid e,e' \in E, \langle e,e'\rangle \in B\}$$
$$\cup \{(\langle o,e\rangle,e),(e,\langle e,1\rangle) \mid e \in E\} \blacksquare$$

What these two trivial theorems say is that nets have "as much" structure as elementary event structures (ignoring the empty event structure); nothing is lost in the passage $S \mapsto \mathcal{N}[S]$. However, this does not work in the opposite direction, as in general N and $\mathcal{N}[\mathcal{E}[N]]$ are not isomorphic. For the net N from Example 1.2 $\mathcal{E}[N]$ and $\mathcal{N}[\mathcal{E}[N]]$ take the following form, where in drawing $\mathcal{E}[N]$ we use the standard graphical representation of partial orders:

$\mathcal{E}[N]$:

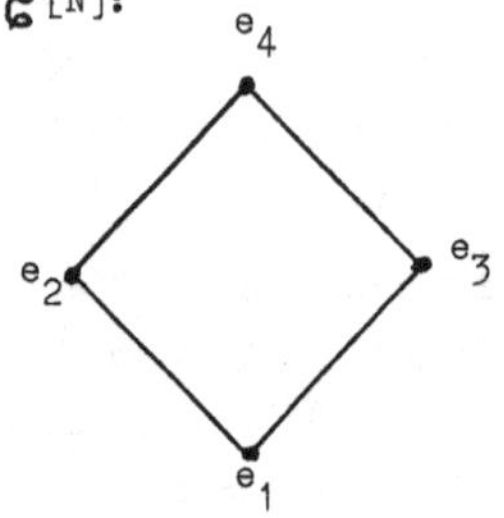

$\mathcal{N}[\mathcal{E}[N]]$:

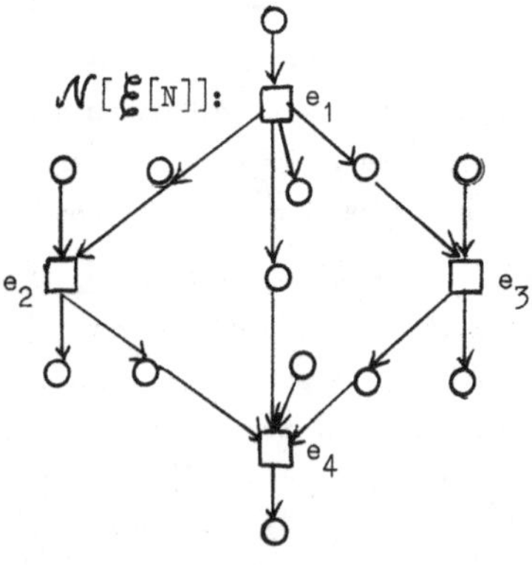

It is natural to ask whether it is reasonable to identify causal nets using the equivalence relation:

$$N_1 \equiv N_2 \text{ iff } \mathcal{E}[N_1] = \mathcal{E}[N_2].$$

From our point of view, it seems that $\equiv$ is an acceptable equivalence relation, although from a net theory point of view, it might have undesirable properties, such as identifying the following K-dense net N_1 with the non K-dense net N_2:

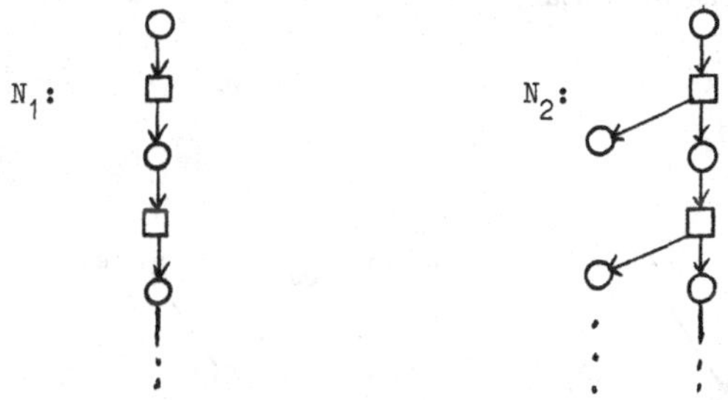

However, we press on for the moment with the connection between elementary event structures and Scott [Sco 1,3] domains of information. Given an elementary event structure, $S = (E,\leq)$, we want some idea of information about a certain set, x, of events having occurred (in the process $\mathcal{N}[S]$). This information can be represented by the set itself, and the intuition behind the causality relation tells us that x must be left-closed, where:

<u>Definition 1.7</u> Let $S = (E,\leq)$ be an elementary event structure, and suppose $x \subseteq E$. Then x is <u>left-closed</u> iff

$$\forall e \in x \; \forall e' \in E: \; e' \leq e \Rightarrow e' \in x.$$

So, as "information points" we choose the left-closed subsets of E. What about their ordering? From the above it follows that x' contains more information than x precisely when x is a subset of x'.

<u>Definition 1.8</u> Let $S = (E,\leq)$ be an elementary event structure. Then $\mathcal{L}[S]$ is the partial order of left-closed subsets of E ordered by inclusion.

<u>Definition 1.9</u> Let $(D, \sqsubseteq)$ be a partial order. An element $p \in D$ is a <u>complete prime</u> (<u>prime</u>) iff for every $X \subseteq D$ (every finite $X \subseteq D$), if $\bigsqcup X$ exists and $p \sqsubseteq \bigsqcup X$, then there exists an $x \in X$ such that $p \sqsubseteq x$.

<u>Definition 1.10</u> A partial order $P = (D, \sqsubseteq)$ is said to be <u>prime algebraic</u> iff for every element $d \in D$, $\bigsqcup P_d$ exists (where $P_d =_{def} \{p \sqsubseteq d \mid p \text{ is a complete prime}\}$), and $d = \bigsqcup P_d$. The set of complete primes of P is denoted $\mathcal{C}_P$.

<u>Theorem 1.11</u> Let $S = (E,\leq)$ be an elementary event structure. Then $\mathcal{L}[S]$ is a prime algebraic complete lattice. Its complete primes are those elements of the form $[e] =_{def} \{e' \in E \mid e' \leq e\}$ $(e \in E)$.

<u>Definition 1.12</u> Let $P = (D, \sqsubseteq)$ be a prime algebraic complete lattice. The elementary event structure $\mathcal{P}[P]$ is defined as $(\mathcal{C}_P, \sqsubseteq \restriction \mathcal{C}_P^2)$. Define $\pi : P \to \mathcal{L}[\mathcal{P}[P]]$ by $\pi(d) =_{def} \{p \in \mathcal{C}_P \mid p \sqsubseteq d\}$.

Theorem 1.13 Let $S = (E, \leq)$ be an elementary event structure; then $\psi : S \cong \mathcal{P}[\mathcal{L}[S]]$ where $\psi(e) =_{def} [e]$. Similarly, let $P = (D, \sqsubseteq)$ be any prime algebraic complete lattice; then $\pi : P \cong \mathcal{L}[\mathcal{P}[P]]$.

Example 1.14 Let S be the elementary event structure associated with the causal net from Example 1.2.

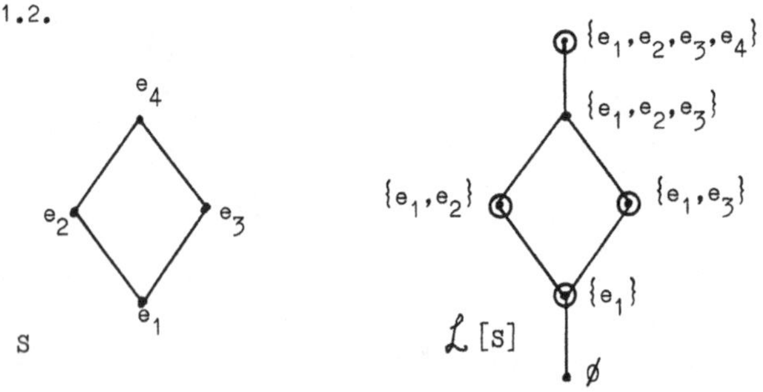

The primes of $\mathcal{L}[S]$ are circled, and it is easy to see that $S \cong \mathcal{P}[\mathcal{L}[S]]$.

Theorem 1.13 shows that elementary event structures and prime algebraic complete lattices are equivalent structures, in the sense that one does not lose any structural information going from one to the other via the $\mathcal{L}$ and $\mathcal{P}$ mappings - in contrast to the earlier result about the relationship between causal nets and elementary event structures. (However, the corresponding categories need not be equivalent.)

The framework we have set up so far, can be pictured as follows:

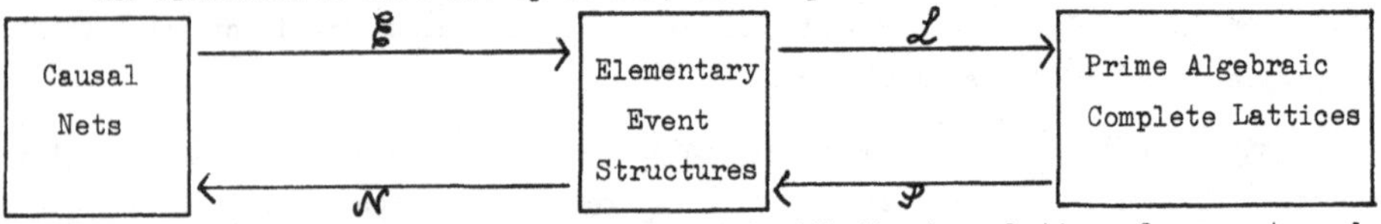

Basically, the rest of this paper is concerned with the translation of concepts and ideas from one side of this diagram to the other. From right to left we get an explanation in the framework of net theory of the Scott idea of information (not a complete one though, as we only deal with a special class of partial orders determined by information content). From left to right we see how net concepts (like events and causality) translate into the idea of partial order of information (not a complete one either, as indicated above). In the rest of this section we shall elaborate a little on this latter translation.

Note that we have deliberately established the links between net theory and the theory of partial orders at the process level. We strongly believe that an understanding of this low level is necessary for an understanding of similar links between higher level systems within the two theories.

Now let us see how some of the basic concepts of net theory translate using the mappings $\mathcal{E}$ and $\mathcal{L}$. Not surprisingly, since we specifically focussed our attention on event occurrences of nets, the concept of an event translates very well. From our construction of $\mathcal{P}[P]$, where P is a prime algebraic complete lattice, it seems that the notion of events translates into the complete primes of P. To see the intuition behind these primes, we shall need the notion of prime intervals of partial orders.

Definition 1.15 Let $(D, \sqsubseteq)$ be a partial order. Define the interval from d to d', $[d,d']$, for $d,d' \in D$ as

$$[d,d'] =_{def} \{d'' \in D \mid d \sqsubseteq d'' \sqsubseteq d'\}.$$

An interval $[d,d']$ is said to be prime iff $d \neq d'$ and $[d,d'] = \{d,d'\}$, in which case d' is said to cover d, which we write as $d \prec d'$.

With our computational interpretation in mind, prime intervals correspond to "steps" of computations or more specifically, occurrences at particular states of the computations. To see how this works formally, define the relation $\lesssim$ between prime intervals by

$$[d_1,d_1'] \lesssim [d_2,d_2'] \text{ iff } d_2' = d_1' \sqcup d_2 \text{ and } d_1 = d_1' \sqcap d_2.$$

Next define the equivalence relation $\approx$ between prime intervals as the equivalence generated by $\lesssim$. This relation represents the intuition behind "occurrences of the same event".

Proposition 1.16 Let $P = (D, \sqsubseteq)$ be a prime algebraic complete lattice. Then for any prime interval $[d,d']$, $\pi(d') \setminus \pi(d)$ is a singleton. Hence if we put

$$pr([d,d']) \in \pi(d') \setminus \pi(d)$$

then pr is a well-defined mapping from the prime intervals of P to $\mathcal{C}_P$.

Theorem 1.17 Let $P = (D, \sqsubseteq)$ be a prime algebraic complete lattice; then the following conditions are equivalent for prime intervals $[d_1,d_1']$ and $[d_2,d_2']$:

1. $[d_1,d_1'] \approx [d_2,d_2']$.
2. $pr([d_1,d_1']) = pr([d_2,d_2'])$.
3. There exists a prime interval $[d_3,d_3']$ such that $[d_1,d_1'] \gtrsim [d_3,d_3'] \lesssim [d_2,d_2']$.

Further, if p is a complete prime of P then: $p = pr([\bigsqcup \{p' \in \mathcal{C}_P \mid p \neq p' \wedge p' \sqsubseteq p\}, p])$.

Now, it is easy to see that the events of a causal net N are in one-to-one correspondence with the events of $\mathcal{E}[N]$, and the events of an elementary event structure S are in one-to-one correspondence with those of $\mathcal{N}[S]$. On the other hand, the events of S are also in one-to-one correspondence with those of $\mathcal{L}[S]$, and the events of a prime algebraic complete lattice are in one-to-one correspondence with those of $\mathcal{P}[P]$.

The situation for translation of conditions is a good deal less pleasant. Our main tool for handling conditions is the extensionality axiom A7, which allows us to identify any condition b with its pre- and postevent (${}^{\bullet}b$ and $b^{\bullet}$). For simplicity, we shall only demonstrate how conditions translate into elementary event structures.

A condition of an elementary event structure S is taken to be any condition of $\mathcal{N}[S]$. By definition this gives a nice one-to-one relationship between conditions of S and $\mathcal{N}[S]$, but, obviously, it is more interesting to see how conditions of a causal net N correspond to certain conditions of $\mathcal{E}[N]$. Define the map, bed, between these two sets of conditions as follows:

$$\forall\, b \in B:\ \mathrm{bed}(b) \begin{cases} (0,e') & \text{if } {}^{\bullet}b = \emptyset \text{ and } b^{\bullet} = \{e'\} \\ (e,1) & \text{if } {}^{\bullet}b = \{e\} \text{ and } b^{\bullet} = \emptyset \\ (e,e') & \text{if } {}^{\bullet}b = \{e\} \text{ and } b^{\bullet} = \{e'\} \end{cases}$$

It follows from the axioms of causal nets that bed is well-defined, and that it is one-to-one; however, in general bed will <u>not</u> be onto. We leave it to the next section to see how the causal dependency and the concurrency relation of causal nets translate nicely into our event and lattice structures.

2. Occurrence Nets

From a computational point of view, all the structures introduced in Section 1 lack the important notion of branching or nondeterminism. This is not inherent in either of our theories, and in this section we shall see a nice correspondence between their different ways of treating nondeterminism.

Within net theory higher level nets may have (forwards or backwards) conflict. Essentially this means that the subprocess "caused by" or "causing" an event or a condition is no longer unique. Net theory includes a thorough treatment of conflicts, mainly at the system level of transition nets. It has been argued that the process level semantics of a transition net is the <u>class</u> of causal nets it unfolds into, where all the choices associated with such an unfolding are "made by the environment". However, from a computational point of view, we would prefer to deal with conflicts at the semantical level, and to express the meaning of a system with conflicts in <u>one</u> semantical object. We deliberately want to stay as close to causal nets as possible, looking for a class of nets with conflicts on a slightly higher level than causal nets. Graphically, this means that we want to allow nets with the following structures:

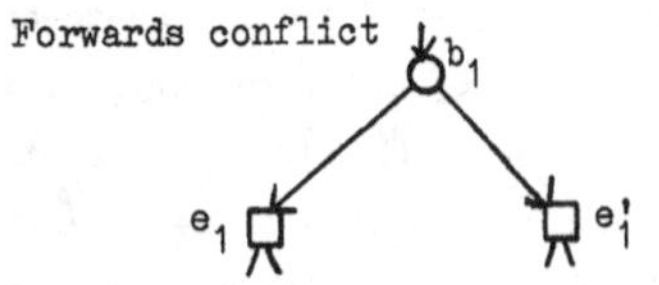

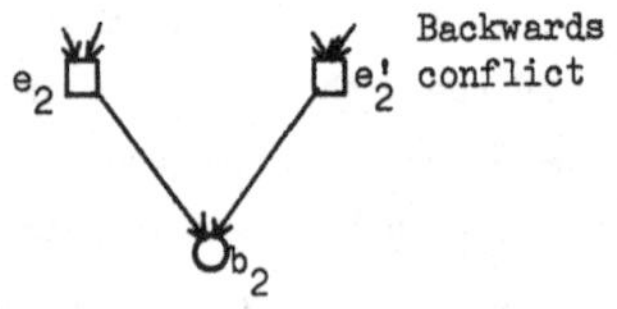

The intuition behind these structures is as follows:

forwards conflict: from the holding of b_1 either e_1 or e_1' (but not both!) may occur, in either case with the same effect as in causal sets.

backwards conflict: the holding of b_2 may have begun from an occurrence of e_2 or e_2' (but not from both!).

For our present purposes it seems best to deal only with forwards conflict, i.e. we shall be looking for a replacement for A4.

<u>Definition 2.1</u> Let $N = (B,E,F)$ be a Petri net satisfying A5 - A7. For any $a \in B \cup E$, let a^- denote the subset of E defined by

$$a^- =_{def} \{e \in E \mid eF^*a\}.$$

Two events e_1 and e_2 are said to be in <u>direct conflict</u>,

$$e_1 \#_{1N}\, e_2 \text{ iff } e_1 \neq e_2 \text{ and } \exists b \in B: \ (bFe_1) \wedge (bFe_2).$$

Two elements of $B \cup E$, a_1 and a_2, are said to be in <u>conflict</u>,

$$a_1 \#_N\, a_2 \text{ iff } \exists e_1, e_2 \in E: (e_1 \in a_1^-) \wedge (e_2 \in a_2^-) \wedge (e_1 \#_{1N}\, e_2).$$

<u>Definition 2.2</u> A Petri net N is an <u>occurrence net</u> iff it satisfies A5 - A7 and

A4': $\#_N$ is irreflexive.

Occurrence nets will be our new class of semantical nets. Elements of E and B still represent unique occurrences and holdings, respectively, and A4' guarantees that no event (or condition) is in conflict with itself (can occur on two different branches of the computation, so to speak).

<u>Definition 2.3</u> For an occurrence net $N = (B,E,F)$, the <u>concurrency relation</u> $co_N \subseteq (B \cup E) \times (B \cup E)$ is defined by

$$co_N =_{def} ((B \cup E) \times (B \cup E)) \setminus (F^+ \cup (F^+)^{-1} \cup \#_N).$$

<u>Proposition 2.4</u> Let $N = (B,E,F)$ be an occurrence net. Then co_N is symmetrical and reflexive. Furthermore, any two elements of $B \cup E$ are related in one of three mutually exclusive ways: causally dependent, concurrent or in conflict.

Before introducing branching in our other theories, let us briefly illustrate how occurrence nets do describe the semantics of transition nets the way we wanted. Assume N is a finite, safe transition net with initial marking. The idea is that its behaviour under the forwards firing rule will be described by an occurrence net with precisely one event for each firing of N, and precisely one condition for each residence of a taken on a place. Now, a particular (finite) behaviour of N may be described by a sequence

(*) $\sigma = M_0\ t_0\ M_1\ t_1 \ldots t_n\ M_{n+1}$,
where the M_i's are markings, M_0 is the initial marking, the t_i's transitions, and $\forall\, i \leq n$: $({}^\bullet t_i \subseteq M_i) \wedge (M_{i+1} = (M_i \setminus {}^\bullet t_i) \cup t_i^\bullet)$.

Notice that we have used safeness. A particular firing of a transition,

t_n, may now be identified with a certain equivalence class of sequences of this form. The equivalence will abstract away from the ordering of concurrent firings of transitions. Take a sequence of the form (*), and assume there exists an $i \leq n-1$ such that $^{\bullet}t_i \subseteq M_{i-1}$ (and hence $^{\bullet}t_i \cap {}^{\bullet}t_{i-1} = \emptyset$). Then "$\sigma$ represents the same firing as σ'" ($\sigma \equiv^{(1)} \sigma'$), where

$$\sigma' = M_0\ t_0 \cdots M_{i-1}\ t_i\ M_i'\ t_{i-1}\ M_{i+1} \cdots t_n\ M_{n+1},$$

and M_i' is the unique marking guaranteeing that σ' is of the form (*). If $^{\bullet}t_n \subseteq M_{n-1}$ (and hence $^{\bullet}t_m \cap {}^{\bullet}t_{n-1} = \emptyset$) then also "$\sigma$ represents the same firing as σ"" ($\sigma \equiv^{(2)} \sigma''$), where

$$\sigma'' = M_0\ t_0 \cdots M_{n-1}\ t_n\ M_{n+1}',$$

and M_{n+1}' is the unique marking guaranteeing that σ'' is of the form (*).

Now, let $\equiv$ denote the reflexive, symmetrical and transitive closure of $(\equiv^{(1)} \cup \equiv^{(2)})$, and let, for any σ of the form (*), $[\sigma]$ denote the equivalence class of σ with respect to $\equiv$. Basically, equivalence under $\equiv$ is the same abstraction from orderings of concurrent firings as introduced in Mazurkiewicz [Maz] for a different purpose.

It is easy to see that each representative of an equivalence class has a unique final transition, and hence we may identify these equivalence classes with firings of the transition net. So, a firing is represented by "the token game history that caused it", and the events of our semantical occurrence net, E, will be this set of equivalence classes. Residences of tokens on places are then represented by the set

$$B = \{\langle e,p\rangle \mid e \in E \text{ is a firing of transition } t, \text{ and the place } p \text{ belongs to } t^{\bullet}\} \cup \{\langle o,p\rangle \mid p \in M_0\}.$$

And finally, the F relation of our semantical net will be

$(e,b) \in F$ iff there exists a place p of N such that $b = \langle e,p\rangle$.

$(b,e) \in F$ iff either $b = \langle [M_0\ t_0 \ldots t_{n-1}\ M_n], p\rangle$, $e = [M_0\ t_0 \ldots t_{n-1}\ M_n\ t_n\ M_{n+1}]$ and $p \in {}^{\bullet}t_n$

or else $b = \langle o,p\rangle$, $e = [M_0\ t_0\ M_1]$ and $p \in {}^{\bullet}t_0$.

Proposition 2.5 The constructed net (B,E,F) satisfies the axioms for occurrence nets. The map f, defined below, from $B \cup E$ to places and transitions of N is a folding:

$$f(\langle o,p\rangle) = f(\langle e,p\rangle) = p,$$

$$f([M_0\ t_0 \ldots t_n\ M_{n+1}]) = t_n.$$

Example 2.6 Below we show a transition net N with initial marking together with its associated occurrence net.

N:

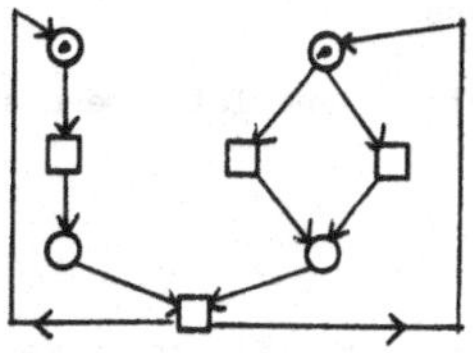

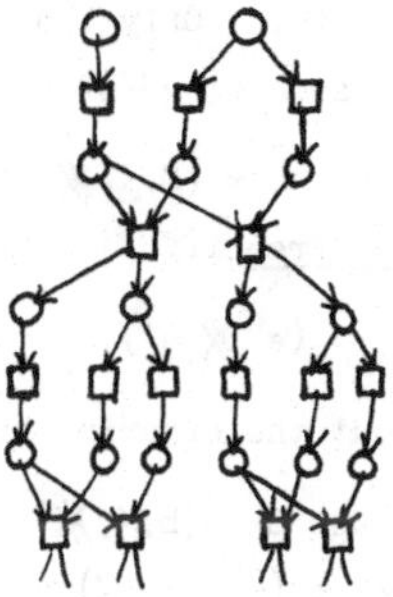

Let us now see how branching is handled in our other theories. Since elementary event structures were our "poorest" structures, it is not surprising that the only way of introducing branching is by adding structure.

<u>Definition 2.7</u> An <u>event structure</u> is a triple $S = (E, \leq, \#)$, where

E1. $(E, \leq)$ is an elementary event structure,

E2. $\#$ is a symmetrical and irreflexive relation in E, satisfying $\forall e_1, e_1', e_2, e_2' \in E$: $(e_1 \# e_2) \wedge (e_1 \leq e_1') \wedge (e_2 \leq e_2') \Rightarrow e_1' \# e_2'$.
$\#$ is called the <u>conflict relation</u>.

<u>Theorem 2.8</u> Let $N = (B,E,F)$ be an occurrence net. Then $\mathcal{E}[N] =_{def} (E, F^* \upharpoonright E^2, \#_N \upharpoonright E^2)$ is an event structure.

<u>Theorem 2.9</u> Let $S = (E, \leq, \#)$ be an event structure (with $E \neq \emptyset$). Then there is an occurrence net $\mathcal{N}[S]$ such that $S = \mathcal{E}[\mathcal{N}[S]]$.

<u>Proof</u> Define the set CE as follows:

$$CE =_{def} \{x \subseteq E \mid \forall e,e' \in x: e \neq e' \Rightarrow e \# e'\}.$$

The events of $\mathcal{N}[S]$ are obviously those of E, and the set of conditions is defined by:

$$B = \{\langle e,x \rangle \mid e \in E,\ x \in CE, \text{ and } \forall e' \in x: e \leq e'\} \cup$$
$$\{\langle o,x \rangle \mid x \in CE,\ x \text{ nonempty}\}.$$

Finally, the F relation is defined as

$$F = \{(\langle e,x \rangle, e') \mid \langle e,x \rangle \in B,\ e' \in x\} \cup$$
$$\{(\langle o,x \rangle, e') \mid \langle o,x \rangle \in B,\ e' \in x\} \cup$$
$$\{(e, \langle e,x \rangle) \mid \langle e,x \rangle \in B\}$$ ■

Things get a bit more interesting when we move on to our lattice structures and generalisations of the mappings $\mathcal{L}$ and $\mathcal{P}$. Intuitively, an event structure represents a class of processes, where $e \# e'$ means that e and e' never occur in the same process. So, not all left-closed subsets of an event structure make sense as information points. Only the conflict free left-closed subsets can be the sets of occurrences at some stage of an associated process.

Definition 2.10 Let $S = (E, \leq, \#)$ be an event structure, and let x be a subset of E. Then x is conflict free iff

$$\forall e, e' \in x: \neg (e \# e').$$

Our idea about the ordering of information points is still the same, though.

Definition 2.11 Let $S = (E, \leq, \#)$ be an event structure. Then $\mathcal{L}[S]$ is the partial order of left-closed (w.r.t. $\leq$) and conflict free subsets of E, ordered by inclusion. What about our characterisation of the structures $\mathcal{L}[S]$? Obviously, we do not any longer get complete lattices. Two points will be inconsistent (have no upper bound) iff their union (as sets of events) meets the conflict relation. But any consistent set of points will have a lub (their union), so the structures will be consistently complete. For a characterisation we need the even stronger condition of coherence (introduced in [Mar]).

Definition 2.12 Let $(D, \sqsubseteq)$ be a partial order. A subset x of D is pairwise consistent iff any two of its elements have an upper bound in D; $(D, \sqsubseteq)$ is said to be coherent iff every pairwise consistent subset of D has a lub. The consistency relation is denoted $\uparrow$; $\not\uparrow$ denotes inconsistency.

Theorem 2.13 Let $S = (E, \leq, \#)$ be an event structure. Then $\mathcal{L}[S]$ is a prime algebraic coherent partial order. Its complete primes are those elements of the form $[e] =_{def} \{e' \in E \mid e' \leq e\}$.

Definition 2.14 Let $P = (D, \sqsubseteq)$ be a prime algebraic coherent partial order. Then $\mathcal{P}[P]$ is defined as the event structure $(\mathcal{C}_P, \leq, \#)$, where $\leq$ is $\sqsubseteq$ restricted to $\mathcal{C}_P$, and for all $e, e' \in \mathcal{C}_P$: $e \# e'$ iff e and e' are inconsistent in P.

Theorem 2.15 Let $S = (E, \leq, \#)$ be an event structure, then $S \cong \mathcal{P}[\mathcal{L}[S]]$. Similarly let $P = (D, \sqsubseteq)$ be any prime algebraic coherent partial order, then $P \cong \mathcal{L}[\mathcal{P}[P]]$.

Example 2.16 Here we show an occurrence net N together with $\mathcal{E}[N]$ and $\mathcal{L}[\mathcal{E}[N]]$.

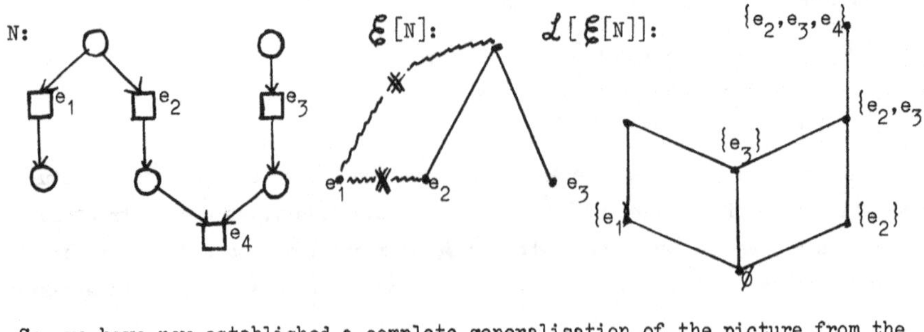

So, we have now established a complete generalisation of the picture from the previous section:

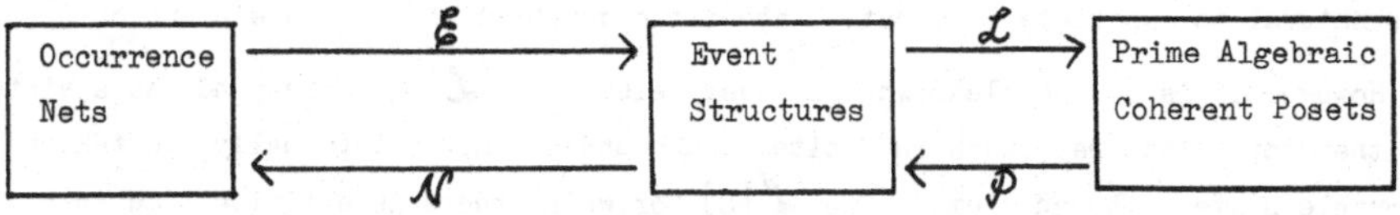

All considerations about translations of events and conditions work just like in Section 1. Formally, Proposition 1.16 and Theorem 1.17 hold for prime algebraic coherent partial orders. Restricting ourselves to these relations on events, the following should now be obvious to the reader.

	Occurrence Nets $N = (B,E,F)$	Event Structures $S = (E,\leq,\#)$	Prime Algebraic Coherent Posets $P = (D,\sqsubseteq)$
Causality	$F^{+} \restriction E^{2}$	$<$	$\sqsubsetneq \restriction \mathcal{C}_P^{\,2}$
Conflict	$\#_N \restriction E^{2}$	$\#$	$\not\uparrow \restriction \mathcal{C}_P^{\,2}$
Concurrency	$E^{2}\setminus(F^{+} \cup (F^{+})^{-1} \cup \#_N)$	$E^{2} \setminus (<\cup> \cup \#)$	$\mathcal{C}_P^{\,2}\setminus(\sqsubsetneq \cup \sqsupsetneq \cup \not\uparrow)$

Finally, let us see what these relations look like in terms of prime intervals of partial orders.

<u>Definition 2.17</u> Let $P = (D, \sqsubseteq)$ be a prime algebraic coherent partial order. The relation $\rightarrowtail$ ("may occur before") on $\mathcal{C}_P$ is defined as follows: $p_1 \rightarrowtail p_2$ iff there exist prime intervals of P, $[x_1,x_1']$, $[x_2,x_2']$, such that $pr([x_1,x_1']) = p_1$, $pr([x_2,x_2']) = p_2$ and $x_1' \sqsubseteq x_2$. The complement of $\rightarrowtail$ is denoted $\not\rightarrowtail$.

<u>Proposition 2.18</u> Let $P = (D,\sqsubseteq)$ be a prime algebraic coherent partial order, and let $p_1,p_2 \in \mathcal{C}_P$. Then

$$p_1 \sqsubsetneq p_2 \text{ iff } (p_1 \rightarrowtail p_2)\wedge(p_2 \not\rightarrowtail p_1),$$
$$p_1 \not\uparrow p_2 \text{ iff } (p_1 \not\rightarrowtail p_2)\wedge(p_2 \not\rightarrowtail p_1),$$

and hence p_1 and p_2 are concurrent iff $(p \rightarrowtail p_2)\wedge(p_2 \rightarrowtail p_1)$.

3. <u>States, Observers and Confusion</u>

In the previous two sections we have associated an event structure S with a computation (computation being understood in a general sense) and have regarded $\mathcal{L}[S]$ as the set of information points of the computation, an element of $\mathcal{L}[S]$ giving some of the events which have occurred but without "remembering" their time of occurrence. In more detail an event structure $S = \langle E,\leq, \# \rangle$ is an abstract description of a computation which picks out certain events related to the computation and represents causality and conflict on E through the relations $\leq$ and $\#$. The facts that the concurrency relation and the relation $\# \cup 1$ are non-trivial in general are due, respectively, to the indeterminacy of the relative speeds in the various subprocesses of the computation and the choice of process that a run of the computation will follow. Having described a computation by an event structure, S, it is natural to associate information about the computation with an element of $\mathcal{L}[S]$.

However it is not so clear whether every element of $\mathcal{L}[S]$ corresponds to a state that the computation may reach in finite or unbounded time. Informally, we take an observable state to be an element C of $\mathcal{L}[S]$ for which there is a finite time in a run of the computation for which events in C are precisely those observed by that time. A state is defined similarly but here time is allowed to be unbounded.

Example 3.1

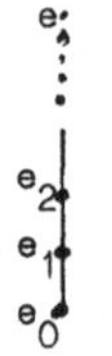

Here S_1 is the (elementary) event structure consisting of an unbounded chain $e_0, e_1, \ldots$ below an event e.

Example 3.2

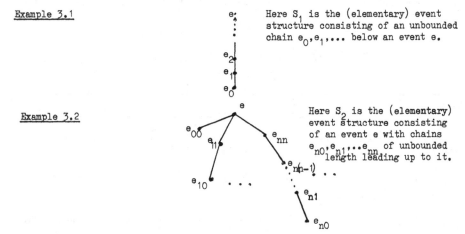

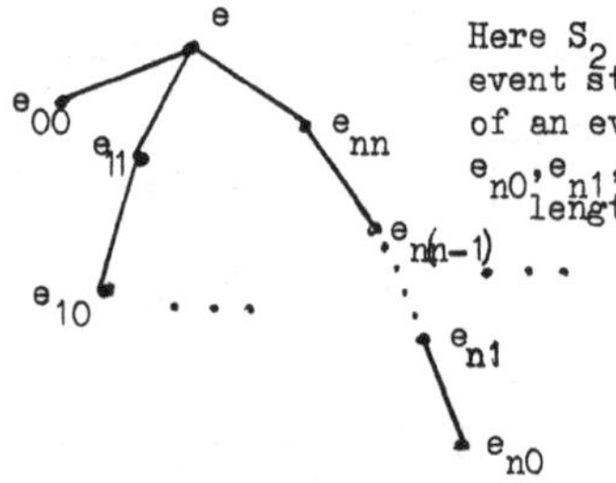

Here S_2 is the (elementary) event structure consisting of an event e with chains $e_{n0}, e_{n1}, \ldots e_{nn}$ of unbounded length leading up to it.

Consider the computations described by S_1 and S_2. First let us suppose there is a uniform lower bound on the extent of time which passes between the occurrences of e and e' if e<e'. Thinking of occurrence nets which induce S_1 or S_2, this is equivalent to supposing there is a uniform lower bound on the extents of the holdings of the conditions. Then as the events called e in S_1 and S_2 dominate chains of unbounded length, if the computations always start with no events having occurred the events e can never occur. Thus for such computations $[e] \in \mathcal{L}[S_1]$ and $[e] \in \mathcal{L}[S_2]$ are not states. This is because for such computations the event structure descriptions S_1 and S_2 contain the redundant element e. If we keep the first assumption for the computations but no longer insist that they start at some definite time the event e in S_2 could now occur. In this case as an extreme, it might be that the event e always occurs sometime in any run of the computation. Then, of course, $\emptyset \in \mathcal{L}[S_2]$ cannot be an observable state as e is not "reachable" from it. Finally we could drop the first supposition and allow e in S_1 to occur, giving $\mathcal{L}[S_1]$ as the set of observable states. Then example 3.1 corresponds to Zeno's paradox and the event e to Achilles' catching-up with the tortoise (a very peculiar computation).

Thus depending on what assumptions we make on the computation and on the event structure description of it the left-closed conflict-free subsets may or may not correspond to the states. Also without extra assumptions the observable states are not derivable from the event structure alone. In making the last statement we are diverging from the approach of conventional net theory where we understand the observable states of a causal net are identified with its cases [Pet 1]. A causal net is said to be K-dense iff every case meets every sequential process. With the above interpretation of a case as an observable state, insisting on K-density for a causal net guarantees that every observable state defines a unique point in every sequential process. As for us the cases of a causal net do not necessarily correspond to observable states we shall not feel bound by K-density. This is why we defined a causal net to satisfy merely A1 to A7 i.e. to be a conflict-free occurrence net. However note we expect a revised version of K-density to hold in a causal net where we restrict the cases in its statement to observable cases.

Referring back to the examples and the ensuing discussion, in this section we shall make some restrictions on the nature of the computations and on our event-structure descriptions of them. With these restrictions we shall be able to identify states with left-closed, conflict-free subsets. We insist that if in an event structure S, for events e and e', $e<e'$ then their occurrences must be separated by at least unit time (we call this the <u>discreteness restriction</u>). As pointed out before, this is equivalent to assuming that the extents in time of the holdings of conditions in an occurrence net including the event structure have a uniform lower bound. Thus we avoid the problems of dense event structures such as the rationals and the reals. We will also assume there is a state of null information, when no events have occurred from which the computation starts. (We call this the <u>initiality restriction</u>.) Note that these assumptions are consistent with our definition of the unfolding of a transition net. At first we shall work with event structures later showing how our results translate to occurrence nets.

We now begin a formalisation of the intuitions above. We first define the concept of an observer which corresponds to a particular run or history of a computation where each event's occurrence is recorded together with the time at which it occurred. Time will be discrete with a starting time zero and we use the symbol "∞" to "record" events which never occur according to a particular observer. An event may never occur either through being in conflict with a pre-observed event, through the computation diverging before the event, or simply through the event being too far from the starting state as in example 3.1. Time will be represented by $\omega \cup \{\infty\}$ ordered as usual.

<u>Definition 3.3</u> Let S be an event structure $(E, \leq, \#)$. An observer for S is a map $O: E \rightarrow \omega \cup \{\infty\}$ such that

1. $e<e' \wedge O(e)<\infty \Rightarrow O(e)<O(e')$
2. $e<e' \wedge O(e) =\infty \Rightarrow O(e') = \infty$
3. $O(e)< \wedge O(e')<\infty \Rightarrow \neg(e \# e')$

We denote the set of observers for S by Ob[S].

The above paragraph explains clauses 2 and 3 in the definition and clause 1 formalises our first restriction on computations. We have already motivated the following definition.

Definition 3.4 Suppose S is an event structure $(E,\leq,\#)$ and $C \in \mathcal{L}[S]$. Say C is an observable state of S iff

$$\exists o \in Ob[S]\ \exists t \in \omega: C = \{e \in E \mid o(e)<t\}.$$

Also say C is a state of S iff

$$\exists o \in Ob[S]\ \exists t \in \omega \cup \{\infty\}: C = \{e \in E \mid o(e)<t\}.$$

We write $O\mathcal{S}[s]$ and $\mathcal{S}[S]$ for the observable states and states respectively, ordered by inclusion.

Definition 3.5 Let S be the event structure $(E,\leq,\#)$. Define $\Delta: E^2 \to \omega \cup \{\infty\}$ by

$$\Delta(e,e') =_{def} \mathrm{Sup}\{ n \mid \exists e_1,\ldots,e_n \in E: e_1<\ldots<e_n \wedge ((e_1 = e \wedge e_n = e') \vee (e_1 = e' \wedge e_n = e))\}.$$

For an event structure S, Δ as defined above gives a "distance measure" on events. From it we obtain a metric on $\mathcal{L}[S]$.

Definition 3.6 For S and Δ as in definition 3.5 we define

$$d: \mathcal{L}[S]^2 \to \omega \cup \{\infty\} \text{ by}$$

$$d(C_1,C_2) = \mathrm{Sup}\{\Delta(e,e') \mid e,e' \in (C_1-C_2) \cup (C_2-C_1)\}.$$

We say for $C_1,C_2 \in \mathcal{L}[S]$ that they are reachable from each other iff $d(C_1,C_2)<\infty$. This concept is easily related to a more standard idea. Define one-step forward reachability by putting for C_1,C_2 in $\mathcal{L}[S]$;

$$C_1 \vdash_1 C_2 \text{ iff } C_1 \subseteq C_2 \wedge (\forall e \in C_2 \setminus C_1: {}^\bullet e \subseteq C_1)$$

Then our reachability is just the least equivalence relation extending $\vdash_1$.

Definition 3.7 For d and $S = (E,\leq,\#)$ as above and $e \in E$, say e has finite depth in S iff $d(\emptyset,[e])<\infty$.

Theorem 3.8 Suppose S is an event structure with metric d on $\mathcal{L}[S]$ as defined in 3.6. Then for $C \in \mathcal{L}[S]$

1. $C \in \mathcal{S}[S]$ iff $\forall e \in C$: e has finite depth in S.
2. $C \in O\mathcal{S}[S]$ iff $d(\emptyset,C)<\infty$.

Corollary 3.9 For an event structure S, $O\mathcal{S}[S]$ is closed under intersections and finite consistent unions.

If an event e of an event structure S is not of finite depth it can never be observed when the computation starts from the initial null state $\emptyset \in \mathcal{L}[S]$. Consequently the states only involve events of finite depth. In this section it is natural to restrict ourselves to event structures in which all events have finite depth. For example this excludes the event structure S_2 (example 3.2), even though $N[S_2]$ is K-dense.

<u>Definition 3.10</u> An event structure S is said to be of <u>finite depth</u> iff every event in S has finite depth.

<u>Theorem 3.11</u> If S is an event structure $(E,\leq,\#)$ the following are equivalent:

1. S is of finite depth.
2. $\mathfrak{S}[S] = \mathcal{L}[S]$
3. $\forall e \in E \ \exists O \in Ob[S]: \ O(e) \in \omega$
4. $\forall A \subseteq E: \ (\forall a_1, a_2 \in A: \neg(a_1 \# a_2)) \Rightarrow \exists O \in Ob[S]: A \subseteq O^{-1}\omega.$

Thus if an event structure S is of finite depth $\mathfrak{S}[S] = \mathcal{L}[S]$, so, by the results of the last section, we can recover S, to within isomorphism, from $\mathfrak{S}[S]$. The event structure $S = (E,\leq,\#)$ can also be recovered directly from the observations of the set E. Precisely:

<u>Theorem 3.12</u> If the event structure $S = (E,\leq,\#)$ is of finite depth then:

$$\leq \; = \bigcap_{O \in Ob[S]} \leq_O \quad \text{and} \quad \# = \bigcap_{O \in Ob[S]} \#_O$$

where $e \leq_O e' \Leftrightarrow_{def} (O(e') < \infty \Rightarrow O(e) \leq (e'))$

and $e \#_O e' \Leftrightarrow_{def} (O(e) \neq \infty \Leftrightarrow O(e') = \infty)$.

So far in this section we have worked with event structures. Here we translate our results to occurrence nets.

<u>Definition 3.13</u> An occurrence net N is said to be of <u>finite</u> depth iff $\mathfrak{E}[N]$ is of finite depth.

In order that we can associate a case of an occurrence net $N = (B,E,F)$ consisting purely of conditions with an observable state of $\mathfrak{E}[N]$ we impose the minor axiom:

A8. $\forall e \in E: {}^{\bullet}e \neq \emptyset \wedge e^{\bullet} \neq \emptyset$.

Note that the non-K-dense net mentioned in section 1 satisfies A8 and is of finite depth, and also that $N[S_2]$ for S_2 in example 3.2 satisfies A8, is K-dense but not of finite depth.

<u>Definition 3.14</u> Let $N = (B,E,F)$ be an occurrence net. A <u>case</u> of N is a ken of co_N. For $C \in \mathcal{L} \circ \mathfrak{E}[N]$ define the <u>frontier of C in N</u>, written $Fr_N(C)$, by

$$Fr_N(C) = (\bigcup \{e^{\bullet} \mid e \in C\} \cup \{b \in B \mid {}^{\bullet}b = \emptyset\}) \setminus \bigcup \{{}^{\bullet}e \mid e \in C\}.$$

In general such a frontier will not be a case. However

<u>Proposition 3.15</u> Suppose $N = (B,E,F)$ is an occurrence net of finite depth satisfying A8. Then for $C \in \mathfrak{S} \circ \mathfrak{E}[N]$, $Fr_N(C)$ will be a case. We call such frontiers <u>observable cases</u> of N and $Fr_N(\emptyset)$ the <u>initial case</u>.

It is now possible to prove a restricted form of K-density.

Theorem 3.16 Let N be a causal net of finite depth satisfying A8. Then every observable case meets every sequential process in N.

Confusion

K-density proved to be a concept which did not translate very well into the framework of event structures and domains. Finally we deal with confusion which fortunately does translate well. Indeed confusion, or strictly confusion freeness, was rediscovered in the work of Kahn and Plotkin on concrete datatypes [Kah] without their knowing it at the time.

The incompatibility of a set of states of a computation stems from the conflict between their constituent events. (This manifests itself as coherence of the domain of states.) In general it is not clear when and where a particular conflict between two events is resolved ("conflict resolution is not objective"). This is because of two violating situations which may occur called symmetric and asymmetric confusion. Within net theory these concepts are introduced formally at the level of transition nets [Pet 2]. The following are the obvious corresponding definitions for an occurrence net.

Definition 3.17 Let N = (B,E,F) be an occurrence net of finite depth satisfying A8. We say N is symmetrically confused iff there are an observable case C and events e,e',e'' such that ${}^\bullet e, {}^\bullet e', {}^\bullet e'' \subseteq C \wedge {}^\bullet e \cap {}^\bullet e' \neq \emptyset \wedge {}^\bullet e' \cap {}^\bullet e'' \neq \emptyset \wedge {}^\bullet e \cap {}^\bullet e'' = \emptyset$. We say N is asymmetrically confused iff there are an observable case C and events e,e',e'' such that ${}^\bullet e \cup {}^\bullet e'' \subseteq C \wedge {}^\bullet e' \not\subseteq C \wedge {}^\bullet e' \subseteq (C \setminus {}^\bullet e) \cup e^\bullet \wedge {}^\bullet e \cap {}^\bullet e'' = \emptyset \wedge$ $\wedge\, {}^\bullet e' \cap {}^\bullet e'' \neq \emptyset$. We say N is confused iff N is symmetrically or asymmetrically confused.

Example 3.18 Symmetric confusion Asymmetric confusion

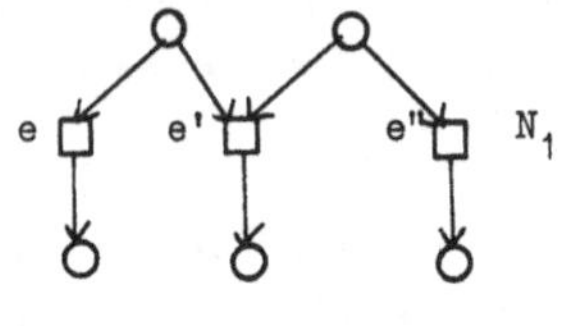

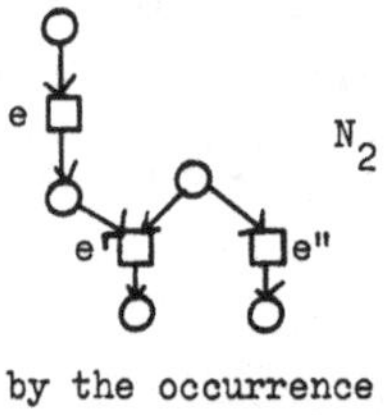

In N_1 the conflict between e and e' may be resolved by the occurrence of e". In N_2 e' and e" may be brought into conflict by the occurrence of e.

Definition 3.19 Let $S = (E, \leq, \#)$ be an event structure. Define $\#_\mu$ by putting for e,e' in E:

$$e \#_\mu e' \text{ iff } e \# e' \wedge [e] \cup [e'] \setminus \{e,e'\} \in \mathcal{L}[S].$$

Theorem 3.20 Let N = (B,E,F) be an occurrence net of finite depth satisfying A8 and define $\#_\mu$ as in 3.19 taking $S = \mathcal{E}[N]$. Then

1. N is symmetrically confused iff $\exists\, e,e',e'' \in E: e \#_\mu e' \#_\mu e'' \wedge \neg(e(\# \cup 1)e'')$
2. N is asymmetrically confused iff $\exists\, e,e',e'' \in E: e' \#_\mu e'' \wedge e < e' \wedge \neg(e < e'')$.

Definition 3.21 Let S be an event structure $(E, \leq, \#)$ of finite depth and let $\#_\mu$ be as defined in 3.19. Then S is said to be confusion-free iff

1. $\#_\mu \cup 1$ is an equivalence relation

and 2. $e < e' \#_\mu e'' \Rightarrow e < e''$.

We can interpret clause 2 above as requiring enablings to respect the $\#_\mu \cup 1$-equivalence classes.

Theorem 3.22 Let N be an occurrence net of finite depth satisfying A8. The following are equivalent

1. N is not confused.
2. $\mathcal{E}[N]$ is confusion-free.
3. $\mathcal{L} \circ \mathcal{E}[N]$ satisfies axiom Q of concrete domains.

Corollary 3.23 Let N be an occurrence net of finite depth satisfying A8, having only countably many events and such that for all events e, ${}^{\bullet\bullet}e$ is finite. Then N is not confused iff $\mathcal{L} \circ \mathcal{E}[N]$ is a distributive concrete domain.

Axiom Q evolved from the intuitions of Kahn and Plotkin in their work on concrete datatypes. There an event is imagined to occur at a fixed point in space and time so conflict between events is localised in that two conflicting events are enabled at the same time and are competing for the same place, or point in space.

Acknowledgements

G. Winskel and G. Plotkin thank the Science Research Council for their support of this research; M. Nielsen thanks the Departments of Computer Science and Artificial Intelligence of Edinburgh University for their hospitality during 1978. We thank H. Genrich and R. Milner for helpful and stimulating discussions.

References

[Bes] Best, E. (1977) A Theorem on the Characteristics of Non-Sequential Processes. Computing Laboratory Technical Report No. 116, University of Newcastle-upon-Tyne.

[Kah] Kahn, G. and Plotkin, G.D. (1978) Domaines Concrets. IRIA Rapport de Recherche No. 336, IRIA, France.

[Mar] Markowsky, G. and Rosen, B. (1976) Bases for Chain-Complete Posets. IBM J. Res. and Develop., Vol. 20, 138-147.

[Maz] Mazurkiewicz, A. (1977) Concurrent Program Schemes and their Interpretations, DAIMI PB-78 (Aarhus Univ. Publ.), July 1977.

[Pet1] Petri, C.A. (1976) Nichtsequentielle Prozesse Arbeitsberichte des IMMD, Bd. 9, Heft. 8, p.57ff. Universität Erlangen-Nürnberg. Also: Non-Sequential Processes, Translation by P. Krause and J. Low. Internal Report GMD-ISF-77-05. Bonn (1977).

[Pet2] Petri, C.A. (1977) General Net Theory. Communication Disciplines. Proc. Joint IBM Univ. of Newcastle Seminar 1976 (ed. B. Shaw) University of Newcastle-upon-Tyne.

[Sco1] Scott, D. (1970) Outline of a Mathematical Theory of Computation. Proc. of 4th Ann. Princeton Conf. on Information Sciences and Systems, pp. 169-176.

[Sco2] Scott, D. (1971) The lattice of flow diagrams. Symposium on Semantics of Algorithmic Languages (ed. E. Engeler) Lecture Notes in Mathematics, Vol. 188, Springer-Verlag, New York, pp. 311-366.

[Sco3] Scott, D. (1976) Data Types as Lattices. SIAM J. Comput., Vol. 5, No. 3, 522-587.

[Sto] Stoy, J.E. (1978) Denotational Semantics: The Scott-Strachey Approach to Programming Language Theory. Cambridge: MIT Press.

AN EXTENSIONAL TREATMENT OF DATAFLOW DEADLOCK

William W.Wadge
Computer Science Department
University of Warwick
Coventry CV4 7AL UNITED KINGDOM

Abstract

We discuss deadlock in reference to a simple equational dataflow language, and devise a test (the cycle sum test) which is applied to the dependency graph of a program. We use Kahn's extensional semantics of dataflow and give a purely extensional (non operational) proof that no program passing the cycle sum test can ever deadlock. The proof is based on the notions of size (length) and completeness in the domain of histories, and should extend to a much wider context.

0. Introduction

The question of termination has always been of fundamental importance in the theory of computation; in fact the single most important theoretical result is the unsolvability of the "halting problem". Of course, termination is of great practical importance as well. A conventional program which fails to terminate for some appropriate input is traditionally considered to be incorrect (or at least only partially correct, complete correctness being defined as partial correctness plus termination).

Recent developments, however, have to a large extent made obsolete the idea that proper programs all stop after some finite number of steps. Many programs now written are intended to perform continuously; for example an operating system, a traffic control system, or (the one we will use) a data flow network. For these programs there is still a notion of 'healthy' behaviour, but it is (superficially) the exact opposite of termination. If such a program halts at some stage, it is usually considered to be in error, the victim of a "crash" or of "deadlock". Obviously, conventional methods for proving termination of conventional programs need not be relevant.

The reason that the traditional notion of termination fails to extend to these more general contexts is that it is an operational notion. Fortunately, it appears that there is a static notion (which refers to data objects, and not computations) which corresponds to termination in simple cases, but also generalizes. We have in mind the notion of completeness.

A complete object (in a domain of data objects) is, roughly speaking, one which has no holes or gaps in it, one which cannot be further completed. In a standard 'flat' domain, all but the minimal elements are complete; in a domain of ordered pairs, the complete elements are those for which the components are complete; in a domain of finite trees, those in which all the leaves are complete; and in a domain of functions, those which are total, i.e. which yield a complete result when given a complete argument.

The distinction between complete and partial (or incomplete) objects could prove to be even more important than that between terminating and nonterminating computations. Complete objects are important because they are mathematically 'conventional', and the collection of complete objects in a domain usually enjoys conventional mathematical properties which are not true of the domain as a whole.

Completeness is, as we said, a static concept, but it also has operational significance. If our programming language has a denotational (mathematical, extensional) semantics, then we have a correspondence between programs and elements of an appropriate domain. From our limited experience, it seems that programs which behave in a healthy fashion will correspond to complete elements of the domain. For example, a Turing machine which always halts computes a total (i.e. complete) function.

It might seem strange that we have defined so important a concept in such a vague and informal way. Unfortunately, there is at present little choice, for it seems that in general there is no way of determining which elements of an arbitrary domain deserve to be called complete.

In many domains the complete elements are exactly the maximal elements, but this need not always be the case; there may be incomplete elements which cannot be completed. In a domain of continuous functions, for example, there may be partial functions (like the as soon as functions of Lucid [2]) which have "essential" singularities. And even if completeness could be defined precisely in the context of standard domain theory (i.e. in terms of the relation of approximation), it would be of little help without methods for proving that objects defined in certain ways must be complete.

Fortunately there appears to be a simple way to extend the notion of domain to give a meaning to "completeness". The remedy is to adopt the methods of topology and introduce a quantitative measure of convergence, related to a metric. Rather than develop a general theory of such domains (at present only partially understood) we instead give an example of the power of the method by using it to justify the correctness of a simple and useful test for deadlock in a simple dataflow language.

1. Data Flow

The term "data flow" refers to a loosely defined operational concept in which computation is controlled by the flow of data through a network ([1], [3], [4], [7]). The model we will use is that of [7]. A data flow network is a directed graph, the arcs of which are communication channels down which data 'tokens' travel, and the nodes of which are processing stations. The diagram shows a simple data flow network which generates in order the sequence 1, 2, 3, 5, 8, ... of Fibonnacci numbers (our nets are continuously operating devices).

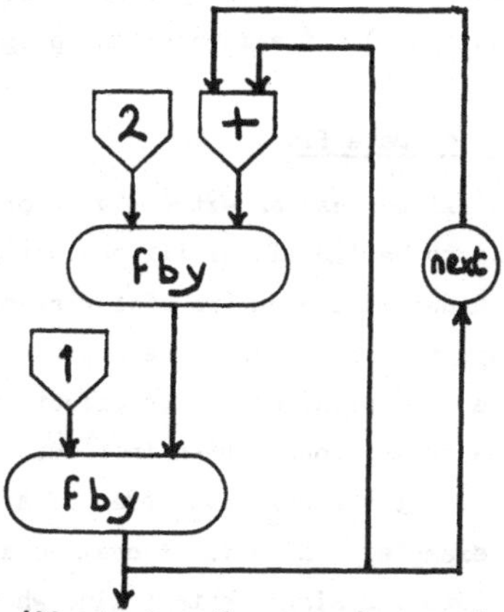

The example network illustrates the use of several important nodes.

The simplest are those like the one labelled "+" which correspond to ordinary operations on data items. The "+" node repeatedly awaits the arrival of tokens on its input lines; as soon as there are tokens on both lines, the two tokens are removed and a token representing their sum is sent down the output line. As with the other nodes, input on the different lines need not arrive simultaneously or even at the same rate, and tokens awaiting processing queue on the arcs. A special case of this kind of node are the 'constant' nodes with no input lines. The node labelled "2" simply generates an endless stream of tokens representing the number 2.

The remaining nodes do not process tokens but merely manipulate them. The "next" node discards the first token which arrives but passes the rest on.The "fby"("followed by") node awaits the first token to arrive on its left input, passes it on as its first output, but after that passes on whatever appears on its second input line. Any tokens which might arrive later on the first input line are discarded (but no input from the second line is discarded). The "fby" node allows arcs to be initialized, though possibly with values computed by other parts of the net. Both nodes have a two state internal memory.

These, of course, are not the only useful nodes. One particularly important one, which we will call the "upon" node (for want of a better name), acts as a valve or gate to slow up the rate of flow of its first argument. As long as 0's arrive down its second input line it sends on copies of the last token it read in from the first input line. When a 1 (representing "true") arrives it ingests the next token on the first line and sends on copies of it until another 1 arrives. For example, if tokens representing 3, 5, 7, 9, 11, ... arrive down the first input line, and tokens representing 0, 0, 1, 0, 1, 1, 0, 0, 1, ... arrive down the second input line, then tokens representing 3, 3, 3, 5, 5, 7, 9, 9, 9, 11, ... will be sent down the output line. This node has an internal 'storage location' capable of holding one data item.

Many other nodes have been proposed or are possible, but even with the few described here one can (as we shall see) write interesting programs.

2. The Extensional Semantics of Data Flow

The nodes just described all possess an extremely important property, namely functionality. A node is said to be functional iff the entire history of its output activity is completely determined by the entire histories of the activities of its input lines. Roughly speaking, this means that there are no random devices in the node itself, and that the rate of arrival of inputs affects only the rate of departure of outputs. A functional node can obviously take into account the order of arrival tokens on a particular line but not the relative order of arrival of tokens on different lines. The canonical example of a nonfunctional node is the 'race' or 'collector' node which passes on down its single output line whatever appears at either of its inputs (choosing at random if tokens are waiting on both lines).

Functionality is extremely important because it allows a simple extensional (i.e. mathematical or denotational) treatment of data flow. It allows us to use mathematical objects to characterise the role or function of arcs, nodes and graphs.

The mathematical object assigned to an arc is a history, namely a record of all the tokens which travelled down the arc. In a 'healthy' net the activity proceeds indefinitely, so that the history will be an infinite sequence of data items; but (as we shall see) it is possible that activity might cease at some finite stage, and so our domain of histories contains all finite and infinite sequences. This domain is a cpo under the subsequence ordering.

The mathematical object which we assign to a node is the function from histories to histories which describes the correspondence between the inputs and the outputs of the node.

Suppose now that we have a net all of whose nodes are functional. Each arc is the output of some node, so that the history corresponding to it is the result of applying the function corresponding to this node to the histories of its input arcs. The history of each arc is therefore defined by a simple equation, and so to a dataflow net there corresponds a set of equations, one for each arc in the net. If the net has cycles in it, this set of equations is recursive. Kahn indicated in [7], and Faustini has proved in [5], that the actual operational behaviour of the net is exactly described by the least fixed point (solution) of the equations.

3. The Equational Dataflow Language

The result just quoted is generally accepted as being very important, but often only as an accomplishment of descriptive semantics. In this perspective histories are used to describe the activity on arcs, functions describe the activities of nodes, and least fixed points of equations describe the activity of nets. From this point of view the result appears somewhat limited, because minor variations in the operational basis (e.g. nonfunctional nodes) cause the whole system to break down.

The real significance of the result emerges only when we reverse the point of view. Arcs and tokens should be seen as operational ways to realize histories; nodes, as implementations of history functions, and nets as devices for computing the solutions of equations. From this perspective many of the variations on pure data flow can be simply rejected as unsuitable for the purposes intended.

One very interesting feature of this new perspective is that data flow programs are not graphs but rather sets of equations. This equational language is quite easy to use and the programs are concise and often very elegant. Here is an equational version of the Fibonnacci program

```
F = 1 fby (2 fby F + G)
G = next F
```

and here is one which generates the stream of factorials

```
I = 1 fby I + 1
F = 1 fby F * next I
```

(fby appears as an infix operator with lowest possible precedence, so that e.g. "2 fby F + G" is the same as "2 fby (F + G)"). Notice that nested expressions are permitted on the right hand side. Subexpressions (like "next I") correspond to 'anonymous' arcs in the dataflow network, i.e. arcs which do not correspond to any program variable.

Here is a merge program

```
XX = X upon XX ≤ YY
YY = Y upon YY ≤ XX
 Z = if XX ≤ YY then XX else YY
```

which has two input (i.e. undefined) variables, "X" and "Y" ("upon", like "fby", has low precedence). Given any values for these variables, the least fixed point of the program gives us the corresponding value of "Z". It is not hard to see that if X and Y are increasing streams of natural numbers then Z is their ordered merge, without repetitions. For example, if X begins 3, 5, 7, 9, 10, ... and Y begins 2, 6, 7, 9, 12, ... then Z begins 2, 3, 5, 6, 7, 9, 10, ...

If we add to the above program the equations

```
S = 1 fby Z
X = 2 * S
Y = 3 * S
```

we have a new program without input variables which generates in order all numbers of the form 2^i3^j (S begins 1, 2, 3, 4, 6, 8, ...).

The following program

```
AA = A upon B < 2
 B = AA fby if B > 1 then B÷2 else next AA
 D = B mod 2
```

generates and concatenates the binary expansions of the numbers in A (so that if A begins 9, 6, 8, 3, ... then D begins 1, 0, 0, 1, 0, 1, 1, 0, 0, 0, 1, 1, 1, ...). If we add the equation

```
A = 1 fby 2 * A
```

D will be the sequence 1, 0, 1, 0, 0, 1, 0, 0, 0, 1, ...

4. Circularity and Deadlock

All the example dataflow programs given so far are recursive, i.e. have variables which are defined directly or indirectly in terms of themselves. This is true in general of all but the simplest programs, whether they generate streams of data (like the Fibonnacci program) or just process them (like the merge program).

The equational programmer uses circularity to bring about repetition (this accounts for its importance) although it is far more general and powerful than simple iteration. In operational terms, the fact that a variable is defined in terms of itself means that the corresponding arc in the net is part of a cycle (loop) in the net. Data tokens travel around and around the loops in a net, usually being transformed in the process. These loops are the 'wheels' that keep the net moving.

Real wheels in real machines have, however, a tendency to seize up and stop, and the same is true of the cycles in a dataflow net. If a net has a cycle in it, it means that some node is directly or indirectly consuming its own output. The possibility therefore arises that the node might starve itself, i.e. might find itself in a situation in which it is waiting for itself to produce data. This is what is usually (although in more general contexts) called deadlock.

Deadlock in a dataflow net can in fact occur. In the simple example

G = 1 fby (2 fby 1 + next next G)

the net turns out two numbers (1 and 2) and then seizes up when the two "next" nodes 'gobble up' the two tokens. Nothing further is produced, and the "+" node spends eternity waiting for its own output.

Another example is the following

Y = 5 fby next X
X = 2 * Y upon P

which deadlocks almost immediately unless the first value of P is 0. If it is 0, the extra copy of the 10 token makes its way past the "next" node and enables the second multiplication.

On the other hand, it is certainly possible to write circular programs which never deadlock provided only that their inputs do not run dry. This is the case with <u>all</u> the example programs given earlier.

Obviously, deadlock does not occur just because a variable is defined in terms of itself. A study of a small number of examples soon reveals that what matters is <u>how</u> a variable depends on itself. For example, in the following very simple healthy program

I = 1 fby I + 1

the variable I depends on itself but in such a way that the <u>present</u> value of I (i.e. the one currently being computed) depends on at most the previously computed value. On the other hand, in the following deadlocking program

J = 1 + J
K = 2 * next K

the present values of J and K depend on the present and future values of J and K respectively.

What is clearly indicated is some sort of requirement which would ensure that the present value of any variable depends only on its previous values.

The first step in formulating such a requirement is to describe more exactly the way in which the outputs of the various nodes depend on their inputs. For example, if

A = B + C

then the value of A being computed depends only on the values of B and C just read in; the output of a "+" node neither leads nor lags the inputs, and the first three (say) values of A require the first three values of B and C. On the other hand, if

A = next D

then the output lags the input by one : the first three values of A require the first four values of D (or at least require that the node read these values in). Conversely, if

A = 3 fby B

then the output leads the second input : the first three values of A require only the first two values of B.

These lead/lag effects are clearly cumulative. If we have

A = 3 fby (5 fby B)

then A leads B by 2, so that the first three values of A require only the first value of B. The effects can also cancel each other: if

A = 3 fby next B

then in general the first n values of A require the first n values of B.

These observations suggest some sort of quantitative measure of this time displacement of dependencies. We therefore associate with each of the arguments of the different operations an integer which (informally speaking) measures how far the output leads the argument in question. The associated numbers are as follows:

(i) 0 is associated with each argument of the "+" node, and in general with each argument of a node computing an ordinary data operation;

(ii) 0 and 1 respectively are associated with the arguments of fby;

(iii) -1 is associated with the argument of next;

(iv) 0 and 1 respectively are associated with the arguments of upon.

When operations are composed, these numbers are added; to find the way in which the value of a whole expression can depend on the values of variables occurring in it,we consider the expression as a tree, trace a path from the root of the tree to the variable, and add up the numbers associated with the operations on the path. For example, if the expression is

(3 fby (next B + next C)) upon (next (P fby B))

then the path to "P" goes through the second argument of "upon" (+1), the argument of "next" (-1), and the first argument of "fby" (0). The sum of these numbers is 0, and so we conclude that in general the present value of the expression could depend on the present value of P. If a variable occurs more than once in an expression, we take the minimum of the path sums (which, in the case of "B" here, is 0).

It should not now be too hard to guess how we can use these numbers to assure ourselves that a variable in a data flow program is not defined in terms of its own present or future values. We look at the graph of the program and form path sums for all paths which start and end with the arc corresponding to the variable in question (i.e. all cycles containing that arc). If every such "cycle sum" is positive, the dependency of that variable on itself is healthy. To make sure that the whole program is healthy, we perform the test for every arc. Equivalently, we make sure that <u>every cycle in the graph of the program has a positive cycle sum</u>.

This is the <u>cycle sum test</u> and our claim is that every program passing the test is immune to deadlock (provided only that its inputs do not deadlock). All the example programs given in the earlier section pass the test. In the graph of the Fibonacci program, for example, there are two cycles, and their sums are 1 and 2.

5. Justification of the Cycle Sum Test

Deadlock is an operational concept and so it might be expected that we will now proceed to an operational proof of our claim. This is possible, and worth doing,but it would be missing the point of this paper, which is to illustrate the possibility and importance of an extensional (non operational) notion of completeness.

The connection between deadlock and completeness is actually quite easy to appreciate. Even in the absence of a precise definition of dataflow deadlock, it is evident that deadlock cannot be present in a net in which the activity on arcs(flow of tokens) goes on indefinitely. In terms of extensional concepts, unceasing activity corresponds to infinite elements in the domain of histories previously described,and we can certainly agree that these are exactly the elements of that domain which deserve to be called complete. The equivalence of the operational and extensional semantics of dataflow tells us that to prove a program deadlock free it is sufficient to prove that its least fixed point is complete (for every complete set of values for its input variables). (Kahn himself noticed this connection between deadlock and completeness).

Our goal therefore is to show that the least fixed point of a set of equations passing the cycle sum test must be complete. We can get a good idea of why this must be the case by examining almost the simplest healthy recursive program,

$$I = 1 \text{ fby } I + 1$$

whose least fixed point <1,2,3,...> is complete. Let f be the function defined by the right hand side, i.e. let f(x) be 1 fby x+1 for any history x, so that the meaning of the program is the least fixed point of f. We know that this least fixed point is the limit (lub) of the sequence $\emptyset$, $f(\emptyset)$, $f(f(\emptyset))$, ... , $f^i(\emptyset)$, ... (where $\emptyset$ is the empty history). This sequence of histories begins

$\emptyset$

<1>

<1,2>

<1,2,3>

and it is easy to see why the limit must be complete - the terms of this sequence increase in length by one on each step. Furthermore, it is easy to see why these lengths increase - the function f increases length, i.e. the length of f(x) (x finite) is one plus the length of x. In fact it is evident that the least fixed point of any length increasing function must be infinite (complete).

Since we measure the dependency of "I" on itself as plus one, it would seem likely that there is some connection between length and the numbers we assigned to the arguments of operations. This is indeed the case. For example, we associated the numbers 0 and 1 with the arguments of upon, and simple calculations will show that (if x and p are finite) the length of x upon p is at least the minimum of the length of x and the length of p plus one. In general we will associate a sequence d of integers of length n with an n-ary operation g on histories whenever the length of $g(x_0,x_1,\ldots x_{n-1})$ is, for any $x_0\ldots x_{n-1}$, at least

$$\min_i(\text{length}(x_i) + d_i)$$

To make these ideas more precise, let H be the domain of histories, let $\hat{\mathcal{N}}$ be the natural numbers plus ∞ (with numerical ordering) and extend addition and subtraction to $\hat{\mathcal{N}}$ in the obvious way.

<u>Definition</u> For any positive integers n and m and any n×m matrix M with components in $\hat{\mathcal{N}}$.

B(M) is the set of all functions g from H^n to H^m such that

$$\text{length}(g(x))_j \geq \min_i (\text{length}(x_i) + M_{ij})$$

for any j and any x in H^n.

The components of the matrix M estimate the way in which the ith input of g effects the jth output. For example, if $g \in B(M)$ and $M_{3,5}$ is 2, then the first k values of the 5th output of g require at most the first k-2 values of the 3rd input.

This association between functions and matrices has the following important property: that composition corresponds to min/sum matrix product. If $g \in B(M)$ and $n \in B(N)$ and if the composition of g and h is defined, then their composition is in B(L) where

$$L_{ij} = \min_k \; M_{ik} + N_{kj} .$$

Now suppose that we have a general dataflow program (for simplicity without input variables) consisting of n equations defining n variables. From these equations we form the n×n matrix (with components in $\hat{Z}$) the ith row of which consists of the numbers describing the way in which the expression on the right hand side of the equation defining the ith variable depends on the other variables. For example, if the program

```
 A = 1 fby 2 * A
AA = A upon B < 2
 B = AA fby if B > 1 then B/2 else next AA
 D = B mod 2
```

then the matrix and its corresponding graph is

	A	AA	B	D
A	1	∞	∞	∞
AA	0	∞	1	∞
B	∞	0	1	∞
D	∞	∞	0	∞

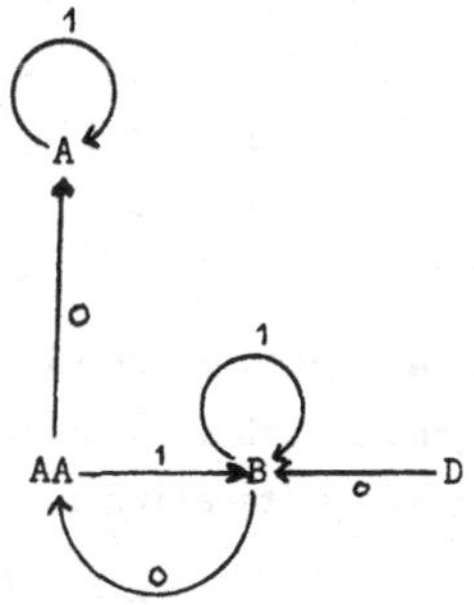

(notice that ∞ signifies no dependency)

This is the matrix of <u>direct</u> dependencies; the corresponding graph is not exactly the dataflow graph of the program, but it is apparent that both graphs pass or fail the cycle sum test together.

It is not hard to see that this matrix M can be associated with the function f from H^n to H^n defined by the equations of the program; in other words, f is in B(M). Thus for any x in H^n we have

$$\text{length}(f(x)) \geqslant M * \text{length}(x)$$

where length has been 'coerced' into a vector-to-vector operation and * is min/sum product. We must somehow put these facts together to conclude that the least fixed point of f is complete (that each component is complete).

If it happens that all the entries of the matrix M associated with f are positive, the result is guaranteed. The reason is that in these circumstances, f increases length in the following sense: the length of the shortest component of $f(x_0 \ldots x_{n-1})$ is always greater than the length of the shortest component of $\langle x_0 \ldots x_{n-1} \rangle$, and this condition easily implies that every component of the least fixed point of f is infinite.

Unfortunately it is almost never the case that all of the entries of the matrix M itself are positive, even when the program (like the example just given) satisfies the cycle sum test. In particular, if the program includes the equation

$$V_i = \text{next } V_j$$

then the i,j^{th} component of M will be -1. The fact that the program passes the cycle sum test means only (in matrix terms) that the diagonal elements of the dependency matrix

$$\min_{1\leq k\leq n} M^k$$

are positive. For example, the dependency matrix of the program just given is

	A	AA	B	D
A	1	∞	∞	∞
AA	0	1	1	∞
B	0	0	1	∞
D	∞	∞	1	∞

A little experiment shows that the problem is that it 'takes time' for the increases in the length of one component to effect the rest. This would suggest speeding up the process by iterating f, i.e. by considering an equation of the form

$$x = f^m(x)$$

for some large m. (The least fixed point of f^m is the same as that of f for any positive m). By what was said earlier we know that f^m is in $B(M^m)$, where exponentiation is with respect to the min/sum product. It is therefore enough to show that some power of M has all positive entries.

We mentioned that M represents the labelled dependency graph of the program. Since we are using the min/sum product, the i,j^{th} entry of M^m must be the 'cost' (i.e. path sum) of the 'cheapest' path <u>of length m</u> from i to j in this graph. Since this graph has n nodes, any path through this graph must consist of a cycle free part of length not greater than n plus a number of cycles, each also of length not greater than n. There are only a finite number of cycle free paths, so that the cost of the cycle free part of any path must be not less than some number b independent of m. On the other hand, each cycle contributes at least +1 to the cost. Thus if m is greater than $(n+1)|b|$, every path of length m will have more than b cycles and will therefore have positive cost. In other words, all the entries of M^m must be positive, as desired.

This completes an informal outline of the purely extensional proof that every program passing the cycle sum test is deadlock free.

6. Application of the Test

The fact that a program passes the cycle sum test means first of all that it is free of deadlock, as we already indicated. The class of programs which pass the test is surprisingly large, and includes all those which correspond to simple iterative algorithms (written in Algol with for-loops). There are, however, quite sensible programs which fail the test but nevertheless do not deadlock, and it would be too restrictive to require that a legal dataflow program pass the test. For these more general programs other methods of proving completeness must be devised.

We also saw that the meaning (least solution) of a cycle sum test approved program is a complete element in the domain of histories. This means that the denotation of the variables are 'conventional' objects, and one very important consequence is the fact that we can use conventional mathematical rules in reasoning about them. For example, we can invoke the equations

$$(I + J) - J = I$$
$$\text{if true then } X \text{ else } Y = X$$

which may not be valid if X, Y, I and J are not complete.

Finally, the fact that a program passes the cycle sum test means that it has a unique solution (since its least solution is maximal) and this gives us a very powerful verification rule. For example, the equations

$$I = 1 \text{ fby } I + 1$$
$$J = 1 \text{ fby } J + 2*I + 1$$

pass the test; furthermore, some simple rules tell us that

$$I^2 = 1 \text{ fby } I^2 + 2*I + 1$$

so that I^2 satisfies the equation defining J. Since this equation has a unique solution, we conclude that $I^2 = J$. Note that this proof involved no induction.

7. Towards a General Notion of Completeness

The proof that a program passing the cycle sum test has a unique, complete solution was purely extensional, and clearly used only a few assumptions about the distinction between complete and partial elements of the domain of histories and the length function. It is quite plausible that the proof could be generalized to any domain equipped with similar notions of 'size' and completeness.

We have already mentioned that there seems to be no way, given an arbitrary domain, to single out a subset of complete elements; nor does there seem to be a general way to introduce a norm. Most interesting domains, however, are not arbitrary, they are not pulled out of hats. They are constructed from simple domains using domain operations (like cartesian product) and recursive definitions. For these domains it seems likely that we can define size and completeness in a natural way. In fact we have already seen a simple example, where we earlier (implicitly) defined the length of a tuple of histories to be the length of its shortest component, so that a tuple is complete iff all its components are.

One specially intriguing property of these (to some extent hypothetical) domains is that the collection of complete elements in a domain would seem to form a metric space, if we define the distance between two complete elements to be 2^{-s} where s is the size of the glb of the elements. In the case of natural number valued histories, the space of complete elements is the Baire space of classical descriptive set theory (see, for example, [8]).

It is not possible (as far as we know) to formulate the cycle sum theorem purely in terms of functions on an abstract metric space. But it is possible, however, if we use instead of a metric a dual notion which we call an "agreement": a function which assigns to any two points a nonnegative element of $\hat{Z}$ which measures how close together the points are, yielding ∞ if they coincide. This approach could allow a fixed point semantics for a large class of 'obviously terminating' recursive programs which would be mathematically 'conventional' in that it could completely avoid reference to partial objects and approximation.

8. Acknowledgements

The cycle sum test was first devised by the author in order to characterize a class of compilable Lucid programs; C. Hoffman used the test in [6]. M. Farah was probably the first to notice that Lucid programs passing the test had unique solutions (which might not be complete because Lucid's as soon as function is incomplete). The importance of the test in the study of dataflow became apparent in the course of supervising Faustini's researches, and the latter helped formulate the present version of the proof.

References

1. Arvind and Gostelow, Dataflow computer architecture: research and goals, technical report no. 113, Department of Information and Computer Science, University of California Irvine.

2. Ashcroft, E.A., and Wadge, W., Lucid, a nonprocedural language with iteration, CACM 20, no. 7, pp 519-526.

3. Davis, A.L., The architecture of DDM-1: a recursively structured data driven machine, report UUCS-77-113, Department of Computer Science, University of Utah.

4. Dennis, J.B., First version of a dataflow procedure language, MAC TM 61, MIT.

5. Faustini, A.A., The equivalence of the operational and extensional semantics of pure dataflow, Ph.D. (in preparation), University of Warwick, Coventry UK.

6. Hoffman, C.M., Design and correctness of a compiler for a nonprocedural language, Acta Informatica 9, pp 217-241 (1978).

7. Kahn, G., The semantics of a simple language for parallel processing, IFIPS 74.

8. Kuratowski, K., Topologie (I), Warsaw (1958).

ON ACHIEVING DISTRIBUTED TERMINATION

Nissim Francez
Department of Computer Science
Technion - Israel Institute of Technology
Haifa, Israel

ABSTRACT

We consider a distributed system based on communication among disjoint processes, in which each process is capable of achieving a post condition of its local space in such a way that the conjunction of local post conditions implies a global post condition of the whole system. We then augment the system with extra control communication, in order to achieve distributed - termination, without adding new channels of communication. The algorithm is applied to a problem of sorted partition.

Key words and phrases: Concurrent programs, distributed processes, disjoint memories, communication, input-output, distributed termination.

The work has been partially sponsored by NSF grant No. MSC 78-673, during my stay at USC, Los Angeles.

1. INTRODUCTION

Recently, Hoare designed a new programming language for concurrent programming called CSP [8], which differs from previously suggested languages such as Concurrent Pascal [1], or Modula [11], on a major design issue. Namely, processes are disjoint, i.e. share no kind of variables whatsoever. All communication among concurrent processes is by means of input-output, which also serves for synchronization. A similar kind of communication is also employed by Milne and Milner [9], without suggesting any specific language for expressing it. Sintzoff [10] uses similar primitives with a different synchronization, based on channel testing. Brinch Hansen [2] suggests procedure calls as a means of communication among otherwise disjoint processes. Thus, the subject of distributed programs gains more and more interest, which is, of course, connected with developments in microprocessor technology as the future implementation tool.

Some of the theoretical problems involved in the semantics of such programs are discussed in [9], as well as in [7], and we are currently working on proof rules for strong (total) correctness of such programs. One of those questions, the problem of distributed termination, is discussed in this paper, where an algorithm for achieving such termination is suggested. Thoughts on some of the issues involved in termination of concurrent programs may be found in [6].

The need for such an algorithm arises, because in general termination is a property of the global state of a concurrent program. It may be hard to distribute the decision to terminate to processes which are aware of their local state, and have only limited information about the state of other processes with which they are connected along a channel of communication. On the other hand, it may be fairly easy to distribute a global post-condition into (a conjunction of) local post conditions. We shall discuss an example, an algorithm for achieving a sorted partition into n subsets, which is a generalization of a problem solved by Diskstra [5] for $n=2$.

2. THE PROBLEM

Suppose we want to design a concurrent program P, which has to achieve upon termination a post condition $B(\bar{y})$, where $\bar{y}$ is the (global) state vector. Suppose also that it is possible to partition $\bar{y}$ into $n(\geq 2)$ disjoint substates $\bar{y}_1,\dots,\bar{y}_n$, and find n predicates (over those substates) $B_i(\bar{y}_i)$, $i=1,\dots,n$ so that

$$(1)\qquad (\bigwedge_{i=1,n} B_i(\bar{y}_i)) \supset B(\bar{y}).$$

Finally, suppose we can design relatively easily n processes $P_1,\dots,P_n$, which have as their state vectors $\bar{y}_i$ respectively, which by means of some communications with each other, exchanging data, can achieve a state $B_i(\bar{y}_i)$ after a finite amount of time (we will call this communication the basic communication).

Then, the concurrent program $P :: [P_1 \| \ldots \| P_n]$ would be a natural solution to the original problem, provided we can enforce termination as soon as all P_i's achieve their favorable state satisfying B_i (such states will be called final). Partial correctness follows from (1). Each P_i is repetitive, of the form

$$P_i = *[g_{i_1} \rightarrow S_{i_1} \; \square \; \vdots \; \square \; g_{i_{k_i}} \rightarrow S_{i_{k_i}}]$$

(where g_{i_j} may involve basic communication).

When the steady state $\forall i \cdot B_i(S_i)$ is reached, all P_i's are in their outer level, with no guard ready.

Since there is no central control which can inspect all P_i's from the outside and decide when to terminate, the P_i's have to establish the required fact by means of some extra control-communication. We call the problem of designing such control communication the problem of distributed-termination.

Obviously, a solution in which each P_i terminates as soon as it finds its own $B_i(\bar{y}_i)$ true is not correct, since there may exist another P_j, which needs some more basic communication with P_i in order to establish the truth of $B_j(\bar{y}_j)$. We will assume another natural property:

(2) No two processes in final states conduct basic communication.

The required solution should be, of course, independent of the specific problem P is trying to solve. It should be a communication scheme that could be inserted into any partially correct solution as above with the slightest possible additions to the basic communication part (for interface with the control communication). The solution should, therefore, be also independent of the number of processes involved, n, and of the specific neighborhood relationships holding among the P_i's (here 'neighbors' means processes with which some P_i is connected by means of a communication channel).

Another important requirement from the solution is, that it does not add new neighborhood relationships, or equivalently, new communication channels. This is important for physical realizations of such a solution. A simpler solution can be obtained if this requirement is deleted.

3. THE PATTERN OF DISTRIBUTED TERMINATION

Let $P :: [P_1 \| \ldots \| P_n]$ be a concurrent program with processes P_i, $i=1,\ldots,n$. Let $\bar{y}$ denote the global state of P, and $\bar{y}_i$, $i=1,\ldots,n$, the total state of P_i, and we assume that all the processes are disjoint and are communicating in some way along channels.

For a process P_i, endotermination is termination depending only on the reachability of some final state, determined by some predicate $B_i(\bar{y}_i)$ over the initial local state. Compare de Bakker [3]. Exotermination is termination depending on the condition that every member of a pre-specified set $T = \{P_{i_1},\ldots, P_{i_k}\}$, $k > 0$, has terminated.

T is called the termination dependency set (TDS), and $T = \emptyset$ by convention in case of endotermination. Normally, if $P_j \in TDS_i$, P_i will communicate with P_j. We avoid here discussion of how the TDS is specified, and how the termination of its members is sensed, which are language dependent issues.

In general the kind of termination a process exhibits may depend on its own initial state as well as on the initial state of its companions. If the processes contain also local (internal) non-determinism [7], then the dependency is on each initial state and each computation! (1) As an example, consider a process P_1, which is ready to accept no more than m messages from its companion P_2, where m is locally determined and $TDS_1 = \{P_2\}$. If P_2 terminates before delivering m messages, P_1 will terminate in an exotermination. If P_2 is willing to send m or more messages, P_1 will terminate in an endotermination.

The concepts of endonontermination and exonontermination are defined analogously. Thus, endonontermination means the unreachability of any final local state. Exonontermination means nontermination of at least one process from TDS.

Some processes are always either endoterminating or endononterminating, or are always either exoterminating or exononterminating. ('Always' here means for each tuple of initial states and each computation.) We call such processes endoprocesses and exoprocesses, respectively. It is a useful language feature to allow syntactically imposing restrictions on a process as to what kind of termination it should exhibit. In CSP [8], one can use a guarded command containing only i/o guards in a way which implies that the process is an exoprocess. Using a mixture of boolean and i/o guards does not allow such a syntactical distinction.

For each program P as above, we now define its communication-graph G_p. G_p contains one node for each P_i in P, and an edge (P_i,P_j), for each pair of processes P_i, P_j s.t. a channel of communication exists between P_i and P_j. Note that channels of communication are directed, and the G_p is a directed graph, which may contain both (P_i,P_j) and (P_j,P_i). We assume that G_p has no self loops, since no process communicates with itself. For convenience, we assume that G_p is weakly connected, i.e., the underlying undirected graph is connected. Otherwise, one has to discuss properties of the weakly connected components. We also assume that the channels are not created and destroyed dynamically, and G_p can be determined syntactically from P. Various properties of P can be expressed in terms of G_p.

(1) In the sequel, we assume that processes have no local nondeterminism, for simplifying the discussion.

which characterizes all potential communications. For example, if G_p is a tree then P obviously cannot deadlock. In Dijkstra [4] there are some dynamic properties expressed with relation to such a graph, again in a context of deadlock freedom characterization.

Here, we are interested in another graph T_p, derived from G_p and the various TDS sets. T_p will reflect all the termination dependencies within P.

The nodes of T_p are the same as those of G_p, one for each process $P_i \in P$. However, the edges of T_p are not in general syntactically determined, since they may depend on the initial states. Let $\bar{y} = (\bar{y}_1, \ldots, \bar{y}_n)$ be a fixed initial state vector.

For each edge $(P_i, P_j) \in G_p$

1. $(P_i, P_j) \in T_p$ iff $P_i \in TDS_j$
2. $(P_j, P_i) \in T_p$ iff $P_j \in TDS_i$.

Thus, T_p contains some of the directed edges of G_p and/or their reversals. All nodes corresponding to endoterminating processes will be sources, having no incoming edges.

<u>The Distributed Termination Pattern Theorem:</u>

P terminates for $(\bar{y}_1, \ldots, \bar{y}_n)$ only if T_p is acyclic.

<u>Proof</u>. If T_p contains a cycle, then a deadlock situation occurs, since no process whose corresponding node lies on the cycle can possibly terminate. (Obviously all nodes on such a cycle correspond to processes which are exononterminating for $\bar{y}$.)

The meaning of this theorem is that whenever P terminates for $\bar{y}$, it has a partial order induced on its processes, which describes a "<u>wave of termination</u>", where all endoterminating processes (for that $\bar{y}$) terminate first, then all processes whose TDS contain only endoterminating processes terminate, and so on.

The acyclicity of T_p is of course not sufficient, because of the possibility of dynamic deadlocks and infinite computations. However, even the necessary condition gives one the general feeling of the way distributed termination is achieved.

Methodologically, it may be easier to impose such a partial ordering syntactically and let the required "termination wave" be apparent from the program text. A similar observation is mentioned by Dijkstra [5], who suggests an algorithm containing one (syntactically) endoterminating process (in our terms) and one (syntactically) exoterminating process. He indicates that an alternative design of the algorithm is possible, involving two endoterminating processes, which would use a different termination pattern but would be harder to verify.

Finally, consider a simple example, expressed in CSP [8] notation. Consider again the process P_1 mentioned above, which is ready to consume no more than m inputs, and terminate if its companion P_2 does so before m messages have been passed. Let P_2 be a process ready to produce no more than k outputs and terminate if its companion P_1 does so before k messages have been passed.

In the program, we omit variable declarations for brevity, as well as the portions of program which process input or generate output, without further communication. We let $P :: [P_1 \| P_2]$ where

$$P_1 :: a := 0; \quad * \quad [a < m,\ P_2?\, x \rightarrow a := a + 1]$$

$$P_2 :: b := 0; \quad * \quad [b < k,\ P_1!\, y \rightarrow b := b + 1] .$$

For this program P we have:

$$G_p = \underset{p_1}{\circ} \longleftarrow \underset{p_2}{\circ}$$

reflecting the directed channel of communication between p_2 and p_1, along which p_2 sends outputs to p_1, and p_1 receives input from p_2.

For T_p, we have three possible cases.

a) $k = m$. T_p has no edges at all, since no termination dependencies exist.

$$T_p = \underset{p_1}{\circ} \qquad \underset{p_2}{\circ}$$

b) $k < m$. In this case, p_2 is endoterminating and p_1 is exoterminating with $TDS_1 = \{P_2\}$.

$$T_p = \underset{p_1}{\circ} \longleftarrow \underset{p_2}{\circ}$$

p_2 will induce termination on p_1.

c) $k > m$. This is the symmetric case, and $TDS_2 = \{P_1\}$.

$$T_p = \underset{p_1}{\circ} \longrightarrow \underset{p_2}{\circ}$$

T_p is acyclic in all three cases, as expected, since P terminates for every initial state (m,k).

As an example the insufficiency of the acyclicity of T_p, consider the following program in CSP [8]:

$$P :: [P_1 :: P_2?\, x \| P_2 :: P_1?\, y \| P_3 :: * \, [P_1?z \rightarrow \text{skip} \square P_2?\, x \rightarrow \text{skip}]]$$

T_p =

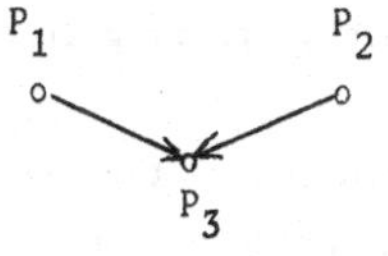

which is acyclic (syntactically!)

However, P_1 and P_2 are engaged in a deadlock, each waiting for an input from the other, thus preventing P_3 from (exo)-termination.

Note that in CSP [8], the TDS is implicit, dependencies being determined by means of i/o guards. Exotermination is expressed by making the whole program an i/o guarded loop.

4. A SOLUTION

Our strategy will be to arrange termination dependencies among $P_1,\ldots,P_n$ so that T_p will be acyclic. We assume that in the original P_i's no dependencies are specified. We want to designate an arbitrary P_{i_0}, which will "collect" all the information about the rest of the P_i's having reached a state satisfying $B_i(\bar{y}_i)$. Having reached the conclusion that <u>all</u> P_i's are in a final state, P_{i_0} will terminate, thus initializing the termination wave, which will eventually reach all P_i's.

The basic idea in the design of the algorithm is to find a spanning tree in G_p's underlying undirected graph (thus not adding new channels!). The control communication will have the following phases:

1) When in final state, the root will initiate a control wave to all its descendants in the spanning tree.
2) The ware propagates through a node P_j as long as $B_j(\bar{y}_j)$ is true too. Freeze the basic communications of node which the control wave passed.
3) Collect answers from all nodes in a subree, and notify father (in the tree) about the state of the subtree (in case $B_j(\bar{y}_j)$ itself is false, there is no need to propage the control wave, and an immediate negative notification can be delivered).
4) If a positive (i.e., asserting that all nodes are in final state) answer reaches the root, it may initiate the termination wave by terminating itself. The TDS's will be induced by the spanning tree so that this wave will spread all the way to the leaves. Note that contrary to the control-waves and answers which are part of the algorithm, the termination wave will be derived from the CSP rules concerning i/o guards [7,8].

In case of a negative answer (meaning that some nodes are not in a final state yet), an unfreezing wave is propagated, allowing the resumption of basic communication.

One has to take care, that at least one basic communication is performed between two consecutive control waves, to eliminate the possibility of an endless control loop.

Let G_p be the communication graph and T_p^* be any spanning tree in the underlying undirected graph of G_p. We now modify $P_1,\ldots,P_n$ to $\bar{P}_1,\ldots,\bar{P}_n$. First, we define for each $\bar{P}_i$ its TDS to be the set containing its father in T_p^*, and only it. The root of T_p^* is specified as an endoterminating process. We have thereby made the dependency graph T_p to coincide with the spanning tree T_p^*, thus guaranteeing that it is acyclic, in accordance with the pattern theorem stated above.

Next, we add to each P_i a control section G_i to be executed as an alternative to the basic communications, and add a small interface section to the basic communication part of P_i.

C_i will depend on the relative position of the node i (corresponding to P_i) in T_p^*. We will distinguish among three cases: the root, an intermediate node and a leaf.

In order to describe C_i, we use a liberal extension of the CSP [8] notation: Let $J = \{j_1,\ldots,j_k\}$ be an index set.

$$\prod_{j\in J} S_j \overset{df}{=} [S_{j_1} \parallel S_{j_2} \parallel \ldots \parallel S_{j_k}] \quad ,$$

$$\bigwedge_{j\in J} q_j \overset{df}{=} q_{j_1} \ \& \ldots \& \ q_{j_k} \quad \text{(conjunction)}.$$

For a node P_i in T_p^*, let $f(P_i)$ be the index of P_i's father, and Γ_i be the set of indices of P_i's sons.

<u>Case 1</u>: P_i is the root.

$$
\begin{array}{l}
C_i :: B_i,\ \text{newwave} \longrightarrow \prod_{j\in\Gamma_i} \bar{P}_j!\underline{ok};\ \prod_{j\in\Gamma_i} \bar{P}_j?a(j);\\
\qquad r := \bigwedge_{j\in\Gamma_i} a(j);\ [r \longrightarrow \text{halt}\\
\qquad\qquad \square\\
\qquad\qquad \sim r \longrightarrow \text{newwave:=false};\ \prod_{j\in\Gamma_i} \bar{P}_j!\underline{resume}\\
\qquad\qquad]\\
\square_{j\in\Gamma_i} \bar{P}_j?\text{ready}(j) \longrightarrow \text{skip}\\
\square\\
\bigwedge_{j\in\Gamma_i} \text{ready}(j) \longrightarrow \text{newwave:=true};\ \prod_{j\in\Gamma_i} \text{ready}(j):=\text{false}
\end{array}
$$

a is a new boolean array, not used in P_i, while <u>ok</u> is a new (control) communication signal, of a type different from <u>boolean</u> and <u>integer</u> (to meet the matching of types required by CSP [8] for i/o).

Thus, whenever $\bar{P}_i$ is in a B_i - state, it may choose to issue a control signal <u>ok</u> to each of its sons in T_p^* (in any order that the sons are ready to accept it). Then, it waits for each son to "answer" with a boolean value. If all answers are true, P_i halts. Otherwise, it sends each son a <u>resume</u> message (to be interpreted by the sons as a permission to resume basic communication, after being 'frozen' by the <u>ok</u> question), and may resume itself some basic communication, or try to initiate another control communication, once a ready signal arrived from each son. The meaning of ready(j) is explained in the sequel. The (new) boolean newwave (initialy true) records the arrival of all ready(j) signals.

Case 2: P_i is an intermediate node.

$$
\begin{array}{l}
C_i :: \bar{P}_{f(P_i)}?\underline{ok} \longrightarrow cm:=false; \\
\qquad [\sim B_i \longrightarrow \bar{P}_{f(P_i)}!false \\
\qquad \square \\
\qquad B_i \longrightarrow \prod_{j\in\Gamma_i} \bar{P}_j!\underline{ok};\ \prod_{j\in\Gamma_i} \bar{P}_j?a(j); \\
\qquad\qquad r:=\bigwedge_{j\in\Gamma_i} a(j);\bar{P}_{f(P_i)}!r \\
\qquad] \\
\square \\
\quad \bar{P}_{f(P_i)}?\underline{resume} \longrightarrow \prod_{j\in\Gamma_i} \bar{P}_j!\underline{resume};\ cm:=true;\ advanced:=false \\
\square \\
\quad \square_{j\in\Gamma_i} \bar{P}_j?ready(j) \longrightarrow skip \\
\square \\
\quad (B_i \vee advanced)\&\bigwedge_{j\in\Gamma_i} ready(j),\bar{P}_{f(P_i)}!true \longrightarrow \prod_{j\in\Gamma_i} ready(j):=false
\end{array}
$$

The array a and the ok signal are as in Case 1. cm is a new boolean variable, whose interpretation is masking basic communications. <u>The $\bar{P}_i$ basic communication part is augmented with cm as a guard</u>. cm is initialized to true.

Thus, as an alternative to its basic communication, $\bar{P}_i$ may accept an ok signal from its father as part of the control wave. Upon receiving such a signal, $\bar{P}_i$ immediately falsifies the basic communication guard cm, which can be set again to true by a resume input from its father, thus "freezing" itself. Then, $\bar{P}_i$ checks its local state. If it is not a B_i - state, it immediately responds with a false to its father thereby breaking the control wave. Otherwise (in a B_i - state) it behaves like the root, propagating the control wave, only instead of using the value of r, the accumulated state of its subtree, it communicates r to his father.

Another set of alternatives is to receive a ready(j) (equal actually to true) from each son, which means a permission to initiate a new ok wave. This message is passed on to the father, in case P_i is in a B_i - state, or some basic communication occurred, which is recorded in the boolean advanced. Initially, advanced=false, and for all j, ready(j)=false.

Case 3: P_i is a leaf.

C_i :: $\bar{P}_{f(P_i)}$?ok → cm:=false;$\bar{P}_{f(P_i)}$!B_i

□

$\bar{P}_{f(P_i)}$?resume → cm:=true;advanced:=false;ready:=true

□

ready&(B_i V advanced),$\bar{P}_{f(P_i)}$!true → ready:=false

ready is a (new) boolean, whose task is to insure that a ready signal to the father is sent only once per control wave.

In all three cases, we also augment the basic communication part of each P_i, which is not the root (why?), with a statement advanced:=true, recording the fact that some advance in basic communication did occur.

Thus, the overall operation of $\bar{P}$ is as follows: Processes are engaged in basic communication as long as possible. Occasionally, the root choses to initiate an ok message, to traverse the tree T_p^*, and wait for a boolean result r, which should be true only if $\forall i \cdot B_i(\bar{y}_i)$=true holds. Whoever receives this ok signal freezes its basic communication, and either spreads the ok message down the tree, or decides that its own state is not a B_i-state. Eventually, each process delivers an answer r to its father, s.t. r=true iff all the processes in its subtree (all "frozen"), are in a B_i-state. Once the root receives its own r, it halts if r is true, and otherwise sends a resume signal to "unfreeze" the whole tree. Once a process receives this message, it delivers it further down the tree and resumes basic communication. Each process not yet in B_i-state, after doing at least one basic communication, signals that another ok-wave is possible. When this signal reaches the root, the whole control cycle may start again. This goes on until $\forall i \cdot B_i(\bar{y}_i)$=true is reached (this is assumed to occur!), which will cause the root to halt eventually, and then the required termination wave will spread down T_p^*, until it reaches all processes of $\bar{P}$, since T_p^* is a spanning tree. Thus, distributed termination has been induced on the original P. We remind the reader again, that the spreading of the wave of termination follows from the language rules of i/o guards, and the construction of T_p^* as a spanning tree. It is not part of the addition. The control communication is used only to determine when can the root terminate!

4. CORRECTNESS

We want to prove now that the above algorithms has the required properties, i.e., that the augmented program

$\bar{P} = [\bar{P}_1 \| \ldots \| \bar{P}_n]$ terminates, with $\forall i \cdot B_i(\bar{y}_i)$=true, given that P is such that $\forall i \cdot B_i(\bar{y}_i)$=true eventually occurs. The proof is informal.

By our construction, $T_{\bar{p}} = T_p^*$ and so is acyclic. Since the root process is the only endoterminating process, we have to prove its termination, which is sufficient by the constructing of $T_{\bar{p}}$ as a spanning tree over $P_1, \ldots, P_n$.

<u>Claim 1</u>: Each non-root $\bar{P}_i$ must eventually be ready for control (<u>ok</u>) communication with its father as its only alternative. Otherwise, it will perform an indefinite number of basic communications, which is impossible by assumption. Note that this alternative is not conditioned, and therefore, cannot be blocked. Note, also, that this control communication <u>may</u> take place earlier, before it becomes the <u>only</u> alternative, depending on the guard scheduling rules.

<u>Claim 2</u>: Whenever some non-root $\bar{P}_i$ receives the control signal <u>ok</u> from its father, it will eventually respond with a boolean r, satisfying

$$r = \begin{cases} \text{true} & \text{iff for all } \bar{P}_j \text{ in } \bar{P}_i\text{'s subtree, } B_j(\bar{y}_j) \text{ holds} \\ \text{false} & \text{otherwise.} \end{cases}$$

This follows by induction on the height of $\bar{P}_i$ in T_p^*. If $\bar{P}_i$ is a leaf, then P_i itself is the whole subtree, and the claim is obvious.

Otherwise, if $\bar{P}_i$ detects a non-B_i-state and answers false, the claim is true immediately. If $\bar{P}_i$ detects a B_i-state, it will attempt to send <u>ok</u> control signals to all its sons. By Claim 1 applied to all the sons, all of them will eventually receive the <u>ok</u> signal, and by the induction hypothesis, since their height is smaller by one, they will eventually respond with an answer r as above. The claim follows because the conjunction of such r's has the same property, when B_i is known to hold. Note that after the response with r, $\bar{P}_i$ is again is the top level, but unable to perform basic communication, since cm=false.

<u>Claim 3</u>: The state of each $\bar{P}_i$ does not change between its response (r) to its father, and the input of a <u>resume</u> signal. Upon receiving <u>ok</u>, cm is set to false, and thus disables any further basic communication, which might change its state. Only the input of the <u>resume</u> signal cases setting cm to true and allows resumption of basic communication.

<u>Claim 4</u>: a) The root cannot initiate two consecutive control cycles, unless some process performed some basic communication; b) After each control cycle, either the root terminates, or another cycle will follow.

4.a follows from the presence of the newwave guard, which is set to true only after all the sons reported with ready(j)=true. Each such response of some P_i depends on receiving ready signals from his own sons, and reporting to the father. This reporting cannot be blocked, and has to occur eventually, again as the only alternative, because either B_i is true, or it is false and then some basic communication has to occur and set advanced to true. For a leaf, ready is set to true upon receiving <u>resume</u>, is not depending on any input from other processes. Hence 4.b follows also.

Proposition. $\bar{P}_{i_o}$ (i_o is the index of the root) terminates, and upon termination $\forall i \cdot B_i(\bar{y}_i)$ holds.

Proof. By the same argument as in Claim 1 and since newwave is initially true, $\bar{P}_{i_o}$ eventually reaches a state where it must send an ok signal to all its sons. By Claim 1, each son will eventually receive this signal, and by Claim 2 will eventually respond with some a . Let $r = \bigwedge_{j \in \Gamma_{i_o}} a(j)$. If r=true, then P_{i_o} terminates, and by Claims 2, 3 the property $\forall i \cdot B_i(\bar{y}_i)$=true follows.

If r=false, P_{i_o} will send resume signals to its sons, etc., (this signal will be accepted, by the note after Claim 2) until everybody can resume basic communication. By Claim 4, some basic communication will have been necessary performed by some $\bar{P}_j$, before a new control cycle like this can be repeated. Thus, only a finite number of such control cycles is possible, and again $\bar{P}_{i_o}$ will terminate.

A simple analysis of the suggested algorithm shows that in the best case, in which $\bar{P}_{i_o}$ first attempts a communication cycle only when $\forall i \cdot B_i(\bar{y}_i)$=true already holds, the number of control communications performed is $2\cdot(n-1)$. Each $\bar{P}_i$ receives once an ok signal, and responds once with an r answer. In the worst case, a control communication can occur between two basic communications, and hence the total number of $4b\cdot(n-1)$, where b is the number of basic communications. (The factor 4 is due to the additional "unfreezing" wave and ready response.) This may grow very fast, and is due to the non-monotonic behavior of the P_i's w.r.t. reaching a B_i-state. The actual number of control communications will depend on the guard scheduling algorithm. Further complexity analysis is beyond the scope of this paper.

5. AN EXAMPLE: SORTED PARTITION

Let S be a non-empty set (i.e., without repetitions) of natural numbers, and let $S = S_1 + S_2 + \ldots + S_n$ be a disjoint partition of S into $n \geqslant 2$ not empty subsets. Also, let $m_i = |S_i|$, the number of elements in S_i.

Consider the following post condition $B(S_1,\ldots,S_n)$

$$B(S_1,\ldots,S_n) \equiv \forall i, j (1 \leqslant i < j \leqslant n)\ \forall p,q(p \in S_i \ \&\ q \in S_j \supset p < q)$$
$$\&\ \forall i\ (1 \leqslant i \leqslant n)\ \ |S_i| = m_i\ .$$

i.e. the final state is such that each subset S_i has the same number of elements as it started with, and the partition is sorted in ascending order of the processes' indices.

The only basic communication allowed is sending or receiving a natural number.

This is a generalization of (a slight modification of) a program presented by Dijkstra [5] for n=2, called there a sorting problem.

One can easily verify that an equivalent specification is given by

$$B(S_1,\dots,S_n) \equiv \forall i(1 \leqslant i < n)\ \forall p,\ q(p \in S_i \ \&\ q \in S_{i+1} \supset p < q)$$
$$\&\ \forall_i (1 \leqslant i \leqslant n)\ |S_i| = m_i.$$

Furthermore, if we introduce the functions $\max(S_i)$ and $\min(S_i)$ with the usual meanings, this can be further transformed to

$$B(S_1,\dots,S_n) \equiv \forall i(1 \leqslant i < n)\ (\max(S_i) < \min(S_{i+1}))$$
$$\&\ \forall_i (1 \leqslant i \leqslant n)\ |S_i| = m_i.$$

This suggests a program organization, in which each process (except P_1 and P_n) has two neighbors with which it communicates, i.e. interchanges natural numbers. The end-processes in the line will have only one neighbor each.

Now we may introduce an additional variable:

lin_i = last input from right neighbor, for $1 \leqslant i < n$.

Then, define for $1 \leqslant i < n$

$$B_i(S_i, lin_i) \equiv \max(S_i) \leqslant lin_i \quad \& \quad |S_i| = m_i.$$

Then one can verify that, with the help of the fact that for $1 \leqslant i < n$, last input from right = last output to left, which is implied by the CSP semantics and the program bellow, one has

$$(\bigwedge_{i=1,n} B_i(S_i, lin_i)) \supset B(S_1,\dots,S_n)$$

which fits our requirement as described above.

Next, we have to find processes P_i, $i=1,n$ such that after a finite amount of basic communication reach their B_i-states, and which conform to property (2) above, and to the linear arrangement of the neighborhood relation.

By generalizing Dijkstra's algorithm in [5], one obtains:

```
        for 1 < i < n:
   Pi :: update; lin:=-∞;
        *[
          mx>lin, Pi+1! mx→Si:=Si-{mx}; Pi+1?lin;Si:=Si+{lin}; update
          □
                    Pi-1?ℓ→Si:=Si+{ℓ}; update; Pi-1!mn;Si:=Si-{mn}; update
         ]
```

where update is defined by (mx:=max(Si); mn:=min(Si)). Each process P_i has a choice between two alternatives:

1) If the largest element in the current value of S_i is larger than the last input, send it to the right neighbor, remove it from S_i, and include in S_i an element received from the right neighbor.

2) Accept any number from the left neighbor, include it in S_i, then send back the smallest member of S_i and remove it from S_i.

In general, each process sends "large" numbers to the right, replacing them with "small" numbers, and similarly, receiving "large" numbers from the left, replacing them by "small" numbers.

For the end-processes we have:

```
P_1 :: update; lin=-∞;
   *[mx > lin, P_2!mx →... (as before)...], and
P_n :: update;
   *[P_{n-1}? ℓ→... (as before)...].
```

By a slight generalization of Dijkstra's argument in [5], one indeed shows that after a finite amount of time, each process reaches a B_i-state. Furthermore, each output guard is adjoined to a guard implying $\sim B_i$, and property (2) also holds.

Note again the non-monotonic behaviour of P_i w.r.t. B_i. It may be possible that some P_i is in its B_i-state, i.e. all its elements are smaller than its right neighbor's and larger than its left neighbor's. However, his right neighbor P_{i+1}, for example, may exchange a number with his right neighbor P_{i+2}, and receive an element smaller than $\max(S_{i-1})$, when this element is passed to P_i, B_i is no longer true. The eventual stability is shown like in bubble sort, where the "big" elements float to the right, whereas the "small" ones float to the left.

Next, we want to augment the program $P :: [P_1 \| \ldots \| P_n]$ with our control sections to achieve distributed termination.

A natural spanning tree T_p^* to choose will have P_1 as root, and P_{i+1} as the only son of P_i, i=1,...,n-1.

We get the following $\bar{P} :: [\bar{P}_1 \| \ldots \| \bar{P}_n]$:

```
      for 1 < i < n:
P̄_i :: update;lin:=-∞;cm:=true; ready:=false; advanced:=false;
   *[cm,mx>lin,P̄_{i+1}!mx →...(as before)...; advanced:=true
    □
            cm,P̄_{i-1}?ℓ →...(as before)...; advanced:=true
    □
              P̄_{i-1}?ok →...cm:=false;
                            [mx>lin →P̄_{i-1}!false
                             □
                             mx≤lin →P̄_{i+1}!ok;P̄_{i+1}?a;P̄_{i-1}!a
                            ]
    □
         P̄_{i-1}?resume →P̄_{i+1}!resume;cm:=true;advanced:=false
    □
         P̄_{i+1}? ready →skip
    □
     (mx≤lin∨advanced),ready,P̄_{i-1}!true →ready:=false
    ]
```

And for the root:

```
P̄1 :: update;lin:=- ;ready:=false;newware:=true;
   *[cm,mx lin,P̄2!mx →...(as before)...
    □
     mx≤lin,newwave   →P̄2!ok;P̄2?a;
                       [a →halt
                       □
                       ~a →newwave:=false;P̄2!resume
                       ]
    □
          P̄2?ready    →skip
    □
             ready    →newwave:=true; ready:=false
     ]
```

And for the end process (leaf):

```
P̄n :: update;cm:=true;advanced:=false;ready:=false;
   *[cm,P̄n-1?ℓ                         →...(as before)...,advanced:=true
    □
                    P̄n-1?ok            →cm:=false;P̄n-1!(mx≤lin)
    □
                    P̄n-1?resume        →cm:=true;advanced:=false;ready:=true
    □
     (mx≤lin∨advanced),ready,P̄n-1!true →ready:=false
    ]
```

CONCLUSION

We have formulated an algorithm that achieves a joint decision of a group of communicating processes to terminate, where each of them is directly aware only of its own local state. The algorithm is based on a general property of disjoint processes, where termination can be either achieved directly, or induced by other terminating processes. We showed how to solve a problem of sorted partition using the algorithm.

We feel that this kind of situations will occur often, in various applications of distributed programming. Recently, we learned that Sintzoff dealt with a similar question(unpublished), and suggested a circular arrangement of the P_i's instead of our spanning tree. He is not concerned with the problem of avoiding new channels.

Currently a research project (jointly with W.P. de Roever) is attempting to construct a formal system, in which the formal counterpart of the sketchy proof presented here could be formulated.

ACKNOWLEDGEMENTS

Zami Ben-Chorin was very helpful by suggesting a bidirectional control communication which did not work, and whose improvement led to the current scheme. With Jorgen Staunstrup, I spent useful time discussing the general concept of distributed termination.

Many thanks to Robin Milner, who refereed the paper, and detected a deadlock possibility in an early version, and helped to improve the presentation, as did another (anonimous) referee.

REFERENCES

1) Brinch Hansen, P.: The Architecture of Concurrent Programming; Prentice Hall, 1977.

2) Brinch Hansen, P.: Distributed Processes - A Concurrent Programming Concept, CACM, 21, 11, 1978.

3) De Bakker, J.W.: Semantics and Termination of Nondeterministic Recursive Programs. Proc. of the 4th Conf. on Automata, Languages and Programming, 1976.

4) Dijkstra, E.W.: A Class of Simple Communication Patterns, EWD-643, 1978.

5) Dijkstra, E.W.: A Correctness Proof for Communicating Processes - A Small Exercise. EWD-607, 1977.

6) Francez, N.: On the Question of Termination of Concurrent Programs, May 1978, submitted to IEEE-TSE.

7) Francez, N., Hoare, C.A.R., Lehmann, J.D., De Roever, W.P.: Semantics of Nondeterminism, Concurrency and Communication, 1978.

8) Hoare, C.A.R.: Communicating Sequential Processes. CACM, 21, 8, 1978.

9) Milne, G. and Milner, R.: Concurrent Processes and their Syntax. Dept. of Computer Science, Edinburgh, 1977.

10) Sintzoff, M.: On Language Design for Program Construction; Centre de Recherche en Informatique, January 1978.

11) Wirth, N.: Modula - A Programming Language for Modular Programming; Software-Practice and Experience, 7, 2, March 1977.

Specifying and Proving Properties of Guardians for Distributed Systems

Carl Hewitt, Giuseppe Attardi, and Henry Lieberman
M.I.T.

545 Technology Square
Cambridge, Mass 02139

ABSTRACT

In a distributed system where many processors are connected by a network and communicate using message passing, many users can be allowed to access to the same facilities. A public utility is usually an expensive or limited resource whose use has to be regulated. **Guardians** are abstractions that can be used to regulate the use of resources by scheduling their access, providing protection, and implementing recovery from hardware failures. We present a language construct called a **primitive serializer** which can be used to express efficient implementations of guardians in a modular fashion. We have developed a proof methodology for proving strong properties of network utilities e.g. the utility is guaranteed to respond to each request which it is sent. This proof methodology is illustrated by proving properties of a hardcopy guardian which manages two printing devices.

I -- INTRODUCTION

I.1 --- Semantics

Programs written for distributed systems with many processors can be plagued by subtle errors arising in unpredictable situations. To limit these problems, it is necessary that the primitives for dealing with concurrency provided by our programming languages have simple intuitive interpretations and completely unambiguous definitions. They should also be powerful enough to express simple solutions to simple or common problems and to admit rigorous proof methods. For both of these reasons we have been looking for primitives whose semantics are mathematically well defined. We want each primitive construct to denote a mathematical object which defines the behavior of the primitive. Our methods of proof are ultimately based on theorems about these mathematical objects.

In a similar vein mathematical semantics must be provided for any well defined specification language. Ideally a specification language should be powerful enough so that it is convenient to express both the partial specifications of the abstractions of the user (such as airline reservation systems and disk head schedulers) as well as the abstractions of the programming language (such as monitors and serializers).

This paper makes use of a description system in which the properties of actors can be described. A distinctive feature of our description system is that it specifies the required behavior of objects rather than their physical representation. Instead of using predicates to state the interface requirements between modules, descriptions are attached to the data manipulated by each module. The idea is to allow properties of actors to be specified in the form of descriptions that appear directly in the code.

I.2 --- Guardians

Guardians are abstractions that can regulate the use of a resource by scheduling its access, providing protection, and implementing recovery from hardware failures which manifest themselves as time-outs. In this paper we develop partial specifications and proofs for an hardcopy server for two printing devices. In a subsequent paper we will present partial specifications and proofs for other guardians such as a readers-writers guardians using different scheduling algorithms, a guardian for a disk spindle that optimizes head motion, etc.

I.3 --- Primitive Serializers

The guardians in this paper are implemented using primitive serializers which are a further development of serializers [Hewitt and Atkinson: 1977, 1979]. Primitive serializers have been given a clear mathematical denotation and are also more flexible than previous serializers in that they have less built-in machinery. Their more primitive character gives them the ability to efficiently implement the facilities (such as queues) that were provided by previous serializers as well as to implement new facilities that were not provided before. Unlike previous serializers, primitive serializers do not have any implicit nondeterminism in the evaluation of synchronization conditions. Additional flexibility comes form the fact that primitive serializers can explicitly deal with actors which act as customers to whom replies should be sent. The concept of customers is a very general and useful notion which can be used in particular to give a precise meaning to the idea of a "waiting process". Customer can be dealt with as any other actor, for instance they can be put into queues for implementing specific scheduling policies. Sending a **Response** to a customer correspond to resuming a waiting process. Primitive serializers are easier to implement efficiently than the serializers developed by [Atkinson and Hewitt: 1977, 1979].

At the same time primitive serializers maintain the advantages of serializers over other published proposals for synchronization primitives such as monitors [Hoare: 1974; Brinch-Hansen: 1973] and Communicating Sequential Processes [Hoare: 1978]. The examples considered in this paper are used to illustrate the advantages of using the actor model for partially specifying and proving properties of guardians.

II -- A DESCRIPTION SYSTEM

II.1 --- Goals

The main goals of our description system are to conveniently use the following kinds of descriptions:

PARTIAL descriptions which enable whatever properties of an object are known to be expressed even if they are incomplete. Partial descriptions are important in partial specifications because it is impossible to arrive at complete specifications for a large software system all at once. They are important in proofs because in a proof some properties are given whereas others must be derived.

INCREMENTAL descriptions which enable us to further describe objects when more information becomes available and are a necessary feature for the use of partial descriptions. Incremental descriptions are important in proofs and incremental specifications because all of the properties are not available at one time but must be derived and evolved with time.

MULTIPLE descriptions which enable us to ascribe multiple overlapping descriptions to an object which is used for multiple purposes. Multiple descriptions are important in multiple specifications and proofs because different properties of an object might be useful in different contexts.

We would like to point out the usefulness of description systems to describe partial specifications for programs. In fact the assumptions and the constraints on the objects manipulated by the program are an integral part of the program and can be used both as checks when the programming is running and as useful information which can be exploited by other systems which examine the program such as translators, optimizers, indexers, etc. We believe that bugs occurring in programs are frequently caused by the violation of implicit assumptions about the environment in which the program is intended to operate. Therefore many advantages can be drawn by a system that encourages the programmer to state such assumptions explicitly, and by a system which is able to detect when they are violated.

Our description system is based on following Axiom of Transitivity of Predication which can be stated as follows:

if (<**description**$_1$> *is* <**description**$_2$>) *and* (<**description**$_2$> *is* <**description**$_3$>)
    then (<**description**$_1$> *is* <**description**$_3$>)

The importance of the above axiom is that it implies that inheritance holds in our description system.

Our description system is designed to allow us to provide multiple partial descriptions of objects. For example (*a* **Cartesian_complex [imaginary_part: 0]**) is a description of an instance of a Cartesian complex number whose **imaginary_part** is 0. Note that we have used the indefinite article "*a*" to mark descriptions of instances of a concept. Descriptions can in turn be multiply described. For example the following command describes (*a* **Cartesian_complex**) as being (*a* **Number**) and as having two attributes, namely a **real_part** which is (*a* **Real**) and an **imaginary_part** each of which must be a **Real**.

(*a* Cartesian_complex) *is* **(*a* Number)** *and*
                (*a* Cartesian_complex [real_part: (*a* Real)] [imaginary_part: (*a* Real)])

Note that by using the concept **Cartesian_complex** twice in the above description that we have specified that every **Cartesian_complex** has two attributes **real_part** and **imaginary_part** which each have as value a **Real**.

Note that the *is* statement is asymmetric so that it would be <u>incorrect</u> to say

(*a* Cartesian_complex) *is* **(*a* Real)**

since a Cartesian complex number is not always a real number. Furthermore it would also be <u>incorrect</u> to say

(*a* Cartesian_complex) *is* **¬(*a* Real)**

since some Cartesian complex numbers are **Real**.

Our description system successfully deals with an important distinction that has plagued most previous systems which rely on inheritance. Given that 3+4i is a **Cartesian_complex** and that **Cartesian_complex** is an **Algebraic_field**, one is not allowed to conclude that 3+4i is an **Algebraic_field**. Note that this mistake will not occur in our system because the rule of transitivity of predication does <u>not</u> apply to the following two descriptions:

3+4i ***is*** **(*a* Cartesian_complex)**

Cartesian_complex ***is*** **(*an* Algebraic_field)**

While **Cartesian_complex** is described as being an **Algebraic field**, an instance of **Cartesian_complex** such as **(*a* Cartesian_complex)** cannot be considered as **an Algebraic field**.

The user can describe a **Real** x as being a **Cartesian_complex** with **real_part** x and imaginary part 0:

(*a* Real) ***is*** **=x** ***and*** **(*a* Cartesian_complex [real_part: =x] [imaginary_part: 0])**

The character = is used to mark local identifiers. Local identifiers play a role in the description system similar to the role played by free identifiers in formulas in the quantificational calculus: they can be bound to any object. For example since

(3 ***is*** **(*a* Real))**

it follows that

(3 ***is*** **(*a* Cartesian_complex [real_part: 3] [imaginary_part: 0]))**

The user can partially describe a **Cartesian_complex** with **real_part** x and **imaginary_part** 0 as being x which is a **Real**:

(*a* Cartesian_complex [real_part: =x] [imaginary_part: 0]) ***is*** **=x** ***and*** **(*a* Real)**

Notice that we have just established a mutual recursion among our descriptions because we have described **Real** in terms of **Cartesian_complex** and vice versa. This will enable us to view either one as the other in the appropriate circumstances.

The above descriptions express some of the relations between **Real** and **Cartesian_complex** numbers. We believe that it is important that a description system allows information to be presented in an incremental fashion. For example it should be possible for the user to later <u>further</u> describe **Cartesian_complex** numbers relative to other kind of numbers.

```
(a Cartesian_complex [real_part: =x] [imaginary_part: =y]) is
    (a Number) and
    (a Polar_complex [magnitude: =r (a Real)])
  such_that
    (r is (x^2 + y^2)^(1 / 2))
```

It is important to realize that in giving the above descriptions the user is not making any commitments as to the physical representation of complex numbers. The possibility is still open that complex numbers will be physically represented in Cartesian, Polar form, some mixture, or still some other alternative physical representation. It is even possible that both physical representations will cohabit in the same system! This last possibility is especially important in distributed systems where the autonomy of nodes on the network must be respected.

II.2 --- Descriptions of Communications

Messages are sent to guardians in **communications**. A request is a communication which always contains a message and a customer:

```
(a Request) is
    (a Communication) and
    (a Request [message: ...] [customer: ...])
```

The concept of a customer subsumes the notion of a **continuation** in the lambda calculus programming languages [A. Church, C. Strachey, L. Morris, C. Wadsworth, J. Reynolds, C. Hewitt, Sussman and Steele, etc.].

Another kind of communication is a **Response** which is either a reply or a complaint:

```
(a Response) is
    (a Communication) and
    (either
        (a Reply [message: (a Message)])
        (a Complaint [message: (a Message)]))
```

III -- PRIMITIVE SERIALIZERS

The design goals for monitors is that they were intended to be a structuring construct for implementing operating systems. There have been some attempts to develop useful proof rules for monitors [Howard: 1976; Gjessing: 1977; Hoare: 1974; Owicki: 1978] Serializers [Atkinson and Hewitt: 1977, 1979] are a further step toward these goals. However the language construct developed by Hewitt and Atkinson may be too complicated to be useful both as a formal foundation and as a basis for the proof methodology. In the study we present here the approach has been reversed. Instead of designing a desirable set of primitives and then trying to describe their semantics in a formal way, we started with a basic primitive with a simple semantics.

The syntax of a simple primitive serializer is the following:

(*create_serialized_actor* behavior)

Primitive serializers are used to create actors whose state may change after the receipt of a communication. A convenient way to express this is by means of the notion of behavior. At any given time a serialized actor has a behavior (which is another actor) and its behavior may change as a result of communications which it receives.

The actor created by *create_serialized_actor* behaves in the following way. It can be either **locked** or **unlocked**. When it is created it is **unlocked**. When the first communication arrives, the serializer becomes *locked* and the communication received is sent to behavior.

A behavior will typically be implemented using a *receivers* expression which has the following syntax:

```
(receivers
    (pattern_for_communication_1 received body_1)
    ...
    (pattern_for_communication_j received body_j))
```

If an actor created by a *receivers* expression receives a communication c which matches any of the

pattern_for_communication$_i$, then the corresponding **body**$_i$ is evaluated to produced the next state. If **c** matches more than one of the **pattern_for_communication**$_i$, then an arbitrary one of the corresponding **body**$_i$ is selected to be executed.

As a result of receiving the communication, the current of behavior will possibly transmit some communications using a command of the form (*transmit_to* t c) transmits the communication actor **c** to the target actor t. In addition it computes a new behavior nb using a command of the form

(*become* nb)

An important consideration in the design of efficient serializers is that they should remain locked for as brief a time as possible.

Note that there are three separate events which must occur before a communication C can be received by a serialized actor T. First it must be transmitted in a transmission event of the form

(*a* Transmission [target: T] [communication: C])

Next it must arrive in a arrival event (synonymous with delivery event) of the form

(*an* Arrival [target: T] [communication: C])

Hardware modules called arbiters are used to establish an arrival ordering for all communications delivered to T. Finally it must be received in a receipt event of the form

(*a* Receipt [recipient: T] [communication: C])

Communications are received in the order in which they are delivered. The receipt event marks a transition in which the target changes from **unlocked** to **locked**. Thus if a serialized actor becomes locked then no more messages can be received until it unlocks.

IV -- A SIMPLE EXAMPLE

IV.1 --- Descriptions of Messages for Checking Account

As a simple example of how primitive serializers can be used, we give the implementation of a very simple checking account guardian.

There are two kinds of messages which must be dealt with by the guardian: **Withdrawal** and **Deposit** which can be described as follows:

(*a* Withdrawal) *is*
    (*a* Message) *and*
    (*a* Withdrawal [amount: (*a* Non_negative_US_currency)])

(*a* Deposit) *is*
    (*a* Message) *and*
    (*a* Deposit [amount: (*a* Non_negative_US_currency)])

which says that both kinds of messages have an attribute named *amount* which must be a non-negative US currency.

(*a* Transaction_completed_report) *is* (*a* Reply)
(*a* Transaction_not_completed [reason: overdraft]) *is* (*a* Complaint)

IV.2 --- A Concurrent Case Expression

Clearly some kind of conditional test is needed in implementations. Use will be made of *select_case_for* expressions of the following form:

```
(select_case_for expression
   (pattern_1 then body_1)
   ...
   (pattern_n then body_n)
   [none_of_the_above: alternative_body])
```

which when evaluated first evaluates expression to produce a value V.

If the value V matches any of the $pattern_i$ then the corresponding $body_i$ is evaluated and its value is the value of the *select_case_for* expression. If the value V matches more than one of the $pattern_i$ then an arbitrary one of the corresponding $body_i$ is selected to be executed. However, if the value of expression can match two different patterns then the Programming Apprentice will warn the user if it cannot demonstrate that the results of executing the bodies are indistinguishable. This rule has the advantage that it makes $body_i$ depend only on $pattern_i$ making it easy add more selections later.

We shall say that two activities are concurrent if it is possible for them to occur at the same. The concurrent case statement facilitates efficient implementation by allowing concurrent matching of expression against the patterns. This ability is important in applications where attempts to determine whether or not conditions hold take large amounts of time.

If the value V does not match any of the $pattern_i$ then alternative_body is executed. This rule provides the ability to have the patterns represent special cases leaving the alternative_body to deal with the general case if none of the special cases apply.

IV.3 --- A Simple Guardian

Using these definitions we can implement the checking account guardian as follows using a primitive serializer:

```
(describe (create_account [initial_balance: =i (a Non_negative_US_currency)])
   [is: (a Serialized_actor [responds_to: (either (a Deposit) (a Withdrawal))])]
      ;responses to deposit and withdrawal messages are guaranteed
   [implementation:
      (create_serialized_actor
            (an Account [balance: i]))])

(describe (an Account [balance: (a Non_negative_US_currency)])
   [implementation:
      (receivers
            ((a Request [message: (a Withdrawal [amount: =a])] [customer: =c]) received
                  (select_case_for balance
                        ((≥ a) then
                           (transmit_to c (a Transaction_completed_report))
                           (become (an Account [balance: (balance - a)])))
                        ((< a) then
                           (transmit_to c (a Transaction_not_completed [reason: overdraft]))
                           (become (an Account)))))
            ((a Request [message: (a Deposit [amount: =d])] [customer: =c]) received
                  (transmit_to c (a Transaction_completed_report))
                  (become (an Account [balance: (balance + d)]))))])
```

We have adopted in this code and in our language a useful convention for giving default values to missing parameters in a function call. For instance in the above code the expression

(*become* (*an* Account))

is considered to be equivalent to

(*become* (*an* Account [balance: balance]))

That is, any paramenter with keyword id, not mentioned in the call, receives the value associated to the identifier id. This convention allows to shorten our notation avoiding to repeat all the parameters that are left unchanged.

V -- IMPLEMENTING A HARDCOPY SERVER

Implementing a hardcopy server on a distributed system provides a concrete example to illustrate the advantages of primitive serializers. The following definition shows a program to create a guardian for two hardcopy devices. The example illustrates how a primitive serializer can be used to implement a guardian that protects more than one resource. Finally, the program below illustrates the use of nondeterminism in primitive serializers since if both devices are idle, then a nondeterministic choice is made which should serve the next Hardcopy_request since it doesn't matter which one is chosen.

V.1 --- A Concurrent Conditional Expression

The implementation of the hardcopy server given below makes use of a conditional construct of the following form:

```
(select_one_of
   (if condition_1 then body_1)
   ...
   (if condition_n then body_n)
   [none_of_the_above: alternative_body])
```

If any $\underline{\text{condition}_i}$ holds then the corresponding $\underline{\text{body}_i}$ is evaluated. If more than one of the $\underline{\text{condition}_i}$ hold then an arbitrary one of the corresponding $\underline{\text{body}_i}$ is selected to be evaluated. However, if it seems to the Programming Apprentice that more than one of the $\underline{\text{condition}_i}$ might hold simultaneously then it will warn the user if it cannot demonstrate that the execution of the corresponding $\underline{\text{body}_i}$ have equivalent effects. The rule of concurrent consideration of conditions encourages programs which are more robust, modular, easily modifiable, and efficient than is possible with the conditional expression in LISP for the reasons which are enumerated in the discussion of the *select_case_for* expression. If none of the $\underline{\text{condition}_i}$ hold then alternative_body is executed.

The reader will probably have noticed that the *select_one_of* construct is very similar to the *select_case_for* construct which we introduced earlier in this paper. The reason for introducing both constructs is that whereas the *select_case_for* construct is often quite succinct and readable there are cases such as the implementation below in which it is desirable to concurrently test properties of more than one actor in a single conditional expression making the use of *select_one_of* preferable.

The *select_one_of* expression is different from the conditionals of McCarthy, Dijkstra, etc. in several important respects. The conditions of *select_one_of* have been generalized to allow pattern matching as in the pattern directed programming languages PLANNER, QA-4, POPLER, CONNIVER, etc. Notice that our concurrent conditional expression is different from the usual

nondeterministic conditional in that if any of the conditions hold then the body of one of them must be selected for execution even if the evaluation of some other condition does not terminate (cf. [Manna and McCarthy: 1970, Paterson and Hewitt: 1971, Friedman and Wise: 1978]).

V.2 --- Implementation of a Hardcopy Server

Below we give the implementation of the hard copy server.

```
(describe (create hardcopy_server =device1 =device2)

  [is: (a Serialized_actor [responds_to: (a Print_request)]
                          [receives: (either
                                       (a Completion [device: (either device1 device2)])
                                       (a Breakdown_report [device: (either device1 device2)]))])]

  [implementation:
   (label the_hardcopy_server    ;the_hardcopy_server is the name of the actor created by serialize
     (create_serialized_actor
       (a Hard_copy_server [queue: (an Empty_queue)] [device1_state: idle] [device2_state: idle]))

     where

     (describe (a Hard_copy_server [queue: (a Queue [each_element: (a Print_request)])]
                                   [device1_state: (either idle printing broken)]
                                   [device2_state: (either idle printing broken)])
      [preconditions: (implies
                         (queue is ¬(a Queue [sequence: []]))
                         (and (device1_state is ¬idle) (device2_state is ¬idle)))]

      [implementation:
        (receivers
          ((a Print_request) =the_request received
             (ponder [queue: (a Queue [all_but_rear: queue] [rear: the_request])]))
                   ;invoke the ponder transition with the_request at the rear of the queue

          ((a Completion [device: device1] [response: =r] [customer: =c]) received
                   ;this communication notifies the serializer that device1 has completed printing
                   ;the value returned by that operation is r and was expected by c
             (transmit_to c r)
             (ponder [device1_state: idle]))

          ((a Completion [device: device2] [response: =r] [customer: =c]) received
             (transmit_to c r)
             (ponder [device2_state: idle]))

          ((a Breakdown_report [request: =r] [device: device1]) received
              (ponder [queue: (a Queue [front: r] [all_but_front: queue])]
                      [device1_state: broken]))

          ((a Breakdown_report [request: =r] [device: device2]) received
              (ponder [queue: (a Queue [front: r] [all_but_front: queue])]
                      [device2_state: broken])))]))])
```

```
(describe (ponder [queue: (a Queue [each_element: (a Print_request)])]
                  [device1_state: (either idle printing broken)]
                  [device2_state: (either idle printing broken)])
  [is: (a Hard_copy_server [queue: (a Queue [each_element: (a Print_request)])]
                           [device1_state: (either idle printing broken)]
                           [device2_state: (either idle printing broken)])]
  [implementation:
   (select_one_of
    (if (queue is (a Queue [front: (a Request [message: =r] [customer: =c])]
                           [all_but_front: =all_but_front_q]))
        and (device1_state is idle)
     then
       (transmit_to device1
               (a Request [message: r]
                          [customer: (create_transaction_manager [request: r]
                                                                 [device: device1]
                                                                 [customer: c])]))
       (become (a Hard_copy_server [queue: all_but_front_q] [device1_state: printing])))

    (if (queue is (a Queue [front: (a Request [message: =r] [customer: =c])]
                           [all_but_front: =all_but_front_q]))
        and (device2_state is idle)
     then
       (transmit_to device2
               (a Request [message: r]
                          [customer: (create_transaction_manager [request: r]
                                                                 [device: device2]
                                                                 [customer: c])]))
       (become (a Hard_copy_server [queue: all_but_front_q] [device2_state: printing])))

    (if (device1_state is broken) and (device2_state is broken) then
       (transmit_to operator "Both printers are broken!")
       (become (a Hard_copy_server)))

    [none_of_the_above:
     (become (a Hard_copy_server))])])
```

Note that a new transaction manager is created to manage each printing request for the hardcopy device.

The actor create_transaction_manager (defined below) creates a serialized actor s wrapped inside a *time_out_if_no_response_after* expression:

```
(time_out_if_no_response_after (10 minutes)
      s)
```

which forwards to s any message it receives and also sends s a Time_out message after 10 minutes if it has received no message in the meantime.

Note that if a manager receives a Time_out message then it sends the hardcopy device an **abort_printing** message waiting 1 minute for the device to respond using the following expression:

```
(send_to d abort_printing [time_out_if_no_response_after: (1 minute)])
```

If the device responds with a Ready_for_next_request_report within 1 minute then the_hardcopy_server is told that the transaction has completed with a response which is a complaint that the allotted time has been exceeded. If the device does not respond to an abort_printing message within 1 minute, then the_hard_copy server is sent a breakdown report for the device and the operator is informed that the device is broken.

The definition given below is assumed to be inside the lexical scope of the above serializer thus making the_hardcopy_server lexically visible.

```
(describe (create_transaction_manager [request: =r] [device: =d] [customer: =c])
  [is: (a Serialized_actor [receives: (either (a Response) (a Time_out))])]
  [implementation: (create_serialized_actor (a Transaction_manager [timed_out: false]))

  where

  (describe (a Transaction_manager [timed_out: (a Boolean)])
    [implementation:
      (receivers
        ((a Response) =the_response received
          (if (not timed_out)
              then (transmit_to the_hardcopy_server
                          (a Completion
                               [device: d]
                               [response: the_response]
                               [customer: c])))
          (become (a Transaction_manager)))
        ((a Time_out) received
          (select_case_for (send_to d (an Abort_printing_request)
                                  [time_out_if_no_response_after: (1 minute)])
            ((a Ready_for_next_request_report) then
              (transmit_to the_hardcopy_server
                     (a Completion
                          [device: d]
                          [response: (a Complaint [message: allotted_time_exceeded])]
                          [customer: c]))
              (become (a Transaction_manager [timed_out: true])))
            ((a Time_out) then
              (transmit_to operator (a Breakdown_report [device: d]))
              (transmit_to the_hardcopy_server (a Breakdown_report [request: r] [device: d]))
              (become (a Transaction_manager [timed_out: true])))))))])])
```

The statement

```
(become (a Transaction_manager [timed_out: true]))
```

has the effect of causing the timed_out state component of the transaction manager to become true. Therefore any response addressed to that actor after its termination will be discarded since the code specifies

```
(if (not timed_out)
    then (transmit_to the_hardcopy_server
                (a Completion
                     [response: the_response]
                     [device: d]
                     [customer: c])))
(become (a Transaction_manager))
```

In particular a response form a device will not be considered after a time out has been generated.

VI -- PARTIAL SPECIFICATIONS OF A HARD-COPY SERVER

Using primitive serializers, we have been able to deal with an important problem in the specification of guardians which allow time out. The problem is that if a guardian is allowed the possibility of time out in a partial specification how is it possible to rule out a trivial implementation which always times out. Our solution to this specification problem is to require that a guardian which receives a Print_request r which satisfies the following description:

```
(a Print_request
    [message: r]
    [customer: c])
```

must eventually send one of the hardcopy devices a communication which satisfies the description

```
(a Request
    [message: r]
    [customer: m])
```

where m is a transaction manager. Furthermore if m receives a response before it receives a time out message then the response must be sent to c. In this way we can specify that a guardian is allowed to time out but disallow the possibility that it can do so without allowing the device the allotted amount of time to complete the transaction.

VII -- PROOFS FOR THE HARD-COPY SERVER

Due to space limitations for this paper, the proofs here assume the absence of breakdowns although they are valid in the presence of time-outs. It is quite easy to extend the proofs to deal with the possibility of breakdowns.

We first show that the constraints on the attributes of the hard-copy server are always met. These constraints are useful in the rest of the proof. In most of the primitive serializers which we have examined, many of the properties of interest about the serializer are constraints which always hold as opposed to merely being preconditions.

The second part of the proof shows that the serializer completes each transition from a state in which it is unlocked to a state in which it is again unlocked. This will be a preliminary result for proving that the preconditions for the hard-copy server always hold. Finally we prove that the guardian always replies to the requests which it receives.

VII.1 --- Checking the Constraints

First we verify that the constraints on the attributes of the hard-copy server always hold, namely:

(queue *is* (*a* Queue [each_element: (*a* Print_request)]))
(device1_state *is* (*either* idle printing broken))
(device2_state *is* (*either* idle printing broken))

The proof that these constraints always hold is by induction.

1. Show that the constraints are true when the hard-copy server is created.
2. Assuming that the constraints are true, show that, whatever communication is received, the next *become* statement will produce a hard-copy server which satisfies the constraints.

It is clear by inspection that each of the three constraints is true when the serializer is created. After a communication is received, the function **ponder** is called with arguments satisfying the constraints in the description of **ponder**. This description can be used and gives us the fact we needed to complete the proof. Now to show that the implementation of **ponder** corresponds to its description, a similar technique can be used. In this proof we will have to use the descriptions for the operations called by **ponder**.

This part of the proof is not very different from the kind of static type checking usually performed by a compiler.

VII.2 --- Proof of the Preconditions

We want to show that whenever the guardian is unlocked, its state satisfies the precondition:

```
(implies
    (queue is ¬(an Empty_queue))
    (and (device1_state is ¬idle) (device2_state is ¬idle)))
```

It is immediate that this precondition holds vacuously at the creation of the hard-copy server since the queue is empty.

The general result can be established by case analysis for each communication received. For instance if the guardian receives a **Print_request r** in a state where the receipt preconditions hold, then the request **r** will be added to the rear of the queue and **ponder** will be called with a non empty queue as an argument. There are two cases to be considered (we are assuming the absence of breakdowns):

> 1: One of the devices is idle. Therefore by the precondition the **queue** contains only the request **r**. The request **r** is removed from the queue and the appropriate message is sent to the idle device. This reestablishes the precondition because the queue is once again empty.
>
> 2: None of the conditions in the **ponder** transition is true, so that the **none_of_the_above** clause applies. Since the queue was not empty, this means that none of the devices was idle. Then the guardian unlocks becoming a hard-copy server with the state of both devices being not idle. Therefore the precondition will hold again also in this case.

The proof that the receipt preconditions hold when the guardian is unlocked is similar for the **Completion** communications and the **Breakdown_report** communications.

VII.3 --- Proof of Guarantee of Service

We can prove that service is guaranteed to all printing requests. If the guardian receives a request when one of the devices is **idle**, the request will be immediately passed on, since the queue will be empty according to the precondition for the hard-copy server.

If none of the devices is **idle**, then the request will be queued.

The following assertion is proved by induction on **n**:

If n requests precede a request R in the queue, then R will be passed to one of the devices after n completion communications have been received by the guardian.

A completion is either one of the following communications:

(a Completion [device: device1] [response: ...] [customer: ...])
(a Completion [device: device2] [response: ...] [customer: ...])

The implementation of the guardian has the property that the hardcopy server will always receive a communication back for each of the requests it sent to a device. By the precondition for the hard-copy server we know if R is in the queue, then there is a request outstanding for either **device1** or **device2**, and a completion or a breakdown report will be received by the guardian.

The first such communication will be received after a number p of print requests have been received by the guardian. p is finite because of the law of finite chains in the arrival ordering of actor systems [Hewitt and Baker 1977].

We can show that each of these p print request will leave unchanged the first n elements in the queue and will not alter the state of the devices. Consider then the effect of the next completion received by the guardian. We show that either the number of requests preceding R is decreased by one in the next unlocked state or the request R is sent to one of the printing devices. Clearly one effect of the completion is that one of the devices will become idle. Therefore the next request will be removed from the queue and passed to the free device. Therefore if n is 0, the request R is served. On the other hand if n is bigger then 0, then removing the first element from the queue reduces by one the number of elements preceding R in the queue.

VIII -- ADVANTAGES OF PRIMITIVE SERIALIZERS

Before proceeding to prove properties of primitive serializers, we would like to discuss some of their advantages over previous proposals for language constructs for synchronization.

VIII.1 --- Control Flow follows Text

Each activity of the serializer is initiated by the receipt of a communication which causes the serializer to become locked. After a new receiver has been computed, it becomes unlocked and is ready to receive another communication. Unlike monitors, serializers have no explicit wait or signal command which cause the execution to be suspended and resumed from different points within the program.

VIII.2 --- Absolute Containment

The guardians which we have implemented using serializers do not give out the resource being protected. Instead they pass messages from the users to the resource implementing a property which we call absolute containment which was proposed by [Hewitt: 1975] and further developed in [Hewitt and Atkinson: 1977] and [Atkinson and Hewitt: 1979] (cf. [Hoare: 1976] for a similar idea using the **inner** construct of SIMULA). The idea is to pass a message with directions to the resource so that it can carry out the directions instead of giving out the resource to the user. An important problem with the usual strategy of giving the resource out is that retrieval of the resource from a process that has gone amuck is often messy. The concept of absolute containment is related to the use of the **inner statement** in [Hoare: 1976].

In addition we have found that absolute containment produces a more modular implementation than any kind of scheme which actually gives out resources protected by guardians. Note that the proof that all requests will receive a response from a network utility that implements absolute containment depends only on the behavior of the resource and the code for the serializer which implements the guardian, but not on the programs which call the guardian. In the usual scheme of giving out the resource, it is necessary to prove that each process which can use the resource will give it back.

Our hardcopy server implements absolute containment by never passing out either of its hardcopy devices to the external environment. Thus there is no way for others to depend on the number of physical devices available. Furthermore there is no problem retrieving the devices from users who have seized them since they are never given out.

VIII.3 --- Modularity in State Change

Primitive serializers directly support a scheduling strategy of receiving each communication and then deciding what actions the communication requires. The possible actions include changing state and sending messages to other actors.

The only way to cause a state change in the programming language used in this paper is to use a primitive serializer. State change can be encapsulated within a serializer in a much more modular fashion than is accomplished by <u>individual</u> **ASSIGNMENT** and **GOTO** commands. In serializers state change and transfer of control are encapsulated in a single primitive that accomplishes them concurrently. We have found that this encapsulation increases the readability and modularity of implementations that require state change.

VIII.4 --- Generality

In our applications we want to be able to implement guardians which guarantee that a response will be sent for each request received. This requirement for a strong guarantee of service is the concurrent analogue to the usual requirement in sequential programming that subroutines must return values for all legitimate arguments. In our applications it would be <u>incorrect</u> to have implementations which did not guarantee to respond to messages received.

The SIMULA subclass mechanism was designed for sequential and quasi-parallel programming. It needs substantial revision for concurrent programming. The monitors of Hoare and Brinch-Hansen represented a substantial step towards generalizing classes for use in concurrent systems. However the use of explicit **wait** and **signal** commands on fifo queues or priority queues makes the scheduling structure of monitors somewhat inflexible. Furthermore it is difficult to prevent deadlock if monitors are nested within monitors. One strategy for implementing guardians with monitors is to use an ordinary SIMULA class whose procedures invoke a monitor which is local to the class. For example a hardcopy server could be implemented as an ordinary class with a **PRINT** procedure which invokes **REQUEST_PRINT**, **START_PRINT**, and **STOP_PRINT** procedures in the monitor. Primitive serializers avoid the two level structure of monitor within class by explicitly dealing with the actors which act as customers to whom replies should be sent. No special commands like **wait** and **signal** are needed because the customers are ordinary actors which can be remembered and manipulated using the same techniques that work for all actors.

The utility of the extra generality in primitive serializers is illustrated by our implementation of the **hardcopy_server** in which we place a request which is not serviced because of the breakdown of a printer at the <u>front</u> of the queue of requests to be serviced. Many synchronization primitives with more built-in structure (such as monitors) permit additions to queues only at the rear.

VIII.5 --- Conveniently Engendering Parallelism

Primitive serializers provide a very convenient method for causing more parallelism: simply transmitting more communications. The usual method in other languages for creating more parallelism entails creating processes (cf. ALGOL-68, PL-1, Communicating Sequential Processes etc.). The ability to engender parallelism by transmitting communications is one of the principle differences between actors and the usual processes in other languages. For example in the implementation of the transaction manager in this paper, both the operator and the_hardcopy_server can be notified that a printer has broken down by simply transmitting the appropriate communications.

VIII.6 --- Unsynchronized Communcation

In actor systems it is not necessary to know whether the intended recipient is ready to receive the communication; a guardian implemented using primitive serializers can transmit communications and then receive more messages before the communications which it has transmitted have been received. In our application involving the implementation of a distributed electronic office system, it is highly desirable that the sending of communication be unsynchronized from the receipt of the communication.

VIII.7 --- Behavior Mathematically Defined

The behavior of primitive serializers can be read directly from the code. These mathematical denotations are intended provide a solid mathematical foundation on which to develop proof techniques and to provide a direct link with the underlying actor model of computation. Mathematical denotations have not yet been developed for the serializers in [Hewitt and Atkinson: 1977] or monitors because of the complexity of these constructs.

VIII.8 --- Encouraging the use of Concurrency

Primitive serializers permit implementations to use near maximum concurrency. In particular in contrast to the usual process model which only allows sequential execution within a monitor or critical region, primitive serializers encourage the use of concurrency in handling messages received. The only limitation on parallelism in systems constructed using ACTI derives from communications received by serialized actors when they are locked.

VIII.9 --- Absence of Deadlock

Primitive serializers have the important advantage that it is possible to guarantee absence of deadlock in actor systems by simply assuring that each individual actor will unlock after it receives a message. Absence of starvation (e.g. that every request received will generate a response) is more difficult to prove.

VIII.10 --- **Ease of Proof**

We have found the above advantages of primitive serializers quite helpful in proving properties of implementations. Furthermore the structure of our proofs follows naturally from the syntactic structure of a primitive serializer. The proof given in this paper that the hardcopy server will always respond to requests which it receives illustrates how primitive serializers facilitate proofs..

IX -- FUTURE WORK

We are encouraged with the experience of using our description system to describe each of the programming problems considered in this paper. However it clearly needs much further development in pragmatic and behavioral descriptive power.

One important area in which work remains to be done is to demonstrate that primitive serializers can be implemented as efficiently as other synchronization primitives as semaphores, monitors, etc. We have designed primitive serializers with this goal in mind. On the basis of some preliminary investigation we believe that they can be implemented at least as efficiently as monitors and communicating sequential processes. The third author has constructed some preliminary implementations in a dialect of the ACT1 language described in this paper which runs on the PDP-10. In the course of the next year, we will continue to work to improve this implementation and to transfer it to the MIT CADR machine where ultimately it can be supported by micro-code.

Another area in which work remains to be done is automating proofs such as the one in this paper. We feel that we are getting close to the point where a Programming Apprentice can do most of such proofs under the guidance of expert programmers. Russ Atkinson is working on automating the proofs for the version of serializers in [Atkinson and Hewitt: 1977] and [Hewitt and Atkinson: 1979]. We hope to be able to use some of the techniques which he has developed in our symbolic evaluator.

X -- CONCLUSIONS

We are encouraged with our initial experience in working with primitive serializers and plan to develop them further. They appear have a number of important advantages over previous proposals for modular synchronization primitives. These advantages include ability to delegate communications [Hewitt, Attardi and Lieberman: 1978] and compatibility with the implementation of unserialized actors [Hewitt 1978]. Event oriented specification and proof techniques are readily adapted to proving properties of guardians implemented using primitive serializers. These properties include the guarantee that a response is sent for each request received and a guarantee of parallelism [Atkinson and Hewitt: 1978]. Note that the property of guaranteed response for each message sent cannot be proved in many models of computation because it implies the possibility of **unbounded nondeterminism** [Hewitt: 1978]. In this paper we have shown how previous work on event oriented specifications and proofs can be extended to deal with time outs.

Partial descriptions like the ones given in this paper are illegal in almost all type systems. The desire to be able make incremental multiple descriptions such as these has been one of the driving forces in the evolution of our description system. The SIMULA subclass mechanism is probably the most flexible and powerful type mechanism in any widely available programming language. However, as a description system, it has some important limitations. It does not support interdependent descriptions or multiple descriptions. Also it does not permit instance descriptions to be qualified with attributions. Furthermore it does not permit descriptions to be further described thus disallowing any possibility of incremental description.

XI -- ACKNOWLEDGEMENTS

During the spring of 1978, the first author participated in a series of meetings with the Laboratory of Computer Science Distributed Systems Group. These meetings were quite productive and strongly influenced both this paper and the Progress Report of the Distributed Systems Group [Clark, Greif, Liskov, and Svobodova: 1978].

This paper has benefited from ideas that sprang up in conversations in the summer and fall of 1978 with Jean Ramon Abrial, Ole-Johan Dahl, Edsger Dijkstra, David Fisher, Stein Gjessing, Tony Hoare, Jean Ichbiah, Gilles Kahn, Dave MacQueen, Robin Milner, Birger Moller-Pedersen, Kristen Nygaard, Jerry Schwarz, and Bob Tennent. The first author would like to thank Luigia Aiello and Gianfranco Prini and the participants in the summer school on Foundations of Artificial Intelligence and Computer Science in Pisa for helpful comments and constructive criticism.

Valdis Berzins, Alan Borning, Richard Fikes, Gary Nutt, Dan Shapiro, Richard Stallman, Larry Tesler, Deepak Kapur, Vera Ketelboeter, and the members of the Message Passing Systems Seminar have given us valuable feedback and suggestions on this paper. Russ Atkinson is implementing a symbolic evaluator for the version of serializers in [Hewitt and Atkinson: 1977]. Vera Ketelboeter has independently developed a notion of "responsible agents" that is very close to the transaction managers described in this paper. Jerry Barber and Maria Simi have developed methods for proving that actor systems implemented with internal concurrency will respond properly to the messages which they receive.

Although we have criticized certain aspects of monitors and communicating sequential processes in this paper, both proposals represent extremely important advances in the state of the art of developing more modular concurrent systems and both have deeply influenced our work.

PLASMA [Hewitt and Smith: 1975, Hewitt: 1977, Hewitt and Atkinson: 1977 and 1979, Yonezawa: 1977] adopted the ideas of pattern matching, message passing, and concurrency as the core of the language. It was developed in an attempt to synthesize a unified system that combined the message passing, pattern matching, and pattern directed invocation and retrieval in PLANNER [Hewitt: 1969; Sussman, Charniak, and Winograd: 1971; Hewitt: 1971], the modularity of SIMULA [Birtwistle et. al.: 1973, Palme: 1973], the message passing ideas of an early design for SMALLTALK [Kay: 1972], the functional data structures in the lambda calculus based programming languages, the concept of concurrent events from Petri Nets (although the actor notion of an event is rather different than Petri's), and the protection inherent in the protected entry points of capability based operating systems. The subclass concept originated in [Dahl and Nygaard: 1968] and adapted in [Ingalls: 1978] has provided useful ideas.

The pattern matching implemented in PLASMA was developed partly to provide a convenient efficient method for an actor implemented in the language to bind the components of a message which it receives. This decision was based on experience using message passing for pattern directed invocation which originated in PLANNER [Hewitt: IJCAI-69] (implemented as MICRO-PLANNER by [Charniak, Sussman, and Winograd: 1971]). A related kind of simple pattern matching has also be used to select the components of messages by [Ingalls: 1978] in one of the later versions of SMALLTALK and by [Hoare: 1978] in a design for Communicating Sequential Processes. However CSP uses assignment to pattern variables instead of binding which was used in PLANNER, SIMULA, and PLASMA.

XII -- BIBLIOGRAPHY

Atkinson, R. and Hewitt, C. "Specification and Proof Techniques for Serializers" IEEE Transactions on Software Engineering SE-5. No. 1. January 1979. pp 10-23.

Birtwistle, G. M.; Dahl, O.; Myhrhaug, B.; and Nygaard, K. "SIMULA Begin" Auerbach. 1973.

Borning, A. H. "THINGLAB -- A Constraint-Oriented Simulation Laboratory", Stanford PhD thesis, March 1979. Revised version to appear as Xerox PARC SSL-79-3.

Brinch Hansen, P. "The Programming Language Concurrent Pascal" IEEE Transactions on Software Engineering. June, 1975. pp 199-207.

Clark, D. G.; Greif, I.; Liskov, B.; and Svobodova, L. "Progress Report of the Distributed Systems Group 1977-1978" MIT Computation Structures Group Memo. October 1978.

Dijkstra, E. W. "Guarded Commands, Nondeterminancy, and Formal Derivation of Programs" CACM. Vol. 18. No. 8. August 1975. pp 453-457.

Friedman and Wise. "A Note on Conditional Expressions" CACM. Vol 21. No. 11. November 1978. pp 931-933.

Gjessing, S. "Compile Time Preparations for Run Time Scheduling in Monitors" Research Report No. 17, Institute of Informatics, University of Oslo, June 1977.

Hewitt, C. and Baker, H. "Laws for Communicating Parallel Processes" MIT Artificial Intelligence Working Paper 134. December 1976. Invited paper at IFIP-77.

Hewitt, C. "Evolving Parallel Programs" MIT AI Lab Working Paper 164. December 1978. Revised January 1979.

Hewitt, C. "Concurrent Systems Need Both Sequences and Serializers" MIT AI Lab Working Paper 179. December 1978. Revised February 1979.

Hewitt, C.; Attardi, G.; and Lieberman, H. "Security and Modularity in Message Passing" MIT AI Lab Working Paper 180. December 1978. Revised February 1979.

Hoare, C. A. R. "Monitors: An Operating System Structuring Concept" CACM. October 1974.

Hoare, C. A. R. "Language Hierarchies and Interfaces" Lecture Notes in Computer Science No. 46. Springer, 1976. pp 242-265.

Hoare, C.A.R. "Communicating Sequential Processes" CACM, Vol 21, No. 8. August 1978. pp. 666-677.

Kay, A. Private communication. November 1972.

Manna, Z. and McCarthy, J. "Properties of Programs and Partial Function Logic" Machine Intelligence 5 B. Meltzer and D. Michie, editors. Edinburgh Univ. Press. 1970. pp 27-37.

Owicki, S. "Verifying concurrent Programs With Shared Data Classes" Formal Description of Programming Concepts edited by E. J. Neuhold. North Holland. 1978.

APPENDIX I --- Implementation of Cells using Serializers

In this appendix I present an implementation of cells [Greif and Hewitt: POPL-75, Hewitt and Baker: IFIP-77] using primitive serializers.

```
(define (create_cell =initial_contents)
   [is: (a Serialized_actor [responds_to: (either (a Contents_query) (an Update))])]
   [implementation:
      (create_serialized_actor
          (a Cell [current_contents: initial_contents]))])
```

where

```
   (describe (a Cell [current_contents: (an Actor)])
        [implementation:
          (receivers
             ((a Request [message: contents?] [customer: =c]) received
                 (transmit_to c (a Reply [message: current_contents]))
                               ;reply sending to the customer the current contents
                 (become (a Cell)))
                               ;unlock the serializer for the next message without changing the behavior
             ((an Update [next_contents: =n]) received
                 (become (a Cell [current_contents: n])))))])
                   ;unlock the serializer with the current contents being n
```

The above definition shows how serializers subsume the ability of cells to efficiently implement synchronization and state change in concurrent systems.

APPENDIX II --- Implementation of Semaphores using Serializers

Semaphores are an unstructured synchronization primitive that are used in the implementation of some systems. The definition below shows how primitive serializers can be used to efficiently implement semaphores.

```
(describe (create_semaphore)
   [is: (a Serialized_actor
              [receives: (either (a Request [message: P])
                                 (a Request [message: V]))])]
   [implementation:
     (create_serialized_actor
           (a Semaphore [queue: (an Empty_queue)]  ;initially there are no waiting P requests
                                [capacity: 1]))])       ;the capacity is initially 1
```

where

```
(describe (a Semaphore [queue: (a Queue [each_element: (a Customer)])]
                       [capacity: (a Non_negative_integer)])
     [preconditions:
        (implies
           (queue is ¬(an Empty_queue))
           (capacity is 0))]
     [implementation:
        (receivers
          ((a Request [message: P] [customer: =c]) received
             (select_case_for capacity
                ((> 0) then
                     (transmit_to c [reply: Did_P])
                     (become (a Semaphore [capacity: (capacity - 1)])))
                (0 then (become (a Semaphore [queue: (queue enqueue c)]))))
                          ;become a semaphore with c enqueued at the rear of queue

          ((a Request [message: V] [customer: =c]) received
             (transmit_to c [reply: Did_V])
             (select_case_for queue
                ((a Queue [front: =c] [all_but_front: =rest_waiting_customers])
                 then
                     (transmit_to c [reply: Did_P])
                     (become (a Semaphore [queue: rest_waiting_customers])))
                ((an Empty_queue)
                 then (become (a Semaphore [capacity: (capacity + 1)])))))))])
```

In [Hoare: 1975] there is an elegant construction showing that monitors can be implemented using semaphores and cells. His technique can be adapted to show that primitive serializers can also be implemented using semaphores and cells.

PRINCIPLES FOR DISTRIBUTING PROGRAMS

Michel Sintzoff
Philips Research Laboratory Brussels

1. INTRODUCTION

In distributed architectures, there are risks of excessive idleness : for instance, the rate of local activities can be hampered by too long periods of waiting for communications. In order to prevent this, the local components should be as independent as possible. We suggest here principles for achieving this.

Assume we are given a non-deterministic, iterative program on the form

```
        S : do S1(x) : B1(x) → s1(x)
(1.1)          ▯ S2(x) : B2(x) → s2(x)
            od
```

Since the variable x is common to S1 and S2, these two components cannot be effectively elaborated in parallel. We propose to construct a logically equivalent, but more distributed, program on the form

```
        T : begin T0(u,v) : ... ;
                do T1(u)        : ... → s1(u) ...
(1.2)            ▯ T2(v)        : ... → s2(v) ...
                 ▯ T12(x,u,v)  : ... → ...
                od
            end
```

The local, private variables u,v replace the global, common variable x in the components T1 and T2 ; these two components can thus be elaborated in parallel. The preliminary T0 initializes the auxiliary variables. The new command T12 uses the local u,v and the global x : it should express the intercommunications needed for restarting T1 or T2 whenever these are blocked because of insufficient local informations. If T1 and T2 can be applied more often than T12, then the new program T is more distributed than the initial program S.

Two problems must be solved. Firstly, how to restore the global information x on the basis of the local ones u,v? This is needed in T12 which expresses updating and intercommunications. Secondly, how to protect the global constraints, as guarded by B1(x) and B2(x), only by use of informations local to T1(u) and T2(v)? This would ensure T is strongly correct provided S is. We shall tackle these two problems by inductive techniques.

2. TOTALIZING FUNCTION

Throughout this paper, the following is assumed. The initially given program S is written, using the notations in Dijkstra, as

(2.1)
$$\begin{array}{lll} S(x) : \underline{do} & S1 : B1 \rightarrow s1 \\ \quad\;\; [] & S2 : B2 \rightarrow s2 \\ \quad\;\; \underline{od} & \end{array}$$

The parts s1, s2 do not contain guards referring to variables common to both of them. Moreover, functions f_ℓ (ℓ=1,2) are known such that $s_\ell(x)$ is equivalent to x := $f_\ell(x)$, where x represents the variables used in S. The elaboration of S is thus equivalent to the application of

(2.2) $$F = \lambda x.\ [B1 \rightarrow F(f1(x)) \mid B2 \rightarrow F(f2(x)) \mid \neg (B1 \vee B2) \rightarrow x\ ]$$

<u>Definition 1</u>. A function t, noted t(x,s1,s2,m,n) = Y, is a *totalizing function* iff the result Y is the set of values which can be yielded from x by some interleaving of m applications of s1 and n applications of s2.

<u>Construction 1.</u> A totalizing function may be defined inductively. We abbreviate t(x,s1,s2,m,n) into t(m,n), and $\bigcup_{y \in Y} f(y)$ into f(Y) :

(2.3)
$$\begin{aligned} t(0,0) &= \{x\} \\ t(i+1,0) &= f1(t(i,0)) \\ t(0,j+1) &= f2(t(0,j)) \\ t(i+1,j+1) &= f1(t(i,j+1)) \cup f2(t(i+1,j)) \end{aligned}$$

The correctness of this construction is clear, after a few observations. Definition 1 can be formalized as follows :

$$\begin{aligned} y \in t(i,j) \quad & \text{iff } \exists\ i1,\ldots,iM,\ j1,\ldots,jM \text{ such that} \\ & i1 + \ldots + iM = i,\ j1+\ldots+jM=j, \text{ and} \\ & y=(f1^{i1} \circ f2^{j1} \circ \ldots \circ f1^{iM} \circ f2^{jM})(x) \end{aligned}$$

This can be written as

$$\begin{aligned} y \in t(i,j) \quad \text{iff} \quad & i=j=0 \text{ and } y=x, \text{ or} \\ & i > 0 \text{ and } \exists z:(y=f1(z) \text{ and } z \in t(i-1,j)), \text{ or} \\ & j > 0 \text{ and } \exists z:(y=f2(z) \text{ and } z \in t(i,j-1)) . \end{aligned}$$

If we now distinguish the cases $i=j=0$, $i > 0 \wedge j=0$, $i=0 \wedge j > 0$, $i > 0 \wedge j > 0$, we obtain (2.3).

<u>Variant</u>. We can restate Definition 1 and Construction 1 in terms of local variables u0, u, v0, v such that

$$\begin{aligned} u = f1^i(u0) \quad & \text{for some } i \geq 0 \\ v = f2^j(v0) \quad & \text{for some } j \geq 0 \end{aligned}$$

If we express t(i,j) as t(u,v), the recurrences (2.3) become

$$
\begin{aligned}
t(u0,v0) &= \{x\} \\
t(f1(u),v0) &= f1(t(u,v0)) \\
t(u0,f2(v)) &= f2(t(u0,v)) \\
t(f1(u),f2(v)) &= f1(t(u,f2(v))) \cup f2(t(f1(u),v))
\end{aligned}
\qquad (2.4)
$$

In other words, the parameter i is represented by the result u of applying i times s1 on u0; and similarly for j and v.

3. PRECONDITION OF PERSISTENCE

Such a precondition guarantees that a given assertion R is established by applications of S1 and S2, and, more crucially, that the choice in interleaving these applications does not matter : the guards B1 and B2 are then persistent all along, so to speak.

Definition 2. A *precondition of persistence* for establishing a predicate R by m applications of S1 and n applications of S2 characterizes a domain from which R is always established by any possible interleaving of m applications of S1 and n applications of S2. It is noted pp(R,S1,S2,m,n) or, in short, pp(m,n).

Construction 2. Here are inductive rules for deriving pp(m,n); we use wp given in Dijkstra and assume $wp(B \rightarrow s,P) = wp(\underline{if}\ B \rightarrow s\ \underline{fi}, P) = B \wedge wp(s,P)$:

$$
\begin{aligned}
pp(0,0) &= R \\
pp(k+1,0) &= wp(S1,pp(k,0)) \\
pp(0,h+1) &= wp(S2,pp(0,h)) \\
pp(k+1,h+1) &= wp(S1,pp(k,h+1)) \wedge wp(S2,pp(k+1,h))
\end{aligned}
\qquad (3.1)
$$

The following properties are easily verified on (3.1) :

$$
\begin{aligned}
pp(k,h) &\supset pp(k',h') && \text{for } k \geq k',\ \ell \geq \ell' \\
pp(k,h) &\supset B1 && \text{for } k \geq 1 \\
pp(k,h) &\supset B2 && \text{for } h \geq 1
\end{aligned}
\qquad (3.2)
$$

The adequacy of (3.1) with respect to Definition 2 is obvious for pp(m,0) and pp(0,n). Assume now (3.1) is adequate for pp(k,h+1) and pp(k+1,h), and let us check it is adequate for pp(k+1,h+1). There are two sets of interleavings for establishing R after (k+1) times S1 and (h+1) times S2 : either to apply S1 once, and then k times S1 and (h+1) times S2, or to apply S2 once, and then (k+1) times S1 and h times S2. *Both* cases are taken care of in the last rule (3.1). Hence, by induction, pp(m,n) derived by (3.1) verifies Definition 2. Moreover, (3.1) yields the weakest precondition of persistence, as can be proved by induction again : if pp(m,n) is a precondition of persistence, then for all $k \leq m$ and $h \leq n$, pp(k,h) must verify (3.1) where the equalities are replaced by implications.

Variant. As was done in (2.4), we can here rewrite (3.1) in terms of the local results u and v yielded by k applications of S1 and h applications of S2, respectively. Thus we again assume u0,u,v0,v such that

$$t(u0,v0) = x$$
$$u = f1^{k}(u0) \qquad \text{for some } k \geq 0 ,$$
$$v = f2^{k}(v0) \qquad \text{for some } h \geq 0 ,$$

and we construct pp(u,v) instead of pp(k,h) :

$$\begin{aligned} pp(u0,v0) &= R \\ pp(f1(u),v0) &= wp(S1,\ pp(u,v0)) \\ pp(u0,f2(v)) &= wp(S2,\ pp(u0,v)) \\ pp(f1(u),f2(v)) &= wp(S1,pp(u,f2(v))) \wedge wp(S2,pp(f1(u),v)) \end{aligned} \tag{3.3}$$

4. FORMATION OF A MORE DISTRIBUTED PROGRAM

We present here our scheme for deriving a more distributed program (1.2) given an insufficiently distributed one.

Construction 3. Let S be given by (1.1) and let Q be a goal-assertion on which S terminates. The parts of T missing in (1.2) are derived as follows ; m,n are new integer variables :

(T0) It establishes $u = u0 \wedge v = v0$
$\wedge pp(B1 \vee B2 \vee Q,\ S1,S2,m,n) \wedge ((B1 \vee B2) \supset (m > 0 \vee n > 0))$

(T1) The command s1(u) is supplemented with m:=m-1. The guard of T1 must protect $m \geq 0$. For instance

$m > 0 \rightarrow s1(u)$; m:=m-1

(T2) Similarly : $n > 0 \rightarrow s2(v)$; n:=n-1

(T12) Its guard is $m=n=0 \wedge (B1 \vee B2)$. Its command t12 is characterized by the following pre- and post-assertions using free variables $\bar{x},\bar{u},\bar{v}$:

pre(t12) : $x=\bar{x} \wedge u=\bar{u} \wedge v=\bar{v}$
post(T12) : $x \in t(\bar{x},s1,s2,\bar{u},\bar{v}) \wedge u=u0 \wedge v=v0$
$\wedge pp(B1 \vee B2 \vee Q,S1,S2,m,n) \wedge ((B1 \vee B2) \supset (m>0 \vee n>0))$

We show hereafter that the new program T is no less correct than the initial one S.

Proposition. The weakest preconditions of strong correctness of the programs S and T with respect to the post-assertion Q are equivalent.

Proof. The thesis is wp(S,Q)=wp(T,Q). The main problem is to prove $wp(S,Q) \supset wp(T,Q)$. Assume Q holds initially ; then T0 establishes m=n=0 by the definition of the precondition of persistence ; all the guards in T1, T2, T12 are false, and T terminates on Q. Assume that $B1 \vee B2$ holds initially, and that S establishes Q after applications of S1 or S2 ; this implies S establishes $B1 \vee B2 \vee Q$ by at least one application of S1 or one of S2 ; hence T0 yields $m > 0 \vee n > 0$, given (3.1) ; T1 or T2 is thus applied at least once, until m=n=0 ; then, Q may be true, in which case T12 is evaluated once to update the global x and to yield $B1 \vee B2$ = false, which terminates T ; if $B1 \vee B2$ = true after the updating, $m > 0 \vee n > 0$ is obtained and T1 or T2 can be applied again. Recall that successive applications of T1 and T2 are safe since, given (3.2),

$$m > 0 \wedge pp(m,n) \supset pp(m-1,n) \wedge B1$$
$$n > 0 \wedge pp(m,n) \supset pp(m,n-1) \wedge B2$$

Moreover, each application of T1(resp. T2) corresponds to an application of S1 (resp. S2). This ensures T terminates for each initial state from which S terminates.

Variants.

A. Cyclic, deadlock-free programs : Assume S is a cyclic program which must not terminate. This means $B1 \vee B2$ must be an invariant of S. We adapt Construction 3 by simply using Q=false : this ensures the invariance of $B1 \vee B2$ in T. The theorem can be adapted accordingly.

B. Elimination of the variables m,n : Let us note pp(u,v) for the variant pp($B1 \vee B2 \vee Q$, S1,S2,u,v) corresponding to (3.3). Assume we can find J1(u,um) and J2(v,vn) such that

$$J1 \wedge J2 \wedge pp(um,vn) \supset pp(u,v)$$

Then the invariance of $J1 \wedge J2$ under s1(u) and s2(v), given um and vn for which pp(um,vn) holds, would ensure pp(u,v), viz. the persistence of B1 and B2 through T1 and through T2. This invariance is of course guaranteed by guards C1(u,um) and C2(v,vn) such that $J_\ell \wedge C_\ell = wp(s_\ell, J_\ell)$, $\ell=1,2$. Here are the corresponding changes in Construction 3 :

post(T0) : $u=u0 \wedge v=v0$

$\wedge\, pp(B1 \vee B2 \vee Q,\ S1,S2,um,vn) \wedge ((B1 \vee B2) \supset (C1 \vee C2))$

T1 : $C1(u,um) \rightarrow s1(u)$

T2 : $C2(v,vn) \rightarrow s2(v)$

guard(T12) : $\neg((B1 \vee B2) \supset (C1 \vee C2))$, i.e. $(B1 \vee B2) \wedge \neg C1 \wedge \neg C2$

post(t12) : $x \in t(\bar{x},s1,s2,\bar{u},\bar{v}) \wedge u=u0 \wedge v=v0$

$\wedge\, pp(B1 \vee B2 \vee Q,S1,S2,um,vn) \wedge ((B1 \vee B2) \supset (C1 \vee C2))$

This form may appear more attractive ; yet, the discovery of J1 and J2 is less easy than the use of $m \geqslant 0$ and $n \geqslant 0$, and it may be more costly to carry the futurity variables um and vn than the integral bounds m and n.

C. Decomposition of intercommunications. Construction 3 implies the intercommunications T12 occur only if *both* T1 *and* T2 are blocked and wait for new data. One may decompose T12 into a new T12 to be applied if T1 is blocked, and a new T21 similarly associated with T2. The guards of T12 and T21 could be $m=0 \wedge B1$ and $n=0 \wedge B2$, respectively. In general, each of T12 and T21 would still interfere with both T1 and T2 because both m and n (or um and vn) must be updated : the intercommunications are thus not fully decomposed.

Heuristics. We suggest a way of obtaining programs which are really more distributed in some sense, and we give a hint for simplifying the derivation of the updating part in the intercommunications.

A. Really more distributed programs. Construction3 perfectly allows to derive a new program T with a malevolent invariant $m=0 \wedge n=0 \vee m=1 \wedge n=0 \vee m=0 \wedge n=1$: this would closely mimick the original S, in spite of the addition of the new, auxiliary operations. It is thus necessary that T0 and T12 yield the highest possible values for the futurity counters m,n ; this ensures the number of independent applications of T1 and T2 is maximized between any two phases of intercommunications. A possible way to express this requirement is to add the following constraint to the post-assertions of T0 and T12 :

$$\neg\, pp(m+1,n) \wedge \neg\, pp(m,n+1)$$

This is still not the last word : an adequate characterization of the policies for updating m and n requires an analytical study of complexity, which is not made here. For instance, greater values for n could be more beneficial than greater values of m.

B. Simpler totalizing function. Construction3 defines a newly updated global value x to be *any one* value in the entire set $t(\bar{x},s1,s2,\bar{u},\bar{v})$ of possible results : one particular interleaving is thereby chosen implicitly. On the other hand, the strict application of (2.3) or (2.4) can be hard especially if f1 and f2 do not commute. We suggest thus to derive *subsolutions* which can be much simpler and are still sufficient for updating. Such subsolutions are defined by non-void solutions of (2.3) or (2.4) where equality is replaced by set inclusion.

5. ILLUSTRATIONS

We detail two simple, typical examples to illustrate the suggested principles of construction.

Cyclic cooperation. We are given a non-terminating program

```
S : do S1 : x-a ≥ 0  →  x:=x-a
    ▯  S2 : x+b ≤ N  →  x:=x+b
    od
```

We assume $a+b \leq N$ holds.

Totalizing function : t(x,s1,s2,m,n), by (2.3) :

$$
\begin{aligned}
t(0,0) &= \{x\} \\
t(1,0) &= \{x-a\},\ldots,\ t(m,0)=\{x-m.a\} \\
t(0,1) &= \{x+1\},\ldots,\ t(0,n)=\{x+n.b\} \\
t(1,1) &= \{x+b-a,\ x-a+b\} = \{x-a+b\} \\
t(i,j+1) &= \{x-i.a+(j+1).b\},\quad t(i+1,j)=\{x-(i+1).a+j.b\} \\
t(i+1,j+1) &= \{x-i.a+(j+1).b-a,\ x-(i+1).a+j.b+b\} \\
&= \{x-(i+1).a+(j+1).b\}
\end{aligned}
$$

Therefore $t(m,n) = \{x-m.a+n.b\}$

which should not be surprise.

Variant $t(x,s1,s2,u,v)$, by (2.4) :

$$t(u,v) = \{x+u+v\} \quad , \quad u0=v0=0 \ .$$

Indeed,

$$
\begin{aligned}
t(0,0) &= \{x-0+0\}= \{x\} \\
t(u-a,0) &= \{x+u-a\} = t(u,0)-a \\
t(0,v+b) &= \{x+v+b\} = t(0,v)+b \\
t(u-a,v+b) &= \{x+u-a+v+b\} \\
&= t(u,v+b)-a \cup t(u-a,v)+b
\end{aligned}
$$

If $ui=f1^{i}(u0) = 0-i.a= -i.a$ and similarly $vj= +j.b$, then the correspondence between $t(i,j)= \{x-i.a+j.b\}$ and $t(ui,vj)= \{x+ui+vj\}$ becomes even clearer.

The precondition of persistence $pp(R,S1,S2,m,n)$, where $R=B1 \vee B2$, is needed for Construction 3, variant A. We apply (3.1) :

$$
\begin{aligned}
pp(0,0) &= B1 \vee B2 = x-a \geq 0 \vee x+b \leq N \\
&= \underline{\text{true}},\ \text{since } a \leq N-b \text{ by assumption} \\
pp(1,0) &= x-a \geq 0,\ldots,\ pp(i,0) = x-i.a \geq 0 \\
pp(0,1) &= x+b \leq N,\ldots,\ pp(0,j) = x+j.b \leq N \\
pp(1,1) &= x-a \geq 0 \wedge x-a+b \leq N \wedge x+b \leq N \wedge x+b-a \geq 0 \\
&= a \leq x \leq N-b \\
pp(i,j+1) &= i.a \leq x \leq N-(j+1).b \\
pp(i+1,j) &= (i+1).a \leq x \leq N-j.b \\
pp(i+1,j+1) &= x-a \geq 0 \wedge i.a \leq x-a \leq N-(j+1).b \\
&\quad \wedge x+b \leq N \wedge (i+1).a \leq x+b \leq N-j.b \\
&= (i+1).a \leq x \leq N-(j+1).b
\end{aligned}
$$

Thus $pp(m,n) = x-m.a \geq 0 \wedge x+n.b \leq N$.

The variant (3.3) yields

$$pp(u,v) = x+u \geq 0 \wedge x+v \leq N$$

since $u = -m.a$ for some $m \geq 0$, and $v=n.b$ for some $n \geq 0$.

Values of m,n which maximize $pp(m,n)$ according to heuristic A are given by $m= x \div a$ and $n = (N-x) \div b$. Construction 3 yields

```
T : begin  u:=0; v:=0; m:=x÷a; n:=(N-x)÷b ;
      do T1 : m > 0       → u:=u-a; m:=m-1
       ▯ T2 : n > 0       → v:=v+b; n:=n-1
       ▯ T12: m=0 ∧ n=0 → x:=x+u+v ; u:=0; v:=0;
                              m:=x÷a; n:=(N-x)÷b
      od
    end
```

The variables m,n are here easily eliminated, following variant B. Indeed, for J1 = u ⩾ um and J2 = v ⩽ vn, we have

$$J1 \wedge J2 \wedge x+um \geqslant 0 \wedge x+vn \leqslant N \supset x+u \geqslant 0 \wedge x+v \leqslant N$$

Values um,vn which maximize pp(um,vn) are um=x and vn=N-x. Hence

```
begin u:=0; v:=0; um:= -x; vn:=N-x ;
  do             u-a⩾ um → u:=u-a
  ▯              v+b ⩽vn → v:=v+b
  ▯   u-a <um ∧v+b >vn → x:=x+u+v; u:=0; v:=0;
                            um:= -x; vn:=N-x
  od
end
```

We simplify this by using -x for um and N-x for vn, and also show how intercommunications can be decomposed (variant C) :

```
begin u:=0; v:=0;
  do  x+u-a ⩾ 0 → u:=u-a
  ▯   x+v+b ⩽ N → v:=v+b
  ▯   x+u-a < 0
    ∨ x+v+b > N → x:=x+u+v; u:=0; v:=0
  od
end
```

It is instructive to observe that

$$x+u \leqslant x+u+v \leqslant x+v$$

The current, global information x+u+v is defined by the last, global update x and the current, local u,v. It is approximated from below by x+u, known in the first component, and from above by x+v, known in the second one.

Terminating competition. Assume a program

```
S : do   x+a ⩽ N → x:=x+a
    ▯    x*b ⩽ N → x:=x×b
    od
```

terminating on $Q = x+a > N \wedge x \times b > N$.

Since +a and ×b do not commute, it is advisable to derive only a subsolution $\bar{t}(i,j)$ of $t(i,j)$, according to heuristic B :

$$\bar{t}(0,0) = \{x\}$$

$$\bar{t}(i,0) = \{x+i.a\}\ ,\quad \bar{t}(0,j) = \{x\times b^{j}\}$$

If $\quad \bar{t}(i+1,j+1) \subseteq \bar{t}(i,j+1)+a \cup \bar{t}(i+1,j)\times b$

$\quad\quad = \bar{t}(i,j+1)+a \quad\quad$ [arbitrary choice]

then $\quad \bar{t}(i,j+1) = \{x\times b^{j+1}+i.a\}$

$$\bar{t}(i+1,j+1) = \{x\times b^{j+1}+i.a+a\} = \{x\times b^{j+1}+(i+1).a\}$$

and $\quad \bar{t}(m,n) = \{x\times b^{n}+m.a\}$

The corresponding subsolution to (2.4) is

$$\bar{t}(u,v) = \{x\times v+u\},\quad u0=0,\ v0=1.$$

The precondition of persistence is derived without much ado ; further details are omitted :

$$pp(m,n) = (x+m.a)\times b^{n} \leqslant N$$

or $\quad pp(u,v) = (x+u)\times v \leqslant N$

Assume $r(x)$ is an auxiliary function yielding u,v such that $pp(u,v) \wedge \neg\, pp(u+a,v) \wedge \neg\, pp(u,v\times b)$. Then we can obtain

```
T : begin  u:=0; v:=1; (um,vn) := r(x) ;
      do u+a ≤ um → u:=u+a
       [] v×b ≤ vn → v:=v×b
       [] (u+a>um ∧ v×b > vn) ∧ (x+a≤N ∨ x×b≤N)
                    → x:=x×v+u; u:=0; v:=1;
                      (um,vn):=r(x)
      od
    end
```

6. DISCUSSION

Problems remain. Program structures richer than (1.1), for instance with S1,S2,...,Sn, and more serious applications, such as a concurrent garbage collector, should be investigated. It is not clear how easy it is to derive and to evaluate a totalizing function, to induce a precondition of persistence, or to ensure the maximality requirement (heuristic A). The possible improvement with respect to distribution should be better evaluated and compared with the cost of the additional operations.

Relationships exist between the suggestions made here and already known ideas. The totalizing function (2.4) amounts to an abstraction function à la Milner : the local contributions u and v can be viewed as a representation of the corresponding global contribution. As in Lamport and Owicki-Gries, the introduction of auxiliary variables allows to reduce the logical interdependencies between modules. Let us assume the existence of the limit K of pp(true, S1,S2,m,n) for $m \to \infty$ and $n \to \infty$; K expresses that S1 *as well as* S2 can always be applied ; it is thus much stronger than the inductive invariant of Keller or the safe invariant of van Lamsweerde and Sintzoff, which only ensure that at least *one of* S1 and S2 can be applied throughout. The idea suggested in Sintzoff for increasing parallelism simply amounts to concentrate all intercommunications in the initialization and the finalization ; here, intercommunications occur periodically. Finally, note the similarity between the local variables u and v, and counters such as -c(k) and p(k), or -np(message) and np(frame), respectively used by Denning and Habermann to verify synchronization between consumers and producers.

7. CONCLUSION

The two concepts presented here, namely the totalizing function and the precondition of persistence, appear to be simple and, yet, to permit a systematic covering of the set of histories of a program by subsets where program components can be applied independently and safely. In spite of the pending problems, the proposed principles already allow to improve or reconstruct some useful techniques of verification or design which are not always well linked.

Acknowledgements. Useful comments were made by M. Broy, J. R. Abrial, A. van Lamsweerde and G. Guiho (in temporal order).

REFERENCES

Denning, P. J., Third generation computer systems, Computing Surveys, 3, 4(Dec. 1971), 175-216.

Dijkstra, E. W., A Discipline of Programming, Prentice-Hall, Englewood Cliffs, 1976.

Habermann, A. N., Synchronization of communicating processes, CACM 15(1972), 171-176.

Keller, R. M., Formal verification of parallel programs, CACM 19(1976), 371-384.

Lamport, L., Proving the correctness of multiprocess programs, IEEE Trans. Soft. Eng., SE-3(1977), 125-143.

Milner, R., An algebraic definition of simulation between programs, Proc. 2nd Intern. Joint Conf. Artif. Intell., 1971, pp. 481-489.

Owicki, S., and D. Gries, An axiomatic proof technique for parallel programs I, Acta Informatica 6(1976), 319-340.

van Lamsweerde, A., and M. Sintzoff, Formal derivation of strongly correct parallel programs, revised version of Report R338, MBLE, Brussels, 1976, to appear in Acta Informatica.

Sintzoff, M., Inventing program construction rules, in : S. Schuman, P. Hibbard (eds.) Constructing Quality Software, North-Holland, 1978, pp. 471-501.

A PETRI NET DEFINITION OF A SYSTEM DESCRIPTION LANGUAGE

Kurt Jensen, Morten Kyng, Ole Lehrmann Madsen
Computer Science Department, Aarhus University
8000 Aarhus C, Denmark

This paper introduces a language for the description of systems with concurrency, and presents a formal definition of its semantics. The language is based on Delta and the semantic model is an extension of Petri nets with a data part and with expressions attached to transitions and to places.

1. INTRODUCTION

The purpose of this paper is to introduce a system description language, Epsilon, based on the Delta language [Delta 75], and to present a formal definition of its semantics by means of a model based on Petri nets ([Petri 73, 75, 76], [Peterson 77]).

During the last decade there has been an increasing need to understand, control and design large, complex systems of men and machines, and thus a demand for concepts and formal languages to conceive and describe systems with concurrency. Mathematics was for a long time the most important tool for analysing such systems. With the advent of the electronic computer, simulation programming languages have become a popular tool for the description and analysis of complex systems, untractable by mathematics. It turned out that the process of carefully creating a system description (i.e. a program) was often at least as beneficial as actually generating the described model (i.e. a program execution in the computer store) and gathering statistics about it. This experience gave birth to the idea of creating a language specially designed for the description of systems, a language without the restrictions necessarily placed on any language executable on a digital computer. The first major attempt in this direction is the Delta language which was created at the Norwegian Computing Center and which draws heavily on the experience from the development and use of Simula ([Simula 70], [Nygaard 70]). Delta is a tool for system specialists and for other groups working with and influenced by data processing systems. It is also a tool for research workers inside other fields such as biology, medicine, and physics.

The conceptual framework behind Delta introduces a large number of new and interesting ideas. The actual language however is not quite as carefully worked out. It is large and complicated, and the relation between some of the language elements is diffuse. The semantics is only informally described although the outline of an abstract machine for "execution" of Delta descriptions has been defined by programming it in the language itself.

It is not clear what kind of information one wants to extract from system descriptions, i.e. what kind of semantics system description languages should have. The situation is more complex than what is found in normal algorithmic languages and none of the existing semantic approaches appear to be satisfactory. As an attempt to clarify the situation, we describe a system description language called Epsilon containing only a few basic primitives and we define its semantics by means of a formal model based on Petri nets. Petri nets are chosen because they contain a number of concepts which are closely analogous to Delta. Moreover, Petri nets are themselves useful tools for the description of systems with concurrency. The semantic model is a further development of formalisms defined in [Keller 76] and [Mazurkiewicz 77].

Since Epsilon is intended for describing systems of interacting objects, such as men and machines, an Epsilon system consists of a nested structure of objects. An object is characterised by the actions it executes and a selected set of attributes, which may be variables, procedures and objects.

State transformations can be described by means of algorithms or by means of equations. An algorithm is used in cases where it is adequate to describe the way in which a given state transformation is carried out. Equations are used, when it is adequate to describe state transformations implicitly by means of the properties which a given set of variables should fulfil, and when it is less relevant how the properties can be achieved.

The variables of an object may be observed by other objects and will then always have well defined values, i.e. intermediate values appearing during an algorithmic state transformation will not be observable from other objects. Interaction between objects may also take place by means of interrupts, that is an object may require another object to execute some specific actions.

Epsilon also contains a concept of time which can be used to describe continuous state transformations.

The use of equations, observation of non-local variables and the time concept are the main features that distinguish Epsilon from normal programming languages. Epsilon is not a complete language, but it does contain the new and essential ideas from Delta.

In section 2 Epsilon is informally introduced by means of an example. Sections 3, 4, and 5 define the semantic model, the abstract syntax, and the formal semantics of Epsilon respectively. Finally section 6 evaluates the approach and discusses future work.

2. INFORMAL DESCRIPTION OF EPSILON

The main features of Epsilon will be introduced by means of an example describing four balls following a circular orbit. The balls may move in both directions or stand still. Elastic collisions may appear between the balls. Two balls which collide will exchange their velocity (speed and direction). An observer may place a "wall" in front of a ball and in this way negate its velocity. It is assumed that no other forces influence the system, i.e. no friction, no gravitation and no loss of energy. All the balls have the same mass and size.

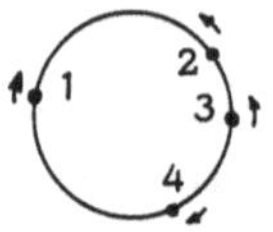

The following semiformal description of the system, Fig. [2.1], introduces the objects and the kind of actions they perform. Formal language elements are written in capital letters with keywords underlined and informal language elements (i.e. not specified in detail) are written in small letters.

An Epsilon system consists of a nested structure of objects. The present system consists of six such objects: four ball objects (lines 2-10), the observer object (11-18) and the system object (1-19) containing the other objects. An object is characterised by a set of attributes (objects, procedures and variables) and an action part.

The declaration (11-18) introduces one object with the name OBSERVER. It has no attributes and its action part (13-17) is a repeated execution of a LET-imperative (14-16). The declaration (2-10) introduces four objects with the names BALL(1), ...,(BALL(4). Each BALL only has one attribute: its position on the orbit (3). Its action part (4-9) is a repeated execution of a LET-imperative (5-8).

The state of an object is a pair consisting of the values of its variables and its stage of execution. The state of an Epsilon system is the set of states for all objects. All objects execute their actions in concurrency.

An object may both observe and change the values of its own variables, but it may only observe variables in other objects.

Objects can interact by means of interrupts; that is, an object, A, may require an object, B, to execute a specific procedure, P, which must be an attribute of B. Each object controls when it wants to accept possible interrupting procedures for execution. Thus, objects may synchronise their actions in two ways: by observing variables and by sending and accepting interrupts. An asynchronous set of objects may be described by restricting all their synchronisation to take place by interrupts. A synchronous set of objects may be described by using observation of variables to synchronise actions.

By means of nesting of objects it is possible to restrict the observability of object-attributes. These and other scope rules will not be defined in this paper.

```
 1 SYSTEM BEGIN
 2 OBJECT BALL(1..4):
 3   BEGIN VAR POSITION : REAL;
 4     REPEAT
 5       LET POSITION = new-position DEFINE POSITION
 6         WHEN crash DO exchange-velocity (crashing-neighbour)
 7         ACCEPT OBSERVER : change-direction
 8       ENDLET
 9     ENDREPEAT
10   END BALL;
11 OBJECT OBSERVER:
12   BEGIN
13     REPEAT
14       LET observe
15         WHEN ready DO INTERRUPT selected-ball BY change-direction
16       ENDLET
17     ENDREPEAT
18   END OBSERVER;
19 END SYSTEM
```

Figure [2. 1]

An object alternates between executing two kinds of actions: event-actions and continuous-actions. Event-actions are instantaneous, indivisible and executed by one object, but possibly in concurrency with actions executed by other objects. Continuous-actions are time consuming, interruptable, and executed in cooperation with continuous-actions executed by other objects. An imperative containing a continuous-action specifies an equation to be fulfilled by the system state but gives no details about how this can be achieved.

Actions are described by imperatives.

The execution of a LET-imperative starts with the execution of a continuous-action. For the LET-imperative (5-8) of a BALL this means that the equation "POSITION = new-position" is constantly satisfied while this continuous-action is executed. The variables following DEFINE (here POSITION) may be changed in order to satisfy the equation. The WHEN-clause (6) describes that the execution of the continuous-action will be stopped when the boolean-expression "crash" becomes true. If this happens the imperative following DO (6) is executed. Similarly the ACCEPT-clause (7) describes that the continuous-action may be interrupted if the OBSERVER sends the interrupt "change-direction". If this happens the BALL will execute the procedure "change-direction". In both cases the execution of the LET-imperative is stopped.

When the OBSERVER executes its LET-imperative (14-16), the equation "observe" will be satisfied. At certain moments of time, the boolean-expression "ready" will be satisfied and the OBSERVER will interrupt one of the BALLs (15).

The system-object executes no actions.

A typical situation in the system will be that all four BALLs are moving around the circular orbit with the OBSERVER merely "observing" them. The BALLs will execute the continuous-action described by the LET-imperative (5-8) and the OBSERVER the one described by the LET-imperative (14-16). The system state will satisfy the equations "POSITION = new position" and "observe".

If two BALLs collide the following event-actions will take place: The boolean-expressions "crash" will be true in the two colliding BALLs. Both of the BALLs will execute the actions described by "exchange-velocity (crashing-neighbour)". Similarly event-actions will be executed if the OBSERVER decides to change the direction of one of the BALLs. The "selected-ball" will then be interrupted and it will execute the procedure "change-velocity".

In Figure [2.2] a more detailed description of the system is given. The description of the BALLs has been extended in order to specify how velocity and position vary. More attributes have been added to each BALL (3-12). Note, however, that some language elements are still informal.

The actions "exchange-velocity" and "change-direction" have been specified as procedures. A sequence of micro-imperatives enclosed within ≪ , ≫ describes one event-action (5, 12, 13) and is thus an instantaneous and indivisible action. Micro- imperatives are normal algorithmic imperatives such as assignment, selection and repetition. The equation "POSITION = new-position" has been specified in detail (15).

TIME is an implicitly defined variable contained in the system object and representing time in the system modelled. TIME is continuously increased. (See 5.4 for a precise description of TIME.)

The boolean-expression "crash" has been separated into two parts (16-17), one for a crash with its left neighbour, and one for a crash with its right neighbour. For the sake of brevity we have not described "left/right-crash" in detail.

EXECUTE is a procedure call (16, 17). PUT is a call-by-value parameter transfer (8, 16, 17); the local variable I in EXCHANGE-VELOCITY is assigned the number of the left/right neighbour. Each BALL has an integer attribute with the name B (2) which for BALL(i) (i = 1, 2, 3, 4) has the value i. P_0, T_0 are used to hold the values of POSITION and TIME at the last collision.

Each BALL starts its actions by an initialisation of its local variables (13). The initial positions, p(B) (13) for the BALLs are assumed to be modulo the length of the orbit. The BALLs cannot pass each other hence it is sufficient to compare their positions directly (without modulo).

```
1  SYSTEM BEGIN
2  OBJECT BALL(B:1..4):
3    BEGIN VAR POSITION, VELOCITY, P₀, T₀: REAL;
4      PROCEDURE CHANGE-DIRECTION:
5        BEGIN « VELOCITY:=-VELOCITY; P₀:=POSITION; T₀:=TIME» END;
6      PROCEDURE EXCHANGE-VELOCITY:
7        BEGIN VAR I: 1..4;
8          INTERRUPT BALL(I) BY NEW-VELOCITY PUT (V:=VELOCITY);
9          LET TRUE ACCEPT BALL(I): NEW-VELOCITY ENDLET
10       END;
11     PROCEDURE NEW-VELOCITY:
12       BEGIN VAR V: REAL; « VELOCITY := V; P₀:=POSITION; T₀:=TIME» END;
13     « POSITION:= p(B);   VELOCITY:=v(B); P₀:=POSITION; T₀:=TIME»;
14     REPEAT
15       LET POSITION=P₀ + VELOCITY * (TIME-T₀) DEFINE POSITION
16         WHEN leftcrash DO EXECUTE EXCHANGE-VELOCITY PUT (I:=B ⊖ 1)
17         WHEN rightcrash DO EXECUTE EXCHANGE-VELOCITY PUT (I:=B ⊕ 1)
18         ACCEPT OBSERVER : CHANGE-DIRECTION
19       ENDLET
20     ENDREPEAT
21   END BALL;
22 OBJECT OBSERVER: ....
23   END OBSERVER;
24 END SYSTEM
```

Figure [2.2]

3. CONCURRENT SYSTEMS

Concurrent systems is a semantic model based upon Petri nets.

3.1 Petri nets

A Petri net PN = (P, T, PRE, POST) is a 4-tuple, where P is a set of places, T is a set of transitions, PRE and POST are functions from T into subsets of P. Moreover

1) $P \cup T \neq \emptyset$

2) $P \cap T = \emptyset$

3) $\forall \, t \in T \, [PRE(t) \cap POST(t) = \emptyset]$

A marking is a function m: $P \rightarrow \{0, 1\}$. A place P is marked if m(p) = 1. If m(p) = 0, p is unmarked. For each $t \in T$ the set COND(t) = PRE(t) ∪ POST(t) are conditions for t. Two transitions t_1 and t_2 are independent iff COND(t_1) ∩ COND(t_2) = $\emptyset$.

A nonempty subset of mutually independent transitions, $X \subseteq T$, has <u>concession</u> in a marking m iff

$$\forall p \in P \quad \begin{bmatrix} p \in PRE(X) \Rightarrow m(p) = 1 \wedge \\ p \in POST(X) \Rightarrow m(p) = 0 \end{bmatrix}$$

where $PRE(X) = \cup \{PRE(t) \mid t \in X\}$ and $POST(X) = \cup \{POST(t) \mid t \in X\}$.

When X has concession in m it may fire. If it fires a new marking m' is reached, such that

$$\forall p \in P \quad \begin{bmatrix} p \in PRE(X) \Rightarrow m'(p) = 0 \wedge \\ p \in POST(X) \Rightarrow m'(p) = 1 \wedge \\ p \notin COND(X) \Rightarrow m'(p) = m(p) \end{bmatrix}$$

where $COND(X) = \cup \{COND(t) \mid t \in X\}$. m' is said to be <u>directly reachable</u> from m, which we write as $m \longrightarrow m'$ or $m \xrightarrow{X} m'$.

3.2 Predicates and relations

Let V be a set of variables, which each may take values in a domain F. Let $A \subseteq V$ be given, and let $[A \rightarrow F]$ denote all total functions from A to F. The set of <u>predicates</u> over A is defined as $[[A \rightarrow F] \rightarrow \{true, false\}]$ and is denoted by $PRED_A$. The set of <u>binary relations</u> over A is defined as all subsets of $[A \rightarrow F] \times [A \rightarrow F]$ and it is denoted by REL_A.

3.3 Expressions attached to transitions

While Petri nets are excellent models for the control flow in a language, they are less suited as models for state transformations in the data part. To remedy this situation we augment Petri nets with a data part containing a set of variables and we attach to each transition t an expression of the form: <u>WHEN</u> GUARD(t) <u>DO</u> REL(t) where GUARD(t) is a predicate over a subset of variables and REL(t) is a binary relation defining a set of possible transformations on the same subset of variables. This set of variables is called the scope of t and is denoted by SC(t).

A transition t has concession only when GUARD(t) is satisfied by the current values of the variables in SC(t). If t fires, one of the possible transformations contained in REL(t) is performed upon the variables in SC(t). Transitions can fire concurrently only if they have disjoint scopes. Thus the firing rule for a subset of transitions is modified by an added requirement on concession for each transition and an added requirement on independence for each pair of transitions.

3.4 Expressions attached to places

As a second extension we attach to each place p an expression of the form: <u>LET</u> EQ(p) <u>DEFINE</u> VAR(p) where EQ(p) is an equation over a subset of variables. This set of variables is called the scope of p and is denoted by SC(p). VAR(p) is a subset of SC(p).

We define a control state to be a marking, while a data state is a set of values for the variables. A system state is a pair consisting of a control state and a data state, such that the data state satisfies all equations attached to places marked in the control state.

An equation is satisfied in a data state iff the predicate constructed from it in the usual way evaluates to TRUE.

The firing of a set of transitions can now be described as the following two steps:

A) The control state is changed according to the modified firing rule, while the data state is changed according to the relations attached to the firing transitions.

B) The equations attached to places marked in the new control state are established. This is done by changing the values of some of the variables in $\cup \{VAR(p) \mid m(p) = 1\}$.

The "intermediate state" between A and B is not considered a system state since there may be equations, which are unsatisfied although they are attached to marked places. Formally we will define the firing of a set of transitions as an instantaneous and indivisible action leading directly from one system state to the next without any intermediate state.

3.5 Concurrent systems

A concurrent system is a triple CS = (CON, INT, INIT) where

- CON, the control part, is a Petri net (P, T, PRE, POST)
- INT, the interpretation, is a pair (DATA, EXP), where
  1) DATA, the data part, is a pair (V,F), where V is a set of variables, which each may take values in domain F.
  2) EXP, the expression part, is a 5-tuple (EQ, VAR, GUARD, REL, SC) consisting of five functions:

     $EQ \ : P \rightarrow \cup \{PRED_A \mid A \subseteq V\}$
     $VAR \ : P \rightarrow \mathcal{P}(V)$
     $GUARD : T \rightarrow \cup \{PRED_A \mid A \subseteq V\}$
     $REL \ : T \rightarrow \cup \{REL_A \mid A \subseteq V\}$
     $SC \ : P \cup T \rightarrow \mathcal{P}(V)$

     such that

     $\forall p \in P \ [EQ(p) \in PRED_{SC(p)} \wedge VAR(p) \subseteq SC(p)]$
     $\forall t \in T \ [GUARD(t) \in PRED_{SC(t)} \wedge REL(t) \in REL_{SC(t)}]$
- INIT, the initial system state, is a system state, (m_I, s_I). See below.

The set of all markings, $M = [P \rightarrow \{0, 1\}]$, are called control states. The set of all data values, $S = [V \rightarrow F]$, are called data states. A pair $(m, s) \in M \times S$ is a system state iff $\forall p \in P \ [m(p) = 1 \Rightarrow EQ(p)(s_{SC(p)})]$, where $s_{SC(p)}$ is the restriction of s to SC(p).

For Petri nets we have defined a set of concepts, such as independence, concession and direct reachability. We will now define similar concepts for concurrent systems. Since the latter definitions are generalisations of the former ones, we will use the same names. To avoid ambiguity, we will prefix the new concepts with "cs-".

Two transitions t_1 and t_2 are cs-independent iff t_1 and t_2 are independent and $SC(t_1) \cap SC(t_2) = \emptyset$.

A nonempty set of mutually cs-independent transitions, $X \subseteq T$, has cs-concession in a system state (m,s) iff

1) X has concession in m
2) $\forall\, t \in X\ [GUARD(t)\ (s_{SC(t)})]$

When X has cs-concession in (m,s), it may fire. If it fires there are two different possibilities:

A) If there exists a system state (m',s') such that

1) $m \xrightarrow{X} m'$
2) $\exists\, s'' \in S\ [\forall\, t \in X\ [(s_{SC(t)}, s''_{SC(t)}) \in REL(t)] \wedge s_A = s''_A \wedge s''_B = s'_B]$

where $A = V - \cup\, \{SC(t) \mid t \in X\}$ and $B = V - \cup\, \{VAR(p) \mid m'(p) = 1\}$

(m',s') is said to be cs-directly reachable from (m,s), which we write as $(m,s) \longrightarrow (m',s')$ or $(m,s) \xrightarrow{X} (m',s')$.

B) If such a system state does not exist, firing of X in (m,s) is a violation.

From now on we will omit the prefix "cs-" and always refer to the definitions of concurrent systems and not to those of Petri nets.

A sequence of system states, $fs = \{(m_i, s_i)\}_{1 \leq i \leq n}$ where $1 \leq n \leq \infty$, is a firing sequence iff $(m_i, s_i) \longrightarrow (m_{i+1}, s_{i+1})$ for all i, where $1 \leq i < n$. fs is finite iff $n < \infty$. A finite firing sequence is maximal iff no transition has concession in (m_n, s_n) and violating iff a set of transitions may fire as a violation in (m_n, s_n). Moreover by definition $fs.FIRST = (m_1, s_1)$, $fs.LAST = (m_n, s_n)$ if $n < \infty$ else undefined, $|fs| = n$, and $(m,s) \in fs$ iff $(m,s) = (m_i, s_i)$ for some i, where $1 \leq i \leq n$.

Having now shown that concurrent systems have a rigorous mathematical definition, we will in the rest of this paper use a more informal notation consisting of the normal graphical notation for Petri nets, augmented with expressions as indicated in subsections 3.3 and 3.4. Scopes will always be implicitly defined by the involved subexpressions for EQ(p), GUARD(t), and REL(t). If EQ(p) or GUARD(t) is omitted this is equivalent to the always satisfied equation, which is denoted by TRUE. If REL(t) is omitted this is equivalent to the identity relation. If VAR(p) is omitted this is equivalent to the empty subset of variables.

3.6 Comparison with similar formalisms

Adding a data part to a Petri net and attaching expressions to transitions have also been proposed in [Keller 76] and [Mazurkiewicz 77]. The attachment of expressions to places is primarily inspired by the LET-imperative in Delta, which allows the values of variables to be defined implicitly by means of equations at the expense of algorithmic transformations. A similar idea is present in assignment systems, [Thiagarajan & Genrich 76].

In the formalism of Mazurkiewicz one is only allowed to attach expressions to transitions in such a way that (Petri net) concurrent transitions get disjoint scopes. Furthermore Mazurkiewicz formalism consists of a scheme and an interpretation. The schemes adhere to the Petri net firing rules. An effect similar to the use of GUARDS are introduced via the interpretation.

In Keller's formalism there is no concurrency between transitions: "if there is any possibility of simultaneous events occurring, such an occurrence can be represented as a sequence of occurrences of events in some arbitrary order." Keller only allows functions on variables, not relations in general. In Keller's terminology this means that our model is "nondeterministic" while his model is "deterministic". Both models are "polygenic".

4. SYNTAX OF EPSILON

In this section the (abstract) syntax of Epsilon is defined using an extended BNF. The use of $\{A\}$ list$\{B\}$ means one or more instances of A separated by B, i.e. A, ABA, ABABA, etc.; list$_0$ indicates that the list may be empty. An optional clause is indicated by opt$\{...\}$.

Syntax

1   <Epsilon-system> ::= SYSTEM < object descriptor>

2   <object-descriptor> ::= BEGIN opt$\{$<decl>;$\}$ <imp> END

3   <decl> ::= <decl>; <decl> | VAR $\{$<id>$\}$ list$\{,\}$: <type>

4 | OBJECT <id> opt $\{$(<id> : <range>)$\}$: <object-description>

5 | PROCEDURE <id>: BEGIN opt$\{$<decl>;$\}$ <imp> END

6   <imp> ::= EMPTY | <imp>; <imp> | EXECUTE <proc-id> <put> <get>

7 | INTERRUPT <object> BY <proc-id> <put>

8 | LET <equation> opt$\{$DEFINE $\{$<var-id>$\}$ list$\{,\}\}$

9     $\{$ WHEN <boolean-exp > DO <imp>$\}$ list$_0$

10    $\{$ACCEPT <object> : <proc-id> <get>$\}$ list$_0$ ENDLET

11 | REPEAT <imp> ENDREPEAT | « <micro-imp> »

12   <object> ::= <object-id> | <object-id>(<range-exp>)

13   <micro-imp> ::= EMPTY | <micro-imp>; <micro-imp> | <var-id> ::= <exp>

14 | IF <selection> FI | DO <selection> OD

15   <selection> ::= $\{$<boolean-exp> → <micro-imp>$\}$ list$\{$ ▯ $\}$

16   <put> ::= opt$\{$PUT($\{$<var-id> := <exp>$\}$ list$\{,\}$)$\}$

17   <get> ::= opt$\{$GET($\{$<var-id> := <var-id>$\}$ list$\{,\}$)$\}$

The syntax of identifiers, types, ranges, equations, and the various expressions will not be specified. <id> is used when an identifier is declared. <object-id> is an application of an identifier declared as an OBJECT, etc. A precise definition of the context dependent parts of the syntax will not be given in this paper. The scope rules resemble those of Algol 60. Only VAR and PROCEDURE declarations may appear in a procedure. Recursive procedure calls are not allowed, neither directly using EXECUTE nor indirectly by means of INTERRUPT (see also sections 5 and 6).

PUT and GET-clauses are call-by-value and call-by-result parameter transfers. In PUT (GET) the leftside (rightside) of the assignments indicates local variables in the procedure whereas the rightside (leftside) is an expression (variable) evaluated at the place of the procedure activation (EXECUTE or ACCEPT).

5. SEMANTICS OF EPSILON

In this section we use concurrent systems to define the semantics of Epsilon. This is done by defining a syntax-directed translation of Epsilon descriptions into concurrent systems. In this paper the translation is only informally defined. It could be formalized using an attribute grammar with concurrent systems as attribute values. In [Pearl 78] a similar syntax-directed translation is formally defined by means of a van Wijngaarden grammar.

The set of behaviours for a concurrent system, defined in section 5.4 by means of firing sequences, constitutes the semantics of the corresponding Epsilon description.

For each language construct a corresponding concurrent system is given. The concurrent system for objects and procedures are defined in section 5.1. For each variable appearing in the description of an object or a procedure there will be a corresponding variable in the concurrent system.

It is important to distinguish between imperatives defined by <imp> (section 4, lines 6-11) and micro-imperatives defined by <micro-imp> (section 4, lines 13-14).

Imperatives and micro-imperatives belong to different levels in an Epsilon description. The action-part is described by imperatives. Imperatives of the form, ≪MIC-IMP≫, are called general-assignment-imperatives. Although defined by a sequence of micro-imperatives a general-assignment-imperative describes one indivisible and instantaneous event-action.

The actual choice of micro-imperatives in Epsilon is of less importance for this paper. We have chosen Dijkstra's guarded commands because they are useful and to illustrate that nondeterministic control structures are simple to define in terms of concurrent systems.

We shall use two levels of concurrent systems to model imperatives and micro-imperatives respectively. At the imperative level there is a single high level concurrent system containing a concurrent subsystem for each imperative in the system.

At the micro-imperative level there is a separate low level concurrent system for each general-assignment-imperative. Each low level concurrent system contains a concurrent subsystem for each micro-imperative in the corresponding general-assignment-imperative. The concurrent subsystems representing imperatives and micro-imperatives are defined in section 5.2 and 5.3 respectively.

A general-assignment of the form ≪MIC-IMP≫ will in the high level concurrent system be represented by one transition having an attached expression of the form DO REL. REL is defined by means of the firing sequences in the low level concurrent system corresponding to MIC-IMP.

The use of Petri nets often leads to large and unstructured nets. This disadvantage can be diminished by the use of levels of concurrent systems. There is no reason to have only two levels. The concurrent systems corresponding to micro-imperatives may use operations like +, *, etc. These will be part of the Epsilon language, and might also be defined using concurrent systems.

The use of concurrent systems at different levels resembles the use of morphisms in Petri nets [Petri 76] and the "structured nets" of [Kotov 78].

5.1 Objects and procedures

Each object is characterized by a set of attributes (objects, procedures and variables) and by an action part.

The actions in the system object are represented by a concurrent system of the form:

[5.1]

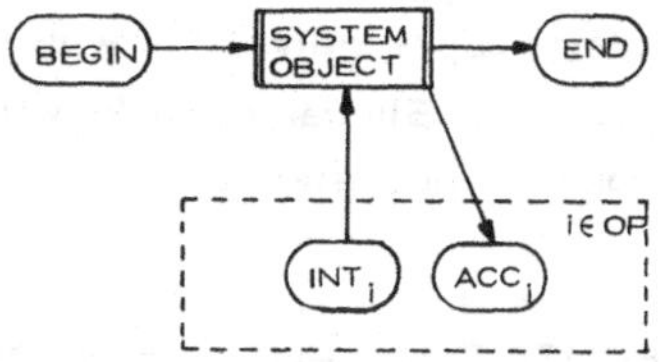

Dashed rectangles are used to indicate a set of identical concurrent subsystems. The text in the upper, righthand corner indicates the name and range of a variable used to give places, transitions, and expressions inside each concurrent subsystem a common subscript. In this simple situation each concurrent subsystem consists of only two places. The range, OP, is the set of all pairs of identifiers, OBJ:PROC, which occurs in one or more ACCEPT-clauses for the system object.

The special rectangle surrounding "SYSTEM OBJECT" indicates a closed concurrent subsystem (i.e. a concurrent subsystem, where no place in the subsystem is a condition for a transition outside the subsystem). The closed concurrent subsystem may have more conditions outside the subsystem than shown (cf. [5.7]).

Each procedure attribute in the system object is represented by a concurrent system of the form

[5.2]

where PROC is the name of the procedure.

Each object attribute in the system is represented by a concurrent subsystem constructed by the same rules as the system object.

Thus in the (high level) concurrent system representing an Epsilon system there is a concurrent subsystem for each object and for each procedure.

The closed concurrent subsystem in [5. 1] and [5. 2] are constructed from the imperatives contained in the object and the procedure respectively. Initially all BEGIN places for objects are marked, all other places are unmarked, and the values of variables are determined by language defined defaults.

5. 2 Imperatives

Each imperative is represented by a concurrent system of the form:

[5. 3]

EMPTY-imperative

The EMPTY-imperative is represented by

[5. 4]

Sequencing

The imperative "IMP_1; IMP_2" is represented by

[5. 5]

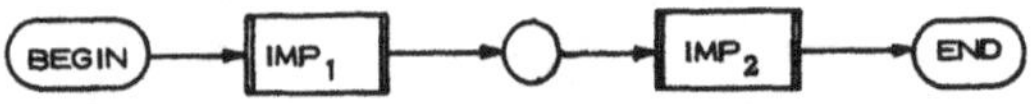

This should be understood as the concurrent system obtained by identifying the END place of the concurrent system representing IMP_1 with the BEGIN place of the concurrent system representing IMP_2. Similar remarks will tacitly be assumed for all following compositions of concurrent systems.

Procedure call

The imperative "EXECUTE PROC PUT($\bar{a}$:= $\overline{exp}$)GET($\bar{b}$:= $\bar{c}$)" is represented by

[5. 6]

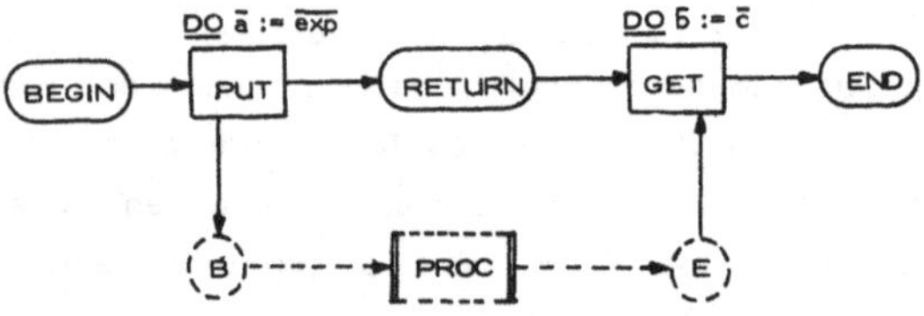

where the subsystem containing B, E, and PROC is the one introduced by the declaration of PROC, see [5. 2].

The "dashed" places, transitions, and directed lines are used to indicate that the corresponding concurrent subsystem is not local to the procedure call, i.e. the subsystem is shared by all calls of the procedure (and all interrupts). The PUT-clause specifies a call-by-value parameter transfer, where the variables $\bar{a}$ (local to PROC) are assigned the values of the expressions $\overline{exp}$ (evaluated in the calling environment). Analogously the GET-clause specifies a call-by-result parameter transfer, where the variables $\bar{b}$ (in the calling environment) are assigned the values of the variables $\bar{c}$ (local to PROC). Note that recursive procedure calls are not allowed.

Interruption

Consider the imperative "INTERRUPT OBJ BY PROC PUT($\bar{a}$:= $\overline{exp}$)" executed by an object OBJ_S. When OBJ is a simple object identifier containing no range expression (OBJ = OBJ_R), the INTERRUPT-imperative is represented by

[5.7]

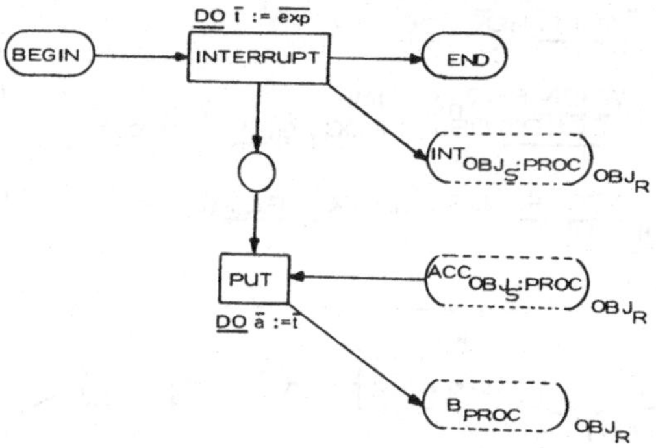

The places $INT_{OBJ_S:PROC}$ and $ACC_{OBJ_S:PROC}$ belong to the concurrent system representing OBJ_R (see [5.1]). B_{PROC} is the BEGIN place for the procedure PROC in object OBJ_R (see [5.2]). When $INT_{OBJ_S:PROC}$ is marked, an interrupt from OBJ_S with procedure PROC is waiting to be executed by OBJ_R. When this interrupt is accepted by OBJ_R, $ACC_{OBJ_S:PROC}$ becomes marked (see [5.9]).

$\bar{t}$ is a set of auxiliary variables used to remember the values of $\overline{exp}$ until OBJ_R is ready to receive them. Each INTERRUPT transition has its own set of auxiliary variables.

Normally OBJ_S is allowed to proceed immediately, without waiting for OBJ_R to accept and execute the interrupting procedure PROC. OBJ_S will be delayed only when $INT_{OBJ_S:PROC}$ is marked already. Note that recursive interrupts are not allowed.

When OBJ contains a range expression (OBJ = OBJ(i)), the INTERRUPT-imperative is represented by

[5.8]

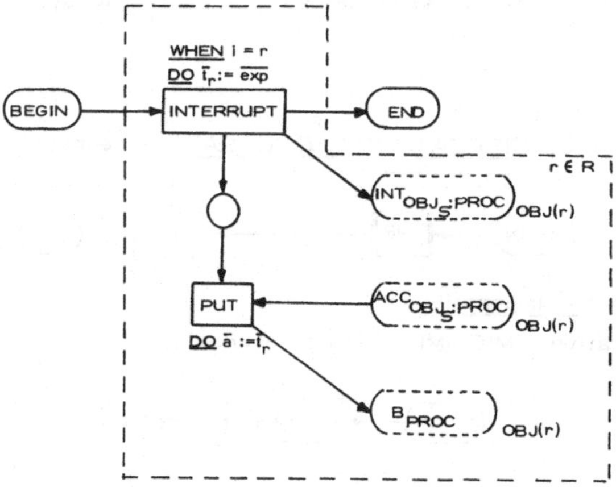

R is the set of values, which the range expression may take.

LET-imperative

The imperative

"LET EQ DEFINE VAR
WHEN BOO_1 DO IMP_1
⋮
WHEN BOO_n DO IMP_n $(n \geq 0)$
ACCEPT OBJ_1:$PROC_1$ GET $(\bar{b}_1 := \bar{c}_1)$
⋮
ACCEPT OBJ_m:$PROC_m$ GET $(\bar{b}_m := \bar{c}_m)$ $(m \geq 0)$
ENDLET"

is represented by

[5.9]

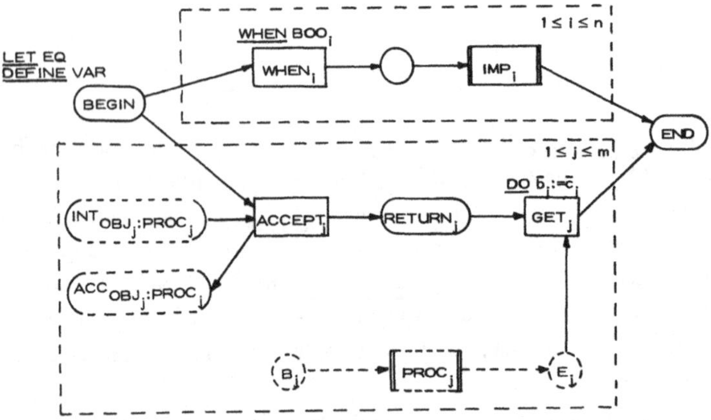

where the subsystem containing B_j, E_j and $PROC_j$ is the one introduced by the declaration of $PROC_j$ in the object, OBJ, executing the LET-imperative, see [5.2]. $INT_{OBJ_j:PROC_j}$ and $ACC_{OBJ_j:PROC_j}$ are defined in [5.1].

The place $INT_{OBJ_j:PROC_j}$ is marked by OBJ_j when it executes an imperative of the form "INTERRUPT OBJ_j BY $PROC_j$", see [5.7].

When the ACCEPT-clause contains range expressions, [5.9] is modified analogously to [5.8].

Repetition

The imperative "REPEAT IMP ENDREPEAT" is represented by

[5.10]

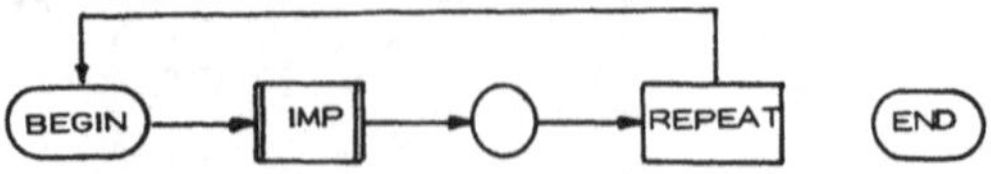

General-assignment-imperative

The imperative "«MIC-IMP»" is represented by

[5.11]

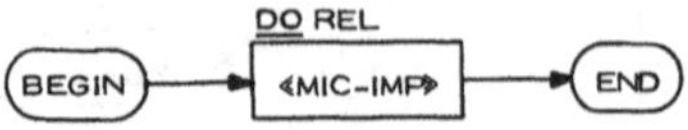

where the relation REL will be defined below by means of a separate (low level) concurrent system, CS, constructed from the micro-imperative MIC-IMP by the rules defined in section 5.3. The variables of CS and the scope of transition «MIC-IMP» are the set of variables, A, observed or changed in MIC-IMP. The variables must all be local to the object. CS has the form

[5.12] 

Let m_B and m_E be the control states for CS in which only BEGIN and END respectively are marked and let a final state be any state of the form (m_E, u). Let FS(s) be the set of firing sequences, fs, where fs.FIRST = (m_B, s). Recalling that F is the value domain for the variables A we define REL as follows:

$$\forall s,r \in [A \to F]\ [(s,r) \in REL \iff$$
$$(\exists fs \in FS(s)\ [fs.LAST = (m_E, r)] \wedge$$
$$\forall fs \in FS(s)\ [fs \text{ is finite} \wedge (fs \text{ is maximal} \Rightarrow fs.LAST \text{ is a final state})])].$$

Let a data state s be given. If it is possible to go into an infinite loop (an infinite firing sequence exists) or to enter a non-final state where no transition has concession, then the above definition implies that there is no r such that $(s,r) \in REL$. In this case the firing of the transition representing the general-assignment-imperative in the data state s is a violation.

5.3 Micro-imperatives

Like imperatives each micro-imperative is represented by a concurrent system of the form [5.12]. In contrast to imperatives BEGIN and END will be the only places outside the closed concurrent subsystem being conditions for transitions inside.

EMPTY-micro-imperative

The EMPTY-micro-imperative is represented by

[5.13] 

Sequencing

The micro-imperative "$MIC\text{-}IMP_1$; $MIC\text{-}IMP_2$" is represented by

[5.14] 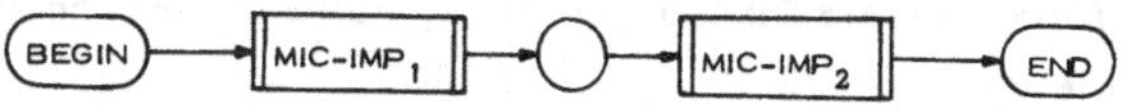

Assignment

The micro-imperative "VAR := EXP" is represented by

[5.15] 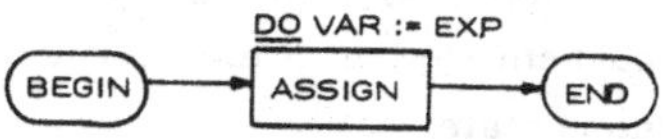

Selection

The micro-imperative (defined in [Dijkstra 75])

"IF GUARD$_1$ → MIC-IMP$_1$

▯ GUARD$_2$ → MIC-IMP$_2$

⋮

▯ GUARD$_n$ → MIC-IMP$_n$ (n ≥ 1)

FI"

is represented by

[5. 16]

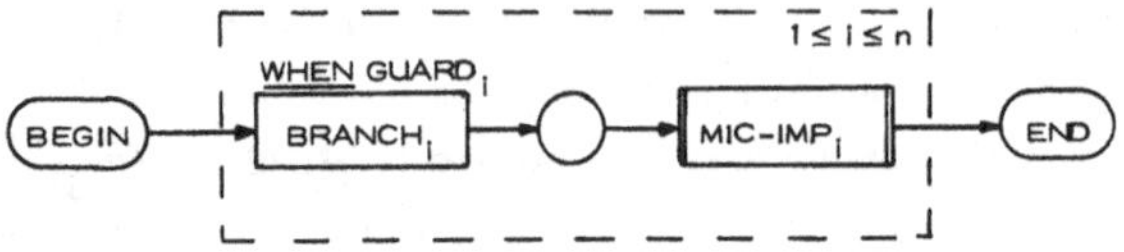

Repetition

The micro-imperative (defined in [Dijkstra 75])

"DO GUARD$_1$ → MIC-IMP$_1$

▯ GUARD$_2$ → MIC-IMP$_2$

⋮

▯ GUARD$_n$ → MIC-IMP$_n$ (n ≥ 1)

OD"

is represented by

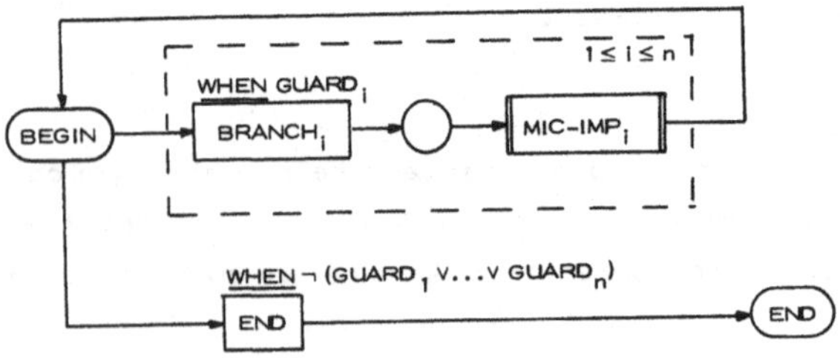

5. 4 Systems

The experience with Delta indicates that a global and continuous time concept is useful and simplifying in the description of a large number of systems, and we have therefore included the variable TIME in Epsilon.

The representation of a continuous time concept by Petri nets has no satisfactory solutions [Petri 76]. For this reason we have chosen not to incorporate incrementation of the variable TIME in the firing rules of concurrent systems, but to treat it separately.

Systems which are most adequately described without a concept of global time, e.g. computer networks and systems containing physical particles with a relativistic behaviour, are described in Epsilon by omitting any use of the global variable TIME.

A behaviour of a concurrent system without TIME is a firing sequence for it starting with the initial system state.

An Epsilon description without global TIME is well-behaved iff all of its behaviours are non-violating.

The behaviours of an Epsilon system with TIME are more complicated, since they are functions from an interval (consisting of the possible values of TIME) into firing sequences. We shall require that in a closed interval of TIME transitions have only concession for a finite number of values of TIME. Furthermore we require that only a finite number of firings take place at any value of TIME. This implies that at most values of TIME no transition has concession and the value of TIME is continuously increased, without changing the marking, until some transition gets concession. Then the value of TIME is kept constant until the concurrent system, by firing of transitions, has reached a system state, where no transition has concession. The value of TIME is again increased and so on. This informal description of behaviours for systems involving global time can be formalised in a way, which contains the corresponding definition for systems without global time as a special instance:

The following definitions are defined relatively to a concurrent system, where FS is the set of firing sequences starting in the initial state (m_I, s_I) and $t_0 = s_I(\text{TIME})$.

A behaviour of a concurrent system is a function $b: J \to FS$, where J is a closed interval of reals and there exists a finite sequence of reals, $t_0 \leq t_1 < t_2 < \ldots < t_{n-1} < t_n \leq t_{n+1}$ with $n \geq 0$, such that

1) $J = [t_0, t_{n+1}] \wedge (m_I, s_I) = b(t_0).\text{FIRST}$

2) $\forall\, t \in J\, [\,|b(t)| > 1 \Leftrightarrow t \in \{t_1, t_2, \ldots, t_n\}]$

3) $\forall\, i \in \{0, 1, \ldots, n\}\ \forall\, t \in\,]t_i, t_{i+1}[\ [b(t_i).\text{LAST} \approx b(t) \approx b(t_{i+1}).\text{FIRST}]$

4) $\forall\, t \in J \forall (m, s) \in b(t)\ [s(\text{TIME}) = t]$

5) $\forall\, t \in J - \{t_{n+1}\}\ [b(t) \text{ is maximal}]$

where $(m_1, s_1) \approx (m_2, s_2)$ iff

a) $m_1 = m_2$

b) $\forall\, v \in V\, [s_1(v) \neq s_2(v) \Rightarrow v \in \cup\, \{\text{VAR}(p) \mid m_1(p) = 1\} \cup \{\text{TIME}\}]$

B(t) is the set of behaviours $b: [t_0, t] \to FS$. An Epsilon description with global TIME is well-behaved iff

$$\forall\, t \geq t_0\ [(B(t) \neq \emptyset) \wedge (\forall\, b \in B(t)\ [b(t) \text{ is finite and non-violating}])].$$

The definition of behaviour given above resembles in some repsects "iterated firing of occurrence" defined in [Moalla, Pulou & Sifakis 78].

6. CONCLUDING REMARKS

In the preceding sections we have presented the kernel of a system description language and a mathematical model used to give a formal definition of the semantics. The presence of the formal definition improves the useability of the language in the description, analysis, and design of systems:

The use as a descriptional tool is enhanced by providing a rigorous basis for an understanding of the language. This basis stresses the use of Epsilon as a tool for hierarchical system description. Furthermore it can be used to isolate the important aspects of given system descriptions and thus be a help in the difficult task of formulating an equivalence-concept for system descriptions.

The formal definition may be used in the analysis of systems to prove global properties of a given system description, e.g. that it is well-behaved. It is an important subject for future work, to formulate suitable global system properties and to develop formal methods for proving them by testing only local properties. This research can draw on a large body of related results in the field of Petri nets. In practical work with large and complicated systems this is most often the only manageable alternative to simulation on a computer system. For a discussion of how to obtain executable programs from system descriptions, see [Kyng 76].

In the design of systems, it will be possible to describe the anticipated design and to analyse it in order to check before implementation, whether it is consistent and has the desired properties. In this way the formulation of the mathematical model and the formal definition improved the design of Epsilon itself.

Comparison with related work

Other uses of Petri nets as a semantic model of languages may be found in [Lauer & Campbell 75] and [Pearl 78] where the semantics for path expressions and a process control language respectively are defined. An attempt to define a formal semantics of the control flow in Delta is reported in [Delta 79]. There the semantics of a large part of Delta is defined using a Petri net model, which is described and analysed in [Jensen 78]. Epsilon is designed using the large number of improvements and simplifications of Delta resulting from this work.

Extensions of Epsilon and the model

In order to get a complete system description language Epsilon has to be enlarged in several respects, e.g. structuring facilities, parameter mechanisms, and control structures. Among the obvious candidates for extensions are classes and subclasses with virtuals as known from Simula. The formal definition of these concepts by means of concurrent systems is straightforward. We do, however, also want to include recursive procedures (and interrupts), reference variables, and dynamic generation (and destruction) of objects, and this calls for an enlargement of the semantic model. In [Delta 79] we used infinite nets (but only finite markings).

At present we are considering a solution based on a model containing labelled tokens representing the identity of the different objects and the different procedure activations. This approach is inspired by [Genrich & Lautenbach 79].

Acknowledgements

We want to thank Antoni Mazurkiewicz and Kristen Nygaard for providing the initial inspiration for this work. Moreover we are grateful to Mogens Nielsen and Erik Meineche Schmidt for stimulating discussions and many helpful comments.

References

Delta, Holbæk-Hanssen, E., Håndlykken, P. and Nygaard, K.: System Description and the Delta Language. Norwegian Computing Center, Oslo 1975.

Delta, Jensen, K., Kyng, M. and Madsen, O.L.: Delta Semantics Defined by Petri Nets. DAIMI PB-95, March 1979, (Comp. Sci. Dept., Aarhus University).

Dijkstra, E.W.: Guarded Commands, Nondeterminacy and Formal Derivation of Programs. Comm. ACM 18, 8 (August 1975), 453-457.

Genrich, H.J. and Thiagarajan, P.S.: Net Progress. Computing Surveys Vol. 10, No. 1 (March 1978), 84-85.

Genrich, H.J. and Lautenbach, K.: The Analysis of Distributed Systems by Means of Predicate/Transition-Nets. Gesellschaft für Mathematik und Datenverarbeitung, Bonn, January 1979 (Draft version).

Jensen, K.: Extended and Hyper Petri Nets. DAIMI TR-5, August 1978.

Keller, R.M.: Formal Verification of Parallel Programs, Comm. ACM 19, 7 (July 1976), 371-384.

Kotov, V.E.: An Algebra for Parallelism Based on Petri Nets. Mathematical Foundations of Computer Science 1978, J. Winkowski (ed.), Springer Verlag (1978), 39-55.

Kyng, M.: Implementation of the Delta Language Interrupt Concept within the Quasiparallel Environment of Simula. DAIMI PB-58, August 1976.

Lauer, P.E. and Campbell, R.H.: Formal Semantics of a Class of High-Level Primitives for Coordinating Concurrent Processes. Acta Informatica 5 (1975), 297-332.

Mazurkiewicz, A.: Concurrent Program Schemes and their Interpretation, DAIMI PB-78, July 1977.

Moalla, M., Pulou, J. and Sifakis, J.: Synchronized Petri Nets: A Model for the Description of Non-autonomous Systems. Mathematical Foundations of Computer Science 1978, J. Winkowski (ed.),Springer-Verlag (1978), 374-384.

Nygaard, K.: System Description by Simula - An Introduction. Norwegian Computing Center, Oslo, 1970.

Pearl, Wegner, E. and Hopmann, C.: Semantics of a Language for Describing Systems and Processes. IST Report 36. Gesellschaft für Mathematik und Datenverarbeitung, Bonn, Mai 1977 (revised January 1978).

Peterson, J.L.: Petri Nets. Computing Surveys Vol. 9, No. 3 (September 1977), 223-252. Commented in [Genrich & Thiagarajan 78].

Petri, C.A.: Concepts of Net Theory. Proc. Symp. Summer School on Mathematical Foundations of Computer Science, High Tatras, Sept. 3-8, 1973, Math. Inst. Slovak Academy of Science, 1973, 137-146.

Petri, C.A.: Interpretations of Net Theory. Interner Bericht 75-07. Gesellschaft für Mathematik und Datenverarbeitung, Bonn, July 1975.

Petri, C.A.: Nichtsequentielle Prozesse. Interner Bericht 76-6, Gesellschaft für Mathematik und Datenverarbeitung, Bonn, June 1976 (translated to English by P. Krause and J. Low).

Simula, Dahl, O.-J., Myhrhaug, B. and Nygaard, K.: Common Base Language. Norwegian Computing Center, Oslo, 1970.

Thiagarajan, P.S. and Genrich, H.J.: Assignment Systems - A Model for Asynchronous Computations. Interner Bericht 76-10, Gesellschaft für Mathematik und Datenverarbeitung, Bonn, November 1976.

Vol. 49: Interactive Systems. Proceedings 1976. Edited by A. Blaser and C. Hackl. VI, 380 pages. 1976.

Vol. 50: A. C. Hartmann, A Concurrent Pascal Compiler for Minicomputers. VI, 119 pages. 1977.

Vol. 51: B. S. Garbow, Matrix Eigensystem Routines – Eispack Guide Extension. VIII, 343 pages. 1977.

Vol. 52: Automata, Languages and Programming. Fourth Colloquium, University of Turku, July 1977. Edited by A. Salomaa and M. Steinby. X, 569 pages. 1977.

Vol. 53: Mathematical Foundations of Computer Science. Proceedings 1977. Edited by J. Gruska. XII, 608 pages. 1977.

Vol. 54: Design and Implementation of Programming Languages. Proceedings 1976. Edited by J. H. Williams and D. A. Fisher. X, 496 pages. 1977.

Vol. 55: A. Gerbier, Mes premières constructions de programmes. XII, 256 pages. 1977.

Vol. 56: Fundamentals of Computation Theory. Proceedings 1977. Edited by M. Karpiński. XII, 542 pages. 1977.

Vol. 57: Portability of Numerical Software. Proceedings 1976. Edited by W. Cowell. VIII, 539 pages. 1977.

Vol. 58: M. J. O'Donnell, Computing in Systems Described by Equations. XIV, 111 pages. 1977.

Vol. 59: E. Hill, Jr., A Comparative Study of Very Large Data Bases. X, 140 pages. 1978.

Vol. 60: Operating Systems, An Advanced Course. Edited by R. Bayer, R. M. Graham, and G. Seegmüller. X, 593 pages. 1978.

Vol. 61: The Vienna Development Method: The Meta-Language. Edited by D. Bjørner and C. B. Jones. XVIII, 382 pages. 1978.

Vol. 62: Automata, Languages and Programming. Proceedings 1978. Edited by G. Ausiello and C. Böhm. VIII, 508 pages. 1978.

Vol. 63: Natural Language Communication with Computers. Edited by Leonard Bolc. VI, 292 pages. 1978.

Vol. 64: Mathematical Foundations of Computer Science. Proceedings 1978. Edited by J. Winkowski. X, 551 pages. 1978.

Vol. 65: Information Systems Methodology, Proceedings, 1978. Edited by G. Bracchi and P. C. Lockemann. XII, 696 pages. 1978.

Vol. 66: N. D. Jones and S. S. Muchnick, TEMPO: A Unified Treatment of Binding Time and Parameter Passing Concepts in Programming Languages. IX, 118 pages. 1978.

Vol. 67: Theoretical Computer Science, 4th GI Conference, Aachen, March 1979. Edited by K. Weihrauch. VII, 324 pages. 1979.

Vol. 68: D. Harel, First-Order Dynamic Logic. X, 133 pages. 1979.

Vol. 69: Program Construction. International Summer School. Edited by F. L. Bauer and M. Broy. VII, 651 pages. 1979.

Vol. 70: Semantics of Concurrent Computation. Proceedings 1979. Edited by G. Kahn. VI, 368 pages. 1979.